GRAVE HISTORY

GRAVE HISTORY

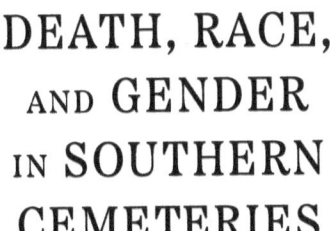

DEATH, RACE, AND GENDER IN SOUTHERN CEMETERIES

EDITED BY **Kami Fletcher**
AND **Ashley Towle**

[THE UNIVERSITY OF GEORGIA PRESS · ATHENS]

© 2023 by the University of Georgia Press
Athens, Georgia 30602
www.ugapress.org
All rights reserved
Designed by Kaelin Chappell Broaddus
Set in 10.25/13.5 Freight Text Pro Medium
by Kaelin Chappell Broaddus

Most University of Georgia Press titles are
available from popular e-book vendors.

Printed digitally

Library of Congress Cataloging-in-Publication Data
Names: Fletcher, Kami, editor. | Towle, Ashley, 1987– editor.
Title: Grave history : death, race, and gender in Southern cemeteries /
edited by Kami Fletcher and Ashley Towle.
Description: Athens : The University of Georgia Press, [2023] |
Includes bibliographical references and index.
Identifiers: LCCN 2023022719 | ISBN 9780820365794 (hardback) |
ISBN 9780820365800 (paperback) | ISBN 9780820365817 (epub) |
ISBN 9780820365824 (pdf)
Subjects: LCSH: Cemeteries—Social aspects—Southern States. |
Southern States—Race relations—19th century. | Southern States—
Race relations—20th century. | Southern States—Social conditions—
19th century. | Southern States—Social conditions—20th century.
Classification: LCC F210 .G76 2023 | DDC 363.7/50975—dc23/
eng/20230524
LC record available at https://lccn.loc.gov/2023022719

CONTENTS

INTRODUCTION
KAMI FLETCHER AND ASHLEY TOWLE   1

CHAPTER 1
The Status Quo Made Picturesque
Nineteenth-Century Macon, Georgia, and Its Garden of the Dead
SCARLET JERNIGAN   16

CHAPTER 2
The Crown Jewel of Kentucky
Louisville's Cave Hill Cemetery
JOY M. GIGUERE   51

CHAPTER 3
Sacred Ground
How a Segregated Graveyard Preserves the Struggles and Successes of an African American Community in Virginia
LYNN RAINVILLE   84

CHAPTER 4
Death Can Not Make Our Souls Afraid
Mosaic Templars of America Zephroes in Macon County, Alabama, 1887–1931
SHARI L. WILLIAMS   113

CHAPTER 5
Jim Crowing the Dead
*A Fight for African American Burial Rights and
Dismantling Racial Burial Covenants*
KAMI FLETCHER   149

CHAPTER 6
"We Have No Further Interest in
These Patients *until They Die*"
*The U.S. Public Health Service's Syphilis Study and
African American Cemeteries in Macon County, Alabama*
CARROLL VAN WEST   171

CHAPTER 7
Profane Memorials
Burying the Martyrs of the Civil Rights Movement
ADRIENNE CHUDZINSKI   198

CHAPTER 8
Cemeteries and Community
*Foregrounding Black Women's Labor and
Leadership in Sacred Site Remembrance Practices*
KANIQUA L. ROBINSON AND
ANTOINETTE T. JACKSON   231

CHAPTER 9
Permanent Reconstruction in
Richmond's Black Cemeteries
ADAM ROSENBLATT, ERIN HOLLAWAY PALMER,
AND BRIAN PALMER   253

CONTRIBUTORS   283

INDEX   287

GRAVE HISTORY

INTRODUCTION

In 1870 Senator Charles Sumner proposed a sweeping civil rights bill that would ban racial discrimination in public spaces, including cemeteries. The bill was a supplement to the 1866 Civil Rights Act and stipulated specific public accommodations to which African Americans could not be denied access. The bill listed public schools, public accommodations, and "cemetery associations incorporated by national or State authority."[1] The supplementary civil rights bill was part of Sumner's larger goal of implementing racial equality in the United States in the wake of the radical changes wrought by the Civil War, emancipation, and Reconstruction. While African Americans had been granted citizenship under the Fourteenth Amendment and Black men were afforded the right to vote by the Fifteenth Amendment, Sumner and other radical Republicans believed that full citizenship would not be achieved until Black people had equal access to public accommodations.[2] According to Sumner, his supplementary civil rights bill would make "the Declaration of Independence in its principles and promises a living letter; make it a practical reality."[3] Allowing African Americans to be buried in a cemetery of their choice, rather than forcing them to be buried in Black cemeteries, was part of Sumner's comprehensive vision of citizenship.

In December 1873 South Carolina congressman Joseph H. Rainey stood before the House of Representatives and delivered an impassioned speech in favor of Sumner's civil rights bill. As a formerly enslaved man, Rainey voiced his support for the bill and questioned the intent of racial discrimination in cemeteries. "Why is a discrimination made against us in the church and in the cemeteries where we go to pay that last debt of nature that brings us all upon a level?" While death might be the ultimate equalizer, burial practices continued to reify racial discrimination and the second-class status of African Americans. As Rainey argued, access to public accommodations, including cemeteries, was a right of citizenship. "I am not a lawyer, and consequently I cannot take a legal view of this matter. . . . I view it in the light of the Constitution—in the light of the amendments that have been made to that Constitution; I view it in the light of humanity; I view it in the light of the progress and civilization which are now rapidly marching over this country."[4]

Sumner and Rainey's vision, unfortunately, was not realized. The final bill passed by Congress in 1875 was a watered-down version of the original, with the clauses covering inclusion in public schools, churches, and cemeteries removed. The bill guaranteed access only to "inns, public conveyances on land or water, theaters, and other places of public amusement."[5]

Intriguingly, much of the debate over the Civil Rights Act of 1875 focused on banning discrimination in juries and public schools. Besides Rainey's speech, there was very little protest over removing cemeteries from the list of public spaces to which African Americans deserved access.[6] In the tumult of Reconstruction, as Americans negotiated ideas about race and rights, burial customs that enshrined racial distinctions largely remained unquestioned and intact. While Rainey was correct that death was the ultimate leveler, burials had a long history of reinforcing hierarchies of power that proved difficult to dislodge.

As the early iteration of Sumner's bill made clear, cemeteries are not simply passive sites of rest and repose, but rather reflections of history, society, and structures of power. This volume interrogates the history of racial segregation in southern cemeteries, in particular, for what it can tell us about how ideas about race, class, and gender were fashioned and reinforced in cities of the dead. Through their cemeteries, white and Black southerners in the nineteenth and twentieth centuries fostered communities of belonging and exclusion. In their continued use and upkeep or neglect of these sacred spaces, southerners demonstrated what was of utmost importance to them. Building on burgeoning scholarship on African American deathways and American cemeteries, this volume starts an important conversation about the relationships southern communities of the living and the dead create, foster, and even dissolve in the midst of social and cultural upheavals.[7]

Grave History is the first volume to use southern cemeteries to interrogate and analyze southern society and the construction of racial and gendered hierarchies from the antebellum period through the dismantling of Jim Crow. Through an analysis of cemeteries throughout the South—representing Alabama, Florida, Georgia, Kentucky, Maryland, Missouri, and Virginia, from the nineteenth through the twenty-first centuries—this volume demonstrates the importance of using the cemetery as an analytical tool for examining power relations, community formation, and historical memory.[8]

Scholars have established that deathways—the ways in which we die as well as the practices that surround death and burial—are ripe for historical, social, and cultural analysis. Beginning in the 1960s, writers such as Jessica Mitford, Geoffrey Gorer, Elisabeth Kübler-Ross, and Ernest Becker insisted that American society had an aversion to death. As evidence they pointed to pushing cemeteries to the outskirts of city limits; hospitalization that separates the dead from the living; and ostentatious funerals that embalm bodies and sanitize the dead.[9] More contemporary scholarship seeks to point out the limitations of such a theory that Americans deny death. In particular, scholars examining the early and antebellum Black experience in southern slaveholding America have exposed the ways in which death was a central facet of the lives of African Americans.

Beginning with the first Africans forcefully ripped from their homes and brought to America as part of the transatlantic slave trade, death has been ubiquitous in the lives of Black people. In "The Black Experience with Death: A Brief Analysis through Black Writings," Maurice Jackson argues that the alarming number of fatalities due to the transatlantic slave trade and plantation slavery came to normalize death and give Black peoples "a different set of expectations [that] form[ed] the secular norm, which specifies that Black people should view death as part of the normal life process, as an inevitable event in a naturalistic context, occurring in the world of experience."[10] Jackson makes clear that death was not de-emphasized and denied but rather accepted; as he points out, spirituals, poems, and literature illustrate how enslaved Black people had a practical and worldly view of death, which they interpreted as the continuation of life. Examining poetry and spirituals, Jackson explains that when the bonded sang about death it was a "covert form of desire for freedom, with death simultaneously representing actual death and freedom—with the obvious realization that the only freedom most of the slaves would find was to occur with death."[11] Jackson particularly cites Claude McKay's 1919 poem "If We Must Die," where death is not denied but welcomed as a noble fate for all Black people fighting back against white supremacy.

Taking up Jackson's contention that death was a common occurrence in Black people's daily lives, contemporary scholars have examined the ways in which Black people in slavery and freedom have used the ubiquity of death as a means to better their circumstances, forge communal and familial bonds, fight for racial equity, and demand justice. Much of this scholarship has focused on slave revolts, suicides, funerals and the rise of Black funeral homes, and mourning culture.[12]

The transatlantic slave trade, plantation slavery, Jim Crow segregation, and the legacies of these institutions dominated the southern landscape for the entirety of the nineteenth and twentieth centuries. Southern funerary culture bears the imprints of these institutions. Slave cemeteries became sites of resistance to white supremacy. For the enslaved, death equaled freedom from bondage, which in turn made last rites and eternal resting places that much more important to Black peoples. Burial grounds in slavery and freedom were important sites of resistance, community building, and remembrance. Scholars have written about slave cemeteries and how bonded people took ownership of certain unused parts of the plantation to create these slave landscapes, purposely hidden burial grounds that were among the trees and near water and slave quarters.[13] Under cover of night, enslaved people properly buried their kin, fictive and blood, and used these spaces to perform second funerals—last rites rituals that served more as memorials and that could occur years after a person died. The burial place was powerful, because the last rites performed there ritualized the decedent into the family of the ancestral spirits. Following emancipation, formerly enslaved people eagerly erected their own private Black cemeteries to properly bury their dead. They formed burial and mutual aid societies in which they combined their money to establish cemeteries and provide proper funerals for their members. Through such actions, African Americans affirmed their familial and communal bonds and built a robust institutional life.[14]

Gender norms are also reflected in southern funeral culture. Corpse care was often the purview of southern women, both white and Black. Through the creation and use of the burial shroud, women provided what historian Jamie Warren calls "corpse care," washing the body and preparing it for burial. This was a frequent part of enslaved women's tasks, giving these women authority over the last legacy and memory of their deceased kin.[15] White plantation mistresses were present during "corpse care," mourning and emoting with enslaved women but also participating by providing funeral caps and shrouds—material culture to which enslaved women had no access. Funeral shrouds, which were made by women, reflect the gendered division of labor within southern funerary culture. In the antebellum and Jim Crow South, shrouds held importance—they aided the appearance of a decaying corpse, elevated the social status of the decedent, and illustrated to their communities the importance of this specialized skill set that women possessed.[16]

The legacy of plantation slavery and Jim Crow is also apparent in the unique funerals Black people developed. Homegoings became symbols of power and acts of political assertion. In *Passed On: African American Mourning Stories*, Karla FC Holloway illustrates how elements of homegoing funerals are products of southern institutions. A homegoing is a celebration of

Black life that resists white oppression and Black subjugation with its long procession and regal attire (for both the decedent and the mourners). The funeral procession was central to homegoings and allowed southern Black people to take up literal public space on the roadways and sidewalks as the procession wound its way to the cemetery. To claim this public space during Jim Crow and to force white southerners to stop and observe Black celebrations of life and death were acts of resistance to white supremacy.[17]

Grave History builds upon this scholarship by focusing on the broader social, cultural, and regional issues engaged by cemeteries in the American South. For the past five decades, scholars have demonstrated that cemeteries were sites of memory and spaces of mourning and are therefore ripe for historical analysis. In his canonical piece on memory versus history, French historian Pierre Nora places cemeteries firmly within the category of memory, calling them *lieux de mémoire* or sites of memory.[18] As sites of memory, cemeteries are simultaneously material, symbolic, and functional expressions of lived experiences and serve as windows to the past. Working to find spaces where marginalized communities find a voice in public society, Elizabethada Wright continues Nora's framework, arguing that cemeteries were ideal sites of memory—not as storehouses or even as museums, but as purposely constructed environs that help the living remember what is forgotten. Wright's analyses that cemeteries are cultural institutions that double as rhetorical spaces pushed scholarship to investigate how cemeteries simultaneously mirror and distort society. Wright asks why cemeteries are not only important but natural rhetorical spaces to help Americans understand marginalized experiences inclusive to gender and race.[19]

Grave History picks up this question and uses cemeteries and the southern communities that created and sustain them to understand how they influenced the creation of an American and regional identity. It interrogates how southern cemeteries were used by discrete groups to create communities of exclusion and belonging based on race, class, and gender. Finally, it explores how cemeteries were sites of power, contestation, and politicization.

This volume focuses on nineteenth- and twentieth-century cemeteries in the South for a few reasons. During the nineteenth century, the rural cemetery movement transformed American deathways. Influenced by the success of Mount Auburn Cemetery in Cambridge, Massachusetts, the first rural cemetery in the United States, cities across the country developed their own rural cemeteries. These new, elaborate, and highly planned cemeteries reflected broader developments in American culture as Americans began to romanticize death and the afterlife. Prior to this cultural turn, white Americans had largely ignored their cemeteries. As Stanley French notes, "Graveyards were treated simply as unattractive necessities to be avoided as much as possible by the living." In the South, corpses were often buried in family plots on privately owned land or in churchyards. The rural, decentralized nature of the region meant that community graveyards were not the norm outside of major cities. But the rise of the rural cemetery movement brought about a significant shift. Cemeteries became spaces that invited the living to interact with the dead and to contemplate the meaning of life and death. Epitaphs on increasingly elaborate graves served as prescriptive literature for cemetery visitors—educating them on the proper roles and virtues to which men and women should aspire.[20]

This volume makes the case that cemeteries serve as useful tools for analyzing transformations in American society. In the case of the South, the history of slavery, emancipation, and Jim Crow are visible within cemeteries, and indeed, those histories are a product of how people buried and remembered their dead. Contributors to this volume explore these issues by employing methodologies that are diverse and on the cutting edge. Most scholarship on cemeteries has tended to focus on gravestone analysis and the material culture of burials. It is our hope that this volume encourages scholars to move beyond these approaches and apply new methods and sources to cemetery studies. Chapters in this volume use genealogical information, archival research, and oral histories. They position cemeteries as outdoor museums and mine grave sites in an effort to collect material biographies. They use technologies such as geographic information system mapping (GIS) to digitally plot grave sites inclusive of race, gender, class, epitaph, and marker type, to draw parallels between living and death patterns. By applying these varied methodologies, the chapters in this volume demonstrate that cemeteries are fruitful spaces to study not simply how people buried their dead but how they continued to use these spaces to make meaning of their lives, foster communities, and struggle for equality and inclusion.

This volume opens with an exploration of how antebellum southerners used the rural cemetery to curate an idealized reflection of their society. Scarlet Jernigan's chapter highlights the importance of analyzing southern rural cemeteries for what they can tell us about antebellum society and how slaveholders, in particular, sought to represent themselves even after death. In doing so, Jernigan's chapter uncovers the antecedents of the Lost Cause, in which white southerners crafted a benevolent image of slavery through the rural cemetery movement. Although they accounted for only 19 percent of the population in Macon, Georgia, in 1860, enslavers bought over half of the 384 lots in the cemetery. By managing impressions in this way, Jernigan argues, white southerners displayed the best of themselves in their Rose Hill

Cemetery while enshrining paternalism, the status quo, and its hierarchy. By comparing Oak Ridge Cemetery—a burial ground for Macon's enslaved people that was founded by white slaveholders, located right across the street—to Rose Hill, Jernigan illuminates how white southerners used the southern cemetery to construct a narrative where slavery was beneficial to white and Black alike, and where slaveholders knew their obligations to care for Black folks. Rural cemeteries, then, can be seen as precursors to Confederate monuments, as they memorialize slave owners' idealized vision of a slave society.

During the Civil War, southern rural cemeteries became battlegrounds of Confederate identity. The rural garden cemetery movement that swept the nation from 1830 to 1870 reflected most Americans' changing ideas about death. Death was no longer to be feared, and so the cemetery became a place where the living and dead communed on a spiritual plane within nature. What followed were imitations of Massachusetts's Mount Auburn Cemetery, consisting of hundreds of acres and marked by life-size monuments and extravagance. White southerners capitalized on the rural cemetery as a means to construct a white southern identity grounded in strict racial segregation. In "The Crown Jewel of Kentucky: Louisville's Cave Hill Cemetery," Joy Giguere reveals how Cave Hill was integral to the formation of a Confederate identity in the state. Significantly, it was women who played a central role in shifting Kentucky from a border state to a bastion of Confederate commemoration. Giguere argues that the death work that southern white women took on, such as brazenly caring for Confederate soldiers' grave sites, aided in the construction of a new identity for white Kentuckians in the postbellum south. In the postbellum era, the white southern community used Cave Hill to cultivate a white southern identity grounded in strict racial Jim Crow customs. Giguere points out that it was after, not before, the Civil War that racially explicit burial policies restricted "colored persons" from admission unless accompanied by a white lot holder.

The subsequent chapters center on how southern Black people from the late nineteenth through the twenty-first centuries have attempted to assume control of spaces of death to challenge racism and preserve their past. In the wake of the Civil War and the tumult of emancipation, African Americans also turned to their cemeteries as a means of constructing meaning from the ruins of the antebellum South. African Americans sought to capitalize on their freedom by reconstituting their kinship networks and constructing their own communities. Just as cemeteries were central to white southerners' community building, so they were for Black people as well. During Reconstruction, African Americans embarked on a flurry of institution building, including churches, schools, and benevolent societies. Black-owned and operated cemeteries were part and parcel of those developments. Lynn Rainville's chapter reveals the fruits of these labors in Charlottesville, Virginia. She documents the lived experiences, struggles, and triumphs of the freed African American women and men in post–Civil War Charlottesville through an analysis of the Daughters of Zion Cemetery. Rainville's essay shows not only how Virginian culture led to the creation of the segregated cemetery in 1873 but also how throughout the twentieth century Black women's mutual aid societies repurposed the deathscape for African American burial needs. As Rainville argues, the Daughters of Zion Cemetery was a place where African Americans exhibited their beliefs about death, kinship, race, and status through their grave markers, botanical plantings, and landscape design.

Shari L. Williams's chapter, "Death Can Not Make Our Souls Afraid: Mosaic Templars of America Zephroes in Macon County, Alabama, 1887–1931," also examines the funerary interests of Black women living in the South. Williams interrogates the meaning of the special gravestones that Zephroes, Black women who were part of the Mosaic Templars of America (MTA), chose for placement on their graves. Williams's analysis of the motivations of these women reveals their familial and community attachments and challenges historians' interpretations of mutual aid societies as the purview of the Black middle class. As Williams demonstrates, in rural Alabama it was working-class African American farmers who joined the MTA. The use of MTA gravestones signaled their commitment to their communities and their desire to achieve more for themselves and their families.

As the optimistic years of Reconstruction gave way to the repressive era of Jim Crow, cemeteries remained sites where white and Black Americans reinforced and contested racial hierarchies. In chapter 5, Kami Fletcher interrogates the premise that death is the great equalizer. In her investigation of restrictive racial burial covenants across the United States, Fletcher shows the insidious effect of Jim Crow segregation on burial patterns that reified and memorialized white supremacy. By following key national, state, and local court cases where African Americans fought against these postmortem white hostilities for inclusion in white cemeteries, the chapter uncovers how Black resistance and struggle for burial rights—the legal right to buy lots and be recognized as legal owners of burial deeds—were an integral legacy of the civil rights movement and a key battleground in the effort to dismantle white supremacy.

Carroll Van West's chapter continues the examination of the painful legacy of Jim Crow on African American communities living in Tuskegee, Alabama. Centering on Creek Stand AME Zion Church Cemetery and Shiloh Missionary Baptist Church Cemetery, where African American victims of the infamous Tuskegee medical experiment were buried, West's chapter shows how African Americans lived under the heritage of the Confederacy and died bearing its scars. Rejecting the idea that their kin would be memorialized as dehumanized specimens, volunteers and civic leaders have taken initiatives as of the early 2000s to designate the cemeteries as landmarks and to take control of their own narrative of just what the Tuskegee study was about and what it means today. As West's chapter demonstrates, cemeteries and the communities that surround and use them are not static memorials to the past, but malleable spaces where the past meets the present. Through monuments and material culture, they tell the experiences of the dead and the living.

Adrienne Chudzinski's chapter takes up this contention by investigating the troubling discrepancy between public historical reverence for martyrs of the civil rights movement and their actual grave sites. Chudzinski investigates the burial sites of Emmett Till, a victim of lynching, and Addie Mae Collins, Denise McNair, Carole Robertson, and Cynthia Wesley, victims of the Sixteenth Street Baptist Church bombing in Birmingham, Alabama. The murders of these young African Americans served as watershed moments in the civil rights movement. But as Chudzinski demonstrates, though public remembrance celebrates these children as martyrs, their final resting places are not afforded the same degree of veneration. As part of an FBI investigation, Emmett Till's casket has undergone several transformations, even suffering desecration in an abandoned shed. The victims of Birmingham's church bombing rest beneath a sea of headstones in a dilapidated cemetery. Worse still, the body of one of the victims is missing, while another is misidentified on her grave marker. Chudzinski traces the enduring struggle to restore a degree of honor and respect to the burial site of each of these victims. To address the incongruences in public and private forms of remembrance, the chapter focuses on the cultural afterlife of these prominent public deaths to explore the tension that separates revered historical narratives from the reality found within cemeteries.

As this volume makes clear, African American cemeteries are in peril of being damaged and destroyed. Antoinette Jackson and Kaniqua Robinson's chapter asks what information we can learn about communities whose cemeteries have been lost in the name of urban renewal. Jackson and Robinson contextualize the rich history of the Black community who buried their dead in three cemeteries collectively known as the Oaklawn Cemetery Complex in St. Petersburg, Florida. These cemeteries are now paved over by parking lots and highways. While the other chapters in this volume ask what we can learn from existing cemeteries, Jackson and Robinson interrogate what we can learn about a community in the absence of their cemeteries. Employing a Black feminist anthropology perspective, the authors contextualize the communities these cemeteries served and, in doing so, excavate the vital role Black women played in the varied social institutions that compose African American deathways. From the church to the hospital and to the funeral home, African American women were integral to providing their community members with a respectable homegoing.

The final chapter provides new directions for how cemeteries can be used to dismantle white supremacy and reckon with the past. Adam Rosenblatt, Erin Hollaway Palmer, and Brian Palmer offer an innovative theoretical framework for thinking about the current disrepair of many African American cemeteries and elucidate new methods local communities can undertake to prevent the demise of these important sites. Drawing on years of activism and volunteer work by Hollaway Palmer and Palmer, as well as field research by Rosenblatt, this chapter tells the story of East End and Evergreen Cemeteries in Richmond, Virginia. They document a space where "structural uncaring"—a set of political and social processes that interpose themselves between a community and the care of its dead—is being disrupted by a sustained volunteer effort to reclaim the cemeteries and reconnect them to families and the Richmond area. As volunteers clear vines and cut overgrown grass, they simultaneously take part in what the authors interpret as a process of racial reckoning with the past. As maintenance of the cemetery continues, the process of upkeep and care evolves but does not end.

As the following essays demonstrate, the communities that cemeteries border and the regions they share make cemeteries a significant place for understanding the social, economic, and political life of specific times and places. With this as its base of understanding, *Grave History* asks readers to consider what burial grounds, graveyards, mausoleums, and memorial parks in the South can tell them about the past and the present. What symbolic or literal, metaphysical or real, and even abstract or distinct imprints from southern culture—past and present—do these cemeteries carry? Grave markers are unique forms of material culture meant to communicate very directly to subsequent generations. At the end of each chapter is an epilogue entitled "Teaching the American South by Learning the Dead." These epilogues provide primary sources and other resources and activities to allow readers to interrogate the complicated history of southern cemeteries for themselves. "Teaching the American South by Learning the Dead" offers classroom lesson plans for both the teacher and the student, and for both the seasoned and the novice cemetery enthusiast. These activities encourage readers to examine cemeteries for their physical organization, iconography, sociodemographic landscape, and identity politics. While readers might not be able to visit each cemetery mentioned in this volume, the epilogues offer an opportunity to do the work of a historian and apply the arguments made in each chapter to their own analysis of the history of southern cemeteries. One of the important aspects of these epilogues is that they *can* be applied to other cemeteries across the United States and perhaps beyond. We want readers who are not from the South to think about what the cemeteries around them can reveal about the past and the present. Thus we hope to spur discussion of the importance of using cemeteries as a lens to explore the past, make sense of the present, and shape the future.

The chapters and epilogues that follow offer new perspectives on southern history and serve as a jumping-off point for additional research into the connections between cemeteries and historical transformations. While each chapter focuses on a different cemetery, some broad themes arise. These chapters make clear that southern culture, policies, politics, and social norms have shaped the creation, development, and function of cemeteries. The institution of slavery left an indelible mark on the landscape of the South that has been preserved in its cemeteries. Segregation of white and Black bodies—even in death—is a vestige of this painful history that Americans continue to wrestle with today.

While race is clearly a factor in the creation and use of cemeteries, gender also is reflected in the southern landscape. The following chapters make clear that women were central to the creation and upkeep of cemeteries and were key political actors and community organizers. Expanding their traditional domestic role as caretakers of the dead, white women organized ladies' memorial associations and raised funds to create rural cemeteries and erect Confederate monuments. They planned Decoration Day festivities to honor the Confederate dead. Through these actions, white women were crucial actors in creating the myth of the Lost Cause. Likewise, African American women organized into mutual aid societies that were charged with creating and maintaining Black cemeteries. Under their stewardship, Black cemeteries such as the Daughters of Zion Cemetery enshrined and celebrated the advances freedpeople made following enslavement. As African Americans fought to dismantle Jim Crow, Black mothers took on a significant role in the fight against white supremacy. While the story of Mamie Till-Mobley demanding an open casket funeral for her murdered son, Emmett, is well known, Till-Mobley was not alone in using the death of a loved one to combat white supremacy. Black women used their role as mothers as a shield in their activist crusades for burial rights and rose up as civic leaders to repurpose burial grounds for Black burial needs, changing and claiming the narrative for their own healing commemorative efforts.

Finally, the preservation, upkeep, and use of cemeteries are political acts and illuminate the stories Americans privilege when it comes to their past. The continued veneration and maintenance of Confederate monuments in cemeteries reflect some Americans' commitment to white supremacy. Likewise, the neglect, disrepair, and destruction of African American cemeteries demonstrate the willful ignorance of some Americans to African American history. As Christopher Petrella notes, "The fight to save . . . historic African American cemeteries around the country demonstrates that the movement for racial justice spans space and time. If Black burial sites are struggling to survive, then so, too, is Black history. Contestations over history, memory, and space reveal just how much is at stake in efforts to preserve the Black past, present, and future."[21] As African Americans struggle to convince white America that Black lives matter, cemeteries remain crucial sites for preserving Black history and remind us that Black deaths matter.

The communities that southern cemeteries serve are reflected in the landscapes of the South and etched in stone on monuments and grave markers within cemetery walls. While cemeteries are places of memorialization and remembrance, the uses to which the living have put the dead changed with the demands of the era. The subsequent chapters disabuse us of the idea that cemeteries are quiet, contemplative spaces. Indeed, southern cemeteries are actually active battlegrounds where Americans—living and dead—grappled and continue to struggle with some of the most pressing issues of our time.

Notes

1. *Congressional Globe*, 41 Cong., 2 Sess., 3434.
2. Please note that the word "Black" is capitalized whereas "white" remains lowercase throughout. The editors have chosen to do so in accordance with the 2020 change by the vast majority of mainstream style guides, including the Associated Press and the *Chicago Manual of Style*. For more, see Nancy Coleman, "Why We're Capitalizing Black," *New York Times*, July 2, 2020, https://www.nytimes.com/2020/07/05/insider/capitalized-black.html; "Black and White: A Matter of Capitalization," *CMOS Shop Talk* (blog), June 22, 2020, https://cmosshoptalk.com/2020/06/22/Black-and-white-a-matter-of-capitalization/.
3. *Congressional Globe*, 42 Cong., 2 Sess., 3738.
4. *New National Era*, December 25, 1873.
5. "Act to Protect All Citizens," 335–37.
6. For more on the Civil Rights Act of 1875, see Murphy, "Civil Rights Law of 1875";

McPherson, "Abolitionists and the Civil Rights Act of 1875"; Foner, *Reconstruction*, 504–5, 532–34, 552–56; Masur, *Example for All the Land*, 224–32; Stanley, "Slave Emancipation and the Revolutionizing of Human Rights."

7. Some of the most influential works on American cemeteries include Laderman: *Sacred Remains*; McElya, *Politics of Mourning*; Rainville, *Hidden History*; Sloane, *Last Great Necessity*; Ryan Smith, *Death and Rebirth in a Southern City*; Roberta Wright and Wilbur Wright, *Lay Down Body*.

8. Please note that Missouri is not traditionally categorized as a southern state. Missouri cemeteries are included in this volume because Missouri was a slave state when it joined the Union in 1820 to counterbalance the free state of Maine that joined at the same time.

9. For more on death denial theory, see Mitford, *American Way of Death*; Gorer, "Pornography of Death"; Kübler-Ross, *On Death and Dying*; Becker, *Denial of Death*.

10. Jackson, "Black Experience with Death," 204.

11. Ibid., 204–5.

12. In recent years, there has been a profusion of scholarship that uses death as an analytical tool to explore power dynamics between white and Black people from enslavement to freedom. See Taylor, *If We Must Die*; Snyder, *Power to Die*; Berry, *Price for Their Pound of Flesh*; Sommerville, *Aberration of Mind*; Warren, "To Claim One's Own"; Fletcher, "African American Mourning Practices and Burial Traditions"; Holloway, *Passed On*; McCusker, "Purple Coffins and Cadillac Hearses"; Suzanne Smith, *To Serve the Living*; Booker, *Nine Years Under*; Plater, *African American Entrepreneurship*.

13. For more on slave cemeteries, see Rainville, *Hidden History*; Roberta Wright and Wilbur Wright, *Lay Down Body*; Jamieson, "Material Culture and Social Death"; King, "Separated by Death and Color"; Garman, "Viewing the Color Line"; Little, "Afro-American Gravemarkers in North Carolina"; Ashcraft, "Carving a Path to Freedom"; Malloy and Malloy, "Slavery in Colonial Massachusetts"; Krüger-Kahloula, "Tributes in Stone and Lapidary Lapses."

14. For more on Black burial societies, see Blassingame, *Black New Orleans*;
Fitzgerald, *Urban Emancipation*; Hinks and Kantrowitz, *All Men Free and Brethren*; Levine, "Single Standard of Civilization"; Rainville, *Hidden History*, 74.

15. Warren, "To Claim One's Own."

16. Ibid.; Rundbland, "Exhuming Women's Premarket Duties"; Aldridge, "Dress in the United States of America."

17. Holloway, *Passed On*; Fletcher, "African American Mourning Practices and Burial Traditions."

18. Nora, "Between Memory and History."

19. Elizabethada Wright, "More Than a 'Heap of Dust.'"

20. French, "Cemetery as Cultural Institution."

21. Petrella, "Gentrification Is Erasing Black Cemeteries."

Bibliography

Primary Sources

"An Act to Protect All Citizens in Their Civil and Legal Rights." *U.S. Statutes at Large* 18, part 3, chap. 114. Washington, D.C.: Government Printing Office, 1875.

U.S. Congress. *Congressional Globe*. 41st Congress. 2nd Session, 1870.

U.S. Congress. *Congressional Globe*. 42nd Congress. 2nd Session, 1872.

Secondary Sources

Aldridge, Ryan Jerel. "Dress in the United States of America as Depicted in Postmortem Photographs, 1840–1900." Master's thesis, Louisiana State University, 2008.

Ashcraft, Mary Ann. "Carving a Path to Freedom: The Life and Work of African American Stonecarver Sebastian 'Boss' Hammond." *Markers: The Annual Journal of the Association for Gravestone Studies* 21 (2004): 12–39.

Becker, Ernest. The Denial of Death. New York: Simon and Schuster, 1973.

Berry, Daina Ramey. *The Price for Their Pound of Flesh: The Value of the Enslaved, from Womb to Grave, in the Building of a Nation*. Boston: Beacon Press, 2017.

Blassingame, John W. *Black New Orleans, 1860–1880*. Chicago: University of Chicago Press, 1973.

Booker, Sheri. *Nine Years Under: Coming of Age in an Inner-City Funeral Home*. New York: Gotham Books, 2013.

Fitzgerald, Michael W. *Urban Emancipation: Popular Politics in Reconstruction Mobile, 1860–1890*. Baton Rouge: Louisiana State University Press, 2002.

Fletcher, Kami. "7 Elements of African American Mourning Practices and Burial Traditions." *Talk Death Daily*, February 8, 2021. https://www.talkdeath.com/7-elements-of-african-american-mourning-practices-burial-traditions/.

Foner, Eric. *Reconstruction: America's Unfinished Revolution, 1863–1877*. New York: Harper and Row, 1988.

French, Stanley. "The Cemetery as Cultural Institution: The Establishment of Mount Auburn and the 'Rural Cemetery' Movement." *American Quarterly* 26, no. 1 (March 1974): 39.

Garman, James. "Viewing the Color Line through the Material Culture of Death." *Historical Archaeology* 28, no. 3 (1994): 74–93.

Gorer, Geoffrey. "The Pornography of Death." *Encounter* 5, no. 4 (1955): 49–52.

Hinks, Peter P., and Stephen Kantrowitz, eds. *All Men Free and Brethren: Essays on the History of African American Freemasonry*. Ithaca, N.Y.: Cornell University Press, 2013.

Holloway, Karla FC. *Passed On: African American Mourning Stories*. Durham, N.C.: Duke University Press, 2002.

Jackson, Maurice. "The Black Experience with Death: A Brief Analysis through Black Writings." *Omega* 3, no. 3 (1972): 203–9.

Jamieson, Ross. "Material Culture and Social Death: African American Burial Practices." *Historical Archaeology* 29, no. 4 (1995): 39–58.

King, Charlotte. "Separated by Death and Color: The African American Cemetery of New Philadelphia." *Illinois Historical Archaeology* 44, no. 1 (2010): 125–37.

Krüger-Kahloula, Angelika. "Tributes in Stone and Lapidary Lapses: Commemorating Black People in Eighteenth- and Nineteenth-Century America." *Markers: The Annual Journal of the Association for Gravestone Studies* 6 (1989): 32–100.

Kübler-Ross, Elisabeth. *On Death and Dying*. New York: Macmillan, 1969.

Laderman, Gary. *The Sacred Remains: American Attitudes toward Death, 1799–1883*. New Haven, Conn.: Yale University Press, 1996.

Levine, Daniel. "A Single Standard of Civilization: Black Private Social Welfare Institutions in the South, 1880s–1920s." *Georgia Historical Quarterly* 81, no. 1 (Spring 1997): 52–77.

Little, M. Ruth. "Afro-American Gravemarkers in North Carolina." *Markers: The Annual Journal of the Association for Gravestone Studies* 6 (1989): 102–34.

Malloy, Tom, and Brenda Malloy. "Slavery in Colonial Massachusetts as Seen through Selected Gravestones." *Markers: The Annual Journal of the Association for Gravestone Studies* 11 (1994): 112–41.

Masur, Kate. *An Example for All the Land: Emancipation and the Struggle over Equality in Washington, D.C.* Chapel Hill: University of North Carolina Press, 2010.

McCusker, Kristine. "Purple Coffins and Cadillac Hearses: The Material Culture of Death and J.C. Oats (Memphis) Funeral Home, 1916–1929." Paper presented at the 101st Annual Meeting and Conference of the Association for the Study of African American Life and Culture, Richmond, Va., 2017.

McElya, Micki. *The Politics of Mourning: Death and Honor in Arlington National Cemetery.* Cambridge, Mass.: Harvard University Press, 2016.

McPherson, James M. "Abolitionists and the Civil Rights Act of 1875." *Journal of American History* 52, no. 3 (1965): 493–510.

Mitford, Jessica. *The American Way of Death.* New York: Simon and Schuster, 1963.

Murphy, L. E. "The Civil Rights Law of 1875." *Journal of Negro History* 12, no. 2 (1927): 110–27.

Nora, Pierre. "Between Memory and History: Les Lieux de Mémoire." In "Memory and Counter-Memory." Special issue, *Representations*, no. 26 (Spring 1989): 7–24.

Petrella, Christopher. "Gentrification Is Erasing Black Cemeteries and, with It, Black History." *Guardian*, April 27, 2019.

Plater, Michael. *African American Entrepreneurship, 1890–1940: The Story of R. C. Scott.* New York: Garland Publishing, 1996.

Rainville, Lynn. *Hidden History: African American Cemeteries in Central Virginia.* Charlottesville: University of Virginia Press, 2014.

Rundbland, Georganne. "Exhuming Women's Premarket Duties in the Care of the Dead." *Gender and Society* 9, no. 2 (1995): 173–92.

Sloane, David Charles. *The Last Great Necessity: Cemeteries in American History.* Baltimore: Johns Hopkins University Press, 1991.

Smith, Ryan K. *Death and Rebirth in a Southern City: Richmond's Historic Cemeteries.* Baltimore: Johns Hopkins University Press, 2020.

Smith, Suzanne. *To Serve the Living: Funeral Directors and the African American Way of Death.* Cambridge, Mass.: Belknap Press of Harvard University Press, 2010.

Snyder, Terri. *The Power to Die: Slavery and Suicide in British North America.* Chicago: University of Chicago Press, 2015.

Sommerville, Diane Miller. *Aberration of Mind: Suicide and Suffering in the Civil War–Era South.* Chapel Hill: University of North Carolina Press, 2018.

Stanley, Amy Dru. "Slave Emancipation and the Revolutionizing of Human Rights." In *The World the Civil War Made*, edited by Gregory P. Downs and Kate Masur, 269–303. Chapel Hill: University of North Carolina Press, 2015.

Taylor, Eric Robert. *If We Must Die: Shipboard Insurrections in the Era of the Atlantic Slave Trade.* Baton Rouge: Louisiana State University Press, 2009.

Warren, Jamie. "To Claim One's Own: Death and the Body in the Daily Politics of Antebellum Slavery." In *Death and the American South*, edited by Craig Thompson Friend and Lorri Glover, 110–30. New York: Cambridge University Press, 2014.

Wright, Elizabethada. "More Than a 'Heap of Dust': The Material Memorialization of Three Nineteenth-Century Women's Graves." In *Women and the Material Culture of Death*, edited by Beth Fowkes Tobin and Maureen Daly Goggin. Farnham, UK: Ashgate Publishing, 2013.

Wright, Roberta Hughes, and Wilbur B. Wright III. *Lay Down Body: Living History in African American Cemeteries.* Detroit: Visible Ink Press, 1996.

CHAPTER 1

The Status Quo Made Picturesque
Nineteenth-Century Macon, Georgia, and Its Garden of the Dead

SCARLET JERNIGAN

"Behold a new city which we now consecrate to the dead! Behold its walls, its gates, and its streets!" wrote one nineteenth-century southerner of the new cemetery in his town. In Macon's municipal rural-style cemeteries Rose Hill and Oak Ridge, "the city of the living clearly rearranged itself in the city of the dead."[1] There, the antebellum town's white citizens both high and low, as well as African Americans both enslaved and free, were to find rest—not side by side exactly but at peace with each other and their respective places in society. These new gardens of the dead—in keeping with the rural cemetery movement—were to be not only picturesque but also class conscious, serving as a "didactic landscape" that would instruct those perambulating there on sunny afternoons.[2] Mapping reveals that Macon's necropolis mirrored the patterns of hierarchy and marginality found in the town's streets. Through Rose Hill and Oak Ridge, white Maconites, including the city's slaveholders, sought to prescribe how the world viewed them and southern civilization. In the postbellum period, both cemeteries underwent significant changes in line with Maconites' altered circumstances.

The City of Macon:
Its Antebellum Demography and Urban Geography

The makeup of antebellum Macon was a predictor of its deathways geography. From Macon's founding in 1823 on the "fall line," directly on the banks of the Ocmulgee River, the town gained importance as an "agrarian city" where commission merchants stored cotton before they shipped it to the coast.³ Macon functioned as a market town for central Georgia, selling just about everything needed for both farm and household—items brought upriver on the Ocmulgee and later overland on the railroad. To bolster the city's commerce, Maconites embraced telegraph service as well as a number of manufacturing establishments. The town's antebellum growth and diversification made the larger rural-style cemeteries Rose Hill and Oak Ridge necessary. As the fifth largest city in Georgia in 1860, Macon had a population of 5,337 whites as well as 33 free and 2,664 enslaved African Americans.⁴ In Macon, as in many southern cities, "slave labor could be found nearly anywhere there was a task to perform," as white urbanites modified slavery to suit their needs.⁵ Though both free and enslaved African Americans would have been ubiquitous on Macon's streets, in the 1860 city directory, which was the principal source for this mapping project, Macon's people of color were virtually invisible.⁶ As scholar Angelika Kruger-Kahloula observed of another slaveholding city, for African Americans "the abodes of the living and the dead were both on the periphery."⁷ Many of the enslaved in the city would have resided in the homes or shops of Macon's slaveholders, in back lots or "yards" behind slaveholders' residences, or in small houses or shanties squeezed into alleys. "Living out" in locations away from slaveholders even under the least favorable conditions provided a measure of independence. An enslaved community formed in East Macon around the Central Railroad depot, allowing for some fellowship, mutual support, and "quasi-freedom."⁸ Even free African Americans did not appear in the 1860 Macon city directory. A similar dearth of records obscures the exact resting places of most people of color within the city's antebellum cemeteries.

For Macon's white population, the 1860 directory reveals the residential patterns of different occupational groups, providing invaluable information necessary for analyzing Rose Hill on Macon's north side. The cemetery mirrored in many ways the socioeconomic patterns in neighborhoods. Dividing white Maconites into seven socioeconomic groups, from most to least prestigious, allows for closer analysis of these groups in both city and cemetery. (See the appendix for a review and explanation of these categories.) Mapping the city shows that those at the lower end of this scale—groups 4 to 7, namely Macon's clerks, middle-class professionals, and skilled and unskilled laborers, who made up over three-quarters of the population—often lived side by side with the more prosperous. (See figure 1.1.) Yet, further inquiry demonstrates that in both city and cemetery, greater wealth—often aligned with slaveholding—often equaled residency in the city's more fashionable areas.

LEGEND

Slaveholders by Group
● Groups 1–3
■ Group 4
▲ Groups 5–7

Nonslaveholders by Group
● Groups 1–3
■ Group 4
▲ Groups 5–7

This map displays the approximate residential locations of 1860 white Maconites. See appendix for an explanation of the factors utilized to determine Maconites' socioeconomic status. The federal censuses of 1840, 1850, and 1860, along with the 1857 Macon tax digest, supplied slaveholding information. The 1860 city directory compiled by Mears and Company provided most of the locations for geocoding. The base map is *Vincent's New Map of the City of Macon*, produced in 1854, used courtesy of the Middle Georgia Archives, Washington Memorial Library, Macon, Georgia. Cartographer: Scarlet Jernigan

FIGURE 1.1. 1860 Macon: Socioeconomic Groups by Slaveholding Status

Being a part of the slaveholding class meant a greater likelihood of living in elite areas of town and of being interred in the city's rural cemetery. Macon's antebellum geography, or "unwitting biography," encompasses the residential choices of the 336 Maconites in the 1860 city directory who either hired enslaved laborers from slaveholders or used their own.[9] The greater their wealth, the more likely Maconites were to be slaveholders or hirers. Of Maconites with residential information gleaned mostly from the 1860 directory, 88 percent of greater merchants and planters in group 1 owned or rented enslaved laborers. In comparison, 58 percent of those in group 3, middling proprietors and city officials, utilized enslaved labor, compared to 7 percent of the skilled laborers in group 5 who were slaveholders or hirers. Though there was no obvious separation between slaveholders and nonslaveholders on Macon's streets, a closer look at the residential topography within the same occupational groups reveals a single pattern. Occupational group 3 had seventy-five slaveholders residing in the city in 1860, compared to fifty-six nonslaveholders. The plotted points in figure 1.2 show the residences of these men and women, while the ellipses indicate clustering. Slaveholders in group 3 were more likely to be living above First Street at higher elevations outside the business district. The data for the sixty-two slaveholders and six nonslaveholders in group 1 denote the same pattern, which also held true for all 336 slaveholders and 1,494 nonslaveholders residing in the city. In all occupational groups, there were fewer slaveholders living in the less affluent areas on the city's perimeter in East Macon, south of Oglethorpe Street, or east of the Southwestern and Central Railroad tracks.[10] (See again figure 1.1.) This trend toward the fashionable was more pronounced in Rose Hill, where slaveholders appeared in numbers that far exceeded their proportions of the population. Though socioeconomic groups 1 through 3 made up only 16 percent of Maconites listed in the 1860 directory, this same bloc constituted almost half of the antebellum lot purchasers in Rose Hill, highlighting the cemetery's elitist leanings.[11]

The wealthiest of these slaveholders included not only planters but also nonagricultural businessmen who sometimes lived alongside planters in the city's most exclusive sections and were subsequently laid to rest beside them in Rose Hill. A number of planters whose agricultural operations were far removed from Macon built mansions in the city and bought lots in Rose Hill instead of choosing residence and interment on their plantations elsewhere. They chose Macon to display their wealth, take advantage of social opportunities, be closer to educational choices for their children, avoid hotels when on business, and secure more stable and visible burial locations. With higher elevations and larger lot sizes, "uptown" College Street and Georgia Ave-

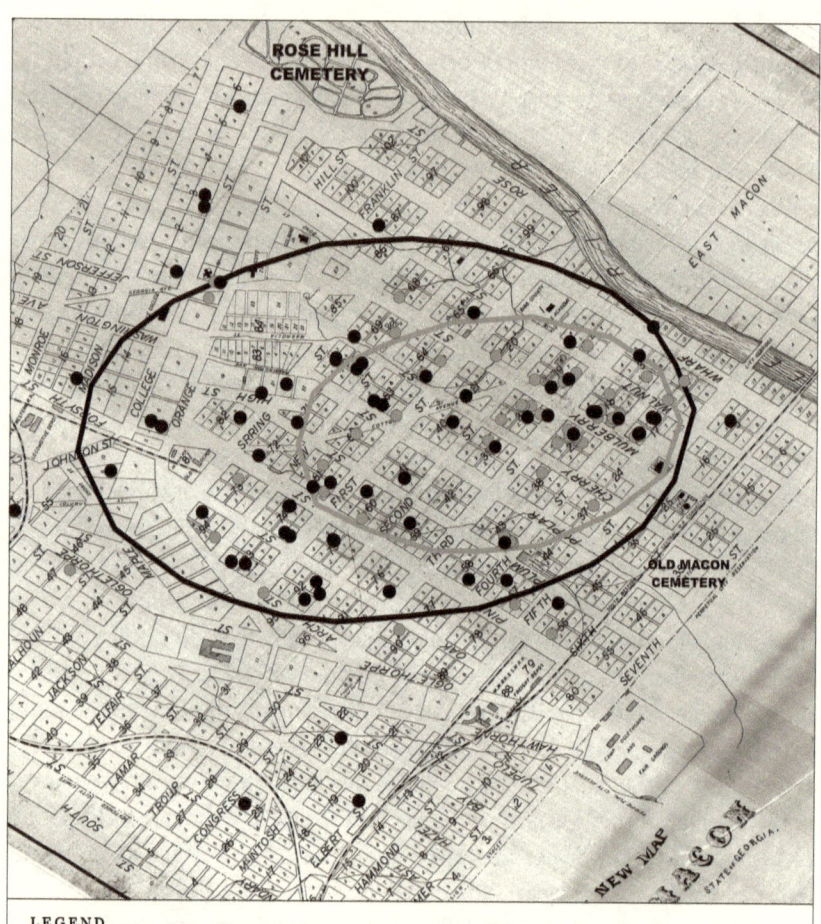

LEGEND

- • Slaveholders
- • Nonslaveholders
- ⬭ Slaveholders
- ⬭ Nonslaveholders

This map displays the approximate residential locations of 1860 white Maconites with known slaveholding condition. The ellipse tool quantifies and visualizes the degree of clustering for the groups in question. See appendix for an explanation of occupational groups. The federal censuses of 1840, 1850, and 1860, along with the 1857 Macon tax digest, supplied slaveholding information. The 1860 city directory compiled by Mears and Company provided most of the locations for geocoding. The base map is *Vincent's New Map of the City of Macon*, produced in 1854, used courtesy of Middle Georgia Archives, Washington Memorial Library, Macon, Georgia. Cartographer: Scarlet Jernigan

FIGURE 1.2. 1860 Macon: Socioeconomic Group 3 Slaveholders and Nonslaveholders

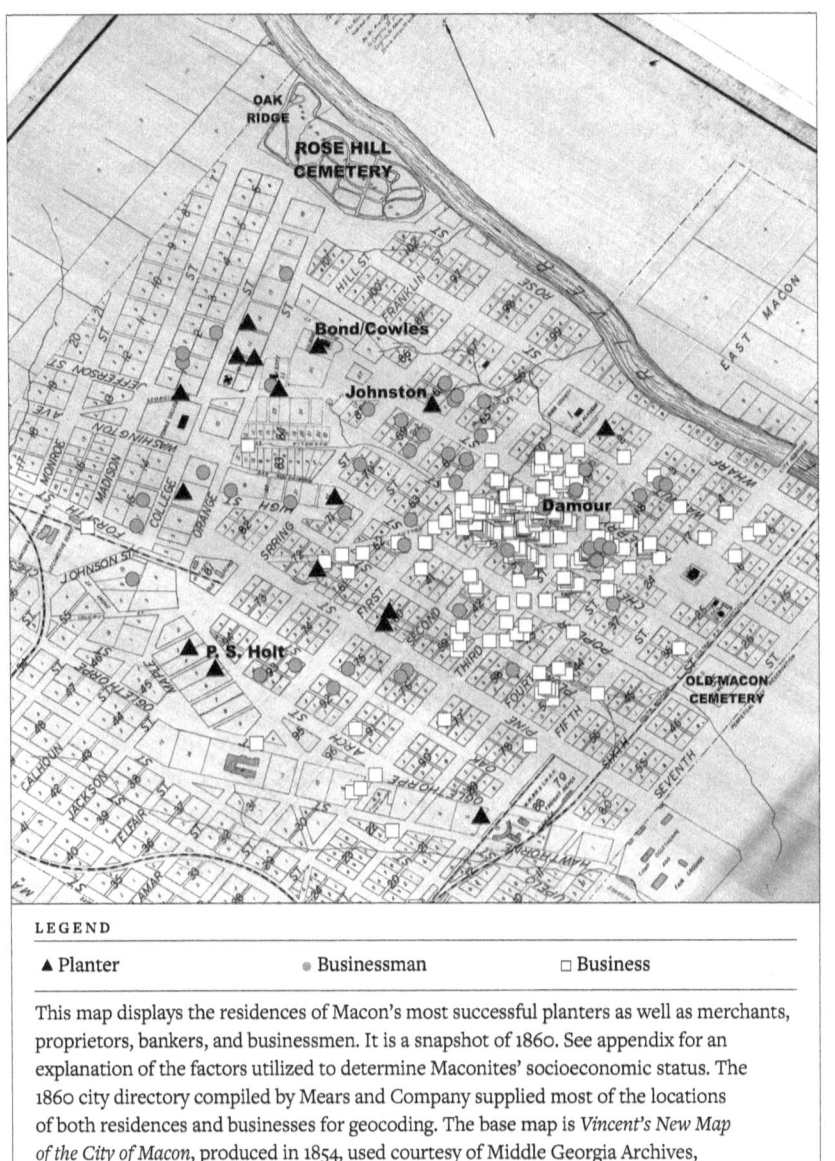

LEGEND

▲ Planter   • Businessman   □ Business

This map displays the residences of Macon's most successful planters as well as merchants, proprietors, bankers, and businessmen. It is a snapshot of 1860. See appendix for an explanation of the factors utilized to determine Maconites' socioeconomic status. The 1860 city directory compiled by Mears and Company supplied most of the locations of both residences and businesses for geocoding. The base map is *Vincent's New Map of the City of Macon*, produced in 1854, used courtesy of Middle Georgia Archives, Washington Memorial Library, Macon, Georgia. Cartographer: Scarlet Jernigan

FIGURE 1.3. 1860 Macon: Socioeconomic Group 1 Planters and Businessmen

nue in particular boasted a number of "superblocks" with the private mansions of the agricultural and nonagricultural crème de la crème.[12] Living on prominences such as these removed residents from city smells and high-traffic dusty streets and allowed them to enjoy any fresh breezes that might be wafting through central Georgia. Though nonagricultural businessman William Butler Johnston built the most spectacular antebellum residence in Macon, the aptly named Italian Renaissance Revival "Palace of the South," his mercantile peers were more likely to live at less fashionable addresses closer to the city's business district, as seen in figure 1.3. Most wealthy planters resided outside the business district uptown; twelve of sixteen planters with homes in the city in 1860 lived above First Street, where the congestion of city businesses started to thin. In comparison, thirty of fifty-two nonagricultural businessmen did so. Almost half of the city's wealthy planters resided above Spring Street, while only 23 percent of greater merchants and proprietors did so. Though this variation could have been due to differences in status consciousness, there were pragmatic reasons why some of the city's wealthiest merchants chose to live downtown, such as the desire to be in proximity to their shops and warehouses.[13] In Rose Hill, the bones of planters and nonagricultural businessmen mingled without the impediment of these pragmatic considerations.

Antebellum Macon's deathways geography imitated in many ways its residential patterns regarding both race and class. The growing number of white planter, commercial, industrial, and transportation workers listed in the 1860 city directory lived in close proximity. There was substantial spatial overlap present among all white occupational groups in the small antebellum city, though slaveholding bestowed an economic advantage, making slaveholders more likely to lay their heads in more fashionable surrounds in both life and death. These slaveholders included agricultural and nonagricultural elites who mingled in both city and cemetery. In contrast, African American Maconites' final resting places were often unknown and unknowable.

Rose Hill:
Class in the Elitist Rural Cemetery

In the rural cemeteries Rose Hill and Oak Ridge, Maconites made class and racial disparities as beautiful as possible, even as they sought to bolster the southern way of life and to gloss over the unpleasant realities of life in antebellum Georgia. Maconites patterned these burial grounds, with Rose Hill for the white population and Oak Ridge for people of color, after the popular rural cemetery movement. Lasting from 1831 into the 1870s, the movement naturalized and beautified burial grounds by placing them on the edge of town, literally in the woods. Each of these picturesque cemeteries was to be a carefully curated wilderness in a style borrowed from eighteenth-century English landscape design used to transform the nobility's great landed estates. This elitist form, transplanted across the Atlantic, aimed to refine Americans, who, according to one concerned writer, "vie with Goth or Vandal in apparent hate of cultured arts." The movement was appropriate for the slaveholding class's purposes, for it was a conservative reform aimed at literally enshrining hierarchy and the status quo.[14] For generations, the dead had packed older city and church graveyards in both North and South, with the high and low of society often lying "indistinguishably intermingled. Magistrates and criminals, preachers, soldiers, merchants, lawyers, doctors, colonial dames . . . [were] all consorting together in promiscuous companionship."[15] "Reform-minded proprietors" in rural-style cemeteries wanted "to avoid such indiscriminate mingling" and instead to establish a more delineated "mirror image of the social groups existing in town." Though Mount Auburn Cemetery outside Boston was the original rural cemetery, southern cities and towns quickly founded their own and modified "cemetery landscape design and use in ways that were distinctive to the region."[16] These variations came into play concerning both the unique white southern hierarchy and the place of free and enslaved African Americans in the South.

Macon's rural cemetery stayed true to both the movement's expansive picturesque model and its class obsession. In the late 1830s, Macon decided to open a new burial ground for its white residents because the Old Macon Cemetery, located on the eastern edge of the city grid, neared capacity. To replace this four-acre utilitarian graveyard, a town committee selected a fifty-acre site on the Ocmulgee River, one-half mile northwest of the city center. Its ridges, dells, and rocky cliffs above the river set it apart from the Old Macon Cemetery's flat landscape. Macon's *Georgia Citizen* described the ambience of Rose Hill with its "various marble monuments, many of them hidden in the depths of the dark green forest, and which can only be found by the intricate windings of various bye-paths."[17] These marble monuments often belonged to the affluent within Rose Hill. Many white working-class and poor Maconites found "some less genteel place of burial," which included the margins of Rose Hill itself.[18] Antebellum Rose Hill had over two hundred recorded white burials in what the interment book often referred to as "Strangers Row." Antebellum Rose Hill's formal, landscaped sections received approximately 1,100 burials, revealing that almost one of every five interments during this period was in Strangers Row. Beyond a minority

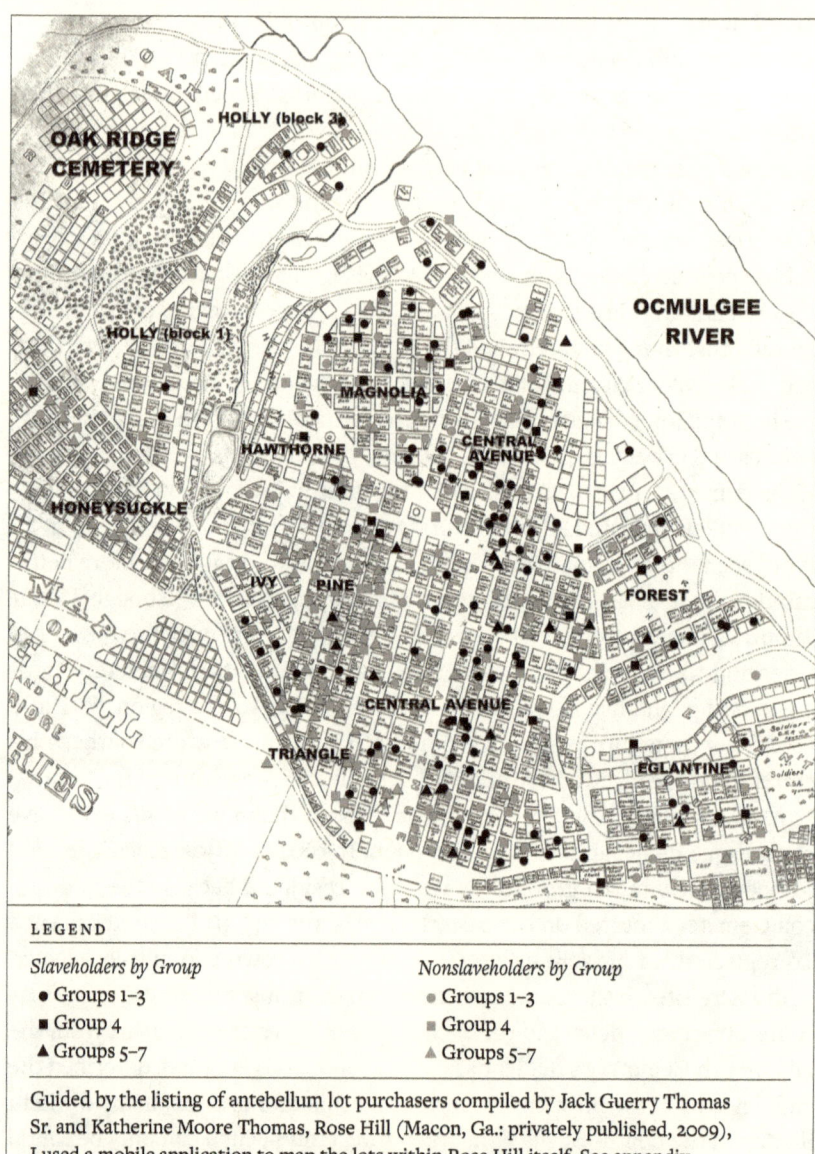

LEGEND

Slaveholders by Group
- Groups 1–3
- Group 4
- Groups 5–7

Nonslaveholders by Group
- Groups 1–3
- Group 4
- Groups 5–7

Guided by the listing of antebellum lot purchasers compiled by Jack Guerry Thomas Sr. and Katherine Moore Thomas, Rose Hill (Macon, Ga.: privately published, 2009), I used a mobile application to map the lots within Rose Hill itself. See appendix for an explanation of the factors utilized to determine Maconites' socioeconomic condition. The federal censuses of 1840, 1850, and 1860, along with the 1857 Macon tax digest, supplied slaveholding information. The base map dates to 1897, when Macon commissioned its city engineer, J. C. Wheeler, to survey Rose Hill and Oak Ridge. The base map is used courtesy of the Middle Georgia Archives, Washington Memorial Library, Macon, Georgia. Cartographer: Scarlet Jernigan

FIGURE 1.4. Antebellum Rose Hill Lot Purchasers: Slaveholding and Nonslaveholding by Socioeconomic Group

listed as paupers, there are twenty-seven Strangers Row burials with known occupations. These working-class whites found rest in "ranges" set aside for the "burial of strangers" or for white Maconites who needed to "select a free lot." These ranges existed along the verges of established burial sections.[19]

The ownership of purchased plots within the cemetery's terraced grid resembled the residency patterns of the living. Those of modest means were often in proximity to the affluent, though they did not mingle "indistinguishably." Certain sections in the burial ground had higher status than others, as the lists of antebellum lot purchasers attest. Holly Ridge was the most exclusive section, with 75 percent of its purchasers in occupational groups 1 to 3. Magnolia followed close behind with 72 percent of the lots held by groups 1 through 3. Honeysuckle and Pine Ridges skewed toward those less well off, with 61 percent of Honeysuckle and 50 percent of Pine's lots purchased by Maconites in occupational group 5, 6, and 7. (See figure 1.4.) As noted above, slaveholders were overrepresented in the cemetery, purchasing over half of the 375 lots sold in the antebellum era. The sections with lot purchaser majorities in socioeconomic groups 1, 2, and 3 also had slaveholding majorities.[20]

Both planters and nonagricultural businessmen, mostly slaveholders, chose high-status locations in Rose Hill. They did so even if they lived in less fashionable surroundings in the city. For example, wealthy grocer John H. Damour resided in the midst of the city's business district but chose a lot at the base of Central Avenue on the Ocmulgee near the Powers, Lockett, and Holt planter family plots. (See figure 1.5.) In many sections of Macon's necropolis, the affluent selected lots near the carriageways or on high ground. It appealed to them that their visitors would have a view from their plot, and "being seen" could continue decades after death if the wealthy chose the most opportune spot for personal or familial memorialization. Favored locations for both the agricultural and nonagricultural elites to cluster included Central Avenue District, block 1, at the cemetery's entrance, which was also at the burial ground's highest elevation. A number of the affluent grouped at the northern edge of Magnolia Ridge. The most exclusive section in the cemetery was Holly Ridge's block 3, where wealthy planters and nonagricultural businessmen were undisturbed in their rest by the less affluent. Separated from the remainder of the cemetery by ravines on either side, "Cowles Hill" monuments were visible from a number of vantage points along the Ocmulgee both inside and outside the cemetery. Merchant and railroad promoter Jerry Cowles of New York and his family lie but a few feet from planter Joseph Bond. Notably, a few years before his demise Bond had purchased Cowles's Greek Revival mansion in

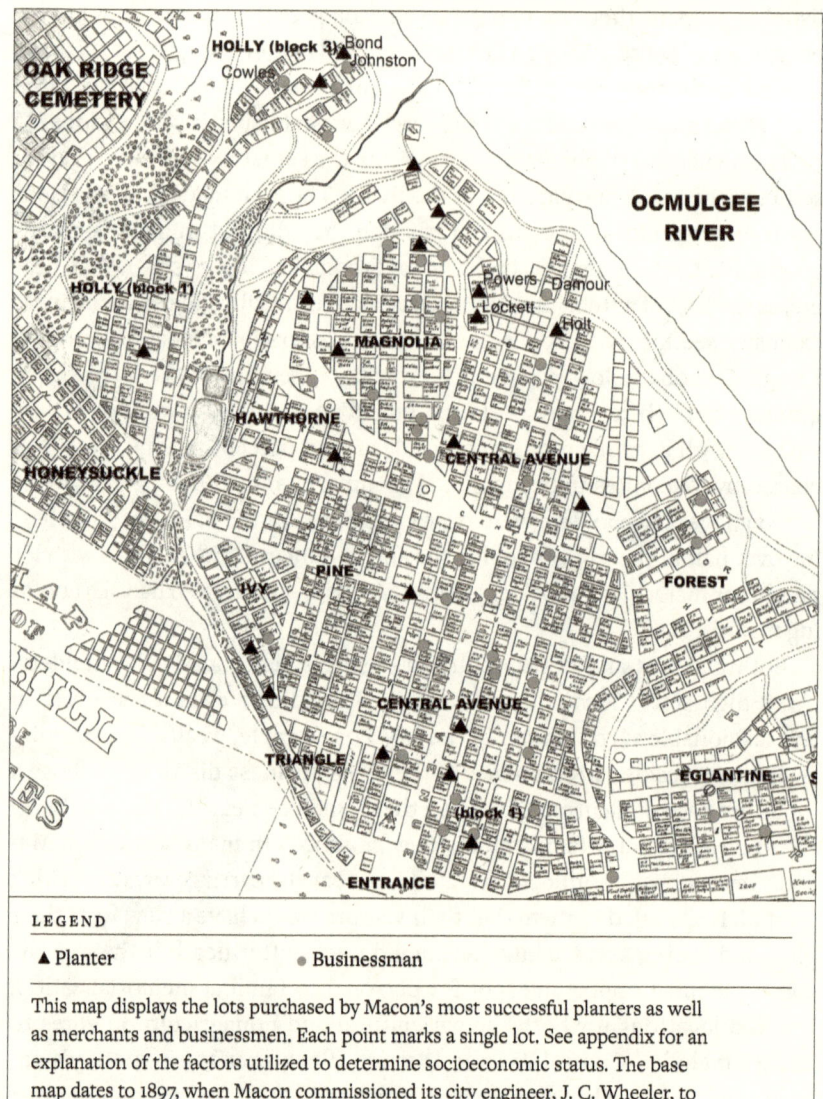

LEGEND

▲ Planter ● Businessman

This map displays the lots purchased by Macon's most successful planters as well as merchants and businessmen. Each point marks a single lot. See appendix for an explanation of the factors utilized to determine socioeconomic status. The base map dates to 1897, when Macon commissioned its city engineer, J. C. Wheeler, to survey Rose Hill and Oak Ridge. It is used courtesy of the Middle Georgia Archives, Washington Memorial Library, Macon, Georgia. Cartographer: Scarlet Jernigan

FIGURE 1.5. Antebellum Rose Hill Lot Purchasers: Socioeconomic Group 1 Planters and Businessmen

northwest Macon after financial reversals had forced Cowles to sell. Bond's lot is adjacent to that of businessman William Butler Johnston, who built the "Palace of the South" in uptown Macon. Upon Bond's unexpected death in 1859, Johnston oversaw the creation of both the Bond and Johnston lots. He hired architects, stone setters, and brick masons to create a "bold bluff" overlooking the Ocmulgee River, accomplished with approximately twelve-foot-high brownstone retaining walls. Stairs leading down to the river connect the Bond and Johnston lots.[21]

Rose Hill burial patterns illuminate how white Maconites organized themselves in regard to status. Though the remains of the rich mingled with Macon's middling sort in many cemetery sections, a healthy proportion of the working class and poor found rest on the "unincorporated" margins, just as the nonslaveholding poor were more likely to live along the city's unfashionable edges.[22] The rural cemetery movement's preoccupation with social rank accommodated well the slaveholding class within the cemetery. The exclusivity of Holly Ridge's block 3, the mixture of both elite businessmen and planters interred there, and Johnston's construction of adjoining lots for the Bond and Johnston families all represent the merchant-planter symbiosis in southern cities such as Macon.

Rose Hill:
Slaveholding and Gender in the Rural Cemetery

A closer look at how white slaveholders chose to represent themselves and their peers in Rose Hill denotes particular narratives about slavery that they subtly or not so subtly promoted. Throughout the cemetery, the slaveholding elites encouraged the less privileged to draw close to the fine monuments in these large family lots and marvel not only at the culture exhibited in sepulchral and lot improvement choices but also at the good deeds of the dead proclaimed in the epitaphs. Of special note were inscriptions citing the upper class's achievements as both "affectionate fathers" and "humane masters." Middling slaveholders contributed more humble and mundane headstones with epitaphs extolling their dead as good Christians and honest neighbors—eulogies often found in nineteenth-century rural-style cemeteries. The prevalence of these epitaphs shored up late-antebellum dogma proclaiming that slavery was not damaging to either slaveholders or the enslaved.

Though Macon's planters did not stand apart as a group from other elites, there are a handful of planter lots in Rose Hill that deserve closer scrutiny because their sepulchre arrangements proved unique in certain respects.

The Macon city council noted in 1859 that many non-Maconites "during the last year have been brought from great distances to be deposited" in Rose Hill.[23] Of these, planters were a notable segment as well as the largest group of slaveholders entombed in the necropolis. In Rose Hill, planters attempted to construct a favorable narrative concerning the "peculiar institution," in the Lockett, Powers, and Bond lots particularly.

Antebellum Americans carefully chose epitaphs that society considered "required reading." These seemingly benign verses could be both a form of social control and propaganda, as evinced by a couple of inscriptions in Rose Hill that directly refer to the deceased's role as "master."[24] Planter John Powers died in Monroe County in 1854 and was interred in the Central Avenue District near the Ocmulgee. Powers's tall pedestal monument in marble includes the following inscription: "The deceased was a strong minded sensible and humane man, as Husband, Parent, Master & Neighbour just and kind." Nearby, Maconite planter Benjamin G. Lockett created a terraced lot complete with fancy wrought-iron fence and impressive retaining wall a number of levels above the nearest carriageway. His kinsman James Lockett died in 1844 in Crawford County. Lockett's epitaph reads in part: "He was a kind husband. Affectionate Father. Humane Master. Charitable Neighbor. Faithful Friend and an honest man."[25] Though these epitaphs have slightly different forms, the messages are fundamentally the same.

Even as abolitionists used "idealized domestic images" to demonstrate the brutality of slavery in contrast to the comforts of a loving family and portrayed slaveholders as incapable of meaningful domestic life, slaveholders employed the same imagery to praise themselves as exemplary family men.[26] In antebellum Rose Hill, Maconites lauded four men as "good fathers," while five were "good husbands." These family men included "humane masters" John Powers and James Lockett, meaning that half of the epitaphs praising fathers and 40 percent of those mentioning exemplary husband also incorporated references to masterhood. Lockett's epitaph describes him as "affectionate," a reflection of the sentimental language associated with the mid-nineteenth-century family, the preservation of which was a foundational purpose of the rural cemetery movement. Not only did these cemeteries include large lots designed to bring generations of kinfolk together in death, but they also promoted intimate nuclear family groupings with the "domestication of death." This garden-style cemetery promoted family as an oasis, an idealized "sanctuary of love and comfort."[27] Lockett's epitaph aligned with the sentimental ideal and pointedly challenged abolitionist claims. Though it did not proclaim the enslaved as part of an "extended family," proslavery advocates certainly did so, as evinced later in the memorialization of Joseph Bond, exposing the slaveholding class's efforts to reconcile a system of "power, fear, and desire, of mistrust and dissimulation," with the "romanticized images of home" circulating at the time.[28]

Both the Lockett and Powers epitaphs use the word "humane" to describe the deceased, an example of proslavery attempts to reconcile slaveholding and virtue. Slaveholders had created an alleged proslavery humanitarianism. Yet, despite their assumed enlightened ideas, even "progressive slaveholders" retained most of the despotic prerogatives over the enslaved.[29] Far from being humane, they dehumanized those they had power over. James Oakes notes, "In law and custom, in ideology and practice, the masters did their best to ignore or sidestep the inescapable humanities of their slaves."[30] Here in the Central Avenue District of Rose Hill, the Powers and Lockett families presented, in marble, a sanitized and romanticized vision of their associations with the enslaved, which was how they chose to see themselves and desired others to view them as well.

Similarly, but on a larger scale, the slaveholding class carefully crafted the narrative surrounding the death and memorialization of Maconite elite planter Joseph Bond. Bond owned six plantations in Lee and Baker counties to the southwest of Macon and at least 273 enslaved individuals.[31] In March 1859, Bond died in an altercation with his brother-in-law's overseer Lucius Brown after Brown beat one of Bond's enslaved waggoners bloody. Earlier Bond had threatened to whip the overseer, a sign of his contempt for a "lower-class" male. As indicated by Bond's threat as well as by his thrashing of Brown with a two-foot-long hickory stick during the dispute, the overseer versus planter dynamic no doubt played a role here. Planters liked to view overseers as the "roughs" whose bad behavior caused "respectables" dedicated to benevolent paternalism to despair.[32] Further evidence of the tension between these groups appears in a letter from Macon-born Oliver Hillhouse Prince Jr. to Maconite elite planter John Basil Lamar: "I cannot tell you how shocked I was at hearing of the death of Joe Bond.... The overseers will take a large portion of this state after a while and Brown will be the Hero of his clan for having slayed the largest cotton planter in the state."[33] Yet, in their commemoration, proslavery newspapers in both Macon and Savannah chose not to air the planter versus overseer dynamic, because they had a different point to make.

For white southerners, Bond's conduct aligned with the prescribed role of not only his class but also his gender and race. Linking Bond's actions to paternalism, Georgia newspapers asserted that this incident illustrated "in bold relief ... a domestic tie of great affection and strength but little inferior to that of parent and child." Savannah's *Daily News* directly responded to abolitionists' accusations, proclaiming that Bond's death was a truer characterization of "the relations of master and servant in the South, than all the effusions of Mrs. [Harriet Beecher] Stowe [the author of *Uncle Tom's Cabin*] and the abolition crew combined."[34] Bond died in what white southern observers deemed an active, self-sacrificial, and public manner—a manner appropriate for his race, class, and gender. According to historian Kenneth S. Greenberg, perishing as a man of action was of particular importance to elite southern men, who desired to die in a way that "demonstrated mastery and control rather than fear and submission." For men such as Bond, the enslaved were the mirror image of their mastery, as these conceptions of manhood connected male power with white supremacy. In this formulation, Bond—a man serving in the role of patriarch—defended an enslaved male whom white society and the law deemed a dependent and thus devoid of manhood rights or masculine prowess.[35]

Though newspapers did their part to glorify Bond, the most lasting memorial to his heroic act was his grave within Macon's necropolis. As a rural-style cemetery, Rose Hill was the depository of local history, providing "landscapes of memory" that placed the "dead and the living in a vast historical narrative."[36] As noted above, elite businessman William Butler Johnston, a friend known for his impeccable taste who often advised Maconites concerning their sepulchre choices, oversaw the construction of Bond's lot overlooking the Ocmulgee. In 1866, a lavish marble funerary monument created by renowned Russian-American sculptor Robert E. Launitz was installed there.[37] It climbed twenty-two feet into the air and cost $25,000. Yet, in March 1859, the Macon *Telegraph*, the "leading voice of the central Georgia plantation interest," found Bond's fresh grave, at that point unadorned, most illuminating: "Standing by his grave, how beautiful are the lessons taught by his life and his death—the lessons of Honor and Duty—honor without sully—duty demanding the sacrifice of his valuable life."[38] Here, the editors directly tied Bond's grave in Rose Hill to a certain narrative about his death, even before his monument and the bluff that would showcase it were in place.

While Georgia newspapers and Macon's garden of the dead presented Bond as the epitome of southern manhood, femininity had its own role to play in southerners' narrative of the region. The configuration of the Bond monument itself, with its five life-sized female sculptures representing devotion, memory, hope, Christian faith, and the angel of resurrection, buoyed the masculinity of Bond with their contrasting femininity. These figures personified beauty, mourning, spirituality, compassion, comfort, and the home—all of which were the domain of women in antebellum America. The

Bond monument and other gravestones in Rose Hill depicted women as the keepers of the home and the backbone of local churches in the South just as they were in the North, and not as females fundamentally warped by the presence of slavery in their midst.[39] In antebellum Rose Hill, epitaphs identified twelve commendable mothers and eight good wives. Thirteen stones hailed Maconite women as good Christians. For instance, the monument to Elizabeth Rosseter Griffin (1813–40) reads, in part, "She was a member of the Methodist Episcopal Church and died resigned to the will of God."[40]

As antislavery advocates proclaimed the corruption of white southern families and the hypocrisy of the region's Christians, Maconites created clearly definable family lots, praised fathers and mothers along with "humane masters," and proclaimed their membership in local churches.[41] An observer can view these inscriptions as simply independent statements made by Maconites or as subtle assertions on their part that they were not devils and that their families were wholesome and good. Whatever their inclinations, white Maconites could "instruct visitors [to the cemetery] in the lessons of history and faith" as well as, if not better than, their counterparts elsewhere. While every rural-style cemetery had societal defects to hide, Macon's garden of the dead camouflaged a system that viewed certain people as property.[42]

Though few monuments in Rose Hill broached directly the role of slaveholder, in Macon's rural cemetery, deathways commemoration was inseparable from slaveholding. Much of the wealth showcased there derived from slavery, as many of Macon's wealthiest residents, mostly slaveholders, lie in the city's necropolis. As James Oakes notes, "In the Old South upward mobility . . . was expressed primarily within the slaveholding class itself." For slaveholders themselves and for those who hoped to one day join them, slaveholding was a symbol of success and financial independence. With its preponderance of the graves of the "master class," Macon's garden of the dead was to be an example of the purported urban progress of the city, even as the burial ground glossed over the inherent commodification and cruelty of slavery.[43]

Oak Ridge:
Racial Burial Segregation in the Rural Cemetery

Racial burial segregation in Macon was a reality of life reflected in the best possible light in the town's northside necropolis, putting to further use the rural cemetery movement's artful display of the southern hierarchy. Upon the opening of Rose Hill, a separate sister cemetery named Oak Ridge—"for the negro population of the city"—began receiving interments. In 1851 the city officially designated the land for Oak Ridge, and the Macon Committee on Cemeteries noted that the section adjoining on the northwest side of Rose Hill contained about ten acres with a "neat entrance, and is enclosed with a substantial fence, neatly white washed, and presenting an appearance creditable to the city."[44] Many of America's rural-style cemeteries set aside portions for "the remains of deceased persons of color," such as Savannah's Laurel Grove, with its fifteen acres in a southwest section earmarked for this use in 1853.[45] Oak Ridge offered many of the same natural beauties, but without the outlay of resources on lot improvement and monuments found in Rose Hill.

The antebellum period saw both enslaved and free people of color laid to rest in Oak Ridge. City records reveal that "a free man of color Hannibal Roe" was interred in Oak Ridge in 1846. Yet, surviving evidence suggests that wealthier African Americans, such as grocer, middling cotton factor, and landowner Solomon Humphries (1801–55), chose burial elsewhere. The overwhelming majority of the antebellum dead entombed at Oak Ridge were enslaved. Monthly sexton reports to the Macon city council indicate at least 950 African American burials from 1840 through 1865. The yearly numbers from that period indicate both uneven reportage and a growing dependence on the cemetery in the 1860s.[46] Macon's slaveholding class met its deathways responsibilities by providing a decent graveyard and paying the appropriate burial fees. With this burial ground, slaveholders demonstrated that they provided for the enslaved in death as they had in life—such was their view of the world. In life, they supplied shelter, food, and clothes. In death, the slaveholding class provided Oak Ridge, which offered an unadorned version of the picturesque.[47] Though antebellum evidence of enslaved Maconites' attitudes toward Oak Ridge is thin, testimony from elsewhere reveals that an intermingling in death was often not what enslaved African Americans desired any more than their white counterparts did, because interment next to slaveholders might link them for eternity. As one formerly enslaved man put it, the grave was "the only resting place of the poor slave."[48]

No matter how African Americans felt about their place in Macon's necropolis, white Maconites, whether they were slaveholders or not, probably viewed Oak Ridge as part of a cemetery complex to be proud of—separate and unequal. Though white Maconites founded Rose Hill's sister cemetery in the 1840s along the northwest edge of Rose Hill, it was not included in the 1854 map of the city, which is an indication of Oak Ridge's place in the minds of white Georgians. As scholar Angelika Kruger-Kahloula observed of American cemeteries writ large: "Hierarchy and marginality are very often displayed in a literal sense."[49]

The antebellum slaveholding class carefully curated their memorialization in Rose Hill, and Oak Ridge was vital to their benign and paternalistic narrative. In the postbellum period, Macon's former slaveholding elite and Rose Hill declined to some extent, even as the city's people of color claimed autonomy in both life and death upon the abolition of slavery. Oak Ridge, which had been a symbol of African American subordination, became an important repository of family history and heritage as people of color built or shored up communities as well as burial places.

Oak Ridge and Rose Hill: Postbellum Changes in the Rural Cemetery

From the city directory to the town's cemeteries, Maconite people of color were more visible after emancipation. Postbellum Macon was a city of red dirt streets, along which whites and a growing number of African Americans lived and worked as there was a "flowering of political, religious, and educational activity" among people of color in the city. In 1878, A. E. Shole published a city directory that included both white and African American Maconites, with people of color identified throughout with a "c" for "colored." Postbellum pallbearers continued to carry the dead to clearly segregated burial grounds, including Oak Ridge.[50] Though one would assume that postbellum freedmen would distance themselves as much as possible from all reminders of slavery, people of color embraced Oak Ridge "as a site for remembrance of lives lost during slavery and identified with this history as their heritage." Organizations such as the Order of the Good Samaritan, the Independent Society, and the Daughters of the Good Samaritan purchased lots for their members. Fashionable and expensive memorials such as that to the Rev. Henry Williams (1843–86), erected by Cotton Avenue Baptist Church, reveal that people of color used the cemetery for their own purposes in the postwar era. A number of notable local African American families are interred there, including that of Professor H. J. T. Hudson, who founded the city's first public high school for African Americans. Oak Ridge's family lots brought together loved ones as freed men and women strengthened family bonds made tenuous by slavery, which had often separated parents from children and wives from husbands. In Oak Ridge, people of color tapped into the sentimentalism of the era that highlighted the precious ties of family. For instance, the epitaph on the obelisk to William B. Clark (1845–88) includes the words "Loving Husband."[51]

Meanwhile, white representation in the city and cemetery also changed. Short story writer Brett Harte wrote of Macon in 1874: "The cemetery seems to cover the whole town."[52] Here, Harte did not present Rose Hill as a place of pride but of melancholy. Postbellum Rose Hill held the handsome, costly monuments and expensive retaining walls of the antebellum slaveholding class who were most invested in the cemetery; however, the wealthy families who had built many of the enclosures were either no longer around to mend them or lacked the funds or interest to do so.[53] For Macon's surviving remnants of the former slaveholding class and their descendants, the decay of Rose Hill possibly fed both nostalgia and resentment.

The Civil War and Reconstruction brought much upheaval to the lives of white and African American Maconites alike, though the rural cemetery remained fertile ground for constructing a usable historical narrative. Rose Hill persisted as an exclusively white domain and, as such, was a "vehicle for the expression of public memory," fulfilling its purpose as that "cultural institution," the rural-style cemetery.[54] In 1872, the white editors of the *Telegraph* resumed their glorification of Bond and his manner of death in two articles. They began, "In Rose Hill Cemetery . . . overlooking the placid waters of the Ocmulgee . . . a massive monument rears its magnificent proportions, inscribed in large letters with the name of 'Bond'." The authors asserted, "The marble monument nor the green sod does not rest upon a form in our beautiful cemetery that, at one time, contained a soul so noble, so generous, so brave, and so true to the responsibilities of the hour as the soul of Joseph Bond." The editors pronounced, "The world should be again reminded of how he [Bond] died, and what he died for."[55] The *Telegraph* articles used the Bond monument in Rose Hill as a springboard to promote "a compassionate portrait of slavery" that served a postemancipation purpose. This trend honored the dead not as individuals but as ideals and as a means "to represent a way of Southern life forever lost through the end of slavery."[56] This retelling promoted a collective memory of what W. Fitzhugh Brundage has called the "willfully recalled and deliberately forgotten past," which included "historical silences" that "omitted slave auctions, beatings, and uprisings" as well as "more mundane hardships."[57] These newspaper articles drew the eye to Bond's grave in Rose Hill and attempted to justify white Georgians' postwar actions. As historian Susan E. O'Donovan notes in her study on the topic, while emancipation had ended the peculiar institution, former slaveholders intended that "the spirit of slavery would outlast the institution from which it had arisen."[58] They proclaimed humanitarian intentions similar to those expressed in the antebellum period, but like the institution from which it sprang, the spirit of slavery was not expressed through benevolent paternalism so much as through violence and coercion. Bloodshed marked almost every election in 1870s Macon until whites all but silenced most African American Maconites at the polls.[59]

Both Rose Hill and Oak Ridge are vital to unlocking the social and cultural history of Macon. In their northside necropolis patterned after the rural cemetery movement of the 1830s to 1870s, antebellum southern whites sought not only to make the hierarchy both beautiful and edifying but also to control their image in perpetuity. Memorialization in Rose Hill was not neutral but instead "represented an attempted conservation in the affairs of the living."[60] This conservation included slavery, and Oak Ridge was an important facet of that attempt, as it stood in the minds of white Maconites as a symbol of their perceived benevolence. Reconstruction ushered in a new period during which former slaveholders "used institutional ways to reassert their power," while freed men and women "acted to derail . . . attempts to resuscitate a now outdated system."[61] In relation to Rose Hill, white southerners waxed nostalgic and continued to promote a particular narrative of the past. Yet, despite white intentions for Oak Ridge, African American Maconites used the cemetery for their own ends, reinterpreting the narrative as their history and transforming a place of subjugation into one of pride.

Appendix

For this project I divided residents into seven hierarchical groups.[62] This categorization was based in part on the status groupings of Alba M. Edwards featured in his 1917 article "Social-Economic Groups of the United States," which describes occupational status trends from 1870 to 1910. This is a flawed system, for Charles B. Nam and Mary G. Powers point out that Edwards, though a "renowned statistician," did not have an empirical structure to classify occupational status in his 1917 attempt. Therefore, I fused this early effort with a largely overlapping system he later devised for 1910 to 1930 occupations, in which he used more scientific classification methods.[63] Edwards's major groupings coincide with Robert A. Margo's division of common labor, artisans, and white-collar workers for 1821 to 1860.[64] Combining information from secondary sources with my knowledge of Macon itself, I reclassified occupations based on the realities of antebellum central Georgia.[65]

To determine where to place Maconites in the seven occupational categories, I utilized my project database, populated with information about over nine thousand antebellum Maconites and individuals tied to the city's history. I extracted data concerning residents' occupations from the 1850 and

1860 federal censuses. The 1860 Macon census provided the occupations of 1,928 individuals, and the 1860 city directory helped clarify vocational designations and proprietorship. To help differentiate between different levels of merchants/proprietors, planters, professionals, and skilled laborers, I took into account wealth and property from the 1840 and 1857 Macon tax digests, the 1850 federal census's accounting of real estate, and the 1860 census's enumeration of both real estate and personal property for Maconites.[66]

TABLE 1.1. Socioeconomic Groupings in Antebellum Macon, Georgia

Group	Occupations Included
1	Greater merchants/proprietors and large manufacturers,* elite or middling planters, † judges,†† elite businessmen
2	Elite professionals,‡ quasi professionals, and kindred: architects, lawyers (elite), ministers (in white churches), physicians (gentlemen), professors
3	Middling merchants/proprietors/manufacturers,* master craftsmen,** managers, political officials, small planters,† bank agents (middling), city officials (mayors, sheriffs), cotton buyers (middling), dentists (elite), editors, hotel proprietors, marshals (U.S.), newspaper proprietors, railroad contractors, railroad officials, slave brokers (middling), speculators (middling), sportsmen (successful), stage contractors
4	Petty merchants/proprietors/manufacturers,* middle-class professionals,‡ low white-collar workers: accountants, agents (lottery, mail, real estate, ticket, etc.), auctioneers, boarding house keepers/proprietors, bookkeepers, civil engineers, clerks (municipal, retail, court), collectors, cotton buyers (small), county officers, draftsmen, governesses, hotel keepers and managers, lawyers (middle class), lottery managers, marshals (city), ministers (in African American churches), newspaper editorial staff (junior), physicians (middle class), postmasters, salesmen, saloon/bar/tavern owners, slave brokers (small), speculators (petty), sportsmen (petty), students (medical/law), superintendents (factory, railroad shops, telegraph), teachers, tellers, telegraph operators, tobacconists, writing masters
5	Foremen, skilled laborers,** farmers, artists, bakers, blacksmiths, boilermakers, boot cutters, boot makers, brickmasons, bridge builders, butchers, cabinetmakers, candymakers, carpenters, carriage makers, cigar makers, clothiers, confectioners, coppersmiths, coroners, county surveyors, daguerreotypists, dentists (old school), deputy sheriffs, dressmakers, druggists, engineers (locomotive, mechanical, stationary), engravers, firemen (locomotive), foremen and overseers (manufacturing), founders, gas fitters, gas makers, gin makers, glaziers, gunsmiths, harness makers, horse traders, housekeepers (hotel), iron fencers, jewelers, machinists, marble cutters, mechanics, midwives, millers, millwrights, molders, overseers (plantation), painters, patternmakers, physicians (homeopathic), plasterers, plumbers, portrait painters, printers, railroad conductors, railroad inspectors, roofers, saddlers, sash makers, sculptors, shoemakers and cobblers, steamboat captains, stonecutters and stonemasons, tailors, tanners, tinners, tinsmiths, turners, varnishers, wagonmakers, watchmakers, wheelwrights
6	Semiskilled workers: apprentices, baggage masters, barbers, barkeepers, bookbinders, cabinet workmen, card strippers, carriage and hack drivers, carriage trimmers, carvers, chair caners, cloth folders, cloth trimmers, constables, cooks, dressers (factory), dyers, express messengers, finishers, housekeepers (residential), horse drovers, jailers, justices of the peace, mail drivers, mattress makers, milliners, office boys, pickers, police officers, policemen, railroad section bosses, scalemen, shavers, seamstresses, shirtmakers, stewards, street overseers, switchmen, warpers, weavers, weighers

Group	Occupations Included
7	Unskilled workers: barkeeps, billiard tenders, boatmen, brickmakers, bridge keepers, ditchers, doffers, draymen, factory laborers, ferrymen, fishermen, fruit sellers, gardeners, guards, mule tenders, nurses, peelers, peddlers, porters, prostitutes, roller coverers, servants, sextons, speeder tenders, spinners, train hands, waggoners, warehouse laborers, washers, watchmen

*Merchants/proprietors/manufacturers were divided based on taxes paid to Macon noted on the 1840 and/or 1857 tax digests, personal property reported on the 1850 and 1860 federal censuses, and/or the number of enslaved reported on the 1840, 1850, and/or 1860 censuses or 1857 tax digest.

    Class 1: greater/large $55.00+ in Macon taxes and/or $30,000+ in personal property or real estate.

    Class 3: middling $20.00 to $54.99 in Macon taxes, $3,000+ in personal property, and/or 5+ enslaved.

    Class 4: small $0.25 to $19.99 in Macon taxes and/or less than $3,000 in personal property.

    A proprietor without supplemental information was entered as a "4."

†Planters and farmers were divided based on taxes paid to Macon noted on the 1840 and/or 1857 tax digests, personal property reported on the 1850 and 1860 federal censuses, and/or the number of enslaved reported on the 1840, 1850, and/or 1860 censuses or 1857 tax digest.

    Class 1: elite and middling planters $55.00+ in Macon taxes and/or $30,000+ in personal property.

    Class 3: small planters $20.00 to $54.99 in Macon taxes, $8,000 to $29,999 in personal property, and/or 8+ enslaved.

    Class 5: farmers $0.25 to $19.99 in Macon taxes, less than $8,000 in personal property, and/or less than 8 enslaved.

    For many planters, most of their property was elsewhere and not included in the Macon tax, but the federal census revealed some personal property and real estate outside of the city. I am not defining planters as those having at least twenty enslaved laborers, as for most of Macon's planters, that information was not included in city records or the federal census. I have relied on other factors.

‡Physicians and lawyers were divided by wealth, which separated elite professionals from those of the middle class. The latter had relatively small practices and less wealth. They were divided here based on taxes paid to Macon noted on the 1840 and/or 1857 tax digests, personal property reported on the 1850 and 1860 federal censuses, and/or the number of enslaved reported on the 1840, 1850, 1860 censuses or 1857 tax digest.

    Class 2: gentleman physicians/elite lawyers $33.00+ in Macon taxes, $10,000+ in personal property, and/or 12+ enslaved.

    Class 4: middle-class physicians/lawyers $0.25 to $32.99 in Macon taxes and/or less than $10,000 in personal property.

**Skilled laborers were divided between master craftsmen, who owned their own establishments, and journeymen.

    Class 3: master craftsmen $20.00+ in Macon taxes, $3,000+ in personal property, and/or 5+ enslaved.

    Class 5: journeymen $0.25 to $19.99 in Macon taxes and/or less than $3,000 in personal property.

††Men were generally chosen to be judges because they were wealthy. Most men identified as judges in Macon were either planters or lawyers.

In a city with over two thousand enslaved laborers by 1850, the enslaved were a sizable proportion of the property held by Maconites. I utilized the 1840 federal census for Macon, which listed the number of enslaved in each household, the 1850 and 1860 federal slave schedules, and the 1857 tax digest, which listed the number of enslaved people for whom individuals paid taxes.[67] Many Maconites inherited the enslaved or hired out and leased enslaved laborers, which was evident in sizable discrepancies between the number of enslaved enumerated with individual Maconites on the 1860 census compared to the 1857 tax digest.[68]

Notes

1. *Laurel Grove Cemetery!*, 17; Wells, *Facing the "King of Terrors,"* 127. In the first quote, the southerner Henry R. Jackson wrote of the new Laurel Grove Cemetery in Savannah in 1853. In the second quote, Wells refers to the rearrangement of the dead in New York, but the same principle applies here.

2. Sloane, *Last Great Necessity*, 54.

3. Goldfield, *Cotton Fields and Skyscrapers*, 30; Eisterhold, "Commercial, Financial, and Industrial Macon." David Goldfield uses the term "agrarian city" to refer to a town that existed largely to process cotton.

4. Only Columbus and Savannah had higher proportions of enslaved people of color, with 37 and 35 percent respectively, compared to Macon's 34 percent. Bellamy, "Macon, Georgia, 1823–1860," 298; Jenkins, "Ante Bellum Macon and Bibb County, Georgia," 422–23; U.S. Department of the Interior, Census of 1860, compendium for the state of Georgia, table 3.

5. Wade, *Slavery in the Cities*, 38.

6. Claudia Goldin argues that the institution's "extreme adaptability" actually made it "more profitable in urban areas." The only hint at the enslaved population was the business directory listing of "slave depots," all three of which were on Poplar Street in central Macon. Goldin, *Urban Slavery in the American South*, 1, 127; *Macon Directory for 1860*, 98.

7. Kruger-Kahloula, "On the Wrong Side of the Fence," 141. Kruger-Kahloula writes about New Haven, Connecticut, which she notes had enslaved laborers until 1848.

8. Vlach, "'Without Recourse to Owners,'" 151, 159; Wade, *Slavery in the Cities*, 74; Haney, "Understanding Antebellum Charleston's Backlots," 87; Reidy, "Masters and Slaves," 113–14 (quotation).

9. The exact number of slaveholders in 1860 Macon is unclear because, first, by the late antebellum period slaveholders hired out nearly one of every three urban enslaved laborers to other employers. In these cases, slaveholders hired out the enslaved to businesses, governments, and individuals for contract terms such as one year. Second, the 1860 census workers sought to enumerate the enslaved in their place of hire rather than by slaveholder and did not specify their status, recording enslaved "usership," as scholar Claudia Goldin terms it, instead of ownership. Further, Joseph Reidy notes in his study of central Georgia that the 1860 slave schedules for Macon list 4,143 enslaved laborers, but the enslaved clearly were not all living and working in the city. Lewis, "Axioms for Reading the Landscape," 12 (quotation); Goldfield, *Cotton Fields and Skyscrapers*, 47; Goldin, *Urban Slavery in the American South*, 19; Rousey, "Friends and Foes of Slavery," 392; U.S. Department of the Interior, Federal Slave Schedules 1860 (hereafter cited as Federal Slave Schedules, 1860); Reidy, "Masters and Slaves," 126; Martin, *Divided Mastery*, 109.

10. *Macon Directory for 1860*; Federal Slave Schedules, 1860; City of Macon, Tax Digest, 1857; U.S. Department of the Interior, Census of 1860, Population Schedules (hereafter cited as Population Schedules, 1860, Macon).

11. Jack Thomas and Katherine Thomas, *Rose Hill*; Rose Hill Cemetery Interment Book 1840–1848, 1854–1879, MF348, Rose Hill Records, Middle Georgia Archives; Rose Hill Deed Book, Book A, 1840–1891, MF349, Rose Hill Records, Middle Georgia Archives; *Macon Directory for 1860*.

12. Orange and Madison Streets, where occupational groups 4 to 7 resided, were largely service streets for College Street. At the time, Maconites referred to the area around Madison and Monroe Streets as "Commoners Run" or "Roe." In this way the "physical orga-

nization of households preserved social distance," despite spatial proximity above Spring Street. Another road with superblocks was Georgia Avenue, running east to west across College. *Macon . . . An Architectural and Historical Guide*, 77; Grigoryeva and Ruef, "Historical Demography of Racial Segregation," 817 (quotation). Angelina Grigoryeva and Martin Ruef are referencing African Americans and whites concerning superblocks, but it is applicable here.

13. Lane, *Architecture of the Old South*, 298; *Macon Directory for 1860*.

14. Harris, "Cemetery Beautiful," 104, 111 (quotation); French, "Cemetery as a Cultural Institution," 70, 89; Farrell, *Inventing the American Way of Death*, 108.

15. Henry T. Blake, *Chronicles of New Haven Green. From 1638 to 1862* (New Haven, Conn.: Tuttle, Morehouse, and Taylor, 1898), 276 (quotation), quoted in Kruger-Kahloula, "On the Wrong Side," 140n.

16. Kruger-Kahloula, "On the Wrong Side," 141 (first, second, third quotations); Giguere, "Localism and Nationalism in the City of the Dead," 850 (final quotation). Here Kruger-Kahloula refers to Grove Street Cemetery in Connecticut, which was a precursor to Mount Auburn Cemetery outside Boston.

17. Earnheart, "Rose Hill Cemetery," 55–56, 131–32, 143–44; W. M. S., "Macon—Rose Hill Cemetery," *Georgia Citizen* (Macon), July 24, 1857. Rose Hill, as a perusal of a map of the cemetery reveals, does not adhere to the rural cemetery ideal of following the natural contours of the topography. Rose Hill is thus something of a hybrid, with the rugged topography and vegetation of a rural cemetery but with a grid layout, resulting in the need for retention walls to create level and stable lots in many areas. Some have compared the effect to terraced gardens in northern Italy. The earliest images of the cemetery, from the late 1800s, show many of these retaining walls. *Art Work of Macon*, 48, 50.

18. Sloane, *Last Great Necessity*, 84–85. David Sloane quotes the 1849 edition of the periodical the *New Englander*, which noted that many had to find "some less genteel place of burial." In other rural-style cemeteries throughout the United States, those who could not afford a family lot either purchased a single grave along the necropolis's edge or lay in the cemetery's potter's field. These "less genteel" interment locations included Fort Hill Cemetery across the river, which had been an active burial site since the establishment of the frontier outpost Fort Hawkins in 1806. Records show that the less affluent also continued using the Old Macon Cemetery, even as those who were financially able had their deceased loved ones moved to Rose Hill, with over sixty reburials in all. Jack Thomas and Katherine Thomas, *Fort Hill Cemetery*; Jack Thomas, *History of Cherry Street Cemetery*, 79–83.

19. Rose Hill Cemetery Interment Book 1840–48, 1854–79; Rose Hill Deed Book, Book A; U.S. Department of the Interior, Census of 1850, Population Schedules, Macon (hereafter cited as Population Schedules, 1850, Macon); *A Compilation of the Acts of the Legislature Incorporating the City of Macon, Georgia, and of the Ordinances Passed by the City Council of Macon, to the 14th February, 1858, Now of Force, Passed 23 June 1854*, 66–67, Macon City Records, Middle Georgia Archives; Hallman and Hallman, *Record of Interments for Rose Hill Cemetery*, v–vi. Most of these graves on the verges cannot be mapped. Interment book listings are inadequate and the original sexton's map is lost. Some of these Strangers Row burials were in areas that cemetery proprietors later officially organized and subsequently sold off to paying customers. For instance, shopkeeper James Hightower received a "free lot" just outside the southwestern boundaries of the Central Avenue District section. A few years later, his lot officially became part of Pine Ridge.

20. Rose Hill Cemetery Interment Book 1840–48, 1854–79; Rose Hill Deed Book, Book A; Jack Thomas, *Rose Hill*; U.S., Census of 1850, Federal Slave Schedules, Macon, Bibb County,

Georgia (hereafter cited as Federal Slave Schedules, 1850, Macon); Federal Slave Schedules, 1860, Macon, Georgia; U.S., Census of 1840, Population Schedules, Macon, Bibb County, Georgia (hereafter cited as Population Schedules, 1840, Macon).

21. *Macon Directory for 1860*, 29; Rose Hill Cemetery Interment Book 1840–48, 1854–79; Rose Hill Deed Book, Book A; Jack Thomas, *Rose Hill*; "Late Jerry Cowles," *Macon Telegraph and Messenger*, May 17, 1877; *Macon . . . An Architectural and Historical Guide*, 52; Courthouse records amassed by architects Brittain, Thompson, Olson, and Bray in restoration of Overlook Mansion, March 1980, Joseph Bond Will and Estate Records Collection, Middle Georgia Archives.

22. Laderman, *Sacred Remains*, 44.

23. City council minutes, December 6, 1859, Book D, p. 361, quoted in Earnheart, "Rose Hill Cemetery," 72n84.

24. "Epitaph" is defined here as wording on the stone beyond a basic biography of birth and death dates, family connections, and place of birth and/or death. Rainville, "Hanover Deathscapes," 568 (quotation), 579; Giguere, "Virtuous Women, Useful Men, and Lovely Children," 1.

25. Rose Hill Cemetery (Macon, Bibb County, Ga.), John Powers and James Lockett headstones, photographed by author, December 21, 2015.

26. Jeffrey Young, *Domesticating Slavery*, 9.

27. These epitaphal statistics are from my own survey of Rose Hill's antebellum stones conducted from 2014 to 2018. Rural cemetery founders feared the increased mobility of the antebellum era, when families scattered. The "domestication of death" focused on the nuclear family and entailed giving the cemetery a homelike appearance with flowers, drapery, domestic furniture, and/or epitaphs such as "Gone Home," intended to make both the deceased and survivors feel at home. Sentimentalism camouflaged death. Linden-Ward, *Silent City on a Hill*, 221; Douglas, *Feminization of American Culture*, 201 (first quotation), 210–13, 223; Rainville, "Hanover Deathscapes," 559, 570; Sloane, *Last Great Necessity*, 11; Jeffrey Young, *Domesticating Slavery*, 8 (second quotation).

28. Johnson, *Soul by Soul*, 3 (first quotation); Jeffrey Young, *Domesticating Slavery*, 7 (second quotation).

29. Wyatt-Brown, *Southern Honor*, 3; Morgan, "Progressive Slaveholders," 408; Chaplin, "Slavery and the Principle of Humanity," 300, 303. This was indicative of the increasingly self-conscious proslavery thought of the late antebellum period, in line with spurious declarations that slavery was a positive good as well as the foundation of aristocratic republican freedom. Genovese, *Slaveholders' Dilemma*, 79.

30. Oakes, *Ruling Race*, xx.

31. Scarborough, *Elite Slaveholders of the Mid-Nineteenth-Century South*, appendix C; Joseph Bond will, 1856, Joseph Bond Will and Estate Records Collection, Middle Georgia Archives.

32. "Sketch of the Life of the Late Joseph Bond," part 1, *Telegraph*, September 17, 1872; "Sketch of the Life of the Late Joseph Bond," part 2, *Telegraph*, September 18, 1872; Collins, *White Society in the Antebellum South*, 7 (quotation).

33. Oliver H. Prince Jr. to John B. Lamar, March 20, 1859, folder 138, Jackson and Prince Family Papers (#00371), Southern Historical Collection.

34. "A Contemporary, in Noticing the Killing of Col. Joseph Bond by the Overseer Brown, Makes the Following Sensible and Feeling Remarks," *Daily News* (Savannah), April 5, 1859.

35. Bloch, *Gender and Morality in Anglo-American Culture*, 140; Greenberg, *Honor and Slav-*

ery, 91–92; Bederman, *Manliness and Civilization*, 20. See Orlando Patterson's *Slavery and Social Death: A Comparative Study* (Cambridge: Harvard University Press, 1982), which is the classic work on the relationship between honor and slavery as regards attitudes toward death. In his articulation, the enslaved were "socially dead." In reality, enslaved men of color did not mirror these beliefs that they were socially invisible as men. Gail Bederman points out that Frederick Douglass resisted a lashing due to what Douglass referred to as "a sense of my manhood." Bederman, *Manliness and Civilization*, 20.

36. French, "Cemetery as a Cultural Institution"; Laderman, *Sacred Remains*, 72 (first quotation); Schantz, *Awaiting the Heavenly Country*, 80 (second quotation).

37. Bond's monument was not erected until 1866 due to its being delayed in Louisville, Kentucky, because of the onset of the Civil War. "The Monument to Mr. Joseph Bond," *Georgia Weekly Telegraph*, November 5, 1866, 4; Samuel Thomas, *Cave Hill Cemetery*, 90.

38. J. A. N., "Col. Joseph Bond," *Telegraph*, March 15, 1859; "Monument to Mr. Joseph Bond"; Reidy, "Masters and Slaves," 178 (first quote); courthouse records amassed by architects Brittain, Thompson, Olson, and Bray in restoration of Overlook Mansion. Voucher 41 shows that in February 1860 Robert E. Launitz received $2,500 from the estate of Joseph Bond as the first payment of a "contract made this day with Mrs. H. S. Bond for a monument."

39. "Monument to Mr. Joseph Bond." Mourning, with its emotional messiness, was considered appropriate for women. Lithographs in the mid-1800s showed women as the primary mourners. Others depicted in these lithographs were not "crumpled by grief," in the words of Mark Schantz. Roark, "Embodying Immortality," 70, 102; Schantz, *Awaiting the Heavenly Country*, 166, 172–75.

40. Again, these epitaphal statistics are from my own survey of Rose Hill from 2014 to 2018. In antebellum America, there were clear formulas for epitaphs and grave sculpture that reinforced the prescribed roles for white men and women. Of the 291 antebellum stones with epitaphs in Rose Hill that went beyond the basics of family relationships, place of nativity, and birth and death dates, 129 inscriptions were religious. Giguere, "Virtuous Women, Useful Men, and Lovely Children," 1; Rainville, "Hanover Deathscapes," 543; Central Avenue District, block 7, Rose Hill Cemetery (Macon, Bibb County, Ga.), Elizabeth Rosseter Griffin headstone, photographed by author, December 28, 2015.

41. Kruger-Kahloula, "On the Wrong Side of the Fence," 141; Boles, *Irony of Southern Religion*, 76–77.

42. Schantz, *Awaiting the Heavenly Country*, 95 (quotation); Berry, *Price for Their Pound of Flesh*, 3.

43. Oakes, introduction to *The Ruling Race: A History of American Slaveholders* (New York: Norton, 1998), xii; Johnson, *Soul by Soul*, 102.

44. "Council Chamber, Sept. 12, 1851," *Telegraph*, September 23, 1851; "Oak Ridge Cemetery 1840 to 1865," interpretive marker, Oak Ridge Cemetery, Macon, Ga., viewed by author, July 2019.

45. *Laurel Grove Cemetery!*, 24 (quotation); Giguere, "Localism and Nationalism," 872–73; Berry, *Price for Their Pound of Flesh*, 89.

46. "Oak Ridge Cemetery 1840 to 1865"; "Unknown, but Not Forgotten," interpretive marker, Oak Ridge Cemetery, Macon, Ga., viewed by author, July 2019; *Macon's Black Heritage*, 35. For years, there has been talk of the use of ground-penetrating radar to determine how many people lie in Oak Ridge. Experts estimate that many bodies were probably buried on top of each other and that there are probably between eight hundred and fourteen hundred unmarked burials. "Finding the Forgotten," *Telegraph*, March 5, 2004; Stanley

Dunlap, "Unknown, Forgotten Could Be Recognized at Historic Macon Cemetery," *Telegraph*, July 2, 2016.

47. Roediger, "And Die in Dixie," 165–67, 171–72; Berry, *Price for Their Pound of Flesh*, 87; Warren, "'To Claim One's Own,'" 120, 122.

48. Roediger, "And Die in Dixie," 180; Oakes, *Ruling Race*, 116–17 (quotation).

49. Kruger-Kahloula, "On the Wrong Side of the Fence," 135.

50. Reidy, "Masters and Slaves," 342 (quotation); *Sholes' Directory of the City of Macon*.

51. Jack Thomas, *Rose Hill*, 545–80; "Oak Ridge Cemetery 1866 to the Present," interpretive marker, Oak Ridge Cemetery, Macon, Ga., viewed by author, July 2019 (first quotation); Oak Ridge Cemetery (Macon, Bibb County, Ga.), William B. Clark headstone, photographed by author, July 2019. Interment in Oak Ridge continues to the present. Though there are no family lots available, burials continue in established plots.

52. Ida Young, Gholson, and Hargrove, *History of Macon*, 325.

53. "Old Records of Rose Hill Interesting Documents," *Telegraph*, December 17, 1905. This article noted that the sexton was attempting to raise funds from the families buried in the cemetery to pay for the cemetery's upkeep. In defense of the city, I should note that Rose Hill was not designed for easy accessibility and upkeep, especially considering all the retention walls that were expensive not only to build but also to maintain.

54. Schantz, *Awaiting the Heavenly Country*, 73 (first quotation); French, "Cemetery as a Cultural Institution," 70 (second quotation).

55. "Sketch of the Life of the Late Joseph Bond," part 1; "Sketch of the Life of the Late Joseph Bond," part 2; "A Contemporary, in Noticing the Killing of Col. Joseph Bond."

56. Burton, "Myths Laid to Rest" (quotations). Burton is talking about slaveholders being a part of antebellum funerals for enslaved persons, but it applies here as well, when slaveholders were using deathways (this time related to the death of a slaveholder) to bolster the image of slavery.

57. Brundage, "Introduction: No Deed but Memory," 6–7.

58. O'Donovan, *Becoming Free in the Cotton South*, 132.

59. Reidy, "Masters and Slaves," 288–89, 294, 391, 398–99, 435–36.

60. Farrell, *Inventing the American Way of Death*, 108.

61. Merritt, *Masterless Men*, 334 (first quotation); O'Donovan, *Becoming Free in the Cotton South*, 133 (second quotation).

62. Historians have explored the pitfalls and problems of ranking occupations and the increasingly complex difficulties of classification. The finer gradations in the occupational structure are not critical to my findings. Griffen, "Occupational Mobility in Nineteenth-Century America," 310–12, 316; Katz, "Occupational Classification in History," 63, 70.

63. Edwards, "Social-Economic Groups of the United States"; Nam and Powers, *Socioeconomic Approach to Status Measurement*, 36–37; Edwards, "Social-Economic Grouping of the Gainful Workers of the United States."

64. Margo, *Wages and Labor Markets in the United States*, 45, table 2.2. Unfortunately, his samples from Georgia were miniscule.

65. Green, "Born of the Aristocracy?"; Katz, "Occupational Classification," 68. In his article "Profile of a Late Antebellum Community," James C. Bonner divided the residents of Hancock County, Ga., into seven occupational groups, including planters. Tyler Anbinder also used an occupational scheme in his study of antebellum Savannah, which shored up my findings in Macon. Bonner, "Profile of a Late Antebellum Community"; Anbinder, "Irish Origins and the Shaping of Immigrant Life in Savannah," 34–35.

66. Population Schedules, 1850, Macon; Population Schedules, 1860, Macon; *Macon Di-*

rectory for 1860; Tax Digest for 1840, Macon City Records, Middle Georgia Archives; City of Macon, Tax Digest, 1857. The 1830 and 1840 censuses did not include vocational information. These sources were not extremely reliable, with self-reported personal and real estate on the censuses relying completely on the honor system and tax lists by local assessors often faulty. There was "gross underreporting" of property within the city on the tax digests, which also did not include wealth held outside the city. Yet, relatively broad socio-economic groupings, as well as reliance on multiple sources to categorize individuals, minimized the impact of unreliable sources. Griffen, "Occupational Mobility," 316, 318. Griffen divided occupations into five levels: unskilled, semiskilled, skilled, and low and high white-collar workers.

67. Population Schedules, 1840, Macon; Federal Slave Schedules, 1860, Macon; Federal Slave Schedules, 1850, Macon; City of Macon, Tax Digest, 1857.

68. Reidy, "Masters and Slaves," 126; Griffen, "Occupational Mobility," 316.

Bibliography

Primary Sources

ARCHIVES

Georgia Archives, Morrow

City of Macon, Tax Digest, Bibb County, Ga., 1857, RG 111-20-33, microfilm drawer 239, box 57

Georgia Historical Society, Savannah

Laurel Grove Cemetery! An Account of Its Dedication with the Poem of the Honorable Robert M. Charlton and the Address of the Hon. Henry R. Jackson, Delivered on the 10th November, 1852, to Which Are Added the Ordinances Establishing and Regulating the Cemetery. Savannah, Ga.: G. N. Nichols, 1853.

Middle Georgia Archives, Washington Memorial Library, Macon

Joseph Bond Will and Estate Records Collection
Macon City Records
Oak Ridge Records
Rees Stereographic Collection
Rose Hill Records

Southern Historical Collection, University of North Carolina, Chapel Hill

Jackson and Prince Family Papers, 1784–1947

PERIODICALS

Daily News (Savannah)
Georgia Citizen (Macon)
Georgia Journal and Messenger (Macon)
Macon Telegraph and Messenger Macon)
Telegraph (Macon)

OTHER PRIMARY SOURCES

Art Work of Macon. Chicago: W. H. Parish, 1894.
The Macon Directory for 1860, Containing the Names of the Inhabitants, Business Directory, and an Appendix of Much Useful Information. Macon, Ga.: Mears and Company, 1860.
Sholes' Directory of the City of Macon, July 1st 1878. Macon, Ga.: A. E. Sholes, 1878.

U.S. Department of the Interior. Census Bureau. Census of 1840. Population Schedules, Macon, Bibb County, Georgia.

U.S. Department of the Interior. Census Bureau. Census of 1850. Population Schedules, Macon, Bibb County, Georgia.

U.S. Department of the Interior. Census Bureau. Census of 1860. Compendium for the state of Georgia.

U.S. Department of the Interior. Census Bureau. Census of 1860. Population Schedules, Macon, Bibb County, Georgia.

U.S. Department of the Interior. Census Bureau. Federal Slave Schedules 1850. Macon, Bibb County, Georgia.

U.S. Department of the Interior. Census Bureau. Federal Slave Schedules 1860. Macon, Bibb County, Georgia.

Secondary Sources

Anbinder, Tyler. "Irish Origins and the Shaping of Immigrant Life in Savannah on the Eve of the Civil War." *Journal of American Ethnic History* 35, no. 1 (2015): 5–37.

Bederman, Gail. *Manliness and Civilization: A Cultural History of Gender and Race in the United States, 1880–1917*. Chicago: University of Chicago Press, 1995.

Bellamy, Donnie D. "Macon, Georgia, 1823–1860: A Study in Urban Slavery." *Phylon (1960–)* 45, no. 4 (1984): 298–310.

Berry, Daina Ramey. *The Price for Their Pound of Flesh: The Value of the Enslaved from Womb to Grave, in the Building of a Nation*. Boston: Beacon Press, 2017.

Bloch, Ruth H. *Gender and Morality in Anglo-American Culture, 1650–1800*. Berkeley: University of California Press, 2003.

Boles, John B. *The Irony of Southern Religion*. New York: P. Lang, 1994.

Bonner, James C. "Profile of a Late Antebellum Community." *American Historical Review* 49 (July 1944): 671–72.

Brundage, W. Fitzhugh. "Introduction: No Deed but Memory." In *Where These Memories Grow: History, Memory, and Southern Identity*, edited by W. Fitzhugh Brundage, 1–28. Chapel Hill: University of North Carolina Press, 2000.

Burton, Kristen D. "Myths Laid to Rest: Death, Burial, and Memory in the American South." *Essays in History* 47, no. 1 (2013): 1–28. https://essaysinhistoryjournal.com/articles/abstract/10.25894/eih.206/.

Chaplin, Joyce. "Slavery and the Principle of Humanity: A Modern Idea in the Early Lower South." *Journal of Social History* 24, no. 2 (1990): 299–316.

Collins, Bruce. *White Society in the Antebellum South*. New York: Longman, 1985.

Douglas, Ann. *The Feminization of American Culture*. New York: Knopf, 1977.

Earnheart, Bruce W. "Rose Hill Cemetery: Derivation, Development, Degeneration." Master's thesis, University of Georgia, 1989.

Edwards, Alba M. "A Social-Economic Grouping of the Gainful Workers of the United States." *Journal of the American Statistical Association* 28, no. 184 (December 1933): 377–87.

———. "Social-Economic Groups of the United States." *Publications of the American Statistical Association* 15, no. 118 (June 1917): 643–61.

Eisterhold, John A. "Commercial, Financial, and Industrial Macon during the 1840s." *Georgia Historical Quarterly* 53 (1969): 424–41.

Farrell, James J. *Inventing the American Way of Death, 1830–1920*. Philadelphia: Temple University Press, 1980.

French, Stanley. "The Cemetery as a Cultural Institution: The Establishment of Mount Auburn and the 'Rural Cemetery' Movement." In *Death in America*, edited by David E. Stannard, 70–89. Philadelphia: University of Pennsylvania Press, 1975.

Genovese, Eugene D. *The Slaveholders' Dilemma: Freedom and Progress in Southern Conservative Thought, 1820–1860*. Columbia: University of South Carolina Press, 1992.

Giguere, Joy M. "Localism and Nationalism in the City of the Dead: The Rural Cemetery Movement in the Antebellum South." *Journal of Southern History* 84, no. 4 (November 2018): 845–82.

———. "Virtuous Women, Useful Men, and Lovely Children: Epitaph Language and the Construction of Gender and Social Status in Cumberland County, Maine, 1720–1820." *Markers: The Annual Journal of the Association for Gravestone Studies* 24 (2007): 1–23.

Goldfield, David R. *Cotton Fields and Skyscrapers: Southern City and Region*. Baltimore: Johns Hopkins University Press, 1982.

Goldin, Claudia Dale. *Urban Slavery in the American South, 1820–1860: A Quantitative History*. Chicago: University of Chicago Press, 1976.

Green, Jennifer. "Born of the Aristocracy? Professionals with Planter and Middle-Class Origins in Late Antebellum South Carolina." In *The Southern Middle Class in the Long Nineteenth Century*, edited by Jonathan Daniel Wells and Jennifer Green, 136–53. Baton Rouge: Louisiana State University Press, 2011.

Greenberg, Kenneth S. *Honor and Slavery: Lies, Duels, Noses, Masks, Dressing as a Woman, Gifts, Strangers, Humanitarianism, Death, Slave Rebellions, the Proslavery Argument, Baseball, Hunting, and Gambling in the Old South*. Princeton, N.J.: Princeton University Press, 1996.

Griffen, C. "Occupational Mobility in Nineteenth-Century America: Problems and Possibilities." *Journal of Social History* 5, no. 3 (March 1972): 310–30.

Grigoryeva, Angelina, and Martin Ruef. "The Historical Demography of Racial Segregation." *American Sociological Review* 80, no. 4 (August 2015): 814–42.

Hallman, Lawrence Edward, and Linda Moore Hallman. *Record of Interments for Rose Hill Cemetery of Bibb County, Georgia: Covering the Time Period between 1840 and 1871*. Macon, Ga.: privately printed, 1996; held at Middle Georgia Archives.

Haney, Gina. "Understanding Antebellum Charleston's Backlots through Light, Sound, and Action." In *Slavery in the City: Architecture and Landscapes of Urban Slavery in North America*, edited by Clifton Ellis and Rebecca Ginsburg, 87–105. Charlottesville: University of Virginia Press, 2017.

Harris, Neil. "The Cemetery Beautiful." In *Passing: The Vision of Death in America*, edited by Charles O. Jackson, 103–11. Westport, Conn.: Greenwood Press, 1977.

Jenkins, William Thomas. "Ante Bellum Macon and Bibb County, Georgia." PhD diss., University of Georgia, 1966.

Johnson, Walter. *Soul by Soul: Life inside the Antebellum Slave Market*. Cambridge, Mass.: Harvard University Press, 1999.

Katz, Michael B. "Occupational Classification in History." *Journal of Interdisciplinary History* 3, no. 1 (summer 1972): 63–88.

Kruger-Kahloula, Angelika. "On the Wrong Side of the Fence: Racial Segregation in American Cemeteries." In *History and Memory in African-American Culture*, edited by Genevieve Fabre and Robert O'Meally, 130–49. New York: Oxford University Press, 1994.

Laderman, Gary. *The Sacred Remains: American Attitudes toward Death, 1799–1883*. New Haven, Conn.: Yale University Press, 1996.

Lane, Mills. *Architecture of the Old South*. New York: Abbeville Press, 1993.

Lewis, Peirce F. "Axioms for Reading the Landscape: Some Guides to the American Scene." In *The Interpretation of Ordinary Landscapes: Geographical Essays*, edited by D. W. Meinig, 11–32. New York: Oxford University Press, 1979.

Linden-Ward, Blanche. *Silent City on a Hill: Picturesque Landscapes of Memory and Boston's Mount Auburn Cemetery*. Columbus: Ohio State University Press, 1989.

Macon . . . An Architectural and Historical Guide. Macon, Ga.: Middle Georgia Historical Society, 1996.

Macon's Black Heritage: The Untold Story. Macon, Ga.: Tubman African American Museum, 1997.

Margo, Robert A. *Wages and Labor Markets in the United States, 1820–1860*. Chicago: University of Chicago Press, 2000.

Martin, Jonathan D. *Divided Mastery: Slave Hiring in the American South*. Cambridge, Mass.: Harvard University Press, 2004.

Merritt, Keri Leigh. *Masterless Men: Poor Whites and Slavery in the Antebellum South*. New York: Cambridge University Press, 2017.

Morgan, Chad. "Progressive Slaveholders: Planters, Intellectuals, and Georgia's Antebellum Economic Development." *Georgia Historical Quarterly* 86, no. 3 (fall 2002): 398–422.

Nam, Charles B., and Mary G. Powers. *The Socioeconomic Approach to Status Measurement*. Houston: Cap and Gown Press, 1983.

Oakes, James. *The Ruling Race: A History of American Slaveholders*. New York: Knopf, 1982.

O'Donovan, Susan E. *Becoming Free in the Cotton South*. Cambridge, Mass.: Harvard University Press, 2010.

Rainville, Lynn. "Hanover Deathscapes: Mortuary Variability in New Hampshire, 1770–1920." *Ethnohistory* 46, no. 3 (summer 1999): 541–97.

Reidy, Joseph Patrick. "Masters and Slaves, Planters and Freedmen: The Transition from Slavery to Freedom in Central Georgia, 1820–1880." PhD diss., Northern Illinois University, 1982.

Roark, Elisabeth L. "Embodying Immortality: Angels in America's Rural Garden Cemeteries, 1850–1900." *Markers: The Annual Journal of the Association for Gravestone Studies* 24 (2007): 56–111.

Roediger, David. "And Die in Dixie: Funerals, Death, and Heaven in the Slave Community 1700–1865." *Massachusetts Review* 22, no. 1 (Spring 1981): 163–83.

Rousey, Dennis C. "Friends and Foes of Slavery: Foreigners and Northerners in the Old South." *Journal of Social History* 35, no. 2 (Winter 2001): 373–96.

Scarborough, William Kauffman. *Elite Slaveholders of the Mid-Nineteenth-Century South*. Baton Rouge: Louisiana State University Press, 2006.

Schantz, Mark. *Awaiting the Heavenly Country: The Civil War and America's Culture of Death*. Ithaca, N.Y.: Cornell University Press, 2008.

Sloane, David Charles. *The Last Great Necessity: Cemeteries in American History*. Baltimore: Johns Hopkins University Press, 1991.

Thomas, Jack Guerry, Sr. *History of Cherry Street Cemetery, Macon, Georgia 1825–1840*. Macon, Ga.: privately printed, 2009; held at Middle Georgia Archives.

Thomas, Jack Guerry, Sr., and Katherine Moore Thomas. *Fort Hill Cemetery, Macon, Georgia 1808–2008*. Macon, Ga.: privately printed, 2014; held at Middle Georgia Archives.

———. *Rose Hill*. Macon, Ga.: privately printed, 2009; held at Middle Georgia Archives.

Thomas, Samuel W. *Cave Hill Cemetery*. Louisville, Ky.: Cave Hill Cemetery Company, 1985.

Vlach, John Michael. "'Without Recourse to Owners': The Architecture of Urban Slavery in the Antebellum South." *Perspectives in Vernacular Architecture* 6 (1997): 150–60.

Wade, Richard C. *Slavery in the Cities, the South, 1820–1860*. New York: Oxford University Press, 1965.

Warren, Jamie. "'To Claim One's Own': Death and the Body in the Daily Politics of Antebellum Slavery." In *Death and the American South*, edited by Craig Thompson Friend and Lorri Glover, 110–30. New York: Cambridge University Press, 2015.

Wells, Robert V. *Facing the "King of Terrors": Death and Society in an American Community, 1750–1990*. New York: Cambridge University Press, 2000.

Wyatt-Brown, Bertram. *Southern Honor: Ethics and Behavior in the Old South*. New York: Oxford University Press, 1982.

Young, Ida, Julius Gholson, and Clara Nell Hargrove. *History of Macon, Georgia*. Macon, Ga.: Lyon, Marshall, and Brooks, 1950.

Young, Jeffrey Robert. *Domesticating Slavery: The Master Class in Georgia and South Carolina, 1670–1837*. Chapel Hill: University of North Carolina Press, 1999.

EPILOGUE

TEACHING THE AMERICAN SOUTH BY LEARNING THE DEAD

Link to the map: http://arcg.is/15GCuD

Orient yourself with the map. If you zoom out a bit, you will see where Rose Hill Cemetery is situated in relation to the modern city of Macon, Georgia. It is at the northern edge of the boundaries of what was the antebellum city and lies alongside the Ocmulgee River, which was a vital waterway in early Macon. Note that this is a modern topographical map, which includes present-day roads and features outside the cemetery, many of which did not exist in the antebellum era. To the north and west of Rose Hill, you will see the newer Riverside and Linwood Cemeteries. To return to Rose Hill, hit the home (house) button at the top left of the map.

Use this map and its features to consider some queries concerning white antebellum Maconites.

Origins

- Make sure you have clicked on the "Content" button at the top left of the page to see the various available layers. Then check the view box to the left of the layer "Rose Hill by Birthplace" to see this layer and uncheck the view box on any other layers. Click on the legend button under the layer title if necessary to see what each color represents on the map. (If you do not see the legend button, click on the title of the layer.)
- Clicking on any mapped point results in a pop-up with information about the individual buried there. Occasionally points are so close together that multiple points are on top of each other. These graves are likely in the same lot, and the deceased may even share a tombstone. When multiple graves share the same mapped point, the pop-up

includes "(1 of ?)" in the top left corner. Use the arrow button at the top right of the pop-up to view the other burials represented by that point.
- To view the data in another format, click the table button under the "Rose Hill by Birthplace" layer. A table will appear at the bottom of the screen with the data for all the points in this layer. Clicking on a record in the table will highlight the corresponding point on the map.

Questions to consider for this layer:

- What stands out about the origins of white Maconites?
    - Are you surprised? If so, why?
    - Given what you know about Macon and the United States in the antebellum era—knowledge provided both by the chapter about Macon and other studies—why might people have moved to Macon?
- What groups of white Maconites are visibly clustered or segregated in the cemetery?
    - Why might these groups cluster?
    - Did you expect more separation between regional groups or more clannish behavior? Why or why not?

Inscriptions

- Uncheck the viewing box for the "Rose Hill by Birthplace" layer and check the "Select Tombstone Inscriptions" viewer box. This layer reveals the surviving antebellum tombstones in Rose Hill that included a line or two indicating where the deceased was born. Use the instructions outlined above to navigate this layer as well.

Questions to consider for this layer:

- Why might Maconites have chosen to include the deceased's state or country of origin on their gravestones?
- What other elements do some of these inscriptions include? (Do not forget the table button to aid in viewing epitaphs in a systematic manner.)
    - Why do you think Maconites chose these particular epitaphs to represent the deceased?
    - What do these epitaphs reveal about what Maconites valued?
    - What do these inscriptions reveal about gender?

Historical Methods

- How is this kind of GIS mapping helpful in the study of the history of a city?
- How does this mapping aid in our understanding of cemeteries in particular?
- What are the drawbacks of GIS mapping in the study of both cities and cemeteries?

CHAPTER 2

The Crown Jewel of Kentucky
Louisville's Cave Hill Cemetery

JOY M. GIGUERE

On Friday, June 10, 2016, the remains of boxing legend Muhammad Ali joined those of other Kentucky notables in an interment ceremony at Louisville's historic Cave Hill Cemetery. On the morning of the funeral procession, and with approval by the Ali family, Louisville artist Maggie Cassaro sprinkled approximately eighty-eight thousand rose petals outside the cemetery gates. As reported by the Louisville *Courier-Journal*, "After Ali's hearse had passed over the floral tribute, the petals became mementos for the crowd, which rushed to gather them after Cave Hill closed its gates."[1] Ali's grave has since become a pilgrimage site for visitors from around the world, and while Cave Hill Cemetery is the final resting place for many famous Kentuckians—most notably Col. Harland Sanders, founder of Kentucky Fried Chicken—the presence of a Muslim African American's remains highlights the degree to which the cemetery has transformed since its creation in 1848 (see figures 2.1 and 2.2).

Established during the rural cemetery movement as a cemetery "for the white race exclusively," Cave Hill had regulations until 1870 prohibiting entrance to African Americans. Until after the passage of the Civil Rights Act of 1964, African Americans could not be buried there.[2] In addition to being the burial place for Ali, the cemetery today holds the remains of local civil rights leaders, including Woodford Porter Sr., Senator Georgia Powers, and Judge Benjamin Shobe. A tour of the gravesites of these leaders was offered in the summer of 2017 as part of the "I Am Ali Festival."[3] Today, Cave Hill is a cultural institution that reflects the diversity and progressiveness of twenty-first-century Louisville, and it also functions as a place where vis-

FIGURE 2.1. Grave of Muhammad Ali, Cave Hill Cemetery (photograph by Jeff Harmening)

FIGURE 2.2. Grave of Col. Harland Sanders, Cave Hill Cemetery (photograph by the author)

itors can learn about the city's history, enjoy the arboreal and floral riches of the landscape, delight in the sepulchral artwork and architecture, and, of course, pay respects to the dead.

    The history of Cave Hill Cemetery, with its winding path toward inclusion and diversity, is in many ways reflective of the history of Louisville, and of Kentucky more generally. Situated on the Ohio River in northern Kentucky, Louisville during the nineteenth century sat at the nexus of North, South, and West—not just geographically, but culturally as well. A gateway city to the West, Louisville blossomed in a relatively short period from a frontier settlement founded by George Rogers Clark in 1778 to an industrial hub of the Upper South by the 1840s. As in other American cities experiencing the parallel developments of urbanization and industrialization during the antebellum period, Louisville's residents fashioned theirs as a modern, cosmopolitan city—its citizens fashionable, its businesses thriving, and its cultural institutions equal to any found farther east. As one visitor from Cleveland described it in 1856, "It is a town in every regard worthy [of] any State in the Union. It has wealth, it has thrift, it has enterprise, it has beauty, it has a big river and many railroads, it has [George D.] Prentice of the *Journal*, and lots of negroes."[4] Kentucky relied far less on the institution of slavery than those states in the Cotton Belt, but even so, the 1860 census enumerated 225,483 enslaved persons, which represented about 20 percent of the state's population.[5] After a short-lived attempt at neutrality in 1861, Kentucky remained loyal to the Union during the Civil War years, but sympathies across the state were deeply divided. The state gave between ninety and one hundred thousand men to the Union cause during the war, many of whom were freed Black persons who served in the United States Colored Troops (USCT), while somewhere between twenty-five and forty thousand men volunteered to fight for the Confederacy.[6] The actual number of Kentucky civilians who harbored prosecessionist feelings remains open to speculation. The contest over loyalty and identity played out on the battlefield but also on the cultural landscape, both during and after the war. Thus Cave Hill Cemetery, an institution established for the enjoyment of the living as much as for the burial of the dead, reflected both the transformations and intransigence of the people who called Louisville home. This essay considers the early history of Cave Hill, from its dedication in 1848 until the end of the nineteenth century, a significant formative era that witnessed the evolution of the Upper South rural cemetery from an institution reflective of national cultural developments to a space of conflict over wartime allegiances and, in the postwar era, a landscape that embodied the multifarious and, at times, contradictory identities of the city and state in which it is located.

Cave Hill Cemetery and the Rural Cemetery Movement

When the Louisville City Council adopted a resolution in November 1846 to set aside a portion of the "City Farm, at Cave Hill," for a city burying ground, the city's new twenty-eight-acre Eastern Cemetery had been in use for only two years. It was nevertheless apparent to the city leadership that more burial space was necessary for the growing urban hub, and so the Cave Hill Farm would be landscaped and transformed into a new cemetery, "an 'Auburn' or 'Laurel Hill,'" as the resolution described.[7] The "Auburn" to which they referred was Mount Auburn Cemetery in Cambridge, Massachusetts, which by this time had been in use for fifteen years and had served as the model for the establishment of subsequent "rural" cemeteries across the country—including Laurel Hill in Philadelphia, Green-Wood in Brooklyn, Green Mount in Baltimore, and Spring Grove in Cincinnati. The rural cemetery movement—a cultural phenomenon that blended burial reform with landscape gardening as well as with the cultural romanticism of the era—thus expanded throughout the Northeast during the 1830s, and by the 1840s it had spread to areas of the Upper South and Midwest. The term "rural cemetery" referred to the aesthetic of the landscape rather than to its location, which tended to be on the suburban outskirts of the nation's major cities.[8] Regarded as the "Westminster Abbey" of Kentucky, the first rural cemetery established in the commonwealth was dedicated in 1844 in the state capital, Frankfort.[9] Louisville followed with Cave Hill, dedicated in 1848, then Lexington in 1849.[10] Frankfort Cemetery earned national recognition in 1845 with the reinterment of the remains of pioneer Daniel Boone and his wife, while Lexington Cemetery became a national pilgrimage site following the burial of statesman Henry Clay in 1852 and the completion and dedication of his impressive tomb on July 4, 1861.[11]

Rural cemeteries in America shared a similar method of applying landscape gardening to fashion what, to visitors, would look like an untouched, "rural" environment, but despite this unifying ideology, the cemeteries varied considerably in size and design. This had much to do with the fact that landscape gardeners had to work with the natural topography of the sites selected for use as cemeteries, and the limitations in some regions regarding which kinds of flowers and trees would most likely thrive. Cemetery proprietors in some cities, such as Richmond, Virginia, and Baltimore, were directly inspired by their visits to Boston to establish their own rural cemetery on the model of Mount Auburn, but the civic leaders of Louisville did not initially intend to lay out Cave Hill as a rural cemetery.[12] Rather, it was the civil engineer Edmund Francis Lee (1811–57), hired by a committee appointed by the city council, who regarded the Cave Hill Farm, with its undulating hills, promontories, and basins, as perfectly suited for landscaping in the new rural aesthetic.[13] By the end of the century, the cemetery, originally encompassing fifty acres, had expanded to 260 acres, with subsequent landscape gardeners building on the work initiated by Lee. Visitors encountered a landscape that, while designed as a rural cemetery, was unlike any established elsewhere across the country, largely due to the natural feature for which the land was named—the Cave Hill. In 1849, the trustees purchased an additional twelve acres in front of the cemetery, through which the landscape gardener, David Ross, laid off an avenue measuring eight hundred feet long and forty feet wide, the sides of which were ornamented with "20 Hemlock Spruce, 20 Balsam Firs, 20 Norway Spruce, 20 upright Junipers, 20 White Pine, 20 Cedars," and between the trees were "160 Dahlies of every variety, and other flowering plants."[14] The gatehouse and clock tower were eventually constructed at the principal entrance in 1881, with the clock and bell installed in 1892.[15] (See figure 2.3.)

By 1895, the cemetery company had nearly twelve thousand feet of water pipe and nine thousand feet of sewer pipe installed, as well as water hydrants for use by lot holders, all of which were fed by the city water company. Among other structures for use by visitors and cemetery staff, the office building was constructed at a cost of $17,000. As was common in rural cemeteries around the country, lot holders reserved the right to adorn their lots with flowers, which meant a profusion of colors and varieties, and the cemetery planted trees of every kind—beech, elm, maple, oak, ash, sweet gum, sycamore, sour gum, dogwood, magnolia, Japanese gingko, cypress, willow, and cedar. While earlier in the nineteenth century the cypress, willow, and cedar had been popular in cemetery landscapes and mourning iconography for their "melancholy significance," sentiment by the end of the century encouraged their removal and replacement with trees of "greater beauty" and fewer melancholy associations.[16]

In the days leading up to the cemetery's formal dedication on July 25, 1848, the *Louisville Daily Courier* ran extensive articles extolling the benefits of rural cemeteries, educating the public on this cultural phenomenon, and thus encouraging the "ladies and gentlemen of the city [to] visit these grounds on the day of consecration, and see the beauties of the place for themselves."[17] Such encouragement was successful, for on that day, "a large assemblage of ladies and gentlemen assembled in the grove, which had been chosen as the place of dedication."[18] The proceedings included an opening prayer by the Reverend Mr. Sehon, the singing of an ode written by Fortu-

FIGURE 2.3. Entrance to Cave Hill Cemetery, ca. 1906, Detroit Publishing Company (courtesy of the Library of Congress Prints and Photographs Division)

natus Cosby in honor of the occasion, a benediction delivered by the Reverend Mr. Gallagher, rector of St. Paul's Church in Louisville, and the principal oration delivered by Connecticut native and Presbyterian minister Edward P. Humphrey.[19]

In the course of his address, Humphrey discussed themes that were commonly heard at rural cemetery dedications—historical and contemporary methods for disposing of the dead; why rural cemeteries were necessary; what made them popular resorts for the living; and what made the cemetery thus being consecrated unique or impressive compared to those elsewhere. From ancient to modern times, disposition of the dead had been marked by "inconsistency of practice and opinion," but now, "it is the persuasion of many, that the Rural Cemetery gives the happiest expression to what is approved in reason and religion, and to what is becoming in sentiment and taste, in respect of this important subject."[20] While the motivation for establishing rural cemeteries near other cities had primarily involved urban expansion and the overcrowding of common and church burying grounds, Humphrey offered an additional reason why such a burial space might be necessary in the South: "The plantations in this region, have been cultivated less than three quarters of a century; and yet in passing from the possession of one proprietor to that of another, the family burial place has, in some instances, gone into neglect and become covered with rank vegetation; or perhaps, the fences have been removed, and the place burned over and 'turned out,' as the expression is, into the common field. Soon even the fact, that the dead are buried there, will be forgotten forever, unless the spade shall accidentally reveal their crumbling relics."[21] Cave Hill and other rural cemeteries established in the South were thus designed not only to protect the inviolability of the urban dead but also to function as an alternative to more isolated farm or plantation burials. At Richmond's Hollywood Cemetery and Memphis's Elmwood Cemetery, promoters made ovations to rural landowners to purchase lots in their institutions.[22] However, it appears that appeals to this demographic proved inadequate. As the *Southern Literary Messenger* complained in 1853, "In wandering over the State of Virginia, we have been struck most painfully with the fact that ... there is no abiding place for the living or the dead. The father plants and the stranger to his blood and family waters. His descendants flee the land of their birth, and are found in distant regions. Change is the order of the day with us, and the graves of our relatives are overgrown with briars and noxious weeds, and the ploughshare sooner or later destroys all vestige of the spot where they rest from their labors."[23] Thus, despite their suburban location bridging the urban and rural landscapes, the rural cemeteries in the antebellum South, like their northern counterparts, primarily catered to the burial needs of urban populations.

Humphrey did not tout Cave Hill's anticipated preeminence compared to other rural cemeteries, though his description still conveyed a sense that Louisville could claim its place on the national roster of cities possessing a cemetery of surpassing beauty. "If it be wanting in the elements of grandeur, it is rich in those of rural beauty," he declared. "The green meadow, the fields of waving grain, the cultivated garden, the homes of our friends half revealed amid the foliage, the sunny lawn, the deep old wood, the shadowy cave, the weary highway, and the gushing and redundant fountain, all are here."[24] Within a year following its dedication, the attractions described by Humphrey in his address had decidedly made Cave Hill a popular resort for visitors as well as a significant institution in the cultural development of Louisville. The *Louisville Daily Courier* happily reported, "We are much gratified with the attention this beautiful place has excited among the people of Louisville." Work had proceeded under the direction of landscape gardener Davis Ross, the trustees had an Egyptian Revival receiving tomb constructed, and "many ornamental monuments" were by that time "in the course of preparation" for placement in burial lots.[25] The rapid embellishment of the cemetery through the work of landscape gardeners and lot holders thus made Cave Hill an attractive destination for travelers in the decade prior to the Civil War. One visitor from Cleveland reported, "A person could while away many an hour among its walks and under its ambrosial shades, among its tombs and inviting by-paths; I was attracted to the spot by idle curiosity, and was enchained there for a half day by its unprecedented loveliness."[26] A traveler from Milwaukee, who lodged for several days at the Louisville Hotel, wrote that Cave Hill "well repays the lover of nature and the beautiful" and that "it is the handsomest spot of ground we saw in Kentucky" and "the most interesting spot in the city."[27] By the end of the decade, Cave Hill Cemetery was rightly regarded as the crown jewel of Kentucky.

As with other rural cemeteries established during the 1830s and 1840s, the trustees of Cave Hill Cemetery established a variety of rules for visitors, which became more elaborate—not to mention specific—over time.[28] Revised cemetery policies published in 1869 listed a number of prohibitions, including rules forbidding "large assemblages" of persons; food and refreshments; unfastened horses; writing on or defacing monuments; any behavior that involved "disturbing the quiet and good order of the place by noise or other improper conduct"; and the discharging of firearms.[29] It was also in the 1869 regulations that the trustees at Cave Hill explicitly laid out policies concerning the racial dynamics of the cemetery. Prior to the Civil War, there was no explicit language regarding burials for people of color at Cave Hill, and according to the Filson Historical Society in Louisville, "some white families occasionally provided burial plots for their servants."[30] After the Civil War, however, Cave Hill became an exclusively white space for burial. In the Rules Respecting Lots and Lot-Owners, Article I states, "This Cemetery is set apart for the burial of the white race exclusively."[31] Some rural cemeteries, such as those in Frankfort, Kentucky, and Memphis, Tennessee, reserved segregated spaces for African American burials; others, including Hollywood Cemetery in Richmond, Virginia, relied on prevailing law and custom regarding separate burial spaces for whites and Blacks and did not articulate within their regulations and bylaws any explicit prohibition on burials for people of color. In Louisville, the trustees found it necessary to make such a separation clear. The city's Eastern Cemetery, established in 1844 as a precursor to Cave Hill, contained ground designated for African American burials. This space, along with the Louisville Cemetery, incorporated by seven prominent African American men in 1886, and Greenwood Cemetery, established in 1898, functioned as the principal burying grounds for the city's Black residents.[32] African Americans could visit Cave Hill, but there were, of course, restrictions: "Colored persons, when admitted, must be accompanied by a lot-holder, or some member of the family of the lot-holder, or may be admitted by the written permit of a Trustee, which must be left with the Gate-keeper, and filed by him."[33]

War in the Cemetery

The onset of the Civil War complicated the racial, gendered, and political dynamics within Cave Hill Cemetery, and by war's end, the traditionally apolitical city of the dead had become both politicized and contested terrain. The cemetery became a site for contests over identity and loyalty even as the war was still in its early stages, when the matter of soldier burials first presented itself. Louisville's General Council passed a resolution in October 1861 for the appropriation of "several acres of ground in Cave Hill Cemetery, for the purpose of burying such United States soldiers as may be buried in this vicinity," a resolution that was then adopted by the city's board of aldermen.[34] When Confederate prisoners began to die in Louisville's military prison and hospitals in the early months of 1862, the local military authorities resisted the idea of burying them alongside the Union soldiers. It was then that Elijah Huffman and Samuel Hamilton, local Confederate sympathizers who worked in the pork-packing business, purchased lots that they donated for the interment of rebel soldiers.[35]

In September 1862, when the city braced for what federal authorities believed to be an imminent Confederate assault on the riverfront city, General William "Bull" Nelson prepared for the invasion by ordering defensive trenches to be dug, including through Cave Hill Cemetery. While the Confederate assault never transpired, the press took note of the damage wrought to the cemetery landscape and also made a rare but revealing reference to the role played by African Americans in the defense of the city, particularly in the cemetery's function as a defensive point. The Louisville correspondent to the *New York Times* reported of Nelson's orders, "If he deems it necessary he will impress us all, niggers included, into some kind of military service. Already one thousand darkies have 'gwine to de *mortifications* to dig trenches.'"[36] Reports and news articles about Cave Hill Cemetery prior to the Civil War never mentioned the presence or role of laborers—Black or otherwise—in the cemetery; they were effectively invisible actors in maintaining the landscape so that it was fit for use by the white living and dead. In this case, however, it is clear that Black workers had a role to play, even if it was in the desecration of the landscape for the sake of better defending the city. Ultimately, the preparations ordered by General Nelson resulted in damage to the graves and monuments, and this became a source of consternation to those in both the North and the South who regarded Cave Hill as an important sacred and cultural institution representative of not just Louisville but of the entire state of Kentucky.[37]

It was also during this period, late in 1862, that Cave Hill was host to a number of high-profile funerals for Union officers. Local newspapers touted these events, with their large processions of mourners, as evidence of the city's loyalty to the Union cause, but such reports ignored tangible evidence that Louisville's population was decidedly far more conflicted.[38] Observant visitors noted that despite reports of lavish Union funerals, a greater share of attention to Confederate graves undermined the message of city unity. For instance, in a letter home to his wife at the end of October 1862, Samuel Patton, of the First Illinois Light Artillery Regiment, visited Cave Hill and described the "rifle pit dug through the farthest side from the Citty," adding that "large numbers of the nicest kind of evergreens have been cut down outside the rifle pit and piled up like a brush fence, to obstruct the advance of cavalry. There is a piece of ground allotted to the soldiers for a berrying ground inside the rifle pit, outside is the graves of rebbels that have died while they were prisoners." Most revealingly, while Patton described nothing of the federal graves aside from their location, he noted, "The secesh of Louisville have adorned their graves with myrtil and flowers."[39]

Patton's final observation was brief, but it indicated a profoundly subversive trend that was occurring in Kentucky's cemeteries during the war—the city's white, female rebel sympathizers were establishing a visual rhetoric of Confederate identity in Louisville by brazenly decorating and caring for the graves of the Confederate dead. This activity became especially pronounced once the major Confederate military threat to the state had been repulsed. It was in 1863 that Gen. Ambrose Burnside, frustrated by the ongoing actions of civilians to aid and abet the rebels, issued General Order Number 38, which declared, "All persons within our lines who harbor, protect, conceal, feed, clothe, or in any way aid the enemies of our country" will be "tried as spies or traitors; and if convicted, will suffer death." There would be no further lenience shown toward rebel sympathizers, as Burnside reasserted: "The habit of declaring sympathies for the enemy will no longer be tolerated in this department. Persons committing such offenses will be at once arrested, with a view to being tried as above stated, or sent beyond our lines into the lines of their friends."[40] Any overt action or behavior that could be deemed supportive of the rebel soldiers or the rebel cause would be regarded as treason, and punishable as such. As historian Kristen Streater has observed, many of the most egregious examples of aid given to the rebels in Kentucky came from white women, and Burnside's order was created in large part to quell their activities. For their actions, "the so-called she-Rebels faced investigations, arrests, imprisonment, and exile for their devotion to the secessionist cause."[41]

Within the cemetery landscape, displays of loyalty to the rebel dead and their cause represented perhaps the only overt expression of devotion that would *not* result in imprisonment or exile from the state. Unionists found the behavior of rebel women in the cemeteries and at funerals appalling, though unprosecutable. Commenting on the behavior of such women in attendance at Union funerals, the Louisville *Daily Democrat* chided, "The Secesh women who attend the funerals of the gallant dead to witness the ceremonies, would display better taste if their precious pretty lips did not curl at the sight of the Federal uniform worn by our officers on such occasions."[42] Despite public censure, however, rebel women in Louisville showed their devotion to the Confederate cause and to its soldiers in their care for the graves of the rebel dead at Cave Hill. Echoing Samuel Patton's observation about rebel graves, but offering greater detail, a wounded Confederate chaplain who visited Cave Hill in the spring of 1863 observed, "A proper burial [has been given] to every Confederate soldier that has died in the city. Here, on the Northern border of Kentucky, [was] a sight that should put to shame many who inhabit cities further South. The grave of every Confederate was raised, sodded, and not a few surrounded with flowers. The name of the soldier, his State, and regiment, was lettered in Black on a neat white headboard around which hung a wreath of myrtle, the Christian offering of the true Southern ladies of Louisville to the noble dead." By contrast, "in the grounds allotted to the burial of the Federal dead," the chaplain "found the graves sunken and uncared for; but few having stones or boards or marks of any kind."[43] From the chaplain's perspective, at least, such inattention to the graves of fallen Union soldiers indicated an underlying apathy on the part of Louisvillians toward the Union dead, and possibly therefore toward the Union cause as well.

As the war entered its final years, public indifference toward the Union cause and lack of interest in commemorating the Union dead became increasingly apparent, especially in light of the city's ultimate failure to raise a monument to the federal soldiers. German residents of Louisville initiated a project early in 1864 to erect a monument to the Union soldiers at Cave Hill Cemetery, and the Louisville *Daily Democrat* encouraged "our loyal people" to turn out en masse for the laying of the cornerstone. The ceremony invitation included the "Mayor and City Council, the heads and members of the various public city offices, Gen. Burbridge and staff, Col. Bruce and staff, and all the heads and members of the various government offices here . . . to join in a grand procession and participate in the ceremonies at Cave Hill." The *Democrat* expressed the hope that people would attend in large numbers to make the ceremony "as imposing and impressive as possible" and that the monument would, when finished, be "an ornament to our place and nation."[44] Three weeks after the cornerstone laying ceremony, a correspondent from an Ohio newspaper attended "a mass meeting at Masonic Temple, the largest hall in" Louisville, the purpose of which was to rally enthusiasm for the soldiers' monument. As it was revealed, there was a lack of funds with which to actually build the proposed monument, and so "about forty influential citizens" called for the meeting and published announcements for several days in four newspapers. The turnout for the meeting included a paltry "five men, seven ladies, and fourteen boys," and after an hour, half of the men and all of the boys had left. Criticizing the lack of commitment to the project in a city considered to be a Union stronghold, the correspondent chastised Louisville's residents: "The object of the meeting was only to raise money to build a monument in memory of one or two thousand deceased soldiers. Patriotism is at a discount here. This is only one instance in which calls have been made for the benefit of soldiers, the people have failed to give their attention."[45] In a further effort to rally public support and funding for the project, a "grand picnic" was held at "Schlieder's garden (Spring Garden)" in May, but the necessary funds were clearly not raised, as the memorial then envisioned was never constructed.[46]

Postwar Memorialization in the Cemetery Landscape

With the close of the war, Cave Hill Cemetery increasingly became a mirror reflecting the social and political transformations that were taking place within Louisville. The absence of decorations on Union soldiers' graves during the war could be explained away because people's efforts were needed elsewhere. With the arrival of peacetime, however, the imbalance of sentiment displayed in the burying ground became increasingly obvious and indicated a clear shift toward, as E. Merton Coulter declared nearly a century ago, the state's waiting "until after the war to secede."[47] White Kentuckians had taken the passage of the Thirteenth Amendment as a betrayal of their trust in the federal government to protect the institution of slavery, and the conservative proslavery unionism that had maintained the state's loyalty during the war quickly dissolved as the state's citizens and political leaders grappled with the ramifications of emancipation and citizenship for African Americans.[48] The result was a growing expansion of Confederate identity and political victories by anti–civil rights Democrats across the state, including in Louisville.[49] The northern press, in witnessing the postwar manifestation of rebellion, did not report kindly on the matter. A correspondent for the *New York Times* visited Louisville in the summer of 1865, and he ventured to Cave Hill to see the graves of the soldier dead. Reporting that the "Louisville Cemetery . . . has not far from 5,000 Union soldiers buried in it," he noted that their graves were "neatly sodded, and kept, as indeed all the grounds are, in fresh and good condition." By contrast, "flowers and creeping vines appear on sundry of [the rebel] graves, while the head-boards, neatly painted, are larger and more seemly than those marking where the Union soldiers lie." Regarding the obvious visual disparity, the correspondent likened what he witnessed at Louisville to the burying grounds in Nashville: "a petty rebel discrimination . . . paint and flowers for those who died to overthrow the government, and plain, rough boards, and often weed-grown graves, for the noble fellows who had poured out their lives to save the country, and maintain our national unity." Despite the minimum amount of care given to the burials of the Union dead, the writer optimistically maintained that in "spite of rebel spleen or malignity the time is coming, if it not yet come, when the whole country will regard as consecrated ground the spot where these noble men sleep."[50] Such may have been the case in other Union states, but with Andrew Johnson's approval to relinquish martial law in Kentucky in the fall of 1865, the state's Confederates and rebel sympathizers were now completely unfettered in expressing their loyalty to the Confederate dead and the Lost Cause.

The spring of 1866 brought with it the first major expressions of collective postwar memorialization in Kentucky in the form of highly attended reburials of Confederate soldiers in Frankfort, Lexington, and elsewhere in the state, and the inauguration of Confederate Decoration Day.[51] Communities throughout Kentucky held ceremonies to decorate the graves of the rebel dead, but Louisville drew especially marked attention for the displays that took place at Cave Hill Cemetery. The *Louisville Weekly Courier* reported on the day's proceedings, which occurred at the end of April, noting that while Louisville "has never been the theater of bloody strife," the city still yielded many war dead from its military prisons and hospitals. "Hospitals are disappearing, and military prisons are ceasing to be, but the grass-covered graves of thousands of deceased soldiers, in our 'Cave Hill' Cemetery, will remain. . . . The dead of the Union army, who perished in hospitals here, were buried by their companions in arms, to the number of thousands. The Confederate captives who breathed their lives away in prison hospitals, were buried by those who held them in captivity." By this time, the graves

FIGURE 2.4. Portion of Confederate burial section, Cave Hill Cemetery (photograph by the author)

of the Union soldiers at Cave Hill had all been sodded, and each grave included a wooden head- and footboard. The graves for the Confederate dead had likewise been sodded and marked with painted headboards that included each soldier's information, if known. Further, rosebushes had been planted on the Confederate graves, prompting the *Courier* to observe, "In rose blooming time the beauty and odor of the place will almost rival a forest of roses in the Vale of Sharon." (See figure 2.4.)[52]

Across the South from 1865 into 1866, white women had been in the process of forming ladies' memorial associations (LMAs) whose purpose was the reburial of Confederate dead and decoration of their graves.[53] Since Kentucky, and thus also Louisville, had remained loyal, the city had no LMA (although by the early 1870s the state would have a chapter of the Confederate Burial Memorial Association, an organization based in Nashville).[54] However, the women who had cared for the graves of the rebel dead at Cave Hill during the war took a prominent role in organizing postwar decoration ceremonies. As the *Louisville Weekly Courier* reported, "a large assembly of ladies" gathered to scatter bouquets and flowers, while a "number of gentlemen were also present, some the heroes of many a hard-fought battle." As with many of the first Decoration Day ceremonies that occurred across the South, this first one at Cave Hill Cemetery took place mostly in silence.[55] Southern newspapers highlighted the especially touching vision of a particular young woman at Cave Hill, "arrayed in the somber robes of mourning," who "paused longest beside" the grave of "a friend, from a Southern State, to whom it had been her privilege to minister occasionally" while he was a military prison captive. Adding further romance to the description, the newspaper revealed that the woman was the daughter of Confederate hero Albert Sidney Johnston, which necessarily elevated her as a symbol of devoted white womanhood. In rhetoric that would come to define the ideology of the Lost Cause, it was also reported that she was accompanied by "a faithful family servant," who, although now free, had remained with his mistress despite her "changed fortunes" and who "gazed reverently upon her as she performed her sad duty."[56] Such descriptions only added fuel to the fashioning of the South's Lost Cause mythology, and the faithful slave narrative in particular.

The following year's Confederate Decoration Day in Louisville was an enormous event, at which "hundreds of vehicles lined the carriage-ways, making the scene one of surpassing animation," with a total crowd of about three thousand. Drawn by curiosity, a reporter from the *Cincinnati Daily Gazette* attended the proceedings and observed that in the Confederate section of the cemetery, there were "about four hundred graves with neat, white headboards upon which the name, age and regiment to which the soldier belonged, were inscribed." All of the southern states were represented in the burials at Cave Hill, and on every grave "a bunch of flowers was laid, and some were decked with wreaths of evergreen." Despite the size of the crowd assembled, "there was no parade, no ceremony and no weeping."[57] Further, despite how outnumbered the Confederate graves were by those for Union soldiers—by 1867 there were over three thousand bodies interred in the national cemetery—the outpouring of mourners for Confederate Decoration Day offered a powerful contradiction to the wartime reality of Louisville as a Union stronghold.[58] Those in attendance also confirmed that the decoration ceremony represented more than simple respect for the dead. Upon overhearing a conversation between two women at the cemetery, the *Gazette* reporter could not help but be struck by the incongruity of the space and the people within it: "Two ladies walking before me, the one remarked: 'Do you know I have a prejudice against Louisville? I think it a sort of a Yank town.' 'Oh,' replied the other, 'you don't know us. There are more rebels here than you have any idea.' And so thought I as I walked a little up the hill to the spot where rest the ashes of some five or six hundred Union dead. Not more than a half dozen have any sort of head-board, except a mere mark at each end, and these no doubt were attended to by distant friends. No one was looking at this little work of 'God's acre,' much less strewing flowers over the nameless graves."[59] Appalled as the *Cincinnati Gazette* reporter was, his observation about the lack of attention given to Union graves at Cave Hill was apt—there was as yet no federal Memorial Day holiday, despite the organization of national cemeteries, and without a major effort on the part of local Union veterans and civilians to decorate the graves, ex-Confederates in the city simply continued with the memorial and decoration practices they had begun during the war. Combined with an increase in conservative Democrat political victories across the state, the enthusiasm exhibited by ex-Confederates to memorialize their dead at Cave Hill and elsewhere revealed the definitive postwar shift in Kentucky's identity from Union to Confederate.[60]

Offering reinforcement of the visual narrative of rebel identity within the cemetery was the press, particularly the *Louisville Weekly Courier*, which was run by ex-Confederate Walter Newman Haldeman. The *Courier* reported on the proceedings twice, and in its first observation praised the "gentle and beauteous creatures" who decorated the graves of the dead, and whose actions were "suggestive of the thought that the world loves and honors those who die for principle, whether the cause in which they die is right or wrong."[61] A week later, the *Courier* went into greater detail and offered special praise for Mrs. Kate Huffman, wife of Elijah Huffman, "the lady to whom the friends of these poor wanderers are indebted that they are not now nameless and unrecognized." For while Elijah Huffman had been instrumental in purchasing the area in Cave Hill where Confederates would be buried, his wife had ensured the erection of headboards to properly mark and identify those interred. She, along with other women from the city, were commended by the paper as "distinguished alike for their noble charity and justness to all."[62]

For northerners who witnessed the scene, such unabashed devotion to the Confederate dead at the expense of care for the graves of Union soldiers was clearly beyond the pale. The *Cincinnati Daily Gazette* attacked the proceedings as "a grand secession glorification" and "a spasmodic kick of the Southern Confederacy, . . . an attempt to glory in their shame, by flaunting the evidence of treason in the face of loyalty." Having witnessed such total disregard for the heroic Union dead, the *Gazette* declared, "It was an insult to the loyal people of this city, and of the nation, and they well knew it."[63] The western correspondent for Rhode Island's *Providence Evening Press* offered similar denunciations, noting the care with which the rebel graves had been marked and decorated with flowers, while those of the Union soldiers had been neglected: "For all outward signs the [Union] graves might have been those of dogs." The Providence paper concluded, "Kentucky Rebelism is to day, rampant and defiant. Kentucky 'Unionism' is the poor, contemptible incarnation of meanness it has always been. . . . Kentucky knows nothing of a true love for the Union. She buried it all in the grave of Henry Clay."[64] Such criticisms of the condition of federal graves at Cave Hill evoked a defensive response from one of the cemetery's trustees, who wrote to the *Courier-Journal* to explain that three-fourths of the "over four thousand" Union soldiers' graves had been "sodded, and many of them were sodded before a Confederate soldier was buried at Cave Hill Cemetery." Clearly offended by the suggestion that Union soldiers' graves had been neglected, he wrote, "The Trustees of the Cemetery are responsible for attention to all the graves in the Cemetery. They had the graves of over three thousand Union soldiers and the graves of over two hundred Confederate soldiers sodded and attended to, just as they attend to all graves in the Cemetery."[65]

The trustee's irate letter to the newspaper addressed the question about the sodding of graves, but it was still painfully obvious that little to no attention had been given to decorating Union soldiers' burials. The outpouring of pro-Confederate sentiment in 1867 in Louisville and the scorn of northern reporters thus put pressure on the city's remaining supporters of the Union cause to do something. "The Rebel ladies have frequently strewn the graves of the Rebel dead with flowers, but heretofore the defenders of the old flag have slept uncared for," and so, members of the Grand Army of the Republic and "loyal ladies took the matter in hand." On the morning of June 20, 1867, a year before the GAR issued General Order Number 11, which designated May 30 as a national Memorial Day, "a very large procession proceeded to the cemetery, where the graves were strewn with flowers, evergreens, and immortelles, by fair hands of loyal women." In the Unionist response to Confederate Decoration Day in Louisville, it was reported that "fully three thousand persons were present."[66] The *Chicago Tribune* magnified the attendance to between "eight and nine thousand persons."[67] (See figure 2.5.)

Regardless of the actual number present in the cemetery, it was duly noted that in the decoration of Union graves, "no negroes were present," which made clear that the emancipationist legacy of the war was not a major priority among those memorializing the dead at Cave Hill.[68] Despite the presence of a small number of United States Colored Troops at Cave Hill Cemetery, the city's Black population was not encouraged to participate.[69] Rather, as Anne Marshall has noted, the city's freedmen and women were active with public celebrations of Emancipation Day and the Fourth of July, but these events took place in churches and civic spaces rather than in cemeteries.[70]

FIGURE 2.5. Portion of Cave Hill National Cemetery with Monument to the Unknown Union Dead, erected in 1914 (photograph by the author)

In further response to the preponderance of attention given to rebels' graves, George Prentice, editor of the Louisville *Journal*, rival to Haldeman's *Courier*, published an elegiac poem about the graves of the Union soldier dead at Cave Hill. Written in the same year as Francis Miles Finch's poem of reconciliation, "The Blue and the Gray," Prentice's was defined by the sectionalism that still split the city's population. Referring to the Union dead as "great sons of fame," the poem in its final verses reinforced the sentiments expressed by the northern press toward Kentucky's Confederates:

> Through all the upper air
> May your life blood in exhalations rise,
> A ghastly cloud of red despair
> To traitor eyes.
>
> And may the lightnings dire,
> Coiled in that cloud, like vengeful scorpions dart
> To blast with their keen fangs of fire
> Each traitor heart.

The proverbial line in the sand had been drawn in the battle over the city's postwar identity, with the soldiers' graves at Cave Hill the new symbolic battleground on which Louisville's residents would stake their claim to legitimacy.

The following year brought the first official celebration of Memorial Day sanctioned by the federal government, and while the Grand Army of the Republic planned to hold an impressive ceremony, Louisville's ex-Confederates received censure for their continued outpouring of attention and money for the decoration of rebel graves. The *Evansville Journal* in southern Indiana chastised the expenditure of an estimated $700 for flowers to decorate Confederate graves, when Louisville's Orphan Asylum—"a State Institution at that"—was on the brink of turning children out to starve for lack of funds.[71] For their part, the southern press remarked on the Confederate Decoration Day ceremonies as "most touching," as they involved depositing "a sealed envelope, a wreath of flowers within, and affectionate mottoes, traced by lady hands, without—tokens sent from the South."[72] When the ceremony for the decoration of Union graves took place on May 30, "soldiers and a large number of citizens" proceeded to Cave Hill to decorate the graves as the bells of the fire department were tolled, while "flags were displayed at half-mast over the Custom-house, Court-house, City Hall, and the newspaper offices."[73]

In 1875, following years of acrimonious competition over the decoration of soldiers' graves, veterans of both armies across the country began to attend each other's memorial observances as a step toward further reconciliation.[74] In giving the principal oration at the Memorial Day observance at Cave Hill that year, United States treasury secretary Benjamin H. Bristow both praised the cemetery landscape and honored the soldier dead. "Our own beautiful Cave Hill," he declared, "with its green sward, its trees and flowers, its marble monuments, bearing names familiar to us all, tells how the people of Louisville cherish the memory of departed friends." The cemetery had continued to expand since its dedication in 1848, and elite Louisvillians had marked the landscape with impressive monuments and statuary to honor their beloved dead. In speaking of the soldiers, Bristow admonished the crowd in attendance, "We are assembled to celebrate the valor and virtue of men who died to preserve the blessings of personal liberty and free government to us and our posterity. The memory of their heroic endurance and daring courage should live in the hearts of succeeding generations, so long as the principles for which they fought and died shall survive, and be valued among men."[75] The Boston *Daily Advertiser* praised Bristow's address as one that not only spoke of the sacrifice of the Union soldiers but "paid a high tribute to the southern soldiery, saying it is impossible to doubt that the masses among them fought for what they believed to be right, however deluded by false theories of government, or the artful teachings of cunning and ambitious leaders."⁷⁶ The impression given was one of mutual respect and firm reconciliation across the city, state, and nation.

Such a message, however, obscured the persistence of Confederate identity and loyalty to the ideology of the Lost Cause that had emerged in Kentucky. Former Confederate officer William C. P. Breckinridge, in his Decoration Day oration for 1879 at Cave Hill, declared, "By the side of these graves we make neither apology nor defense." Breckinridge noted that time had brought forth a new generation for whom the war was history, who had been taught that the Confederates were "rebels and traitors, who fought to preserve human slavery.... Upon these graves and the graves of all our dead and the good name of all our living this charge has been made." This, in Breckinridge's view, was a false charge, and he admonished the gathered crowd to remember their duty to love and honor their "martyrs to liberty, who died for the right, and gave their lives in defense of truth."⁷⁷ Despite national ovations toward peacemaking in the decade following the war, with a particular emphasis on reconciliation between white male combatants, Breckinridge's address hit a nerve in the North, and the *New York Times* reported on the proceedings with the title "Kentucky Traitors." Labeling his address "The Plea Made for Its Sons Who Left Their State to Fight against the Union," the *Times* reprinted large sections of Breckinridge's oration to show readers its "animus."⁷⁸ Louisvillians, however, remained unfazed by such criticism. The city's residents continued to turn out in large numbers for Confederate Decoration Day in addition to Memorial Day, and whereas efforts to raise funds for the construction of a Union soldiers' monument at Cave Hill failed, the "ladies of Louisville" rallied in support of a monument project that ultimately would be successful: the construction of a Confederate soldiers' monument.⁷⁹

Immediately following the Confederate Decoration Day ceremony in 1887, women from the leading families of the city formed the Kentucky Women's Confederate Monument Association, the result of which would be the raising of funds for the erection and dedication in 1895 of a seventy-foot-tall monument to the Confederate dead at the intersection of Second and Third Streets, the principal elite neighborhood in the city where white residents promenaded and rode their carriages. The Confederate Soldiers' Monument (figure 2.6) was ultimately one of seventy-two Confederate monuments dedicated across the state, a startling number, especially since only two were ever erected to the Union (one of which is shown in figure 2.5).⁸⁰ Upon its completion and for years afterward, the Louisville Confederate Soldiers' Monument was the starting point for the Confederate Decoration

FIGURE 2.6. Louisville Confederate Soldiers' Monument, ca. 1906, Detroit Publishing Company (courtesy of the Library of Congress Prints and Photographs Division)

Day parade to Cave Hill, and so, while it was geographically apart from the cemetery, the two spaces remained tied together as part of the Confederate commemorative landscape in Louisville.[81]

Becoming a City for *All* the Dead

As the city continued to develop into the twentieth century, both the Louisville Confederate Soldiers' Monument and Cave Hill Cemetery remained fixtures reminding residents and visitors of the city's past. Even as the cemetery's managers continued to expand the grounds and modify the plantings in response to changes in taste, public attention to Cave Hill focused on its two primary historical components—first, as a rural cemetery, one of great beauty for which the city could claim great pride; and second, as the burial site of several thousand Civil War soldiers, with the national cemetery and the Confederate burial section neighboring each other and perpetually highlighting the divided identity of the city's and the state's residents. The cemetery again modified its bylaws and regulations in 1901, reaffirming that Cave Hill was reserved for the burial of whites only and establishing clear rhetoric concerning how people of color—assumed to be servants of white families—could enter the grounds. Upon the application of a lot owner, "servants (white or colored)" could attend to and care for their employer's lot as if they were themselves the lot owner; further, people of color who wished to simply visit the cemetery had to be "accompanied by an owner of a lot certificate, or some member of the family, or [could] be admitted by the written permit of a Manager or the Secretary."[82]

Cave Hill Cemetery was a space that was clearly marked for white use and reflected the identity of elite white Louisvillians; however, despite the apparent fixedness of race relations, there were exceptions that revealed the greater social complexity of this Border South city. On Monday, November 3, 1890, an enormous funeral was held for the Reverend Dr. William J. Simmons, "the colored educator and divine." According to the notice published in the *Courier-Journal*, the funeral would be held at the Fifth Street Baptist Church. From there members of the Masonic Unity Lodge, Number 12, would escort the remains to Cave Hill Cemetery, where they would "be deposited in a vault *for the present* [emphasis added]." Simmons's remains were ultimately interred at Eastern Cemetery nearby, but given his stature as a spiritual leader within the Black community in Kentucky and nationally, and the expectation that his was "probably . . . the largest colored funeral ever held in this city," clearly the Cave Hill Cemetery trustees made an exception to allow his body to rest, albeit temporarily, in their burying ground.[83] Despite the entrenchment of Jim Crow in Louisville, the seeds for the city's future transformations could be witnessed in the temporary entombment of Simmons's remains. The cemetery did not abandon its discriminatory policies until the 1960s, but since then it has become as socially and culturally diverse as it is visually pleasing to anyone who takes the time to visit. As a sign of the cemetery's further evolution and social progress in the twenty-first century, Gwen Mooney currently serves as its sixth president and first female executive since its dedication in 1848. In describing her vision for the cemetery, she has stated, "We want to make this a learning center," and she shares the sentiment that has been evident since the nineteenth century—"Cave Hill is truly a gem for the city of Louisville and the state of Kentucky."[84] Cave Hill has indeed been a gem, but it has also been a mirror, a reflection of Louisville in microcosm in its 175-year history. Its landscape and monuments, the dichotomy of Union and Confederate burials, and the individuals and families who are buried there (as well as those who are not, due to a long history of exclusion) all reflect the complex history and transformations of Louisville, as well as the shared values and conflicted identities of the city's residents.

Notes

1. "Highlands on Alert for Ali Procession," *Courier-Journal* (Louisville, Ky.), June 9, 2016, A5; "Roses for Ali," *Courier-Journal*, June 19, 2016, A15.

2. *Rules, Regulations, and By-Laws of Cave Hill Cemetery*, 74–75. According to the section labeled "Rules Respecting Visitors," under Article II, "Colored persons" could enter the cemetery in the company of a lot holder or a family member of a lot holder or with the written permission of a cemetery trustee. Regarding the entry of African Americans beginning in 1870, see the May 31, 1870, snippet from the *Louisville Daily Commercial* quoted in Thomas, *Cave Hill Cemetery*, 16. Also see "Memorial Day, Honors to the Dead of the Republic," *Cincinnati Daily Gazette*, May 31, 1870, 2.

3. Rose, "Louisville's Hidden Figures"; "I Am Ali Festival."

4. "Louisville—Its Commerce—Beauty—Politics—Public Buildings, &c.," *Plain Dealer* (Cleveland), April 30, 1856, 2. George D. Prentice was a native of Connecticut and moved to Louisville in 1830, where he founded the Louisville *Journal*. Known as a poet as well as a journalist, Prentice earned a national reputation through his newspaper, which consolidated in 1868 with the *Courier* to become the Louisville *Courier-Journal*, "the best known and ablest conducted newspaper in the South," according to *Frank Leslie's Popular Monthly* 20 (November 1885).

5. In Jefferson County, where Louisville is located, there were 2,664 slave owners, 8,708 Black and mulatto slaves, and 2,006 free people of color in 1860. See "Jefferson County (Ky.) Slaves, Free Blacks, and Free Mulattoes."

6. Marshall, *Creating a Confederate Kentucky*, 2.

7. "Proceedings of the City Council," *Louisville Daily Courier*, November 12, 1846, 3.

8. For a comprehensive history of Mount Auburn Cemetery, see Linden, *Silent City on a Hill*. For the rural cemetery movement overall, see French, "Cemetery as Cultural Institution"; Bender, "'Rural' Cemetery Movement"; Sears, *Sacred Places*, 99–103; Sloane, *Last Great Necessity*, 44–64; McDannell, *Material Christianity*, 103–31; Smith, *Rural Cemetery Movement*; Cothran and Danylchak, *Grave Landscapes*; Giguere, "Localism and Nationalism in the City of the Dead."

9. Johnson, *History of the Frankfort Cemetery*, 6. See also *Frankfort Cemetery in Kentucky*.

10. For general histories of these cemeteries, see Thomas, *Cave Hill Cemetery*; Milward, *History of the Lexington Cemetery*.

11. Kammen, *Digging Up The Dead*, 129–34; Coleman, *Last Days, Death, and Funeral of Henry Clay*.

12. *Plan, Prospectus, and Terms, for the Establishment of a Public Cemetery, at the City of Baltimore*, 5; Lancaster, "Green Mount"; *Historical Sketch of Hollywood Cemetery, from the 3d of June, 1847, to 1st Nov., 1875*, 5.

13. Thomas, *Cave Hill Cemetery*, 9–10.

14. "Cave Hill Cemetery," *Louisville Daily Courier*, July 11, 1849, 2.

15. Thomas, *Cave Hill Cemetery*, 64–65.

16. "In Cave Hill—The Story of the Beautiful Cemetery," *Courier-Journal* (Louisville), June 16, 1895, 17.

17. "Cave Hill Cemetery," *Louisville Daily Courier*, July 13, 1848, 2. For another extensive article explaining the history of the rural cemetery movement, along with information pertaining to the act of incorporation for the cemetery, see "Rural Cemeteries," *Louisville Daily Courier*, July 20, 1848, 2.

18. "The Dedication of Cave Hill Cemetery," *Louisville Daily Courier*, July 27, 1848, 2.

19. "In Cave Hill—The Story of the Beautiful Cemetery," 17.
20. Humphrey, *Address Delivered on the Dedication of the Cave Hill Cemetery*, 4–5.
21. Ibid., 9.
22. "Respect for the Dead—Elmwood Cemetery," *Daily Eagle and Enquirer* (Memphis, Tenn.), June 17, 1854, 2; *Historical Sketch of Hollywood Cemetery, from the 3d of June, 1847, to 10th July, 1889*, 3, 4.
23. "Memorials of the Dead," *Southern Literary Messenger* 19 (September 1853), 543–44.
24. Humphrey, *Address Delivered on the Dedication of the Cave Hill Cemetery*, 17.
25. "Cave Hill Cemetery," *Louisville Daily Courier*, July 11, 1849, 2.
26. "Louisville—Its Commerce—Beauty—Politics—Public Buildings, &c.," *Plain Dealer* (Cleveland), April 30, 1856, 2.
27. "A Visit to Cave Hill Cemetery," *Daily Milwaukee News*, June 10, 1859, 1.
28. Rural cemeteries across the country regularly grappled with issues of misbehavior within their boundaries. Rules and regulations for visitors thus became standard, though Mount Auburn Cemetery initially did not have any until it became clear regulations were necessary after its first year in operation. For more on issues of behavior in the rural cemeteries, see Giguere, "'Too Mean to Live.'"
29. *Rules, Regulations, and By-Laws of Cave Hill Cemetery*, 74–75.
30. African American Genealogy and History Sources at the Filson Historical Society.
31. *Rules, Regulations, and By-Laws of Cave Hill Cemetery*, 75.
32. African American Genealogy and History Sources at the Filson Historical Society; "Louisville (KY) Cemetery."
33. *Rules, Regulations, and By-Laws of Cave Hill Cemetery*, 74.
34. "Meeting of the Council," *Louisville Daily Democrat*, October 18, 1861, 2; "Board of Aldermen," *Louisville Daily Democrat*, October 22, 1861, 1.
35. Walden, *Confederate Soldiers and Civilians Buried in the Confederate Sections*, i.
36. "Our Louisville Correspondence," *New York Times*, September 28, 1862, 2. For a more detailed overview of Nelson's preparations for General Bragg's aborted attack on Louisville, see Clark, *Notorious "Bull" Nelson*, 137–52.
37. *New Albany Ledger* (October 3, 1862); "Affairs in Kentucky," *New York Times* October 6, 1862), 2; "General News Summary," *Mercury* (Charleston, S.C.), January 8, 1863, 2.
38. "The Funeral of Brigadier-General Jas. S. Jackson," *Louisville Daily Democrat*, October 12, 1862, 3; "Funeral of Lieut. Col. Jouett and Major Campbell," *Louisville Daily Democrat*, October 14, 1862, 2; "Funeral of Lieut. Col. Jouett and Major Campbell," *Louisville Daily Democrat*, October 12, 1862), 2. Several interments of notable officers at Cave Hill Cemetery were temporary—their remains were later removed to other, permanent burial places. For example, see "The Remains of Gens. Terrill and Webster, Etc.," *New York Times*, October 12, 1862; "Funeral of Lieutenant John A. Williams," *Louisville Daily Democrat*, October 19, 1862, 2.
39. Samuel Patton to Nellie Patton, Louisville, Ky., October 27, 1862. Patton Family Papers, Filson Historical Society.
40. Streater, "Not Much a Friend to Traiters," 249.
41. Ibid., 258.
42. *Louisville Daily Democrat*, October 14, 1862, 2.
43. "The Graves of Confederate Soldiers in Kentucky," *Daily Southern Crisis* (Jackson, Miss.), March 30, 1863.
44. "Monument to Union Soldiers," *Louisville Daily Democrat*, February 21, 1864, 2.
45. "Letter from Louisville," *Xenia Sentinel* (Ohio), March 15, 1864.

46. "For the Benefit of the Union Soldiers' Monument at Cave Hill Cemetery," *Louisville Daily Democrat*, May 11, 1864, 3. There are two Union soldiers' monuments on the grounds at Cave Hill Cemetery. The earlier is the Bloedner Monument, carved by August Bloedner in 1862 and dedicated to thirteen soldiers of the Thirty-Second Indiana Volunteer Infantry Regiment, also known as the First German Regiment, who fell at Rowlett's Station, Kentucky, in December 1861. This monument was originally dedicated at Fort Willich, where the soldiers were buried, but was then removed to Cave Hill Cemetery in 1867, along with the soldiers' remains. The original monument was removed in 2008 for conservation and a copy put in its place in 2010. The second Union monument is the Unknown Union Soldiers' Monument, a rough, boulder-shaped memorial, which was erected in 1914. See "Cave Hill National Cemetery, Louisville, Kentucky," National Park Service.

47. Coulter, *Civil War and Readjustment in Kentucky*, vii.

48. Lee, "Unionism, Emancipation, and the Origins of Kentucky's Confederate Identity."

49. Marshall, *Creating a Confederate Kentucky*, 32–54.

50. "Kentucky," *New York Times*, August 5, 1865.

51. Decoration Day as a regional, and then national, phenomenon manifested among different groups at different times after the war. African Americans in Charleston, S.C., turned out to decorate the graves of federal soldiers on May 1, 1865, and this is generally regarded as the first "Decoration Day." Ex-Confederates began to hold Decoration Day ceremonies to lay flowers and honor the rebel dead beginning in the spring of 1866, while the general order that created Memorial Day was not issued until 1868. See Jabbour and Singer Jabbour, *Decoration Day in the Mountains*, 116–30; Blair, *Cities of the Dead*, 49–76; Blight, *Race and Reunion*, 64–97.

52. "A Solemn Festival—A Floral Offering to the Confederate Dead," *Louisville Weekly Courier*, May 2, 1866, 2. The "vale of Sharon" is a Biblical reference to an area in modern-day Israel that was renowned for its flowers ("I am a rose of Sharon, a lily of the valleys," Song of Solomon 2:2).

53. For the most comprehensive study on southern LMAs, see Janney, *Burying the Dead but Not the Past*.

54. Marshall, *Creating a Confederate Kentucky*, 83.

55. "A Solemn Festival—A Floral Offering to the Confederate Dead," *Louisville Weekly Courier*, May 2, 1866, 2.

56. "An Incident of the Floral Offering Day," *Anderson Intelligencer* (Columbia, S.C.), May 24, 1866.

57. "Letter from Louisville," *Cincinnati Daily Gazette*, April 29, 1867, 1.

58. The cemetery's official count of soldiers buried in the soldiers' sections (not including those in private family plots) was 3,339 Union and 225 Confederate as of 1869. See *Rules, Regulations, and By-Laws of Cave Hill Cemetery*, 39, 41–42.

59. "Letter from Louisville," 1.

60. For more on the political and social transformations that took shape in Kentucky after the war, see Marshall, *Creating a Confederate Kentucky*, 32–80.

61. "The Graves of the Confederate Dead," *Louisville Weekly Courier*, May 1, 1867, 2.

62. "The Confederate Dead in Cave Hill Cemetery," *Louisville Weekly Courier*, May 8, 1867, 1.

63. "Making Treason Respectable," *Cincinnati Daily Gazette*, May 3, 1867, 1.

64. "Our Western Correspondence," *Providence Evening Press*, May 8, 1867, 5.

65. "The Dead of the War at Cave Hill Cemetery," Louisville *Courier-Journal*, August 27, 1867, 2.

66. "Honors to the Loyal Dead," *Evening Telegraph* (Philadelphia), June 20, 1867.

67. "Decorating the Graves of Union Soldiers—Imposing Ceremonies," *Chicago Tribune*, June 20, 1867, 1.

68. "Honors to the Loyal Dead," *Evening Telegraph* (Philadelphia), June 20, 1867.

69. In comparing the records from Veterans Affairs at http://www.interment.net/data/us/ky/jefferson/cavehill/index.htm and in the cemetery records database at Cave Hill Cemetery, I've been able to confirm only five individuals who served in the USCT who were buried during the 1860s: Eleim Johnson (died April 15, 1865), Spencer Price (died July 12, 1863), Walter Scott (died November 25, 1864), Jack Warner (died September 15, 1864), and Jared Woodson (died July 10, 1865). By the time of the Union decoration event in 1867, there were approximately four thousand federal soldiers buried at Cave Hill, so these individuals would have represented 0.0125 percent of the burials; their graves were intermixed with those of white soldiers, so it is entirely possible that the city's Black residents were unaware of their presence in the cemetery. For the online Cave Hill Cemetery burials database, see https://www.cavehillcemetery.com/search/.

70. Marshall, *Creating a Confederate Kentucky*, 92.

71. *Evansville Journal* (Indiana), May 1, 1868.

72. *Daily Memphis Avalanche* (Tennessee), April 29, 1868, 1.

73. *Evansville Journal* (Indiana), June 1, 1868.

74. "A Day of Reconciliation," *Boston Daily Advertiser* (June 2, 1875).

75. *Address of Hon. B.H. Bristow*, 3.

76. "A Day of Reconciliation," *Boston Daily Advertiser*, June 2, 1875.

77. Breckinridge, *Plea for a History of the Confederate War*, 5–11.

78. "Kentucky Traitors," *New York Times*, June 2, 1879,, 3.

79. "Confederate Dead Remembered," *New York Times*, May 29, 1887, 2.

80. Marshall, *Creating a Confederate Kentucky*, 205n.

81. For a more complete history of the Confederate Soldiers' Monument, including its removal and relocation to Brandenburg in 2016, see Giguere, "(Im)Movable Monument."

82. *Charter, By-Laws and Rules and Regulations of Cave Hill Cemetery Co.*, 70–71.

83. "The Dead Educator," *Courier-Journal* (Louisville), November 3, 1890, 2.

84. "Change Coming to Cave Hill," *Courier-Journal*, June 24, 2015, A3.

Bibliography

Primary Sources

MANUSCRIPTS

Filson Historical Society

Patton Family Papers

NEWSPAPERS AND PERIODICALS

Anderson Intelligencer (Columbia, S.C.)
Boston Daily Advertiser
Chicago Tribune
Cincinnati Daily Gazette
Courier-Journal (Louisville, Ky.)
Daily Eagle and Enquirer (Memphis, Tenn.)
Daily Memphis Avalanche
Daily Milwaukee News
Daily Southern Crisis (Jackson, Miss.)
Evansville Journal (Indiana)
Evening Telegraph (Philadelphia)
Louisville Daily Courier
Louisville Daily Democrat
Louisville Weekly Courier

Mercury (Charleston, S.C.)
New Albany Ledger
New York Times
Plain Dealer (Cleveland)

Providence Evening Press (Rhode Island)
Southern Literary Messenger
Xenia Sentinel (Ohio)

PUBLISHED PRIMARY SOURCES

Address of Hon. B.H. Bristow, Delivered on the Occasion of the Decoration of Soldiers' Graves at Cave Hill Cemetery, Louisville, Kentucky, May 29, 1875. Washington: A. S. Taylor, 1875.

Breckinridge, William C. P. *A Plea for a History of the Confederate War: An Address at the Decoration of the Confederate Graves in Cave Hill Cemetery, Louisville, Kentucky, May 26, 1879.* Louisville: John P. Morton and Co., 1887.

Charter, By-Laws and Rules and Regulations of Cave Hill Cemetery Co. Louisville: Courier-Journal Job Printing Company, 1901.

Historical Sketch of Hollywood Cemetery, from the 3d of June, 1847, to 1st Nov., 1875. Richmond: Baughman Brothers, 1875.

Historical Sketch of Hollywood Cemetery, from the 3d of June, 1847, to 10th July, 1889. Richmond: Baughman Stationary Co., Printers, 1893.

Humphrey, Edward P. *An Address Delivered on the Dedication of the Cave Hill Cemetery; Near Louisville; July 25, 1848.* Louisville: Courier Job-Room, 1848.

Plan, Prospectus, and Terms, for the Establishment of a Public Cemetery, at the City of Baltimore, to Be Called the Green Mount Cemetery. Baltimore: John D. Toy, Printer, 1838.

Rules, Regulations, and By-Laws of Cave Hill Cemetery: With the Dedicatory Address and Topographical and Descriptive Notices. Louisville: John P. Morton and Company, 1868.

Rules, Regulations, and By-Laws of Cave Hill Cemetery: With the Dedicatory Address and Topographical and Descriptive Notices. Louisville: John P. Morton and Company, 1869.

WEBSITES AND DATABASES

African American Genealogy and History Sources at the Filson Historical Society. https://filsonhistorical.org/wp-content/uploads/African-American-History-Genealogy-Sources.pdf.

Cave Hill Cemetery Burials Database. https://www.cavehillcemetery.com/search/.

Cave Hill National Cemetery, Louisville, Kentucky." National Park Service. https:/www.nps.gov/nr/travel/national_cemeteries/Kentucky/cave_hill_national_cemetery.html.

"I Am Ali Festival." https://alicenter.org/event/i-am-ali-festival/.

"Jefferson County (Ky.) Slaves, Free Blacks, and Free Mulattoes, 1850–1870." Notable Kentucky African Americans Database. Last modified Jan. 10, 2023. http://nkaa.uky.edu/nkaa/items/show/2376.

"Louisville (KY) Cemetery." Notable Kentucky African Americans Database. Last modified Aug. 17, 2020. http://nkaa.uky.edu/nkaa/items/show/2249.

Veterans Affairs Records of Burials at Cave Hill Cemetery. Interment.net. http://www.interment.net/data/us/ky/jefferson/cavehill/index.htm.

Secondary Sources

Bender, Thomas. "The 'Rural' Cemetery Movement: Urban Travail and the Appeal of Nature." *New England Quarterly* 47 (June 1974): 196–211.

Blair, William. *Cities of the Dead: Contesting the Memory of the Civil War in the South, 1865–1914.* Chapel Hill: University of North Carolina Press, 2004.

Blight, David. *Race and Reunion: The Civil War in American Memory*. Cambridge, Mass.: Belknap Press of Harvard University Press, 2001.

Clark, Donald A. *The Notorious "Bull" Nelson: Murdered Civil War General*. Carbondale: Southern Illinois University Press, 2011.

Coleman, John Winston. *Last Days, Death, and Funeral of Henry Clay: With Some Remarks on the Clay Monument in the Lexington Cemetery*. Lexington, Ky.: Winburn Press, 1951.

Cothran, James R., and Erica Danylchak. *Grave Landscapes: The Nineteenth-Century Rural Cemetery Movement*. Columbia: University of South Carolina Press, 2018.

Coulter, E. Merton. *The Civil War and Readjustment in Kentucky*. Chapel Hill: University of North Carolina Press, 1926.

Finck, James W. *Divided Loyalties: Kentucky's Struggle for Armed Neutrality in the Civil War*. El Dorado Hills, Calif.: Savas Beatie, 2012.

Frankfort Cemetery in Kentucky. Frankfort: Kentucky Genealogical Society, 1988.

French, Stanley. "The Cemetery as Cultural Institution: The Establishment of Mount Auburn and the 'Rural Cemetery' Movement." *American Quarterly* 26, no. 1 (March 1974): 37–59.

Giguere, Joy M. "Localism and Nationalism in the City of the Dead: The Rural Cemetery Movement in the Antebellum South." *Journal of Southern History* 84, no. 4 (November 2018): 845–82.

———. "'Too Mean to Live, and Certainly in No Fit Condition to Die': Vandalism, Public Misbehavior, and the Rural Cemetery Movement." *Journal of the Early Republic* 38, no. 2 (Summer 2018): 293–324.

———. "The (Im)Movable Monument: Identity, Space, and the Louisville Confederate Monument." *Public Historian* 41, no. 4 (November 2019): 56–82.

Jabbour, Alan, and Karen Singer Jabbour. *Decoration Day in the Mountains: Traditions of Cemetery Decoration in the Southern Appalachians*. Chapel Hill: University of North Carolina Press, 2010.

Janney, Caroline. *Burying the Dead but Not the Past: Ladies' Memorial Associations and the Lost Cause*. Chapel Hill: University of North Carolina Press, 2008.

Johnson, Lewis Franklin. *History of the Frankfort Cemetery*. Frankfort, Ky.: Roberts Printing Co., 1921.

Kammen, Michael. *Digging up the Dead: A History of Notable American Reburials*. Chicago: University of Chicago Press, 2010.

Lancaster, Kent R. "Green Mount: The Introduction of the Rural Cemetery into Baltimore." *Maryland Historical Magazine* 74, no. 1 (1979): 62–79.

Lee, Jacob F. "Unionism, Emancipation, and the Origins of Kentucky's Confederate Identity." *Register of the Kentucky Historical Society* 111, no. 2 (Spring 2013): 199–233.

Linden, Blanche M. G. *Silent City on a Hill: Picturesque Landscapes of Memory and Boston's Mount Auburn Cemetery*. Amherst: University of Massachusetts Press, 2007.

Marshall, Anne E. *Creating a Confederate Kentucky: The Lost Cause and Civil War Memory in a Border State*. Chapel Hill: University of North Carolina Press, 2010.

McDannell, Colleen. *Material Christianity: Religion and Popular Culture in America*. New Haven, Conn.: Yale University Press, 1995.

Milward, Burton. *A History of the Lexington Cemetery*. Lexington, Ky.: Lexington Cemetery Company, 1989.

Rose, Julia. "Louisville's Hidden Figures: Cave Hill Cemetery Offers Civil Rights Leaders Tour." WHAS11 News, July 7, 2017. https://www.whas11.com/article/news/local/louisvilles-hidden-figures-cave-hill-cemetery-offers-civil-rights-leaders-tour/454970423.

Sears, John F. *Sacred Places: American Tourist Attractions in the Nineteenth Century.* Amherst: University of Massachusetts Press, 1989.

Sloane, David Charles. *The Last Great Necessity: Cemeteries in American History.* Baltimore: Johns Hopkins University Press, 1991.

Smith, Jeffrey. *The Rural Cemetery Movement: Places of Paradox in Nineteenth-Century America.* Lanham, Md.: Lexington Books, 2017.

Streater, Kristen L. "'Not Much a Friend to Traiters No Matter How Beautiful': The Union Military and Confederate Women in Civil War Kentucky." In *Sister States, Enemy States: The Civil War in Kentucky and Tennessee,* edited by Kent T. Dollar, Larry H. Whiteaker, and W. Calvin Dickinson, 245–64. Lexington: University Press of Kentucky, 2009.

Thomas, Samuel W. *Cave Hill Cemetery: A Pictorial Guide and History of Louisville's "City of the Dead."* Louisville: Cave Hill Cemetery Company, 2001.

Walden, Geoffrey R. *Confederate Soldiers and Civilians Buried in the Confederate Sections and National Cemetery, Cave Hill Cemetery, Louisville, Kentucky.* Louisville: G. R. Walden, 1996.

EPILOGUE

TEACHING THE AMERICAN SOUTH BY LEARNING THE DEAD

The learning exercises outlined in this section could be completed at Cave Hill Cemetery in Louisville but are equally applicable to any of the similarly designed rural cemeteries established east of the Mississippi River during the nineteenth century. The following list provides a selection of major rural cemeteries by year of establishment:

Mount Auburn Cemetery (1831), Cambridge, Mass.
Mount Hope Cemetery (1834), Bangor, Maine
Laurel Hill Cemetery (1836), Philadelphia, Pa.
Green-Wood Cemetery (1838), Brooklyn, N.Y.
Green Mount Cemetery (1839), Baltimore, Md.
Allegheny Cemetery (1844), Pittsburgh, Pa.
Albany Rural Cemetery (1844), Albany, N.Y.
Spring Grove Cemetery (1844), Cincinnati, Ohio
Frankfort Cemetery (1844), Frankfort, Ky.
Swan Point Cemetery (1846), Providence, R.I.
Cave Hill Cemetery (1848), Louisville, Ky.
Bellefontaine Cemetery (1849), St. Louis, Mo.
Hollywood Cemetery (1849), Richmond, Va.
Lexington Cemetery (1849), Lexington, Ky.
Magnolia Cemetery (1850), Charleston, S.C.
Oakland Cemetery (1850), Atlanta, Ga.[1]
Elmwood Cemetery (1852), Memphis, Tenn.
Oakdale Cemetery (1852), Wilmington, N.C.
Greenwood Cemetery (1852), New Orleans, La.

Landscape Design Exercise

Upon arrival to the cemetery, first visit the main office, where you should be able to get a cemetery map. Depending on the size of the cemetery, you may choose to walk or drive from section to section.

Rural cemeteries incorporated a variety of common elements, regardless of where they were established. Take note of the following aspects of the landscape and try to answer the accompanying questions:

1. Does the cemetery have a principal gateway at the entrance? If so, can you identify the architectural style (e.g., Gothic Revival, Egyptian Revival, Romanesque)? Are there only entrance posts, an archway, or a full carriage gateway with lodges on either side? Are there any signs that indicate when the entrance was constructed, and if so, is it the original entrance?

2. As you travel from section to section in the cemetery, observe the design of the landscape—the size of the roadways and footpaths, whether the ground is hilly, whether there are water features (ponds, streams, etc.), the kinds of plant life (trees, bushes, flowers). Based on the landscaping details alone, can you identify older versus newer sections of the cemetery that may have been added in the years or decades after it was first established? How does the landscaping design change from one area of the cemetery to the next? What does this tell us about the aesthetic values of the public and how they changed over time?

3. As an extension of #2, take note of the gravestone and monument designs, styles, sizes, and materials. What kind(s) of iconography (imagery) do you see on the grave markers and from what time periods? What trends and changes can you observe in terms of material and style from one section of the cemetery to the next?[2] How are the grave markers laid out within the section—are they in neat rows, or do they appear to be more in a scattered pattern? Are they vertical or flush to the ground? If there are side-hill tombs or freestanding mausoleums, where are they located? Are they all concentrated together within the cemetery or scattered around?

4. Taking all together your observations from #1 through #3, consider the following: What changes can you observe in the landscape over the course of time? What do these changes indicate about public taste in landscape design, attitudes toward death and mourning, and advances in technology?

Necrogeography Exercise

For this exercise, you will consider the necrogeography of the cemetery—that is, the locations of the dead within the cemetery landscape.

1. As you travel through the cemetery, consider how the ranks and status of the living were preserved in death—for example, the size and complexity of grave markers and monuments provide an indication as to the relative wealth of an individual or family, as well as their standing within the community. Some rural cemeteries were designed so that the burials of wealthy and working-class people appear intermixed on the landscape. In others, public lots for individual burials were separate from those areas where larger family lots were available for sale. By observing the distribution of monument sizes and family versus individual burial plots, consider not only how socioeconomic rank was preserved, but the degree to which the classes were physically separated or allowed to intermingle in death.

2. The identification of race in any historical landscape presents a greater challenge to students and scholars alike. If possible, before entering the cemetery, inquire at the front office whether a separate section containing the burials for people of color is located anywhere in the cemetery. Some cemeteries, such as Laurel Hill Cemetery in Philadelphia, barred the burials of African Americans and the poor when it was founded. Others, such as Frankfort Cemetery in Kentucky, established a separate "colored" section. Many cemeteries maintained segregationist burial policies and practices until well into the twentieth century, so in addition to identifying the absence or presence of "colored" burial sections, you may be able to acquire information from the cemetery office concerning integrated Black burials, when they began, and their locations in the cemetery. By examining the necrogeography of race in the rural cemetery, you can then consider the broader nature of racial politics and segregation within the community of the living in that particular city or state.

3. In many rural cemeteries across the country, soldiers' burial sections and national cemeteries were established within their boundaries during or shortly after the Civil War. As you look at the cemetery map, ask yourself: Is there a national cemetery or soldiers' section present? Is there a Confederate soldiers' burial section? If both exist, how are they related geographically—are they near each other, or on opposite ends of the cemetery? How large are the soldiers' burial sections compared

to each other? Is there a central soldiers' monument in either or both sections? How might the presence or absence of a central monument speak to the popular sentiment of the community in the aftermath of the war?

4. Based on your observations of the cemetery landscape (including plants and other landscaping features), monuments, and the necrogeography of the space, how does the cemetery you are in possibly reflect the region where it is located? Does it bear features that make it more distinctively northern or southern? What aspects of the cemetery landscape, in your view, appear universal and transcend regional variation, and what others might be inherently unique to the local area? Is there visual evidence contained within the landscape that, if you didn't know what town or city you were in, could tell you whether this was a northern or a southern burial landscape?

Notes

1. Oakland Cemetery, which originally consisted of six acres when it was established in 1850, was not initially designed as a rural cemetery, but the rural cemetery aesthetic was increasingly applied as the cemetery expanded during the 1850s and 1860s.

2. A good resource to help with understanding gravestone symbolism/iconography is Douglas Keister, *Stories in Stone: A Field Guide to Cemetery Symbolism and Iconography* (Salt Lake City: Gibbs Smith, 2004).

CHAPTER 3

Sacred Ground

How a Segregated Graveyard Preserves the Struggles and Successes of an African American Community in Virginia

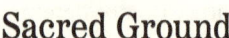

LYNN RAINVILLE

Southern cemeteries are experiencing a resurgence in visits from mourners, preservationists, and tourists, as well as from researchers conducting historical analysis. The perceptive visitor will notice that many public burial sites permanently preserve the residential segregation that African Americans experienced in life. This mortuary segregation was an integral feature of most southern cemeteries until the second half of the twentieth century. In this chapter I focus on the groundbreaking solution that one benevolent group in Charlottesville, Virginia, devised to ensure that they did not have to bury their loved ones in the "Negro" or "colored" section of a predominantly white cemetery.

In the decade after the Civil War, African Americans in Charlottesville had one main option for burial in their urban midst: the newly created Oak Hill Cemetery, which opened in 1863 and was later called Oakwood. The earliest public cemetery in the city, Maplewood, had opened in 1827 but had reached capacity by the war's end and ceased selling new plots.[1] Both of these public options were internally segregated. In 1873, to avoid this inequality in death, members of the Daughters of Zion benevolent society purchased land across the street from Oakwood, surrounded on other sides by a tanyard and by Black-owned property. To the southeast was the fourth urban cemetery, privately owned by the local synagogue and referred to as the Hebrew Cemetery. Two decades later, in 1895, a local newspaper columnist opined that "in every progressive town or city in the country cemeteries are given such attention as [to] make them prominent feature[s] of the place; and we hope our people will not consider money spent in their direction ill advised or useless." The same author described the Daughters of Zion initiative as "a cemetery opposite 'Oak Hill' on the north" owned by "the colored people."[2]

The Role of Mutual Aid Societies in Burying the Dead

The Daughters of Zion were a mutual aid society, but despite the gendered terminology, the group included a small number of men. In other communities the lodge was referred to as the Sons and Daughters of Zion.[3] Although men were a part of the organization, women played a central role in decision-making and led the group's charitable activities. In this chapter I explore the many ways its founders responded to and, to some degree, overcame the racial segregation that prevailed in the communities of the living and the dead. I also demonstrate how individual gravestones and their spatial patterning within this cemetery reveal the challenges that members of Charlottesville's Black community faced and solutions they found to better manage their lives in the Jim Crow–era South.

Historians are beginning to more fully appreciate the cultural and political significance of African American secret societies, including mutual aid organizations and sororal and fraternal orders.[4] These groups, in the words of scholars Theda Skocpol and Jennifer Lynn Oser, "provide mutual aid to members and regularly enact moral rituals stressing shared values and identities."[5] Members of the Daughters of Zion included what W. E. B. DuBois described as the "Talented Tenth," the top 10 percent of the local community, educated and socioeconomically mobile, who worked to help the remaining 90 percent of the African American community attain social and economic parity.[6] Other contemporary lodges included the Good Samaritans, the Eastern Stars, the Daughters of Samaria, the Independent Order of Saint Luke, True Reformers, Knights of Pythias, Freemasons, Elks, Odd Fellows, and the Victoria Tabernacle. Most, if not all, of these organizations in Charlottesville were founded after the Civil War by newly freed men and women.[7] While many of the Black fraternal organizations and most Black churches formed "burial societies" to take care of the sick, assist families with funeral expenses, and bury the dead, the DOZ went one step further and negotiated the purchase of approximately two acres of land.

The site they selected was located across the street from the Oakwood Cemetery, which was segregated into "white" and "negro" zones. By proactively purchasing their own burial ground, Charlottesville's African American community could bury their dead on their own terms, without the shadow of Jim Crow segregation laws. To ensure that the cemetery could not become segregated by race over time, legal language in the deeds dictated that each "section shall be used exclusively for the burial and interment of Colored persons."[8] In postemancipation Charlottesville, the opportunity to purchase a cemetery plot would have been an important step toward claiming full citizenship. For some families, such a plot may have been the first piece of land they owned. Over the next several decades, Charlottesville's increasingly successful African American population buried their dead here.

While the social, emotional, and economic motivations of the DOZ are clear, the timing is less so. One can imagine the strong motivation to establish new burial grounds just after the end of the Civil War, but why wait almost a decade? Perhaps it took a while to amass the funding or to negotiate the land deal. Another important local phenomenon was a series of religious revivals in the 1870s; one local preacher, the Reverend M. T. Lewis, was so talented that he shared his sermons, illustrated by a "magic lantern" to project scenes from Biblical scriptures, with audiences throughout Virginia.[9] In 1873, Lewis became the pastor of the Delevan Baptist Church in Charlottesville. Over the next decade he led his congregation to raise funds for a new building, allowing them to move out of a repurposed hotel into a brand-new structure, which was christened the First Colored Baptist Church.[10] Perhaps the "daughters," many of whom belonged to this congregation, were inspired by these religious revivals and turned their attention to their families' eternal afterlife. Whatever the motivations or catalysts, in January 1873 the society paid $480.61 towards a $600 bill of sale for almost two acres.

The 1873 deed explains that the site would be "for the use of the Charitable association of colored women of Charlottesville, known and styled as 'The daughters on Zion' And used exclusively as a burying ground."[11] This task was complicated by nineteenth-century statutes making it difficult for women to fund and own property in their names. Accordingly, three men served as the titular trustees for the female-led and operated organization. Each man was married to one of the women in the DOZ; in 1877, when the men signed a series of leases for burial plots, fifty-five-year-old Jesse Cole[s] was married to fifty-four-year-old Jane, sixty-one-year-old Robert Goens (also spelled Goins or Goings) was married to sixty-six-year-old Martha Patsy, and fifty-year-old Jesse Cary was married to thirty-six-year-old Nancy.[12] Three decades later, men, most likely spouses of DOZ members, were still serving as the legal representatives and trustees of this predominantly female organization.[13] Despite the occasional legal role for men, this organization provided Black women in Charlottesville with a sense of identity, civic commitment, professional roles, and economic negotiations.

Recovering the Stories of the Dead

The youngest of these three female founders of the cemetery was Nancy Baker Gatewood Cary, who was born into slavery in Charlottesville in 1840. Her parents were originally from Fredericksburg, Virginia; in the years after the war, her father, Armstead Gatewood, was a gardener, while her mother did not list an occupation in either the 1870 or 1880 federal census.[14] Both of her parents and several of her siblings were illiterate.[15] Nancy and her second husband, Jesse (1827–97), could read but not write.[16] Just after the war ended, Nancy—the mother of sixteen—was "keeping house" while her husband worked as a carpenter. She also became active in the DOZ and served as president in 1907.[17] She died in 1927 and was buried next to her husband in the cemetery she helped to establish.[18] She was survived by only five of her children. The occupation on her death certificate, "housewife," does not properly highlight her contributions to this important benevolent society.[19] As a testament to the impact that she had on her community through her charitable work, at her funeral ministers officiated from three different churches—Ebenezer Baptist, First Baptist, and Mount Zion Baptist.[20]

Members of all three of these congregations are buried at the Daughters of Zion Cemetery. First Baptist (formerly the Delevan Church, located in a former temperance inn known as the Delevan Hotel) was founded in 1864 after its members were dismissed from a nearby white Baptist church.[21] In 1873, Rev. Lewis arrived and began a decade-long campaign to construct a new building for the congregation. In 1877, the cornerstone of this structure was laid by the Jefferson Lodge of the African American Freemasons, illustrating the important bonds among churches, Masonic societies, and the postwar Black community. Several of the men buried in the DOZ Cemetery were also leaders in the Piedmont Industrial and Land Improvement Company. This talented group of businessmen raised funds to purchase numerous city lots and other buildings to increase home ownership and opportunities among African Americans in Charlottesville.[22] Three years after the Delevan Church was founded, the Mount Zion Baptist Church was established; its pastors and male members also had strong ties to the Jefferson Masonic Lodge and local Black leaders.[23] The Ebenezer Baptist Church was founded later, in 1892, by the Rev. Alexander Truatt.[24] Over the course of just two generations, Charlottesville's African American community had founded several congregations, raised the money to build impressive, brick churches, and focused their attention on the education (both primary school and professional development) of their members.

Another early leader of the DOZ was Maria Harris Mayo (1846–95), who served for a time as its vice president.[25] Like Nancy Cary, Maria was born into slavery. But in contrast to Nancy, who was a lifelong resident of Charlottesville, Maria left Virginia sometime in the late 1880s and moved to Connecticut with her husband, Thadeus Mayo, and their five children.[26] They were by no means the only Charlottesville residents to move north in the years following the Civil War. For example, the Reverend Lindsey Baxter Goodall migrated to Ansonia, Connecticut, in the early twentieth century, where he served as pastor of the Macedonia Baptist Church, although he ultimately returned to Virginia and died in a city just to the west of Charlottesville.[27] Their reasons for leaving Virginia are not documented, but they may well have been part of the larger exodus of more than six million African Americans from the South to the North as a result of discrimination in housing, employment, schooling, and transportation practices.

The DOZ was a local variant of national organizations such as the Odd Fellows, Knights of Pythias, and the Good Samaritans. Inscriptions on gravestones within the DOZ Cemetery note the membership of one decedent in the all-male "Williams Lodge No. 11 of the Improved Benevolent and the Protective Order of Elks of the World" and another in the all-female "Queen Esther Temple No. 7." Both were Richmond chapters of national benevolent organizations. Although these seem to be the only tombstones that suggest affiliations with benevolent societies, archival sources indicate that many of the decedents belonged to one or more groups. For example, Betsy Toler (died March 18, 1893) and Martha Slaughter (died in 1895) belonged to both the Daughters of Zion and the Good Samaritans.[28] Martha Patsy Goins—who helped establish the cemetery—and her husband, Robert Goins, were among the founders of Delevan Baptist Church in Charlottesville. In communities throughout the South, Black residents founded institutions, such as Masonic lodges, to rebuild their communities after the forced familial and professional separations imposed by slavery. In Charlottesville, the charitable associations partnered with segregated schools, churches, Black-owned businesses, and political parties to train future leaders and professionals.

The purchase of a cemetery lot was not the DOZ's only foray into land ownership. In the 1880s, the benevolent society purchased one or more floors of a three-story, downtown Charlottesville building that took the name Zion Hall. It was located in the growing African American neighborhood of Vinegar Hill, about half a mile from the cemetery. It shared the space with several other fraternal societies, including the True Reformers and the Victoria Tabernacle Lodges. Together, these organizations provided an important cultural and religious center of the African American community. During the first half of the twentieth century, Zion Hall also served as a place of worship (for the burgeoning Ebenezer Baptist Church), the "City Colored Day Nursery" (which still operates today, a few blocks away, as the Barrett Early Learning Center), and the Charlottesville office of the National Dental Association. All of these professional and social institutions were negatively affected when the building and the surrounding neighborhood were razed in the 1960s as part of an "urban renewal" project that decimated dozens of Black businesses and residences in Vinegar Hill.[29]

Six decades after its founding, membership in the Daughters of Zion plummeted, and the rate of burials in the cemetery reflected this decline. It isn't clear what caused the decrease, but it may represent the different priorities of younger people, migrations to the North, and the simple reality that older generations were dying off. In an overview of African American fraternal associations, Skocpol and Oser observe that while sometimes "creative organizers managed to scale one of [these organizations] up into something grander," for the most part locally based groups "flitt[ed] through the historical record at a dizzying pace."[30] In the 1931 Charlottesville city directory the DOZ is not listed under "Societies—Benevolent and Fraternal." Younger prospective members may have joined other, more active groups, such as the Court of Calanthe, the Good Samaritans (a 1929 grave marker in the DOZ Cemetery notes the deceased's membership in this group), the Household of Ruth, or the Improved Order Shepherds and Daughters of Bethlehem.[31] The Charlottesville city directory of 1931 did not list the DOZ Cemetery as a separate entity; instead it included only Oakwood Cemetery and the nearby, independent Hebrew Cemetery.[32] A document from a 1933 court case revealed that "all the members of the said organization known as the Daughters of Zion are now dead, and ... [the] organization has disbanded and become extinct."[33] The same year the organization lost the title to its meeting hall, which it had owned for almost half a century.[34] Burials continued in the cemetery after this point, but it is unclear who supervised them. Five years after the cemetery was excluded from the Charlottesville city directory, it reappeared in the 1936 issue but under an incorrect name: "Oakwood Cemetery (for Colored)."[35] The cemetery deteriorated for decades until the city of Charlottesville stepped in and claimed ownership of the site in 1971, noting that it was "heavily overgrown and appear[ed] not to have been maintained for twenty to thirty years."[36] After a deed search failed to turn up any living owners of the property, the city acquired control and is now responsible for the maintenance of the property under the jurisdiction of the Parks and Recreation Department. The cemetery received only intermittent visits from mourners until 2015, when a local group of remarkable and successful women revitalized the mission and created a nonprofit called The Preservers of the Daughters of Zion Cemetery.[37]

Mapping History, Grave by Grave

The fourteen decades of burials within this African American cemetery reveal broad social, economic, racial, and political themes in Black culture and history. The first thing that strikes a modern-day visitor is the bipartite landscape. Unlike its white counterpart across the street (Oakwood Cemetery), the DOZ Cemetery site ranges from a rolling surface to an almost unmanageably steep slope. There is no evidence that a wall or fence ever enclosed the site, but an entrance road, referred to as an "alley" in an 1877 deed, once divided it into two halves.[38] This point of egress would have allowed horse-drawn hearses to pull in.[39] Like many urban American cemeteries founded in the late nineteenth century, the mortuary site was divided into rectilinear plots that were sold to finance the perpetual care of the markers and the attendant landscaping. Burial plots were sold in at least two sizes: twenty by twenty feet and nine by eighteen feet.[40] Some families easily filled the space with close relatives, including those from multiple generations and lateral relationships, such as grandparents and cousins. In other cases, it appears that plots were subdivided to accommodate singular burials of widows, small children, or impoverished members of the community. Most of these burials lack the alignment seen within larger plots, and they were placed in the steeper and less desirable portions of the cemetery. Moreover, after two recent geophysical investigations revealed hundreds of additional unmarked burials in these steep and occasionally waterlogged areas of the cemetery, it is clear that either many of the individuals buried here lacked markers or that the markers were made from wood or other impermanent materials.[41]

The ground-penetrating radar (GPR) research suggests that there may be over one thousand burials at this site.[42] Today, only about 140 grave markers are extant. The majority are carved from two popular raw materials, marble and granite. All but a handful contain the decedent's name and death date. Beyond those commonalities, the markers display a wide variety of stone sizes, motifs, epitaphs, and inscriptions. Only a quarter contain a personalized message, such as a quote from the Bible, a piece of biographic information, or a sorrowful aphorism. The three most popular inscriptions—"Asleep in Jesus," "Gone but Not Forgotten," and "At Rest"—are commonly found in late nineteenth- and early twentieth-century gravestones of both Black and white individuals. Other inscriptions occur singularly but display broader themes in commemorating the dead, such as trust in God ("God will take care of me," "In God we trust," and "We loved thee well but Jesus loved thee best") or fatalistic observations ("She hath done what she could" and "Death is certain, the hour unseen"). Some families selected excerpts from scripture or poems: "With songs let me follow his flight and mount with his spirit above. Escaped to the mansions with light and lodged in the Eden of Love," and "Yet again we hope to meet thee / When the day of life is fled / When in heaven with joy to greet thee / Where no farewell tear is shed."[43]

Very few of these inscriptions are biographical or truly personal in nature. Aside from the gendered pronouns, they could be interchangeable among any number of individuals. Who would not want to "trust in God," "escape to the mansions with light," and be "in heaven with joy"? The half-dozen personalized stones are generally "in memory of" an individual or memorialize a "beloved" husband, wife, or mother. Two recognize the kindness of the deceased: one reads, in part, "As a Father devoted; As a son affectionate; As a friend kind and fair," while the other refers to a "tender mother and faithful friend."[44] These inscriptions may appear uniquely biographical, but they are found on many gravestones in cemeteries across the country. Moreover, the local Black undertakers played an important role in setting community standards and expectations for a "good death" and appropriate burial. For example, the funeral director and his assistant at the J. F. Bell Funeral Home (founded in 1917) advised mourners on burial details. This Black-owned business continues today as the oldest family-run funeral home in central Virginia.[45] Other historic, Black funeral homes included the Johnson Brothers, Barcus and Kelser Undertakers, A. C. Mabrey, Ferguson, Abbot, Irving-Way Hill Company Inc. (now Hill and Wood), and Jas. A. Perley and Sons. The founders of these businesses—including John F. Bell and Robert Kelser, were active community leaders. The burgeoning funeral home industry began to replace at-home wakes and contributed to mortuary trends, such as standardized gravestone symbols and inscriptions. Meanwhile, the shape and material of the predominantly marble and granite markers were also influenced by industrialization and standardization.[46] At the DOZ Cemetery, many of the stones were carved by W. D. Duke, a local, white "dealer in Marble and Granite Monuments and Tombstones."[47] Other stones may have been purchased at the local W. A. Hartman Memorial Company or from mail-order catalogs such as Sears, Roebuck, and Company or Montgomery Ward.

To understand the unique contributions and struggles of the decedents in the DOZ Cemetery, we must turn to other resources, including census records, newspaper articles, photographs, oral histories, and legal documents. When such additional research is paired with individual headstones, these burial sites become outdoor museums that highlight African American culture and history. What do the life stories of the African Americans buried in the DOZ Cemetery tell us about broader socioeconomic and racial trends in American history?

The earliest documented burial was of Annie Buckner, a girl who died at the age of five or six just a few months after the members of the DOZ took possession of the land in 1873. Though we do not know the cause of her death, Annie's tragically short life may well reflects the health hazards associated with nineteenth-century childhood. Annie's gravestone also lists her sister, who died eight years later, in 1881, when she was only two. Although their deaths occurred years apart, the dual inscriptions are evenly spaced across the vertical dimension of the stone, suggesting that an earlier, perhaps impermanent memorial marked Annie's grave and was later replaced by a stone commemorating both children. Two adjacent graves contain memorials to their brother, John T. Buckner, who died in 1888 at the age of three, and their sister Susie, who lived the longest, dying at the age of twenty-eight in 1910.[48] Her obituary hints at the racism that Black families faced even when their white neighbors attempted to emphasize and mourn their losses. Published in the white-run and authored paper, the obituary describes Susie's father, Anthony Buckner, as "one of the city's most worthy colored residents."[49] This back-handed compliment highlights the perceived distinctions between whites and Blacks. In Anthony's own obituary, penned by a white author in 1923, this racial categorization continues with the assessment that Buckner was "a typical representative of the old school of colored servants." The writer refers to Buckner's childhood during "the era of slavery" when he was enslaved by a white family and then forced to "accompany his young master as a personal servant, according to the custom prevailing in southern families at that day and served throughout the four years of strife."[50] The phrase "four years of strife" is, of course, a reference to the Civil War; recent scholarship provides a much clearer window into what types of tasks these body servants undertook during their time with white soldiers.[51] After Anthony was freed he worked at the University of Virginia for four or five years before striking out on his own and founding a grocery store on Charlottesville's Main Street. His social and economic mobility set the stage for his son's national successes. George W. Buckner (1886–1928) also began as a Charlottesville merchant, but he went on to teach at Booker T. Washington's Tuskegee Institute and to serve on the National League on Urban Conditions in New York.[52] He eventually worked as a successful banker in St. Louis until his untimely death at the age of forty in 1928.[53]

Anthony's wife, Louisa E. Buckner, died in 1909 at the age of fifty-eight, and two years later, he was married again, this time to fifty-two-year-old Mary Churchman. When Anthony himself died, at the age of seventy-eight, Mary and George had a marker placed on his grave in the Daughters of Zion Cemetery with the inscription "Erected by his wife and son." Yet when Mary died twelve years later, in 1934, she was buried not alongside her husband but in the segregated cemetery just south of the DOZ burial ground.[54] This family patterning is an important reminder that although spatial proximity within a cemetery can provide an invaluable source of genealogical information, it may not tell the entire story.

The gravestones in the Buckner family plot reveal kinship connections and some of their personal and professional successes. But none of these accomplishments are highlighted directly in their inscriptions. Among the more than 140 surviving stones, only four provide specific information about the decedent's occupation. All four of these individuals were men engaged in occupations that conferred a high degree of respect and required many years of education: one was a school principal, one was a doctor, and two were ministers.

The Reverend Jesse Herndon was a member of the local Jefferson Masonic Lodge, and upon his death in 1889 at the age of thirty-nine, he was buried under a marble marker that features a hand holding an open Bible and an inscription referring to his leadership of the Mount Zion Baptist Church. The second clergyman, M. T. Lewis, also died young, at the age of forty, in 1883. His is the most elaborate memorial in the cemetery: a solid gray marker topped by a "cushion" carved in stone. The face of the memorial, embellished with architectural flourishes, bears personal information on one side and a Masonic symbol on the other. Surrounding part of the marker is an iron fence, with posts topped by vases, evoking a container for an "eternal flame."

The presence of members and clergy of different churches is striking, as these individuals (or their families) deliberately chose this particular cemetery rather than a churchyard for their burial site. Their decision likely reflects not only the esteem in which the Daughters of Zion were held, but also the prestige associated with the Masonic lodges and charitable associations.

Of course, Black churches themselves were also critical social and religious institutions. Between 1868 and 1900 at least twenty-four Black churches were founded in Charlottesville, but their attrition rate was high. By 1910 only fifteen Black churches were listed in the city business directory. Five churches were located within half a mile of the DOZ Cemetery: Ebenezer Baptist, Wesley Chapel, Zion Union, Mount Zion, and First Baptist on West Main. Despite their names, neither Zion Union nor Mount Zion had a direct connection to the Daughters of Zion society. In addition to trying to meet their members' spiritual, social, and financial needs, several of the churches offered membership in "burial societies." These associations provided a form of insurance: for a small monthly fee, members were assured that their burial needs would be provided for when they died. This assistance supplemented the help from mutual aid societies such as the DOZ.

The third grave that bears a biographical inscription is that of Benjamin Tonsler. His marker, a plain rectangle with only a few carved flowers, includes the words "Erected by Alumni of Jefferson Graded School & Friends." Jefferson was an all-Black school in Charlottesville, and Tonsler was its first principal, serving in the role for thirty years. A tribute published in the local newspaper after his death praised "his earnestness and devotion to the upbuilding of his race ... [that] ... earned [him] a high place in the estimation of the school authorities of the State." The article continues, "It may be justly said without exaggeration that he measured up to the high standard which was set by Booker Washington and men of his stamp."[55] Tonsler's home still stands, about a mile from the cemetery. When he died in 1917 his family and neighbors purchased elaborate floral arrangements that included banners with the names of the donors. The flowers were shaped into anchors (a reference to his faith), stars, the letter "V" (signifying victory over death), and wreaths. A photograph of Tonsler sat near the coffin, displayed prominently in an ornate frame.[56] This elaborate mortuary display emphasized the social status and economic standing of the deceased as well as of the mourners. Some sociologists have traced the practice of elaborate funerals back to African traditions that held that the "good dead" continued living in the afterlife, and generous funerals and grave goods "helped settle them properly in the worlds beyond."[57]

The last of the four DOZ Cemetery graves that bears a biographical inscription is that of Dr. Robert Leo Whittaker. On his stone the acronym "M.D." is added after his name, followed by an eroded quote, most likely from the Bible, that is hard to decipher. Dr. Whittaker graduated from Hampton University in 1897 and Leonard Medical School at Shaw University in 1904. He moved to Newport News, Virginia, in 1905 and worked in a private practice until his unexpected death in 1912. The hospital he had planned to build for African Americans was completed by his colleagues in 1915 and named Whittaker Memorial Hospital in his honor.[58]

Many individuals buried at the DOZ Cemetery accomplished much in the face of social and economic challenges—as did their descendants. One example is Margaret Terry, the daughter of cemetery founder Nancy Gatewood Cary and her first husband, George Hailstock. Margaret was born enslaved in 1857 in a house on Charlottesville's High Street. Her schooling began alongside the white children she served. In a 1937 interview, Margaret related that her owner, Kitty Benson, complained to her own children, "I can't see why Margaret always knows her lesson and you all do not," before proceeding to whip them.[59] Later, Margaret continued her schooling in the North when she accompanied Philena Carkin, a white teacher who had worked in Charlottesville during Reconstruction, to Concord, Massachusetts. In 1884, Margaret married Egbert Terry (1860–1938), whom she had met a decade earlier while teaching in the Virginia public school system, including at Charlottesville's segregated Jefferson Elementary School. The couple taught for a combined 122 years. A 1927 newspaper article highlighting their accomplishments mentions some of the hurdles that Egbert had to overcome: "Born free as Professor Terry was during slavery days it was against the law for him to be taught to read or write, but his desire for knowledge, then as now, was so great that even the law of a sovereign state did not prevent this eager child from studying."[60]

Egbert Terry's obituary revealed that he was a Mason and claimed that he was the "oldest Negro Mason" in Virginia. Just after he and his wife retired in the spring of 1937, a newly built segregated school in Ivy, Virginia (a few miles from Charlottesville), was named in their honor.[61] Interestingly, both Terrys are buried across the road in the segregated section of Oakwood, and not at DOZ Cemetery. Given their death dates, in 1938 and 1950, this may reflect the decline in physical condition of the DOZ Cemetery. More broadly there is a generational gap between decedents born before 1920 and their children: of the cemetery's legible headstones, only four list birth dates after 1920.

In other words, subsequent generations chose to be buried elsewhere. This demographic shift signals changing domiciles, as the younger generations migrated north or to larger southern cities to find employment or education. Charlottesville did not provide African Americans with education beyond grade school until 1927, when Jefferson High School opened.[62] The absence of more recent burials may also signal the expansion of burial options for African Americans after the end of segregation in the 1960s. By that time, the adjacent Oakwood Cemetery was no longer segregated, and in the 1980s new "memorial parks" were opened within the city limits. Younger generations may have found those options more appealing, or they may have lost the social memory and association with the long-defunct Daughters of Zion organization.[63]

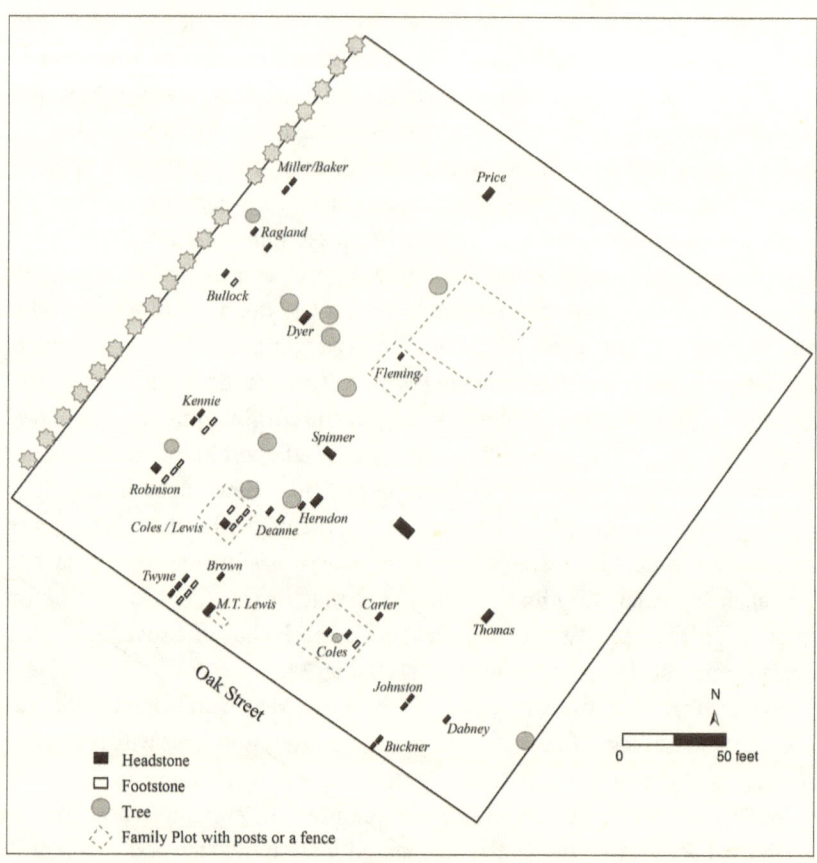

FIGURE 3.1. Map of the extant gravestones that date to the first generation of burials in Daughters of Zion Cemetery, between 1873 and 1900 (map by the author)

Many cemetery studies focus on the distribution of burials as a static pattern to be interpreted and studied. Instead, scholars should view burial grounds as neighborhoods of the dead. And, just like living communities, neighbors change over time. In the mortuary version, of course, old neighbors rarely move away, but new neighbors are added regularly. At the DOZ Cemetery, the rate of interments between 1885 and 1934 was roughly two per year.[64] The constant addition of new "residents," as well as the purchase of additional family plots, reveals a wide range of community connections. The challenge for genealogists, anthropologists, and sociologists is how to recreate these past community connections or social networks. The obvious connections to investigate include kinship ties (either consanguineal or through marriage), occupational or professional peers, residential neighbors (in life), and church members.

One of the subtle connections that decedents have is generational. This does not refer to the decade in which they died, but rather to the cohort with whom they lived. For example, there are only four individuals with preserved stones in the DOZ Cemetery who were born before 1820: Eliza Carter (1819–84), Robert Buckner (1803–1901), and Delila (1795–1895) and Phillip Johnson/Johnston (1813–78).

All four are buried in the southeast quadrant of the cemetery, indicating the original core of the burial ground before it expanded to the north, down the hillside, and west toward a line of houses. Delila lived to the age of one hundred years, five months, and thirteen days. Born in 1795, she lived through the formation of a new republic, a war that threatened to destroy that entity, emancipation, Reconstruction, and the restrictive covenants of segregation. On the local level, she and her family epitomize the struggles and successes of nineteenth-century Black families. She was enslaved by the Rives family of Charlottesville and served them for three-quarters of her long life. At least three of her children were born enslaved: Caroline Watson (born 1839), Lucy Johnson (born 1840), and Philip Johnson (born 1849). Upon her death, her obituary stated, "Lilah Johnson (colored) died this morning at her home near the University of Virginia. She was probably the oldest person in Albemarle county."[65] Throughout this long life, neither the horror of forced bondage nor the economic pressures of Reconstruction separated her from her husband or children.

As her health declined, her daughter Caroline was able to care for her. Unfortunately, two surviving documentary sources cast doubts on Delila's veracity. In an article published a few months before her death, a white columnist writes that Delila "talks fluently of the days of Jefferson, Madison, and Monroe" but then emphasizes that she only *"claims* to have known" them (emphasis added). The subtitle of that piece was "Old Colored Woman Who Claims to Be 100 Years Old." Further, the author questions the truthfulness of her ethnographic account of growing up in early nineteenth-century Charlottesville as "worth listening to whether accurate or not."[66] The same skepticism was repeated in her obituary, where a white author reported that "Lilah" "claimed to be one hundred years old."[67]

The gravestones highlighted in this chapter are just a fraction of the life stories that are revealed by a tour of the DOZ cemetery and by reading accompanying documentation, such as the Facebook page maintained by the Preservers of the Daughters of Zion. Each grave marker illustrates part of an individual's biography, as well as other narratives, such as socioeconomic status, religious beliefs, and community history. For some of us, our gravestones will be the last artifact, physical or ephemeral, that will commemo-

FIGURE 3.2. Overview of the Daughters of Zion Cemetery: the Rev. M. T. Tonsler's grave is in the foreground, behind the ornamental iron fence (photograph by the author).

rate our lives. This results in fields of mortuary memorials that serve as significant sites of cultural memory.

Unfortunately, mortuary rituals can also enforce and codify racist practices. The purchase of land for the Daughters of Zion Cemetery would not have been necessary if the so-called public cemetery located just across the street to the south did not divide its burials into "white" and "colored" sections during the nineteenth century. Gravestone inscriptions document segregated educational institutions, such as Benjamin Tonsler's epitaph that recognizes him as the principal of the "Jefferson Graded School." A handful of stones memorialize the institution of slavery, such as Jane Coles's 1887 marker, which reads "In Memory of our faithful Mammie." Although the purchaser of this gravestone is not identified by name, one presumes it was a member of the white family that enslaved Jane between her birth in 1845 and emancipation in 1865. In obituaries, white newspaper writers offered moralistic judgments about their Black neighbors. The white community divided Blacks into so-called worthy and unworthy individuals—a paternalistic carryover from the antebellum period when favored slaves were given condescending and misleading kinship titles such as "aunt" and "uncle." Far from conveying respect, these titles overlooked surnames (some, but not all, enslaved people had last names) and presumed a naturalized relationship between whites and Blacks.

In the postbellum period, in the face of widespread prejudice and inequality, some members of the white community made a point of praising African Americans who presumably pleased them in some way or whom they considered "well behaved." Not surprisingly, the former category included individuals who served the white community in some capacity, often employees at the nearby University of Virginia or professionals who offered goods or services, such as grocers, washerwomen, or merchants. Several of the obituaries for individuals interred in the DOZ Cemetery referred to this status within the white community. For example, when Jesse H. Cary died in 1897, a white author wrote that he was "one of Charlottesville's most worthy colored citizens."[68] Upon her death in 1915, Margaret Lewis was described as an "old-time colored nurse," who cared for a Mr. John Shepherd. "'Aunt Margaret' as she was familiarly called, was held in high esteem by all who knew her," the *Daily Progress* continued. "She was kind, gentle and faithful in her duties. She was born a slave more than 70 years ago, having belonged to the Meade family. She was the mother of 13 children all of whom, together with her husband, have been dead a number of years."[69] Despite the reference to her large family, her headstone stands with just two footstones, for P. C. Lewis and C. E. Lewis. It is not clear where the rest of her family is buried. An even more telling obituary described a local barber, J. P. Fleming, as "industrious and obliging."[70] In segregated Charlottesville, the white community devalued the professional and leadership skills of their African American neighbors.

A final subtle but relevant connection between the DOZ Cemetery and the surrounding white community is its complicated relationship with the University of Virginia. In 2013, university president Theresa Sullivan formed a commission to investigate its involvement in slavery. Community members uncovered multiple connections between individuals buried at the cemetery and the university. For example, the Coles family served the faculty and students for decades. George E. "Buck" Cole worked as a custodian in the high-status East Lawn student rooms. His mother, Addie Golden Coles (1869-1944), was born in a two-story outbuilding called the Crackerbox, located behind one of the campus's stately pavilions that line its central lawn. His grandmother, Jeanetta Dabney (1829-91), may have been enslaved by professor of modern languages Maximilian Schele de Vere. Mrs. Coles and Mrs. Dabney, as well as several other Coles family members, are buried at DOZ Cemetery.[71]

Preserving Deathscapes and
Their Histories for Future Generations

One of the most remarkable aspects of the DOZ Cemetery is its ongoing significance and the efforts of a committed group of descendants and community members to preserve its stories. Even though the last burial occurred in 1995, this sacred site is more relevant today than ever. I first visited the site in 2002, a year after a dedicated and talented University of Virginia undergraduate, Ted Delaney, finished a thesis on the cemetery. The site was overgrown, several gravestones had toppled (or been pushed over), an enormous poison ivy vine hung over one of the largest family plots, and the concrete in the singular barrel vault had cracked so extensively that the underlying brick framework was visible. Because of its proximity to the much larger and better-kept Oakwood Cemetery, most Charlottesville residents referred to the site as an extension of that segregated burial ground. Few knew its more unusual history. I read through Delaney's thesis carefully. As an archaeologist I was interested in spatial patterns and mortuary symbolism, so I mapped the site with a laser transit and looked for correlations between the design of the stones and the people they memorialize. The map enabled me to decipher some of the hard-to-read names (by recognizing the kinship associations within plots and other unmarked but relevant clusters). In 2003, I added this material to a now-defunct website. For the first few years after I uploaded content online, I received a handful of emails each month with feedback or additional information from descendants or knowledgeable community members.

My research, along with that of several other local historians, aided in the successful effort to begin preserving and better appreciating this site. The current, ongoing chapter is led by descendants and community members. In 2015, a modern-day version of the Daughters of Zion organized themselves into a group called The Preservers of the Daughters of Zion Cemetery, or The Preservers for short. Preserver Edwina St. Rose, who is descended from University of Virginia barber W. L. Brown and the Bullock family (including local land speculator and entrepreneur Burkley Bullock), along with Bernadette Whitsett-Hammond, who is descended from the Reverend G. W. Lewis and Mary Nelson Lewis, founding members of Charlottesville's Ebenezer Baptist Church, sought the assistance of landscape architect Liz Sargent and architectural conservator Shelley Sass to create a plan to guide the restoration and preservation of the cemetery. Following a presentation before the city council, the city of Charlottesville subsequently allocated $80,000 to implement the preservation plan.[72] Under the direction of archaeologist Steve Thompson, the Preservers embarked on their mission, which included addressing erosion and the decaying tree canopy, repairing and replacing broken markers, erecting a fence on the western border, and identifying the number and names of the individuals buried at the cemetery. Preserver Robert King, whose forebear Ida Burton is buried at DOZ Cemetery, took the lead in cleaning the stones and in coordinating volunteers.

In just a few years, the Preservers have organized an annual community event known as Decoration Day, held on the Sunday before Memorial Day; collaborated with the University of Virginia, the Albemarle Charlottesville Historic Society, and others to present exhibits that tell the stories of the individuals buried at the historic cemetery; earned external grants; connected with and learned from dozens of descendants; and received extensive news coverage.[73] In 2017, the BeCville Project, a community-based group comprising several neighborhood associations, funded the construction of a $3,200 grave marker to commemorate burials of unknown individuals.[74]

In December 2017, Edwina St. Rose presided over the dedication of the "Memorial to the Unknown." The commemorative service included a piece by local African American poet Shirley Parrish, titled "A Tribute to the Ancestors," a musical selection by James Bryant, a prayer of dedication by Rev. Dr. Lehman D. Bates II of Ebenezer Baptist Church, and concluding remarks by the other mainstay in the organization, Bernadette Whitsett-Hammond. After the service at the cemetery, the audience was invited to Tonsler Park Recreation Center for refreshments and an archaeological overview by Thompson, who presented the results of a ground-penetrating radar study of the cemetery.[75] The service was a testament to the multitude of community members who have made the research and its recognition possible.

The Preservers' hard work has received a number of honors. In 2016, a local historic preservation group, Preservation Piedmont, recognized the Preservers with their Martha Gleason Award, given for outstanding preservation efforts. And in 2017, Charlottesville's City Planning Commission honored the Preservers with the Citizen Planner of the Year Award.

In August of 2017, white supremacist and white nationalist groups converged on Charlottesville and held a Unite the Right rally to assert their "white civil rights." They provoked a series of encounters with peaceful protesters and beat one Black counterprotester. Later in the day, one of the white nationalists drove his car down a narrow street, killing one woman, and injuring dozens of others.[76] In the aftermath of these tragic events of August 2017, as the Charlottesville community has tried to more honestly address the prevalent racial and economic disparities in the city, interest in the roots of today's African American community has flourished. Charlottesville has hosted several exhibitions, lectures, theatrical performances, and festivals that reveal these rich, historic antecedents and the barriers that Black families have faced there for centuries. Throughout 2018 the Preservers continued to post dozens of informative, biographical Facebook posts about the burials at DOZ Cemetery. Much of this work was thanks to the efforts and research acumen of St. Rose and local historian and Preserver Jane Smith.[77] Together with descendants of those buried in the cemetery, they documented many of the biographical vignettes discussed in this chapter. To complement the Facebook page, Preserver Dede Smith created an audio tour of the DOZ Cemetery.[78]

Using this work as an example of the value associated with visiting and studying these gravesites, the Preservers asked former Virginia General Assembly delegate David J. Toscano, a Democrat whose district included all of Charlottesville and parts of Albemarle County, to introduce legislation to help fund the preservation and care of the site. Upon its passage, the bill provided $69,730 to support "the preservation and care of historical African American graves and cemeteries" throughout the Commonwealth of Virginia.[79]

In 2019, just days before the two-year anniversary of the August 2017 Charlottesville tragedy, the Preservers of the DOZ collaborated with the Holsinger Studio Collection at the University of Virginia Library to open *Gone but Not Forgotten*, a monthlong exhibit sponsored by the Albemarle Charlottesville Historical Society, the University of Virginia, Preservation Piedmont, and a community-based group called Charlottesville Unity Days. The exhibit included a collection originally presented in April 2017 by UVA professor Lisa Goff's Hands-On Public History course, with portraits and biographical material about many of the individuals buried at the cemetery.[80] This community-based research helps to ensure that the lives and contributions of the individuals buried at the DOZ Cemetery will not be forgotten.

Notes

1. Of Grave Concern: A Web Publication Dedicated to the Preservation and Research of Maplewood Cemetery, Charlottesville, Virginia, https://sites.rootsweb.com/~vaogc/; "Oakwood Cemetery," African American Cemeteries in Albemarle and Amherst Counties, http://www2.vcdh.virginia.edu/cem/db/cemetery/details/OKW/.
2. "Our Cemeteries," *Daily Progress* (Charlottesville, Va.), March 28, 1895.
3. For example, in Abingdon, Virginia, the Grand Lodge Number 1 was called Adopted Sons and Daughters of Zion. "Abingdon: Fraternities and Societies," *Southwest Examiner* (Abingdon), August 7, 1886, 3.
4. Dunbar, "Hidden in Plain Sight," 625.
5. Skocpol and Oser, "Organization despite Adversity," 370.
6. Hughey and Parks, "Editorial: Black Fraternal Organizations," 598.

7. Cross-White, *Charlottesville: The African American Community*, 42, 48.

8. Deed Book 71, 417–18 (March 28, 1877), note 70, Cornelia Gilmore's plot, Albemarle County Circuit Court, Clerk's Office.

9. Untitled news item, *People's Advocate* (Alexandria, Va.), June 17, 1876, 3.

10. McKinney, *Keeping the Faith*, 52.

11. Deed Book 68:2, 443–45 (probated February 26, 1874), Albemarle County Circuit Court, Clerk's Office.

12. The reference to the three men as trustees is found in Deed Book 71, 417–18 (March 28, 1877), Albemarle County Circuit Court, Clerk's Office. The ages are approximate, as census records, death certificates, and gravestones are not always in agreement. The ages here are calculated from their entries in the 1870 census.

13. An 1899 deed lists J. H. Brown and Charles James as trustees of the DOZ Cemetery, Deed Book 10, page 172 (November 16, 1899). Charles James was also listed as a trustee in a 1907 deed. Deed Book 19, 14 (September 23, 1907), Charlottesville Circuit Court, Clerk's Office.

14. U.S. Department of the Interior, Census Bureau, Census of 1870, St Anne's Parish, Albemarle, Virginia.

15. U.S. Department of the Interior, Census Bureau, Census of 1880, Charlottesville, Albemarle, Virginia.

16. Ibid.

17. U.S. Department of the Interior, Census Bureau, Census of 1870, St. Anne's Parish, Albemarle, Virginia. Their sixteen children are documented on the 1900 U.S. census. U.S. Department of the Interior, Census Bureau, Census of 1900, Ward 3, Charlottesville City, Virginia. Documents from a 1907 legal proceeding refer to Nancy as the president of the DOZ. Chancery Records Index, 1907-009, Library of Virginia, https://www.lva.virginia.gov/chancery/full_case_detail.asp?CFN=540-1907-009#img.

18. Virginia, U.S., Death Records, 1912–2014, Ancestry.com.

19. Virginia, U.S., Death Records, 1912–2014, Ancestry.com.

20. "Funeral Services for Nancy B. Cary," *Daily Progress* (Charlottesville, Va.), May 28, 1927, 5, http://search.lib.virginia.edu/catalog/uva-lib:2603135/view#openLayer/uva-lib:2603140/5179/2072.5/3/1/0.

21. "Delevan Baptist Church."

22. "Land Improvement Company," *Richmond Planet*, May 17, 1890, 4.

23. "Legacy of Love"; Sargent, Historic American Landscape Survey Submission, 3.

24. "Ebenezer Baptist Church: History."

25. *Turner's Annual Directory for the City of Charlottesville*. Maria Mayo's death date was obtained from a gravestone in Ansonia, New Haven County, Connecticut. "Maria Mayo," Find a Grave, https://www.findagrave.com/memorial/107373952/maria-mayo.

26. "Mayo" (obituary), *Richmond Planet*, August 31, 1895.

27. "Celebrating Our History without Losing Sight of Our Destiny"; "The Rev. L.B. Goodall" (obituary), *Daily News Leader* (Staunton, Va.), March 16, 1950.

28. "Mrs. Betsy Toler" (obituary), *Richmond Planet*, April 1, 1893; "Charlottesville Letter," *Richmond Planet*, May 11, 1895.

29. Cross-White, *Charlottesville: The African-American Community*, 39, 53, 74.

30. Skocpol and Oser, 375.

31. Charlottesville, Virginia, City Directory for 1931, 499, U.S. City Directories, 1822–1995, *Ancestry.com*.

32. Charlottesville, Virginia, City Directory for 1931, 452, U.S. City Directories, 1822–1995, Ancestry.com.

33. Delaney, "Daughters of Zion Cemetery Project," 7, citing Albemarle County Deed Book 79, 110–11 (May 25, 1933), Charlottesville Circuit Court, Clerk's Office.
34. Delaney, "Daughters of Zion Cemetery Project," 13–14, citing Albemarle County Deed Book 19, 14 (September 23, 1907), Charlottesville Circuit Court, Clerk's Office.
35. Charlottesville, Virginia, City Directory for 1936, 382, U.S. City Directories, 1822–1995, *Ancestry.com*.
36. "City Asked to Operate Cemetery," *Daily Progress*, July 24, 1971, 3.
37. The group focuses most of their communications and shares their research through a Facebook page (https://www.facebook.com/daughtersofzioncemetery/) and a website (https://daughtersofzioncemetery.org).
38. Delaney, "Daughters of Zion Cemetery Project," 5, citing the Albemarle County Courthouse Deed Book 71, 417–18 (March 28, 1877).
39. Rainville, *Hidden History*, 152.
40. Delaney, "Daughters of Zion Cemetery Project," 22, citing Albemarle County Deed Book 71, 417–18 (March 28, 1877), Albemarle County Circuit Court.
41. NAEVA Geophysics Inc., *Geophysical Investigation Report*, 1; Rivanna Archaeological Services, "Daughters of Zion Cemetery" (ground-penetrating radar map).
42. Ibid.
43. Rainville, *Hidden History*, 154.
44. Ibid.
45. "Serving the Charlottesville Community since 1917."
46. Rainville, "Hanover Deathscapes," 560–61.
47. Advertisement for W. D. Duke, Charlottesville City Directory, 1902, 41, *Ancestry.com*.
48. Rainville, *Hidden History*, 157.
49. "Death of Susie J. Buckner," *Daily Progress*, September 3, 1910, 1–2.
50. "Colored Merchant Dies Suddenly," *Daily Progress*, December 27, 1923, 1.
51. Levin, *Searching for Black Confederates*.
52. "A Local Colored Man Make Good," *Daily Progress*, June 5, 1918, 1.
53. Missouri State Board of Health, Bureau of Vital Statistics, death certificate, "George W. Buckner," March 18, 1928, https://www.sos.mo.gov/images/archives/deathcerts/1928/1928_00011705.PDF.
54. She was buried March 21, 1934, at Oakwood Cemetery. Certificate of Death, "Mrs. Mary Churchman Buckner" of Charlottesville, March 17, 1934, Virginia Department of Health, Richmond.
55. "A Colored Educator Dead," *Daily Progress*, March 6, 1917, 1.
56. Rufus W. Holsinger, *Tonsler Flowers* (photograph), March 9, 1917, Holsinger Collection, Special Collections, University of Virginia Library.
57. Kuyk, "African Derivation of Black Fraternal Organizations," 577.
58. "Graduates and Ex-Students," 250; "Whittaker Memorial Hospital"; Departure Point Films, *The Story of Whittaker Memorial Hospital*.
59. Interview with Mrs. Margaret Terry by Susie R. C. Byrd, May 21, 1937, Library of Virginia Collections, cited in Perdue, Barden, and Phillips, *Weevils in the Wheat*, 285–86.
60. "Colored Man and Wife Have Taught 105 Years in State," *Richmond Times-Dispatch*, September 4, 1927, 21.
61. "Old Albemarle Negro Teacher Dies after Lifetime of Service," *Richmond Times-Dispatch*, October 6, 1938, 6.
62. Cross-White, *Charlottesville*, 77.
63. Rainville, *Hidden History*, 156.

64. Delaney, "Daughters of Zion Cemetery Project."
65. "Death of a Centenarian," *Daily Progress*, November 23, 1895, 1.
66. "A Centennarian," [sic], *Daily Progress*, July 11, 1895.
67. "Death of a Centenarian," *Daily Progress*, November 23, 1895, 1.
68. Untitled news item, *Daily Progress*, March 1, 1897, 1.
69. "Old Nurse Dead," *Daily Progress*, February 27, 1915, 1.
70. "Death of 'Penny' Fleming," *Daily Progress*, September 1, 1905, 1.
71. "And Remember the Old Cracker Box?," *University of Virginia Alumni News*, December–January 1963, 10–11.
72. "Grave Concern: Local Group Preserves Historic Black Cemetery," *C-VILLE Weekly*, June 8, 2017, https://www.c-ville.com/grave-concern-local-group-preserves-historic-Black-cemetery/.
73. Emily Hays, "Historical Society Starts a New Chapter with Daughters of Zion Exhibit," *Charlottesville Tomorrow*, May 27, 2018 (updated November 9, 2018), https://www.cvilletomorrow.org/articles/historical-society-daughters-of-zion-exhibit-2018.
74. Raennah Lorne, "BeCville Announces Community Project Winners," *C-VILLE Weekly* June 21, 2017, https://www.c-ville.com/becville-announces-community-art-project-winners.
75. *Dedication of the Memorial to the Unknown* (dedication ceremony program), December 16, 2017. In possession of the author.
76. Matthew, "On Charlottesville," 269, 276, 340.
77. Earlier, in the first decade of the twenty-first century, both Ted Delaney, a University of Virginia undergraduate, and Dr. Scot French, then a history professor and digital scholar at the University of Virginia, conducted foundational research into the Daughters of Zion, the cemetery, and many of the families buried at the site.
78. "Daughters of Zion Cemetery," University of Virginia Arts and Sciences Institute for Public History, last modified February 8, 2023, http://publichistory.as.virginia.edu/daughters-zion/audio-tour.
79. Virginia Rev. Code §10.1-22.11, Disbursement of Funds Appropriated for Caring for Historical African American Cemeteries and Graves (amended March 2018). For more on Virginia HB360 and its progress through the legislature, see Trackbill.com, https://trackbill.com/bill/virginia-house-bill-360-historical-african-american-cemeteries-adds-daughters-of-zion-cemetery-in-charlottesville-to-list/1506885/. In 2019, seven more cemeteries were added to the funded bill. Virginia's Legislative Information System, http://lis.virginia.gov/cgi-bin/legp604.exe?191+sum+SB1128.
80. "Daughters of Zion Cemetery," University of Virginia Arts and Sciences Institute for Public History, last modified February 8, 2023, https://publichistory.as.virginia.edu/about-0.

Bibliography

"Celebrating Our History without Losing Sight of Our Destiny." Macedonia Baptist Church, Ansonia, Connecticut. https://macedoniabcac.org/church-history.

Cross-White, Agnes. *Charlottesville: The African-American Community*. Dover, N.H.: Arcadia, 1988.

Delaney, Ted. "Daughters of Zion Cemetery Project: Final Report." Undergraduate honors thesis, Department of History, University of Virginia, 2001.

"Delevan Baptist Church." Nomination materials for the National Register of Historic

Places, (104-0376), 2008. chrome-extension://efaidnbmnnnibpcajpcglclefindmkaj/https://www.dhr.virginia.gov/wp-content/uploads/2018/04/104-0376_Delevan_Baptist_Church_1982_NR_materials_82001802.pdf.

Departure Point Films. *The Story of Whittaker Memorial Hospital*. Newport News, Va.: Newport News Public Library, 2020. https://www.youtube.com/watch?v=36VmlmlL6DM.

Dunbar, Paul Lawrence. "Hidden in Plain Sight: African American Secret Societies and Black Freemasonry." *Journal of African American Studies* 16, no. 4 (December 2012): 622-37.

"Ebenezer Baptist Church: History." Ebenezer Baptist Church. https://www.ebc113.org/history.

"Graduates and Ex-Students." *Southern Workman* 46, no. 4 (April 1917): 249-52.

Hughey, Matthew W., and Gregory S. Parks. "Editorial: Introduction: Black Fraternal Organizations: Systems, Secrecy, and Solace." *Journal of African American Studies* 16 (2012): 595-603.

Kuyk, Barbara. "The African Derivation of Black Fraternal Organizations in the United States." *Comparative Studies in Society and History* 25, no. 4 (1983): 559-92.

"A Legacy of Love: 150+ Years of Church History." Mount Zion First African Baptist Church. https://www.mtzionfabc.org/our-history.

Levin, Kevin M. *Searching for Black Confederates: The Civil War's Most Persistent Myth*. Chapel Hill: University of North Carolina Press, 2019.

Matthew, Dayna Bowen. "On Charlottesville." *Virginia Law Review* 105, no. 2 (2019): 269-341.

McKinney, Richard I. *Keeping the Faith: A History of the First Baptist Church, 1863-1980, in Light of Its Times, West Main and Seventh Streets, Charlottesville, Virginia*. Charlottesville, Va.: First Baptist Church, 1981.

NAEVA Geophysics Inc. *Geophysical Investigation Report: Daughters of Zion Cemetery, Charlottesville, Virginia*. December 9, 2016. Prepared for the city of Charlottesville, Virginia.

Perdue, Charles L., Jr., Thomas E. Barden, and Robert K. Phillips, eds. *Weevils in the Wheat: Interview with Virginia Ex-Slaves*. Charlottesville: University of Virginia Press, 1992.

Rainville, Lynn. "Hanover Deathscapes: Mortuary Variability in New Hampshire, 1770-1920." *Ethnohistory* 46, no. 3 (Summer 1999): 541-97.

———. *Hidden History: African American Cemeteries in Central Virginia*. Charlottesville: University of Virginia Press, 2014.

Rivanna Archaeological Services. "Daughters of Zion Cemetery" (ground-penetrating radar map). https://rivarch10.maps.arcgis.com/apps/View/index.html?appid=70d8f8165f30409c95ccba4833ac89098&fbclid=IwAR0QAE6Z9hYAfvvRbBbV5v8wV629658FYPewhm57auwcSAesW8PDxq5H18g.

Sargent, Liz. Historic American Landscape Survey Submission, May 29, 2016. In author's possession.

"Serving the Charlottesville Community since 1917." J. F. Bell Funeral Home. https://www.jfbellfuneralhome.com/history.html.

Skocpol, Theda, and Jennifer Lynn Oser. "Organization despite Adversity: The Origin and Development of African American Fraternal Associations." *Social Science History* 28, no. 3 (Fall 2004): 367-437.

Turner's Annual Directory for the City of Charlottesville. Yonkers, N.Y.: E. F. Turner, 1889.

"Whittaker Memorial Hospital." Nomination form for the National Register of Historic Places (DHR-12105072), 2009. chrome-extension://efaidnbmnnnibpcajpcglclefindmkaj/https://www.dhr.virginia.gov/wp-content/uploads/2018/04/121-5072_Whittaker_Memorial_Hospital_2009_FINAL_NR.pdf.

EPILOGUE

TEACHING THE AMERICAN SOUTH BY LEARNING THE DEAD

Unlike some primary sources, gravestones are usually accessible to a wide audience. You don't need to make an appointment in an archive or read hundreds of pages in a hard-to-locate book. Instead, you simply need to locate a public, historic burial ground and go for a stroll. For the past two decades I have been encouraging local residents to visit cemeteries outside of the somber occasion of a funeral. There is much to learn from gravestone inscriptions, epitaphs, carved symbols, naming practices, headstone placement, and the landscape of the dead.

When you are conducting such research, the first step is to produce a map of the stones; the distribution of graves will be critical to understanding the subtle patterning of burials based on race, class, and gender. Maps are also the foundation to creating a walking tour of the site. The next step is to research and create minibiographies of the dead. Third, record the symbols carved into the stones, the flowers, geometric patterns, religious symbolism, and more recent laser-carved portraits. The diversity of symbols will vary by region, class, gender, religious denomination, and ethnicity. Finally, collect a sample of inscriptions from the stones, including quotes from secular and religious texts as well more personalized epitaphs. This information serves as the historic data that can be woven into brochures, websites, and walking tours.[1] Below I share a handful of examples that I have worked on in Virginia, as well as a few specific educational projects that the Preservers of the Daughters of Zion Cemetery have created.

When I started studying historic African American cemeteries in 2001 I was committed to sharing my research with a wide audience, so I designed a website where genealogists and community members could search for specific people, gravestones, or cemeteries.[2] Today there are many commer-

TABLE 3.1. Collecting Biographical Information about People Buried in a Cemetery

Step 1	Collect information about the deceased's name, birth and death date, age at death. Look at nearby stones to see if you can determine other kinship connections, such as parents or siblings.
Step 2	Enter the information in an online genealogical program (most public libraries subscribe to one or more of these services and several offer free accounts). In addition to federal census entries (which will usually allow you to build a family tree for the deceased), look for marriage certificates, veteran service records, city directories (which often list occupations), and public "family trees" that provide more biographical information.
Step 3	Work with modern-day community members to locate descendants to "check your work" and see if it is permissible to share the information with local historical societies, genealogical groups, or libraries. This information is the foundation to building more complete local histories and including the successes and contributions of African Americans.

cial options for uploading this type of information, including findagrave.com and billiongraves.com. I recommend sharing the information collected from a historic cemetery through one of those sites to avoid the technological upkeep associated with an individual website. Social media is another effective way to share biographical and historical information uncovered in a cemetery. Several organizations in Virginia are doing an excellent job engaging descendants, visitors, and researchers through their various profiles. For example, the Preservers of the Daughters of Zion Cemetery regularly share their research on their Facebook page: https://www.facebook.com/daughtersofzioncemetery/.

Websites and social media posts are useful ways to share information about a cemetery, but the most powerful response will come from an in-person visit. A decade ago I realized that the most effective way to encourage this habit was to start with children. I partnered with Professor Patrice Grimes at the University of Virginia's Curry School of Education to bring her aspiring teachers to the Daughters of Zion Cemetery once or twice a year for a guided tour.

Since all communities have cemeteries and they are often not far from public schools, they make for a convenient, albeit unusual, field trip. When the education students visited the site, I demonstrated how they could use the stones as primary sources to teach American history. Many of the history topics required by Virginia's Standards of Learning can be addressed by a careful study of the mortuary iconography, biographical data, and socioeconomic patterning of the gravestones. In a historic African American cemetery, students can also trace the history of slavery, emancipation, Reconstruction, segregation, and the civil rights movement. Gravestone data can also be used to teach elementary students about family ties, the chang-

FIGURE 3.3. Graduate students in education visiting the cemetery to integrate gravestone data

FIGURE 3.4. A selection of gravestones from the Daughters of Zion Cemetery that illustrate patterns in genealogical data, motifs, and inscriptions (photographs by the author)

ing popularity of given names, the meaning of funerary symbols, and the euphemistic adjectives and nouns used to describe death and dying.

Older students can calculate the average death date, determine the percentage of males and females or adults versus children, learn spatial skills by mapping the gravestones, or apply Visual Thinking Strategies (VTS) by closely examining the stones. College students can embark on more detailed

TABLE 3.2. Analyzing a Gravestone

Step 1	Draw a gravestone.
Step 2	Gravestone Venn Diagram. Compare your gravestone to a classmate's: How are they similar? How are they different? 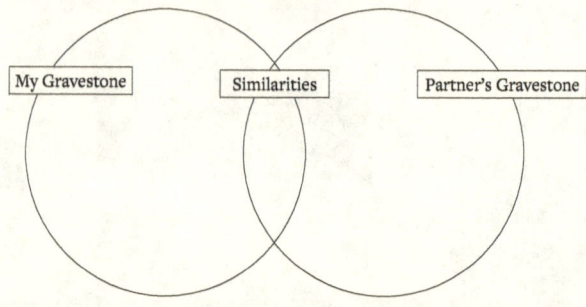
Step 3	Visual Discovery. Draw and identify any symbols on your gravestone. Answer the following questions: What symbols do you see? What words do you see? Identify any geometric shapes.
Step 4	Interpret the Evidence. What do you think the symbols mean? Most shapes carved into gravestones are motifs, reoccurring designs that represent what people thought about death. What emotions or messages do your motifs convey?
Step 5	Historic Inscriptions. Record any words that are legible on the gravestone. Collect a sample of two dozen inscriptions and divide the nouns and adjectives into two columns: optimistic and pessimistic. Is one category more popular than the other? If so, why do you think that is the case?

studies of the socioeconomic backgrounds of the deceased and oral histories with surviving family members and reconstruct a social history of the community. Teachers can compile this research into a tour that guides students through different chapters in local history.

Students of all ages can learn about our shared history from these sites. In Daughters of Zion Cemetery, the Preservers have worked with Dede Smith to create a walking tour that guides visitors to fourteen "stops" as they stroll through the cemetery.[3]

They partnered with the University of Virginia's Institute of Public history to host a website and share this information widely. Research is ongoing into the lives of the individuals buried at the site. Websites, social media accounts, and tours are an ideal way to share this information and locate more leads. More traditional outlets work as well. Over the past two decades I have been interviewed by local radio stations, television shows, and newspapers.[4] I have received hundreds of significant research leads from descendants and local residents from this outreach. The Preservers have also uncovered invaluable photographs, documents, and stories from their

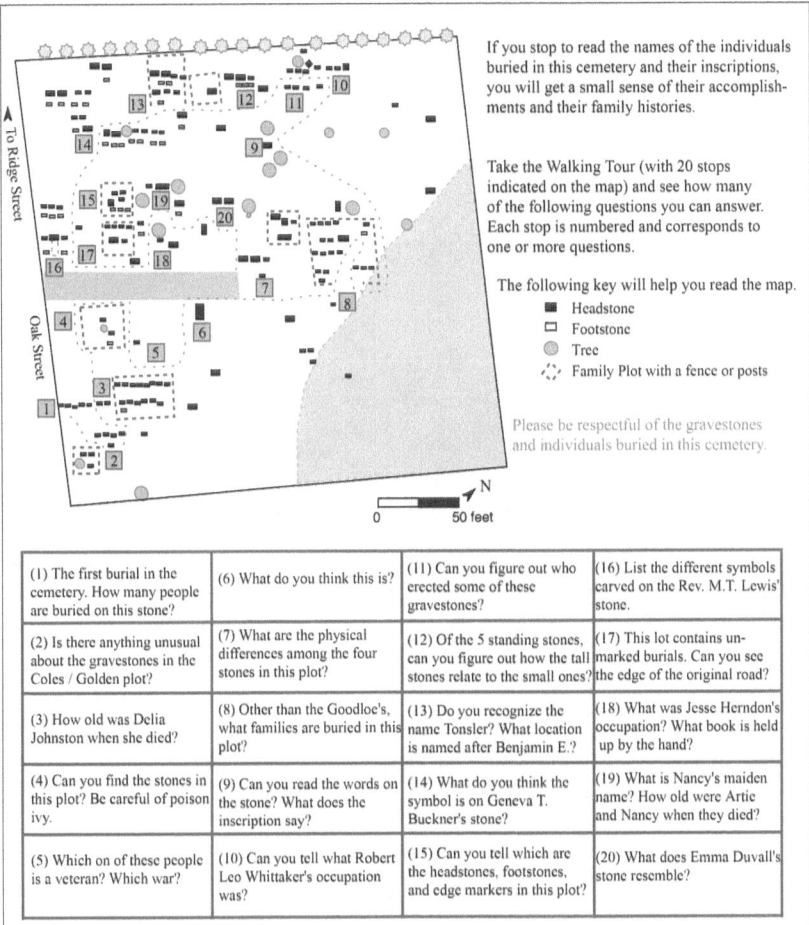

FIGURE 3.5. A "history hunt" designed for fourth and fifth graders to learn about Black history by taking a walking tour of the Daughters of Zion Cemetery (map and guide by the author)

work with descendants. For example, Robert King, the great-grandson of Ida Bell Burton (1893–1946), helped identify the location of her gravestone and shared ornate photographs and significant genealogical data.[5] The Preservers have gone one step further and organized some of their finds into an exhibition that opened in the fall of 2019 at the local Albemarle Charlottesville Historical Society.[6]

The information compiled from these mortuary sites illustrates historic narratives and national values including the worth of the individual, the role of the family, the variety of religious beliefs, struggles for freedom and equality, and the importance of patriotism. Through their monuments, cemeteries reveal ideas about social mobility, gender, race, and attitudes about

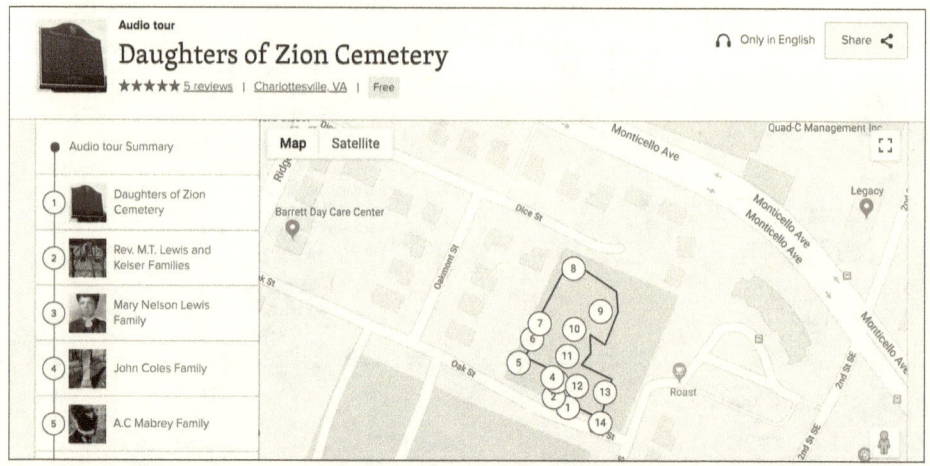

FIGURE 3.6. Excerpt from an audio tour of the Daughters of Zion Cemetery designed by Dede Smith, https://publichistory.as.virginia.edu/daughters-zion/audio-tour

death and the afterlife. Cemeteries are instructional spaces that, if read correctly, have much to teach us about our social and moral values, and about our shared history.

Notes

1. See, for example, "Walking Tour of the Daughters of Zion Cemetery," African-American Cemeteries in Albemarle and Amherst Counties, http://www2.vcdh.virginia.edu/cem/CemSearch_Tour_Zion.shtml.

2. "African American Cemeteries in Albemarle and Amherst Counties," http://www2.vcdh.virginia.edu/cem/. I stopped updating the site in 2011.

3. "Daughters of Zion Cemetery," University of Virginia Arts and Sciences Institute for Public History, last modified February 8, 2023, http://publichistory.as.virginia.edu/daughters-zion/audio-tour.

4. "Dr. Lynn Rainville Shared Her Experience Compiling Her Latest Work, 'Hidden History,'" interview on *Virginia This Morning*, WTVR CBS6 (Richmond), March 27, 2015, https://www.youtube.com/watch?v=i6hqOlO2ygQ; "Saving the Remains of the Day," *Tribune* (Charlottesville), January 1, 2009, 1.

5. "Burton, Ida Bell," https://daughtersofzioncemetery.org/the-people/burton-ida-bell/.

6. "Gone but Not Forgotten Exhibit," Facebook event, August 2, 2019, https://www.facebook.com/events/2032269490401128/.

CHAPTER 4

Death Can Not Make Our Souls Afraid
*Mosaic Templars of America Zephroes in
Macon County, Alabama, 1887-1931*

SHARI L. WILLIAMS

In 1881, the Tuskegee State Normal School opened about twelve miles north of Warrior Stand. Located in the southeast corner of Macon County, Alabama, Warrior Stand is both a rural village and Macon County's voting Precinct Four. Its name comes from Big Warrior, also known as Tustanagee Thlucco, a principal chief of the Mvskoke (Muscogee) Creek Nation, who owned and operated a tavern at Warrior Stand during the 1800s.[1] Prior to the Normal School's opening, Booker T. Washington, its principal, frequently visited Precinct Four's villages to meet with Black parents to learn about their struggles and to recruit their children into the Normal School's first class of students.[2]

As Washington developed amicable relationships over the years with families from Macon County's rural districts, he encouraged Black self-determination and took note of their receptivity to his message by way of their achievements. In 1912, Washington brought their otherwise obscure successes into the public limelight. He published an article in a political and social science journal that highlighted the aspirational African Americans who lived in what he called "Negro farming communities." Washington described how African American residents in the farming communities breathed life into visions of freedom by becoming landowners and building their own churches and schools.[3]

Washington did not mention that cemeteries existed near or on the grounds of most Black churches in these communities. At that time, he certainly would not have viewed ordinary rural cemeteries to be particularly significant. But the Black cemeteries that Washington passed decades ago

FIGURE 4.1. Narcissie Carter headstone, Boromville AME Zion Church Cemetery (undated photograph by Jon Chrismond, findagrave.com)

still dot the landscape today. Several are now on the Alabama Historic Cemetery Register. The Creek Stand AME Zion Church Cemetery, in south Macon County, and the Shiloh Missionary Baptist Church Cemetery in Notasulga, in north Macon County, are on the National Register of Historic Places.[4]

A common feature of many of these important cemeteries is the presence of distinctive Mosaic Templars of America (MTA) headstones. From 1883 until 1930, the MTA operated as one of the largest and most successful Black-owned and operated businesses in the world. In this chapter, I explore the lives of thirty Warrior Stand Precinct Four women who obtained these headstones. I focus on why and how the women joined the MTA and the symbolism and significance of their headstones within several contexts: racially polarized, rural life and death for both Black and white people; rural Black family and community life; death traditions; and class.

In studying these contexts, I determined that the women's choices to join the MTA reflected their familial and communal mindsets and their desire to belong to the sisterhood of Zephroes, the name that the MTA gave to its women members. I intentionally avoid correlating women's membership with socioeconomic class according to traditional labels. Although it is tempting to label the women as middle class just because their membership reflected their progressive thinking, I considered that the women lived during an amazing aspirational period during which rural Blacks struggled to advance and to attain equality. This period began immediately after emancipation, and although it was interrupted by the Great Depression, rural African Americans' push for equality continued until the civil rights movement, when they and their experiences took center stage in the struggle to overthrow Jim Crow.

Certainly, an early twentieth-century Black elite and middle class existed in more densely populated rural towns such as Little Rock, Arkansas, where the MTA began. Members of such groups, and working-class African Americans who resided in the rural hamlets surrounding larger towns and cities, surely recognized distinctions between the haves and the have-nots and possibly used the labels "upper class," "middle class," and "lower class." Nevertheless, these distinctions in and of themselves are not useful for understanding the motivations of the Precinct Four women who joined the MTA. Some scholars assign a class hierarchy to rural African Americans, placing Black landowners on a rung above tenant farmers and sharecroppers. However, Precinct Four's Black landowners, tenants, and sharecroppers alike existed in a segregated world beneath a Jim Crow ceiling, not permitted to freely operate as full citizens. Over time these working-class agriculturalists exerted tremendous effort to improve their social and economic situations, and their collective aspirational and communal mindsets blurred and complicated class distinctions. MTA membership and the MTA headstone signaled those aspirations and therefore functioned implicitly as forms of resistance to Jim Crow.

Mosaic Templars of America
from Arkansas to Alabama

Charles E. Bush and Chester W. Keatts, both formerly enslaved, achieved their entrepreneurial vision to provide burial insurance to African Americans when they founded the MTA in 1882 and incorporated it in 1883 in Arkansas. The company initially operated as the Order of Moses. The biblical story of Moses delivering the Israelites from bondage and leading them to the Promised Land inspired the early MTA leaders' vision to model the company on the tenets of fraternity and mutual benevolence, which meant those who purchased insurance simultaneously became MTA members. Unlike other Black fraternal organizations that formed because they were excluded from existing groups operated by whites, the MTA leaders conceived and established a unique Mosaic enterprise. Keeping with trends of the day among Black fraternal organizations, the MTA leaders created elaborate secret rituals for various occasions, including the initiation of members into the order and the burial of its members.[5] The company mushroomed from its humble Little Rock beginnings and received its first approval to sell insurance outside Arkansas when it obtained an Alabama charter in 1887.[6] This milestone paved the way for interested women in Warrior Stand Precinct Four to obtain death insurance and meet their social needs through Zephroe sisterhood.

Among women in Precinct Four, interest in the MTA was likely spurred by specific circumstances and events. As a group, the women's ancestry can be traced to the rugged interstate route of the 1800s called the Federal Road. From the 1830s cotton boom until the mid-1850s, the Federal Road provided passage to a mass of white emigrants traveling in oxen-drawn covered wagons from Georgia, Virginia, South Carolina, and other Eastern Seaboard states to present-day Alabama. The emigrants forcibly brought enslaved people to perform the backbreaking labor required to establish settlements and produce cotton crops in the fertile Black Belt.[7]

The original free and forced emigrants and their descendants who lived into the first decades of the twentieth century witnessed sweeping social, political, and economic change, including the failure of Reconstruction, which brought on the nadir of race relations. The nadir began at the turn of the century and encompassed national reunification among whites and the cruel era of Jim Crow. Reunification succeeded at the expense of Black people, with the creation of false myths and harmful imagery designed to demonize Blackness. It inspired nationwide white supremacist unity to propel New South economic recovery. Reunification gave birth to Jim Crow, which shaped widespread anti-Black culture and embedded institutional and structural racism in American life.[8] Rampant anti-Black racism in its many nefarious forms drove traumatized Black people such as the Precinct Four women to seek membership in all-Black fraternal organizations to find solace and a sense of belonging.[9]

Other influences on the Precinct Four women were MTA cofounder Charles E. Bush and Booker T. Washington, as well as the Tuskegee Plan, a long-range strategy for uplift that included extension outreach to Black rural communities from the Normal School, which later was called the Tuskegee Normal and Industrial Institute.[10] Bush and Washington enjoyed a close friendship based on mutual respect and a shared belief in Black self-help and advancement. Bush was a charter member of the National Negro Business League (NNBL), which Washington founded in 1900. Sometime after 1900, Bush delivered a commencement address at Tuskegee Institute.[11] In 1913, MTA leaders invited Washington to deliver the keynote speech at the dedication of the MTA's National Grand Temple headquarters building in Little Rock. In 1914, the MTA held its triennial convention on the institute's campus. The event garnered national publicity and drew a throng of three thousand delegates and a large number of visitors. The *Mobile Weekly Press* reported on the prominent women MTA leaders who attended, noting that "the Mosaic Templars know no sex in its representation."[12]

Washington marshaled extension personnel, teachers, and ministers to spread advice, educational programs, and encouragement to rural district residents according to the Tuskegee Plan.[13] Information spread as well through Goodwill tours, excursions to the rural districts that Washington organized so that invited faculty from the institute and other dignitaries could observe firsthand the progress made by Black farm families.[14] The plan also offered conferences for farmers, ministers, and teachers, county-wide fairs, and the Movable School, headed by the first United States Department of Agriculture cooperative extension agent, Thomas M. Campbell, a Black man who supervised field work in a multistate region. Large numbers of proud Black people from Macon County's rural districts attended the institute's commencement ceremonies each year.[15]

Washington himself joined the MTA in 1913. This news likely spread easily by word of mouth throughout the rural districts by way of frequent interactions between the villagers and institute extension personnel. Due to a 2005 fire that destroyed the MTA's National Grand Temple in Little Rock, no records exist to reveal when each of the thirty Precinct Four women purchased MTA insurance and joined chambers after Alabama gained its charter in 1887.[16]

Chambers existed as subordinate bodies within the MTA's tiered organizational structure, which placed the national governing body at the top tier and the state body and local bodies at the lower tiers. As with fraternal organizations in existence today, Precinct Four Zephroes paid fees, dues, and insurance premiums to support the local, state, and national bodies. As they met their financial obligations, Precinct Four Zephroes helped to build the MTA's national endowment fund, which in turn financed the death benefit that their families ultimately received. This fiscal reciprocity constituted the heart of the MTA's mutual aid commitment to its members.[17]

The MTA typically assigned female members to chambers and male members to temples. Chambers and temples were affiliated under a lodge. The MTA's national headquarters periodically advertised membership campaigns to recruit "organizers" or "deputies" to set up lodges. Headquarters charged deputies a fifteen-dollar charter fee and permitted them to charge each new member a joining fee. The deputy would then pay headquarters the charter fee from the total collected from new members and retain the balance for a profit. This structure incentivized would-be deputies to set up as many lodges and recruit as many members into the lodge's affiliated chambers and temples as possible.[18]

MTA headstones in Precinct Four reveal that both men and women belonged to chambers there.[19] A plausible explanation is that the area lacked sufficient numbers of men and women to conform to the gendered division of members, so the deputy organizer resolved the issue by establishing coed chambers. The Precinct Four women belonged to one of the following local chambers: Moores Choice [sic], Shealey's Pride, Smith Prospect, Tatum Home, and Walters Choice [sic].

In keeping with its goal to promote "self-help, thrift, and industry," the MTA ingeniously built in an entrepreneurial component at the local level through its system for establishing lodges, chambers, and temples. As deputy organizers established lodges and collected joining fees from new members, they benefited financially, but they also helped to sustain the MTA's ability to execute its mutual benevolence plan. The MTA strategy succeeded nationwide. By 1908, membership grew from fifteen to eleven thousand. By 1913, the company reported an endowment surplus of $71,198.26.[20] Sadly, this method for generating a revenue stream likely contributed to the MTA's insolvency during the Depression, when Black Americans especially suffered tremendous financial losses and could no longer pay charter and joining fees and premiums. The MTA ceased operations by the end of the 1930s.

Precinct Four Zephroes by
Cemetery and Chamber Affiliation

Table 4.1 lists thirty Precinct Four Zephroes whose graves are marked with MTA headstones. The table also lists vital information, if available. Figure 4.2 is a map that depicts the approximate location of each church cemetery that is listed in the table.

The cemeteries shown on the map are in close proximity according to today's drive times, but from the 1800s well into the first decades of the twentieth century, rural people depended on horse- or mule-driven wagons to travel between villages. The five-mile trip from Warrior Stand to Creek

Table 4.1. Burials: Precinct Four Zephroes

Church Cemetery	Name on Headstone	Maiden Name	Date of Birth– Date of Death	Age at Death	Chamber
Antioch	Moore, Malinda	Unknown	1853–1928†	75	Tatum Home 3655 Hannon
Antioch	Wright, Pollie	Chambliss	1888–1928	40	Tatum Home 3655 Hannon
Boromville	Brown, Francis	Unknown	1846–unknown	unknown	Unknown‡
Boromville	Brown, Malinda	Unknown	unknown–1926	unknown	Walters Choice 4259 Hurtsboro
Boromville	Carter, Narcissie	Unknown	1873–1923	50	Walters Choice 4259 Hurtsboro
Boromville	Henderson, Mary L.	Not Married	1896–unknown	unknown	Unknown‡
Boromville	Key, Carrie	Tolbert	1850–1928	78	Walters Choice 4259 Hurtsboro
Boromville	Key, Cornelia	Unknown	1874–1922	48	Vinces Choice 4174 Auburn
Boromville	Kitchen, Martha	Borom	1885–1925	40	Unknown‡
Boromville	Lewis, Belle	Collins or Cooper	1853–1923	70	Unknown‡
Boromville	Tolbert, Effie	Not Married	1869–1921	52	Walters Choice 4259 Hurtsboro
Creek Stand	Ellison, Clara	Borom	1847–1931	84	Tatum Home 3655 Hannon
Creek Stand	Marshall, Pearlie	Myhand	1894–1926	32	Vinces Choice 4174 Auburn
Creek Stand	Pace, Sallie	Comer	1859–1928	69	Walters Choice 4259 Hurtsboro
Sweet Pilgrim	Benson, Arzela	Unknown	1892–1918	75	Moores Choice 3593 Roba
Sweet Pilgrim	Brown, Ellen	Sistrunk	1843–1918	75	Moores Choice 3593 Roba
Sweet Pilgrim	Germany, Adaline	Harris or Moore	1876–1929	53	Moores Choice 3593 Roba
Sweet Pilgrim	Harris, Susan	Henderson	1819–1919†	100	Moores Choice 3593 Roba
Sweet Pilgrim	Hendon, Leila	Parker	1899–1927	28	Unknown‡
Sweet Pilgrim	McBryde, Jayne	Unknown	1832–1925	93	Moores Choice 3593 Roba
Sweet Pilgrim	Moore, Nettie	Unknown	1858–1923	65	Moores Choice 3593 Roba

Table 4.1. Burials: Precinct Four Zephroes (*continued*)

Church Cemetery	Name on Headstone	Maiden Name	Date of Birth–Date of Death	Age at Death	Chamber
Sweet Pilgrim	Moore, Frances	Germany	1844–1928	84	Moores Choice 3593 Roba
Sweet Pilgrim	Hann, Carrie	Hand or Hann	1883–1919	36	Moores Choice 3593 Roba
Sweet Pilgrim	Reed (Reid), Eliza	Moore	1840–1925†	85	Moores Choice 3593 Roba
Sweet Pilgrim	Wright, Emmaline	Harris or Moore	1856–1920†	64	Moores Choice 3593 Roba
Warrior Stand*	Grear, Ada	Thomas	1880–1924	44	Unknown‡
Warrior Stand*	Jackson, Parthenia	Unknown	1840–1917	77	Smith Prospect 3326 Roba
Warrior Stand*	Moore, Everena/Everline	Perry	1891–1921	30	Unknown‡
Warrior Stand*	Reese, Octavia	Robinson	1894–1917	23	Shealey's Pride 3168 Tuskegee
Warrior Stand*	Tatum Feebee	Henderson	1842–1925†	83	Tatum Home 3655 Hannon

*The racially segregated Warrior Stand Cemetery contains graves of early African American residents, early white settlers, and descendants of both groups. It is located in a heavily wooded area about a half mile north of the Cooper Chapel AME Zion Church. The survey of African American graves in the Warrior Stand Cemetery is incomplete to date, so there may be additional MTA headstones that are not included in this chapter.

†Dates of birth recorded in vital records do not match dates of birth listed on headstones, indicating possible errors made by the chamber official who completed the headstone request form. An example is Eliza Reid, who indicated in a pension deposition taken in 1924 that she did not know her own age but thought that she was twenty-three years old in 1865.

‡Unknown dates of death and chambers are due to illegible headstones that are worn, damaged, or sunken.

Stand takes about six minutes by car, but traveling the same distance by horse and wagon takes about an hour. Limitations on social interactions imposed by slow-moving horse and wagon transportation and low population density account in part for the formation of the self-contained farming communities in Precinct Four that Booker T. Washington described.

Each cemetery shown is still in active use, and except for the Warrior Stand Cemetery, which is affiliated with the Cooper Chapel AME Zion Church, the cemeteries carry the name of the church that maintains it. Precinct Four Zephroes are buried in the cemeteries of the churches they attended, not according to their chamber affiliations. The spatial arrangement of the five cemeteries in Precinct Four does not explain how the MTA named chambers in the area nor how it assigned chamber numbers. Nor do records

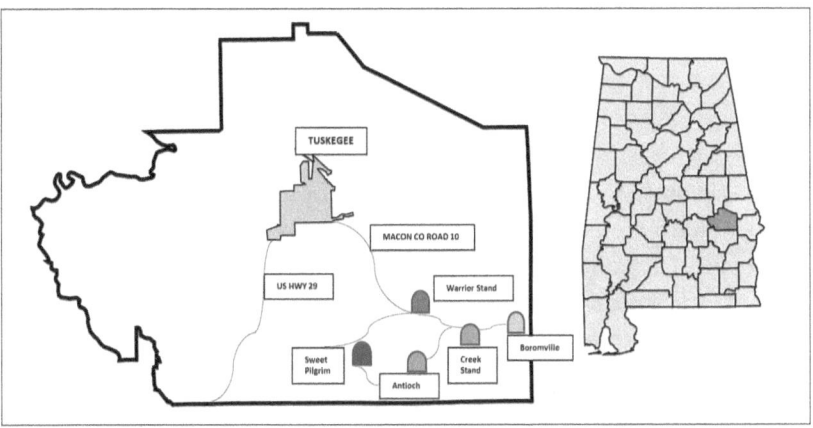

FIGURE 4.2. Map of five Macon County Precinct Four cemeteries (map created in 2007 by Arkyan, Creative Commons cc-by-sa-2.5, https://commons.wikimedia.org/wiki/File:Macon _County_Alabama_Incorporated_and_Unincorporated_areas_Franklin_Highlighted.svg, and modified by the author). The image on the right shows the state of Alabama with Macon County highlighted. The image on the left shows Macon County with the approximate locations of Precinct Four cemeteries. Not to scale. Cemetery gps latitude/longitude coordinates from Findagrave.com: Antioch 32.2806015,-85.5381012; Boromville 32.2997960, -85.4439070; Creek Stand 32.290220, -85.4897800; Sweet Pilgrim 32.29771988, -85.6166992; Warrior Stand 32.3027992, -85.5389023.

exist to explain how often the Precinct Four Zephroes met and where they held chamber meetings. A clue is that most of the women who are interred in the Sweet Pilgrim Cemetery lived in close proximity to each other and belonged to the Moores Choice Chamber. Additionally, several women who attended the Dawkins Church (now Sweet Pilgrim Church) were related by blood or by marriage. For example, Zephroe Susan Harris (born in 1819) was the matriarch of the Moore/Harris family. Her daughters Adaline Germany, Emmaline Wright, and Eliza Reid belonged to the MTA. Eliza's son Frank Reid was married to Zephroe Carrie Hann. Eliza's brother Turner Moore was married to Zephroe Nettie Moore.

The Walters Choice Chamber, however, included women from Boromville and Creek Stand. The Tatum Home Chamber included women from Antioch, Creek Stand, and Warrior Stand. That Precinct Four women either joined a chamber as charter members or through initiation upon the recommendation of a current member possibly accounts for the crossing of village boundaries among Walters Choice and Tatum Home Chamber members. Apparently, the deputy organizer's selection of charter members, and existing social and family relationships that influenced recommendations for initiation, dictated who belonged to which chamber. Kinship and the neighborhood makeup obviously shaped the membership of the Moores Choice Chamber. Blood and allied family members resided within the community that immediately surrounded the Sweet Pilgrim Cemetery, and those buried in the cemetery who have MTA headstones all belonged to the Moores Choice Chamber. A similar pattern exists in the Boromville Cemetery. Of legible headstones at Boromville, the predominant chamber is Walters Choice. This pattern is not so obvious for members buried in the Antioch, Boromville, Creek Stand, and Warrior Stand Cemeteries, where there are fewer MTA headstones and they represent different chambers. Tatum Home Chamber members are buried at the Antioch, Creek Stand, and Warrior Stand Cemeteries. Apparently, social and kinship relationships across village boundaries also shaped the membership of the Tatum Home Chamber.

It appears that each chamber's number reflects the number of its charter. The MTA chartered its first temple—Zephroe Temple number 1—in 1883 in Arkansas, and that temple in turn generated the very first women's chamber, Lone Star Chamber number 1.[21] It seems this pattern continued during the MTA's expansion, because most Precinct Four chambers numbered in the three thousands, a sequence that makes sense given the growth of the MTA from the time that it chartered Zephroe Temple number 1 in 1883 and the state of Alabama received its MTA charter in 1887, four years later.

Precinct Four Life and Death in White and Black

Unfortunately, Precinct Four women did not leave behind memoirs, diaries, or the like to tell us in their own words about their motivations for joining the MTA. But the sources that do exist—census and vital records, historical interpretations of Black death traditions, and documentation of activities in their communities—reveal much about their actions and responses to Booker T. Washington's call for self-determination. Sources indicate that they sought to follow Washington's guidance, but despite their zeal to advance, they could not obliterate racial and cultural prejudice that reinforced anti-Blackness and the myths it generated in matters of life and death. To explore the prejudice and mythology that circumscribed them, I turn to *the words of a white contemporary*, (Anna) Eva Chandler Gagnon, who penned a coming-of-age memoir titled *Home Place*.

Eva Chandler was born to an affluent family in 1885, two years after the MTA's incorporation. Her father, a former Confederate soldier, operated a plantation in Creek Stand where Black sharecroppers toiled year after year. She married Ernest Gagnon in 1918 and self-published her memoir in 1964 after her husband's retirement.

As a white female brought up during the emergence of the Lost Cause narrative and Jim Crow legislation, Gagnon wrote vivid anecdotes and stories about African Americans with an odd mix of disdain and fascination. She admitted that she perhaps saw her life on the plantation through "rose colored glasses" and recalled that listening to the "negroes laughing and singing together in the evenings" as they finished their work at sunset was "perhaps one of the nicest times on the plantation."[22] But her memory of mythical Black depravity is evident in her recollection that her family "lived surrounded by negroes," and while they "never thought of locking the [house] doors at night," they locked the corncribs and smokehouse doors, presumably because they feared "the negroes" would steal food otherwise.[23]

In describing the up-close but complex relationships that once existed among southern Blacks and whites who lived in places such as the Chandler plantation, Ralph Ellison declared that "Southern whites could not walk, talk, conceive of law or justice, or think about family, sex, and love without responding to the presence of Negroes."[24] The phrase "experience religion" can be added to Ellison's list, based on historian Eugene Genovese's argument that understanding religion's influence in the South during slavery requires studying how it differed based on race. The Southern planter class, he pointed out, used religion to maintain the racially oppressive social order, while African Americans used it to resist their oppression.[25]

After emancipation, African Americans rushed to challenge their oppression and show themselves to be worthy citizens in two ways: they legally solemnized their marriages, and they built their own churches and schools.[26] African Americans in Precinct Four followed this trend. The Sweet Pilgrim Baptist Church formed in 1863, while both the Antioch Baptist Church and the Cooper Chapel AME Zion Church at Warrior Stand formed in 1870. Between 1905 and 1913 African Americans in Precinct Four's rural districts constructed fifty-three schoolhouses at a total cost of $40,000.[27]

In 1895, the year Gagnon celebrated her tenth birthday, a group of African American Creek Stand residents—landowners and tenant farmers— assumed the responsibility as trustees of the Creek Stand AME Zion Church to oversee the construction of a building to replace the brush arbor where they held worship services. The village's white physician, Dr. James Ellison, a former slaveholder and Chandler family friend, donated a three-acre parcel of land in 1893 and sold a parcel of undetermined size to the trustees in 1894.[28] In her memoir, Gagnon commended Ellison's donation but not the agency of the trustees. She instead described a camp meeting held at the Creek Stand church as being "protracted" and lasting for six weeks, during which time, she claimed, the people were emotionally charged in their shouting and singing.[29]

As she matured, Gagnon remained curious but skeptical about the Black tenants, sharecroppers, and domestic servants who surrounded her family. She admitted that a death on the plantation made everyone sad, even the white people, but she surmised that Blacks overall were inherently lazy workers and mothers were neglectful, charging that the Black infant mortality rate was high and that "they [Black people] were careless with their babies, and only the strong survived."[30]

Debra Gray White's seminal work on the gendered oppression of enslaved women challenges the notion of ubiquitous slave infanticide and Gagnon's broad-brush claim that African Americans were careless with their children. White surmised that some premeditated murders of Black babies by their mothers did occur in the antebellum South, ostensibly to spare those children from lives of crushing bondage. But more likely, Black infants succumbed to crib death, now called Sudden Infant Death Syndrome (SIDS).[31]

Citing statistics derived by sociologist Michael P. Johnson from 1850 and 1860 census mortality records, White noted that a high percentage of enslaved infant deaths due to suffocation correlated with what are now known to be predisposing factors, such as age, the time of year when the death occurred, and lack of prenatal care due to lower socioeconomic status. White concluded, "We can suppose that some of the infant deaths that planters attributed to infanticide and some blamed on maternal carelessness were actually due to causes which even today baffle medical experts."[32]

White concluded that planters found it easier to blame enslaved women for infant deaths than to objectively investigate the real causes, some of which would adversely implicate the unhealthy conditions that planters themselves imposed on enslaved pregnant women and their children, unborn and born.[33] Similar predisposing factors for SIDS—low socioeconomic status and lack of prenatal care—likely persisted among many of the Black sharecropping families who toiled on the Chandler plantation. Gagnon's cavalier claim about Black maternal carelessness parroted uninvestigated and unsubstantiated allegations passed down since antebellum days.

Gagnon's commentary on Black death extended to bereavement. She observed that when one of their own died, Black mourners displayed the body in the cabin for friends and family to view prior to a church funeral and burial in the nearby cemetery. She stated that the mourners inside the cabin would "scream and scream everytime some friend or relative came to the cabin" and the screams were "terrible to hear."[34]

Cultural scholar Charlton D. McIlwain places a cultural and metaphysical contextual frame around Gagnon's description of screaming Black mourners. He explained that while some contemporary white and Black people alike can display attachments to the bodies of deceased loved ones, the dominant society detaches and "views the dead body in simply material terms." African Americans, however, traditionally exhibit a lingering attachment to the body because they believe it is sacred in both life and death. McIlwain noted that these beliefs are manifested through interaction with the body, such as touching and carrying on conversations with the deceased, and an aversion to cremation so as to keep the body intact.[35]

McIlwain's metaphysical explanation of Black emotionalism speaks to the open expression in Black church worship and Black mourning that Gagnon observed. McIlwain posed that African American mourning settings mirror Black church worship settings, where upbeat music is played and worshippers sway, clap their hands, participate in call-and-response, shout, and testify. He called these "attuned settings" and argued that they create a "mood and atmosphere" in which free emotional expression is acceptable because it "contributes to, rather than disturbs such an atmosphere; such spaces are both created by these behaviors, and such spaces exist to invite such behavior."[36] By McIlwain's definition, attuned spaces would include the emotionally charged events that Gagnon described—the Creek Stand church camp meeting where Blacks worshipped and sharecropper cabins on the Chandler plantation where they mourned. Conversely, McIlwain claimed, white church worshippers and mourners frown upon outward displays of emotion, considering such behavior to be improper and disruptive.[37]

McIlwain's cultural and metaphysical explanations illuminate the racial and cultural differences that influenced Gagnon's perception that Black mourners "seemingly enjoyed seeing a funeral procession" and that "the funeral service would last all day."[38] As with open emotionalism, scholars reveal that the behaviors she observed evince meaningful rituals that acculturated enslaved people passed on to sanction the funeral as the rite to celebrate the deceased person's homegoing. Historian John Blassingame concluded that no expense was spared for these elaborate occasions. Long periods of mourning, long funeral processions, adorned caskets, and displays of open emotion characterized the homegoing celebration.[39] McIlwain offered yet another perspective about the homegoing celebration, noting that historically, oppressed African Americans perceived the transition to the hereafter to be an exodus, making death a milestone event of sorts within the Black community.[40]

Gagnon contrasted emotional Black mourners with forward-thinking African Americans who planned for death: "Even yet, they make plans to be 'laid away' properly, and some of societies we read stories about are really burial societies. They [Blacks] paid about five cents a month, and this entitled them to a decent funeral."[41] Yet even as she praised African Americans who purchased burial coverage, Gagnon seemed to contradict herself as she told a derisive anecdote about a deceased Black woman named Liz.

In the story, which came to Gagnon from an unnamed source, a "lady of the house" (a white woman) overheard her cook, Mary, and other Black servants gossiping as they watched Liz's funeral procession pass by. Mary charged that Liz had purchased burial insurance using the money set aside for her family's groceries and clothing. As the hearse, eight buggies, and a crowd of mourners streamed by, Mary declared,

"Heah she come on her las' ride, an' she sho' done herself proud wid shiny blac' hearse an' dem hi' steppin' hosses fum de lib'ry stable. Unk-h-h. Jest ter see all dat you would think dat Liz wuz a good, find 'omen, when us all knows jes' how mean an' stingy she wuz, squeezin' her nickles ontil her man an' dem po' li'l chillunees had'dly had ernuff ter eat, much les'ter wear. Ah hopes you is 'joying you las' ride, an' dat you cums ter de judgment seat, dey' won' be too hard on you fer all de mean things you done ter yo' man an' dem po' chllun when you beat 'em fer nuthin'. May you res' better dan you deserb.[42]

This disparaging story caps off Gagnon's discussion of Black burial rituals, but it should not be the last word on the subject. On one hand, her portrayal of Black servants as gossiping and Liz as selfish perpetuates negative stereotypes that impugn Black women's moral character. On the other, Gagnon's recollections provide a rare glimpse into African American rural life in the early 1900s, although the view is tainted by racial prejudice.

Without more information, we cannot know whether Liz actually drained the family finances. Perhaps the truth is that she wisely planned, and not at her family's expense, for a homegoing celebration in keeping with traditional African American death rituals. Presumably, the MTA's death benefit enabled Precinct Four Zephroes to plan for their own homegoing celebrations according to traditions passed down from enslavement. But the women's signature headstones suggest that their views about life and death differed somewhat from those held by their ancestors.

It is true that the death benefit provided discretionary funds for Zephroe family members and friends to adhere closely to the activities traditionally associated with African American homegoing observances since enslavement. This would include a proper viewing of the body, funeral service, cemetery burial, and perhaps even the repast—a dinner for family and friends

FIGURE 4.3. MTA engraved symbol (photograph by the author, 2014)

held immediately following the graveside service. But the markings on the MTA's signature Vermont marble headstones imply a difference between the meanings Zephroes ascribed to life and death and those of their enslaved ancestors, differences that evolved from Black gains made since emancipation and that were rooted in the era's ethos of Black self-determination. The women's direct encounters with the people and programs of the Tuskegee Institutes and their constant exposure to the doctrine of self-help evidently inspired their racial pride. With this prominent backdrop, the women could celebrate death as an exodus as did their ancestors, but they could also proudly celebrate lives lived according to high moral character.

The luminous white headstones with thin gray veining featured the classic MTA symbol containing three Vs, the abbreviation for the Latin phrase "Veni, vidi, vici" ("I came, I saw, I conquered"). Members who wanted this special headstone, which became available after the company established a national monument department in 1914, were assessed a tax of fifty cents.[43] Members' willingness to pay the tax suggests that many viewed the headstone as more than a fancy grave marker: it also symbolized postmortem regalia that reflected the deceased member's aspirational consciousness and practice of self-help and virtuous living.

The MTA required chamber officers to complete and sign each headstone request form on behalf of the entire chamber to certify the deceased member's good standing at the time of death (see figure 4.4). The criteria for good standing included living uprightly, providing aid, attending meetings regularly, and paying dues, fees, and assessments.[44] The emphasis on upright

FIGURE 4.4. MTA monument claim form (photograph by Bryan McDade, 2013; courtesy of the Mosaic Templars Cultural Center, Little Rock, Arkansas)

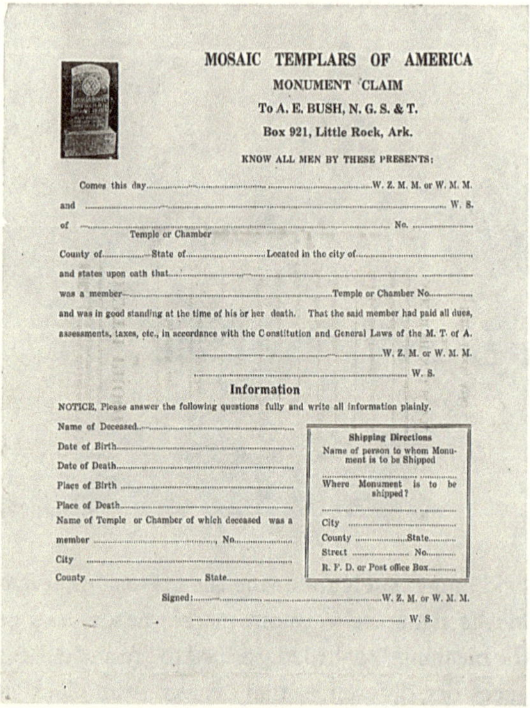

MOSAIC TEMPLARS OF AMERICA
MONUMENT CLAIM
To A. E. BUSH, N. G. S. & T.
Box 921, Little Rock, Ark.

KNOW ALL MEN BY THESE PRESENTS:

Comes this day .... W. Z. M. M. or W. M. M.
and .... W. S.
of .... No. ....
Temple or Chamber
County of .... State of .... Located in the city of ....
and states upon oath that ....
was a member .... Temple or Chamber No. ....
and was in good standing at the time of his or her death. That the said member had paid all dues, assessments, taxes, etc., in accordance with the Constitution and General Laws of the M. T. of A.

.... W. Z. M. or W. M. M.
.... W. S.

Information

NOTICE. Please answer the following questions fully and write all information plainly.

Name of Deceased ....
Date of Birth ....
Date of Death ....
Place of Birth ....
Place of Death ....
Name of Temple or Chamber of which deceased was a member ...., No. ....
City ....
County .... State ....

Shipping Directions
Name of person to whom Monument is to be Shipped
....
Where Monument is to be shipped?
....
City ....
County .... State ....
Street .... No. ....
R. F. D. or Post office Box ....

Signed: .... W. Z. M. or W. M. M.
.... W. S.

living symbolized in the headstone and in chamber rituals projects the Precinct Four Zephroes' resistance to stereotypical notions held by Gagnon and like-minded whites who characterized Black women as immoral.

Zephroe Symbols, Pledges, and Chamber Rituals

While enjoying the affirmational aspects of MTA membership, Precinct Four's churchgoing Zephroes also embraced their namesake and role model Zipporah, the wife of Moses, a woman of color who was noted for her beauty. In Exodus 4:24–26, God is ready to punish Moses with death for neglecting his obligations as the prophet and leader of the Israelites. Understanding that she needs to take immediate steps to save Moses, Zipporah cuts off the foreskin of Gershom, their youngest son, to honor the covenant with God and reawaken Moses to his standing and obligations. Her action spares the lives of her husband and the Israelites.

Precinct Four Zephroes channeled Zipporah through their promises to take care of their people—MTA sisters and brothers, and widows and children. For example, Zephroe Sallie Pace and her husband, Albert, sold an acre of land in 1907 at market cost to the trustees of the Creek Stand School to

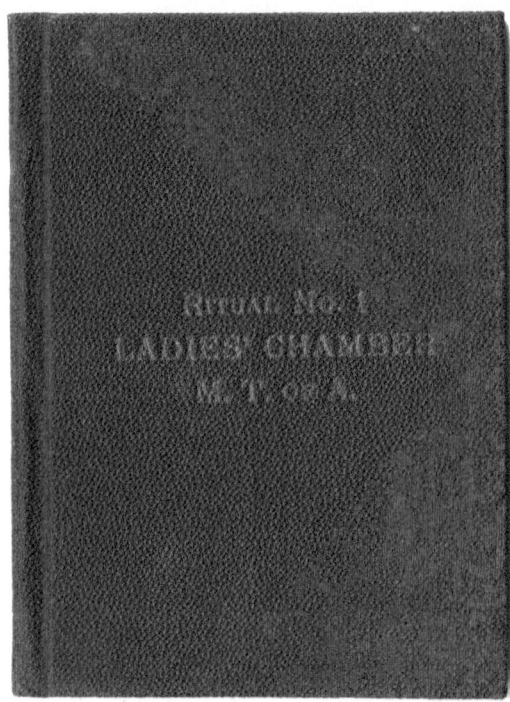

FIGURE 4.5. *Ritual No. 1, Ladies' Chamber, Mosaic Templars of America*, pe1609 (Arkansas State Archives, Little Rock)

erect a school building. Precinct Four's parents, ministers, and teachers likewise rallied within and across their respective communities to build schoolhouses, lengthen school terms, and take care of the sick.[45]

The MTA's chamber rituals encouraged such benevolent acts. In 1884, the MTA published *Ritual No. 1, Ladies' Chamber, Mosaic Templars of America* to be used by Zephroes nationwide. The book contained detailed instructions for conducting a regular business meeting, dedicating a new chamber, initiating new members, installing officers, and funeralizing deceased members. It contained topics on self-help; communal care of widows, mothers, and children; and loyalty and benevolence.

Zephroes pledged to assist and defend each other and their brother Templars, obey all laws and rules, and attend meetings as regularly as possible. The chamber dedication ceremony called upon members to embrace collectivism—the greater good of family and community—and to symbolically put to death selfish individualism by giving help to each other and the order and by accepting help as well. The highest officer, the Most Worshipful Zipporah (MWZ), led the women in singing the dedication ode. The first stanza of the ode—"Death can not make our souls afraid if God be with us there; we may walk through its darkest shades, and never yield to fear"—signified members' symbolic death to self-interest, their adoption of collectivism, and their devotion to each other and to God.[46]

Literacy, Financial Resources, and Class Distinctions among Zephroes

Two basic conditions obviously needed to exist for chambers to operate. First, candidates for Most Worshipful Zipporah and other offices had to be literate so they could read, understand, and follow the ritual book. According to census records from 1870 to 1920, only a few Zephroes in Precinct Four could read and write, and therefore there was a small pool from which officers could be selected. Some women, including Clara Ellison and Martha Kitchen, were listed as illiterate in an earlier census but literate in subsequent census years, which indicates that they learned to read and write, possibly in conjunction with their MTA chamber activities.[47]

The second condition was that women needed the financial means to pay fees, dues, and premiums. According to a 1910 national advertisement, the MTA charged three dollars per year for a burial insurance premium, with an option to pay quarterly installments of seventy-five cents. At death, the policy paid a benefit of $300. Burial policy holders could pay an additional fifty-cent tax if they wanted to qualify for a headstone.[48]

A 1913 ad indicated that for $8.95 per year, a woman could purchase life insurance that paid a benefit of $300 at maturity or death, and $50 at the time of death for burial. Under this policy, a woman policyholder would receive two dollars per week if she became ill.[49] The advertisement presented the minimum cost for a life insurance policy based on age and did not emphasize that policy expiration dates and the amount of the benefit paid to the member depended on the member's age at the time of initiation. The MTA offered Class C policies to older members aged fifty to fifty-five, fifty-five to sixty, and sixty to sixty-five. If a person joined between sixty and sixty-five years of age, their policy did not expire until seven years elapsed. At expiration or death, they received a benefit payment of $300. Younger people qualified for Class A and B policies in the age groups of fifteen to twenty, twenty to twenty-five, twenty-five to thirty, thirty to thirty-five, thirty-five to forty, forty to forty-five, and forty-five to fifty. The maturity period corresponded to age, as did the amount of the benefit payment for these groups. For example, if a person joined at thirty-forty years of age, the policy expired in twenty years and the MTA paid a benefit of $1,000.[50] Information is lacking about the types and classes of policies the Precinct Four women obtained.

While it may be tempting to rigidly connect MTA membership with the traditional categories of upper, middle, and lower class, such a correlation is risky. A woman's ability to afford burial insurance and the headstone tax reflected not only her income but also her household expenses. At the same time, we should also resist the urge to correlate education level and gross income with socioeconomic class. Several of the Precinct Four Zephroes owned homes but could not read or write, while several who rented homes for their entire lives were literate. Furthermore, all of the women belonged to the agricultural working class, and their incomes varied from year to year. In addition, community and family assets factored largely into the economic status of individual women in Precinct Four, most of whom existed within a tight web of blood, fictive, and allied family kinfolk who provided mutual financial and social support.

The label "working class" best describes the Precinct Four Zephroes, because it more clearly reflects the robust aspirational period between enslavement and the clear emergence of a distinct contemporary urban Black middle class after World War II. Focusing on the women's material assets, rather than annual gross income, allows a more accurate analysis of economic stratification.

Material assets for this purpose include the categories used on the agricultural schedule of the 1880 federal census—the value of land rented or owned, the value of farm production, the number of acres planted in cotton, and the number of cotton bales produced. The 1880 Macon County agricultural schedule names individual farmers, making it possible to determine whether familial assets held by the women's kinfolk, including spouses and in-laws, affected the women's economic status. The 1900, 1910, and 1920 population schedules of the census disclose details about the women's economic status in their own households over time. These schedules report whether heads of household owned or rented their homes and, for those in the former category, whether the individual paid a mortgage or owned the home free and clear. The schedules also report literacy and occupational status.

The 1880 agricultural schedule for Precinct Four lists farmers who owned or rented a minimum of forty acres of land (improved, unimproved, and wooded) and who reported income from farm production (goods sold, consumed, or on hand). Renters paid landlords a fixed amount of money. The agricultural schedule is one of the earliest but most obscure forms of recognition of economic aspiration and achievement among Black men living in remote rural areas, because it identifies those who established viable farms in the fifteen short years after the Civil War.

In 1880, census enumerators counted all heads of household—who were typically men—on the separate population schedule. Enumerators also

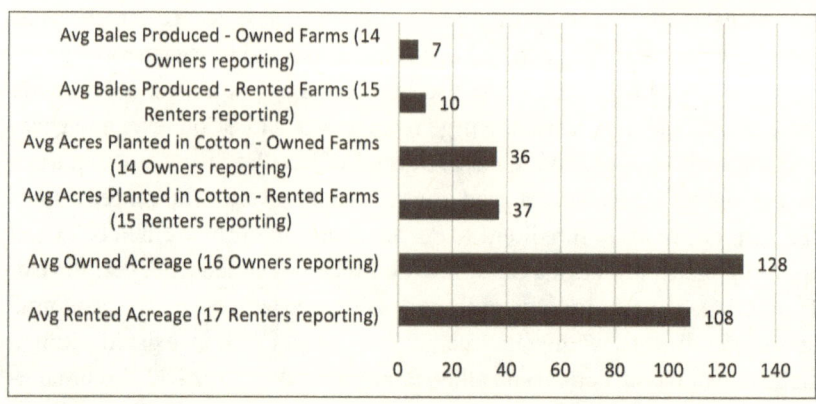

FIGURE 4.6. Land and Cotton Assets: Precinct Four African American Farmers 1880

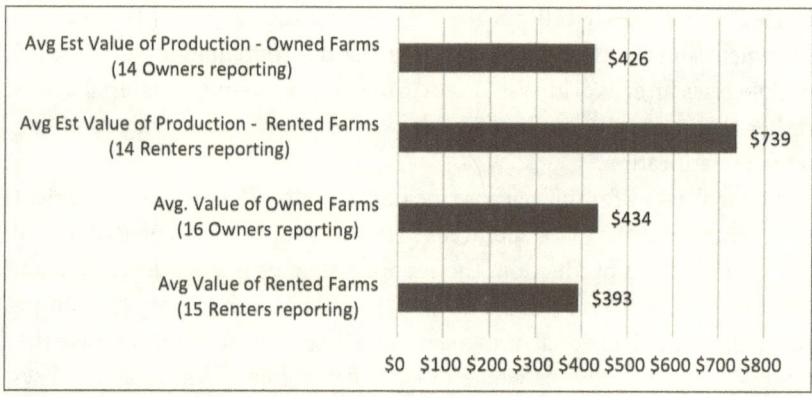

FIGURE 4.7. Land Values: Precinct Four African American Farmers, 1880

listed members of each man's household, typically his wife and children, along with race and year of birth. I cross-referenced names on the agricultural schedule against names and other vital information provided on population schedules and checked marriage, death, and other census records to determine which Black men listed on the agricultural schedule were related to one or more of the thirty Zephroes.

I found that seventeen renters were kin to one or more of fourteen Zephroes. Sixteen Black farm owners appeared on the 1880 agricultural schedule, but I determined that only one was related by blood to a Zephroe: Edmon Swanson, the father of Zephroe Malinda Moore. Only two African American sharecroppers were found, and there was no apparent connection between them and any of the Precinct Four Zephroes.

The majority of the Black farmers reported the value of their farms and of their farm production. Most said that they planted cotton and reported the number of bales produced. Figure 4.6 compares land and cotton assets reported by Black renters with those reported by Black owners. Figure 4.7 compares land values and estimated values of farm production between the same two groups. The analysis indicates that minimal differences existed between the assets held by renters and those held by owners, and in some cases, the renters outpaced the owners.[51]

Five Zephroe Profiles Reveal More

The revelation of parity between renters and landowners based on material assets underscores the complexities of identifying the vectors of socioeconomic stratification among the Precinct Four Zephroes prior to the turn of the century. Nonetheless, economic information provided in federal census population schedules from 1900 to 1930 is useful for crafting profiles of the women that more clearly describe the connection between 1880 material assets and women's ability to pay expenses associated with their MTA memberships (1890 census records for Precinct Four are not available, since they were badly damaged or destroyed in a 1921 fire at the Department of Commerce). Profiles of Parthenia Jackson, Clara Ellison, Carrie Hann, Pollie Wright, and Martha Kitchen include additional census information and further connect 1880s familial assets to financial situations that provided the means for these women to join the MTA.[52]

Clara Ellison and Parthenia Jackson, both born during the 1840s, are among the oldest of the Precinct Four Zephroes. Both women worked as farm laborers after they were married, and both retained their financial stability after their spouses died, no doubt aided by the material assets that had been held within their respective families since 1880.

According to the 1880 census, Benson Jackson, husband of Parthenia, rented ninety acres valued at $180. He valued his farm production at $580. By 1900 Benson had died, but Parthenia Jackson was not an indigent widow. She rented her home and worked as a midwife.[53] Clara Ellison's husband, Isom, was renting a sixty-five acre farm at the time of the 1880 census. He died before 1900, after which she also lived free from indigency. Her father, Abe Borom, was renting land in 1880 but eventually purchased land that she apparently inherited by 1910, when she was listed as a landowner on the census. In 1920, she resided in the household of her son Lewis, who worked as a farmer on his own account, meaning he was self-employed. In 1930, Clara Ellison resided in the household of her daughter, who also owned land. From 1870 to 1920 the census reported that she could not read and write, but by 1930 it reported she was literate. Jackson and Ellison both possessed eco-

FIGURE 4.8. Parthenia Jackson headstone, Warrior Stand Cemetery (photograph by Elvin D. Lang, 2021; courtesy of the Alabama Historical Commission)

FIGURE 4.9. Clara Ellison headstone, Creek Stand AME Zion Church Cemetery (photograph by the author, 2009)

nomic stability that could have enabled Jackson to become a midwife and Ellison to learn to read and write.[54]

Carrie Hann and Pollie Wright, born in the 1880s, benefited from material assets held by male and female kin. Hann's mother, Winny Hand (née Swanson), rented a 212-acre farm valued at $1,062 in 1880. The same year, Hann's paternal grandmother, Polly Chambliss, farmed forty acres valued at $300. The census listed no occupation for Hann in 1900, when she was fourteen years old, which contrasts with her peers in the community who worked as farm laborers.[55]

Pollie Wright's father-in-law, Dow Wright Sr., farmed forty acres in 1880. He produced goods valued at $350. Pollie's husband, Dow Wright Jr., was a tenant farmer with employees. In 1920, he rented their home and worked as a farmer on his own account.[56] Both Carrie Hann and Pollie Wright were literate, neither worked as farm laborers while in their teens, and both married into families that possessed substantial material assets relative to their neighbors. Carrie Hann married Frank Reid, the son of Harbard Reid (sometimes spelled Harbord Reid), a successful farmer, and Pollie's husband, Dow, was an employer.

FIGURE 4.10. Carrie Hann headstone, Sweet Pilgrim Baptist Church Cemetery (undated photograph by Jon Chrismond, findagrave.com)

FIGURE 4.11. Pollie Wright headstone, Antioch Missionary Baptist Church Cemetery (undated photograph by Jon Chrismond, findagrave.com)

Martha Kitchen also belonged to the group of Zephroes who were born during the 1880s. Her father, Charlie Borom, rented a forty-acre farm valued at $120 in 1880. He produced goods consumed and sold valued at $600. Her father-in-law, William Kitchen, also rented a farm in 1880. His 140-acre farm was valued at $640, and he produced goods valued at $400. By 1910 Martha and her husband, Aaron Kitchen, rented a farm. The enumerator listed no occupation in 1910 and 1920 for Martha, who by 1920 could read and write. In 1920 the couple lived in a rented home, and Aaron was farming on his own account.[57]

Familial material assets since 1880 are the common thread among these five women. Their financial situations are representative of one-third of the thirty Zephroes. Figure 4.13 provides an overall profile of Precinct Four's Zephroes based on available information. The majority were born after 1865 and before 1900 and died before 1931. Most lived in rented homes, and about one-third could read and write. One-third benefited from having relatives and/or spouses who emerged as viable farm operators by 1880. Two-thirds did not have that advantage but between 1900 and 1920, most transitioned from being farm laborers to homemakers, with their husbands working as

FIGURE 4.12. Martha Kitchen headstone, Boromville AME Zion Church Cemetery (undated photograph by Jon Chrismond, findagrave.com)

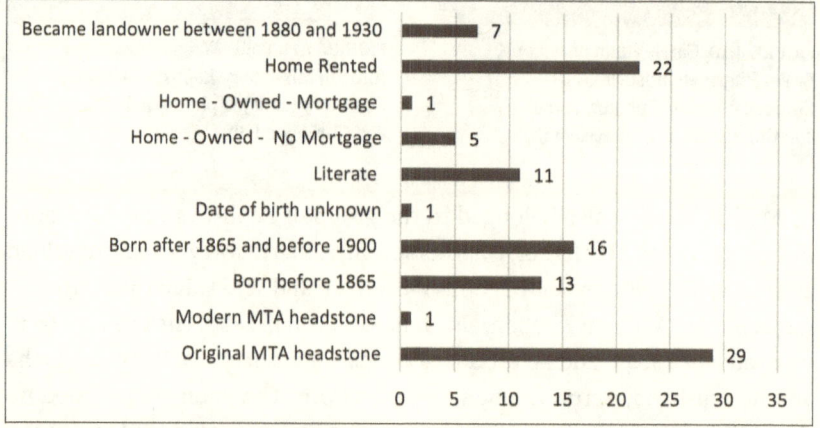

FIGURE 4.13. Profile of Precinct Four Zephroes

self-employed farmers. Other Zephroes—including some who benefited from assets held by relatives in 1880 and some who did not—were single or widowed heads of household working as self-employed farmers by 1920.

The overall profile suggests that minimal socioeconomic stratification existed among the Precinct Four Zephroes, although some had benefited from generational asset building since 1880. Yet we cannot make this conclusion with certainty, because we lack specific information about the assets each woman acquired between 1900 and 1920. A case in point involves the Sweet Pilgrim Zephroes who were related to Frank Reid and his brother

Dow, including Carrie Hann, Eliza Reid, Adeline Moore, Emmaline Moore, Frances Moore, and Nettie Moore.

Frank Reid provided specific information, in his own words, about how he became a prosperous farmer. He and his brother Dow both attended Tuskegee Institute but did not graduate. Regardless, Booker T. Washington's "urgent insistence" on Black landownership inspired Reid, his father, Harbard, and Dow.[58] Harbard Reid, who served in the United States Colored Troops Infantry during the waning years of the Civil War, prospered for nearly a quarter of a century as a renter of one thousand acres that he and his relatives jointly leased.[59] Harbard and his wife, Eliza (Zephroe Eliza Moore Reid), experienced enslavement on plantations located within Precinct Four as members of familial communities consisting of blood and allied relatives who eventually assumed the surnames Moore and Reid. Harbard Reid drew a veteran's pension to supplement his agricultural earnings.[60] In the early 1900s, he and his sons purchased 605 acres. Harbard died in 1909 and bequeathed land to Eliza and to his children.[61] Eliza began collecting a widow's pension in 1910.[62]

In 1911, the Reid brothers owned spacious homes and operated one of the largest and most successful farms in Macon County. Their enterprise included a steam gin, a grist mill, a general store, and a post office. One account credited the brothers with elevating their community, called Dawkins Crossroads, to "one of the most prosperous in the county."[63]

Frank Reid quantified his family's assets based on acreage owned, land value, and bales of cotton produced. He also reported that two maternal uncles—Turner Moore, who was married to Zephroe Nettie Moore, and Moses Moore, the spouse of Zephroe Francis Moore—became landowners during the first decade of the 1900s.[64] If firsthand information like that provided by Frank Reid existed for each of the Precinct Four women from 1900 to 1930, a clearer picture would emerge about if and how they prospered over time.

Although shared aspirations blurred and complicated class lines among this group of working-class Black Americans, we can say with certainty that the Reids fared well relative to others around them. It is plausible that the Zephroes who were related by blood or marriage to the Reids also fared well.

Women from Boromville, Creek Stand, and Warrior Stand such as Belle Lewis, Clara Ellison, Sallie Pace, and Octavia Reese eventually owned their farms and/or homes. This suggests that several Precinct Four women possessed greater financial means to join the MTA but that women with lesser means joined regardless. The sources just do not indicate the degree of economic stratification among them, nor do they reveal whether the women held life insurance policies or the less expensive burial insurance. We do know that all at least paid the fifty-cent annual tax to qualify for a headstone and that Eliza Reid also paid the MTA life insurance premium for $300 of coverage.[65]

It is clear that while women's decisions to join the MTA hinged on their financial resources, their desire to join meant more than buying insurance. It meant belonging and finding solace among like-minded women. In a word, they made it work financially, often with the help of their families and communities. Citing the influence of Booker T. Washington, Frank Reid stated, "We have encouraged the people of our community as much as possible to secure homes, buy lands, live decently, and be somebody."[66] It is unknown whether Frank Reid himself belonged to the MTA and was influenced by its tenets. He died well after the early 1930s, when the MTA closed its doors for good. Regrettably, MTA members from Precinct Four, both men and women, who died after the MTA's insolvency will remain unknown.

Conclusion

The first MTA headstone I ever laid eyes on belonged to Clara Ellison, my maternal great-grandmother. Initially, I thought she had belonged to an organization like the Order of the Eastern Star, but after several years of digging for information about her headstone and its symbols, I met Frazine Taylor, a renowned African American author, archivist, and genealogist, at a cemetery preservation workshop in Tuscaloosa on the University of Alabama campus. When I showed Frazine a photo of Clara Ellison's headstone, she knew exactly what the symbols meant, and she proceeded to tell me about the MTA and how ubiquitous the headstones are across the South. Her explanation and my subsequent research on the MTA caused me to question my own perceptions of my rural ancestors. These perceptions stemmed largely from information found or lacking in written sources instead of from an investigative process that reached beyond what Michel-Rolph Trouillot calls the "silences in our historical narrative" to explore more deeply what is visible, invisible, spoken and unspoken, symbolic, spiritual, and not fully understood.[67] Since then, I realize that in the absence of knowing my great-grandmother personally (she died twenty-five years before my birth), and not having a memoir written by her such as the one that Eva Chandler Gagnon left to her family, I can still learn about her life by asking questions about her daily challenges imposed by internal and external forces, and by interrogating her options to respond based on her material, psychological, physical, and cultural reserves.

Mosaic Templars of America headstones speak to us about the collective challenges African Americans faced due to racial oppression and about their responses to those challenges in the form of affiliating with fraternal organizations. We know that these headstones embody the visions of MTA founders Bush and Keatts who invested their respective talents and business savvy in building a benevolent Black institution to serve the needs of Black people. But the headstones also embody the visions of ordinary African Americans such as the Precinct Four women and men, who aspired to defy barriers and who worked diligently to attain their own versions of independence and freedom.

At this time in our history, when monuments across America still exist that represent the racist worldview that influenced Eva Chandler Gagnon's erroneous perceptions of African Americans, MTA headstones deserve our attention more than ever. Some still stand tall, pristine, and legible, while others sadly and to our shame are sunken, broken, or covered with grime. Regardless, all MTA headstones can unlock intricate stories about aspirational African Americans, their cemeteries, and their communities along many themes, including race, class, and gender, and within local, state, regional, and national contexts. When combined, such stories reveal more exhaustive narratives about African American lives and contributions. I believe my great-grandmother, her sister Zephroes, and her brother Templars in Precinct Four and elsewhere expressed their longing to be rediscovered in this way when they chose to be memorialized by the immortal words "I came, I saw, I conquered!"

Appendix A

Table 4.2. Land Owners and Renters: Kinfolk of Precinct Four Zephroes

	Name as It Appears on Agriculture Schedule (Alternate Spellings Shown in Parentheses)	Relationship to Precinct Four Zephroe(s)	Precinct Area and Page Number on 1880 Agricultural Schedule on Ancestry.com
1.	Abe Borom	Father of Clara Ellison	Beat 4, page 31
2.	Charlie Borom	Father of Martha Kitchen	Beat 4, page 27
3.	Polly Chambliss	Paternal grandmother of Pollie Wright	Beat 4, page 15
4.	Isom Ellison	Husband of Clara Ellison	Beat 4, page 28

Table 4.2. Land Owners and Renters: Kinfolk of Precinct Four Zephroes (*continued*)

Name as It Appears on Agriculture Schedule (Alternate Spellings Shown in Parentheses)	Relationship to Precinct Four Zephroe(s)	Precinct Area and Page Number on 1880 Agricultural Schedule on Ancestry.com
5. Henry Germany	Spouse of Adeline Germany, brother-in-law of Eliza Reid, and Emmaline Germany	Beat 4, page 11
6. Alax Harris (Alex Harris)	Spouse of Susan Harris, father of Emmeline Wright and Adeline Germany, stepfather of Eliza Reid	Township 14, page 10
7. Benson Jackson	Spouse of Parthenia Jackson	Beat 4, page 7
8. Wyatt Key	Husband of Carrie Key	Beat 4, page 30
9. William Kitchen, Sr.	Father-in-law of Martha Kitchen (married to Aaron Kitchen)	Beat 4, page 31
10. Henry Pace	Father-in-law of Sallie Pace	Beat 4, page 28
11. Moses Moore	Spouse of Frances Moore	Township 14, page 9
12. Turner Moore	Spouse of Nettie Moore, brother of Eliza Moore, half-brother of Adeline Germany and Emmaline Wright, brother-in-law of Carrie Hann	Township 14, page 10
13. Harmon Read (Harbord Reid)	Spouse of Eliza Reid, son-in-law of Susan Harris, father-in-law of Carrie Hann, brother-in-law of Adeline Germany and Emmaline Wright	Township 14, page 10
14. Preer Tolbert	Father of Effie Tolbert	Beat 4, page 27
15. Weny Swanson (Winny Swanson)	Mother of Carrie Hann, in-law of Eliza Reid	Beat 4, page 16
16. Dow Wright Sr.	Father-in-law of Pollie Wright (married to Dow Wright Jr.)	Beat 4, page 15
17. Fletcher Wright	Husband of Emmaline Wright, son-in-law of Susan Harris, brother-in-law of Eliza Reid, Adeline Germany, and Carrie Hann	Township 14, page 10

Appendix B

Source Citations for Five Zephroe Profiles

POLLY WRIGHT PROFILE

U.S. Department of the Interior, Census Bureau, Census of 1900, Warrior Stand, Macon, Alabama, Enumeration District 111, s.v. "Pollie Chambliss," Ancestry.com.

U.S. Department of the Interior, Census Bureau, Census of 1910, Precinct 4, Macon, Alabama, Enumeration District 128, s.v. "Pollie Wright," Ancestry.com.

CARRIE HANN

U.S. Department of the Interior, Census Bureau, Census of 1900, Warrior Stand, Macon, Alabama, Enumeration District 111, s.v. "Carrie Hand," Ancestry.com.

MARTHA KITCHEN

U.S. Department of the Interior, Census Bureau, Census of 1910, Precinct 4, Macon, Alabama, Enumeration District 127, s.v. "Martha Kitchen," Ancestry.com.

U.S. Department of the Interior, Census Bureau, Census of 1920, Warrior Stand, Macon, Alabama, Enumeration District 128, s.v. "Martha Kitchen," Ancestry.com.

CLARA ELLISON

U.S. Department of the Interior, Census Bureau, Census of 1870, Warrior Stand, Macon, Alabama, s.v. "Clara Ellison," Ancestry.com.

U.S. Department of the Interior, Census Bureau, Census of 1880, Warrior Stand, Macon, Alabama, Enumeration District 117, s.v. "Clara Ellison," Ancestry.com.

U.S. Department of the Interior, Census Bureau, Census of 1900, Warrior Stand, Macon, Alabama, Enumeration District 110, s.v. "Clarra Ellison," Ancestry.com.

U.S. Department of the Interior, Census Bureau, Census of 1910, Precinct 4, Macon, Alabama, Enumeration District 128, s.v. "Clara Elison," Ancestry.com.

U.S. Department of the Interior, Census Bureau, Census of 1920, Warrior Stand, Macon, Alabama, Enumeration District 129, s.v. "Clara Ellison," Ancestry.com.

U.S. Department of the Interior, Census Bureau, Census of 1930, Warrior Stand, Macon, Alabama, USA, Enumeration District 44-9, s.v. "Clara Ellison," Ancestry.com.

PARTHENIA JACKSON

U.S. Department of the Interior, Census Bureau, Census of 1880, Warrior Stand, Macon, Alabama, Enumeration District 117, s.v. "Pat Jackson," Ancestry.com.

U.S. Department of the Interior, Census Bureau, Census of 1900, Warrior Stand, Macon, Alabama, Enumeration District 111, s.v. "Parthinia Jackson," Ancestry.com.

Notes

1. The Creek Nation is a Muskogean-speaking society of indigenous North American peoples who by the eighteenth century inhabited an expansive territory that stretched from present-day Georgia to present-day Alabama.
2. Washington, *Up from Slavery*, 53.
3. Washington, "Rural Negro Community."
4. The Creek Stand AME Zion Church Cemetery is on the Alabama Historic Cemetery Register and the National Register of Historic Places; the Shiloh Baptist Church Cemetery is on the Alabama Register of Landmarks and Heritage and the National Register of Historic Places; and the Sweet Pilgrim Baptist Church Cemetery and the Warrior Stand Cemetery are on the Alabama Historic Cemetery Register. Alabama Historical Commission, "Alabama Register of Landmarks and Heritage"; Alabama Historical Commission, "Alabama Historic Cemetery Register"; National Park Service, National Register of Historic Places.
5. Bush and Dorman, *History of the Mosaic Templars of America*, 41.
6. Ibid., 161.
7. Williams, *Silent for a While, but Not Idle*, 9.
8. Cox, *Dreaming of Dixie*, 2, 7, 15, 25, 36.
9. Hope, "For the Memorable Fight," 7–9.
10. Shaw, "Negro Progress on the Tuskegee Plan"; Mayberry, *Role of Tuskegee University*, xiv.
11. Bush and Dorman, *History of the Mosaic Templars of America*, 61.
12. Ibid., xxiv, 35, 46, 65. See also "Mosaic Templars Meet in Tuskegee," *Montgomery Advertiser* (Alabama), July 22, 1914; "Mosaic Temples," *Mobile Weekly Press* (Alabama), August 1, 1914.
13. Washington, "Rural Negro Community," 86. Washington credited the *Messenger*, a newspaper created especially for farmers, preachers, and teachers, for "pushing forward the movement."
14. "Dr. Washington and Party Take Southern Trip into Macon County," *Messenger* (Tuskegee, Ala.), June 17, 1910; "Tuskegee Teachers Visit Macon Farms," *Montgomery Advertiser*, April 4, 1911.
15. Mayberry, *Role of Tuskegee University*, 53, 63, 65, 73; "Minister's Institute," *Messenger*, May 1, 1908; "Macon County Fair a Great Success," *Messenger*, November 13, 1908; "Colored Teachers' Institute, Macon County," *Messenger*, July 24, 1908. See also Landrum, "Educating Macon County's Children." The essay is based on oral histories provided by Ella Ellison Davis, Lula Ellison Drane, Willie Mae Ellison Brown, Georgia Carter Echols, and Narcissis Pace James. The essay describes attendance at one- and two-room schools in Macon County during the 1920s, 1930s, and 1940s. Regarding attendance at Tuskegee Institute's commencement ceremonies, the essay explains, "The highlight occurred at the close of the academic year when students attended Commencement Day at Tuskegee Institute (now Tuskegee University). Adults and school children arrived by car, truck, and bus from all over Macon County to participate."

16. Hope, *For the Memorable Fight*, 5.

17. Bush and Dorman, *History of the Mosaic Templars of America*, 176–80.

18. MTA membership campaign advertisement, *Freeman* (Indianapolis), January 29, 1910.

19. Examples are Fred Lloyd, Creek Stand Cemetery, Tatum Home Chamber, and Joe Moore, Isaac Echols, and Jim Reed, all Sweet Pilgrim Cemetery, all Moores Choice Chamber.

20. Bush and Dorman, *History of the Mosaic Templars of America*, xix; MTA membership campaign advertisement, *Freeman* (Indianapolis), September 6, 1913.

21. Bush and Dorman, *History of the Mosaic Templars of America*, 135–36.

22. Gagnon, *Home Place*, 3, 10.

23. Ibid., 14.

24. Ellison, *Shadow and Act*, 116.

25. Genovese, *Roll Jordan Roll*, 235. Also see 280–84.

26. Edwards, "Politics of Marriage and Households in North Carolina during Reconstruction," 7–10.

27. Cornerstones on the Cooper Chapel, Sweet Pilgrim, and Antioch churches; historic marker at Creek Stand AME Zion Church; "Negroes of Rural Districts of Alabama Building School Houses," *Montgomery Times*, May 26, 1913.

28. Gagnon, *Home Place*, 22; Macon County Record Book 4, 169–70 (J. E. Ellison to Steve Pace et al., October 6, 1894) and 171–72 (J. E. Ellison to Steve Pace et al., March 3, 1893), Macon County Courthouse, Tuskegee, Alabama.

29. Gagnon, *Home Place*, 22.

30. Ibid., 11.

31. White, *Ar'n't I a Woman?*, 87–89.

32. Ibid., 89.

33. Ibid.

34. Gagnon, *Home Place*, 11.

35. McIlwain, *Death in Black and White*, 84–86.

36. Ibid., 88–91; Stanley, "Disappearance of a Distinctively Black Way to Mourn."

37. McIlwain, *Death in Black and White*, 82–83.

38. Gagnon, *Home Place*, 11.

39. Blassingame, *Slave Community*, 21.

40. McIlwain, *Death in Black and White*, 39.

41. Gagnon, *Home Place*, 11.

42. Ibid., 11–12.

43. Bush and Dorman, *History of the Mosaic Templars of America*, xviii, 169–71; "Research MTC Members/Gravestones," Arkansas Heritage, https://www.arkansasheritage.com/mosaic-templars-cultural-center/collections-research/research-mtc-members-gravestones.

44. MTA membership campaign advertisement, *Freeman* (Indianapolis), January 29, 1910; Jones, "Mosaic Templars of America."

45. Macon County Deed Record Book 11, 169; Barnard and Jones, Farm Real Estate Values in the United States by Counties, 6; editor's columns, *Messenger*, April 17, 1908, and May 1, 1908. In the April 17 column, the editor reported that families in "public school communities" joined together to grow, cultivate, and sell cotton produced on two to three acres to generate funds to improve schoolhouses or lengthen the school term. He stated that ministers and teachers cooperated to hold rallies in the churches to raise money for schools and "to increase the interest of the parents in their children." After a tornado ripped through several south Macon County communities in the spring of 1908, the editor

reported that "quite a number of the people have given to the suffering, money, bed clothing, and food" and that neighbors held a mass meeting in the Tuskegee courthouse to organize a sustained relief effort.

46. *Ritual No. 1, Ladies' Chamber, Mosaic Templars of America*, 13–16, 19–22.
47. See Appendix B.
48. MTA membership campaign advertisement, *Freeman* (Indianapolis), January 29, 1910.
49. MTA membership campaign advertisement, *Freeman* (Indianapolis), September 6, 1913.
50. Bush and Dorman, *History of the Mosaic Templars of America*, 141–42.
51. See Appendix A Table 4.5: Land Renters and Kinfolk of Precinct Four Zephroes.
52. See Appendix B.
53. Ibid.
54. Ibid.
55. Ibid.
56. Ibid.
57. Ibid.
58. Reid, "Story of a Farmer." Based on dates provided in Reid's essay, it is likely he wrote it between 1903 and 1906.
59. Ibid. See also "Reid, Harbord Pension File." Reid pension file courtesy of Johanna Robinson.
60. Reid, "Story of a Farmer"; "Reid, Harbord Pension File." Harbord Reid's file consolidates documentation related to his pension application and that of his widow, Eliza. The file provides the names of their enslavers and genealogical information about his siblings and her mother and siblings. The file also provides the names of their children.
61. "Harbard Reid," Alabama, U.S., Wills and Probate Records, 1753–1999,.
62. "Reid, Harbord Pension File."
63. Reid, "Story of a Farmer."
64. Ibid.
65. Fannie Reid Johnston deposition, "Reid, Harbord Pension File."
66. Reid, "Story of a Farmer."
67. Trouillot, *Silencing the Past*, 24–26.

Bibliography

Primary Sources

ARCHIVAL SOURCES

Macon County, Alabama, Deed Record Book 4, 1894–1897, Macon County Courthouse, Probate Records Office.

Macon County, Alabama, Deed Record Book 11, Macon County Courthouse, Probate Records Office.

"Reid, Harbord Pension File #1247.500:930.135, Federal Military Pension Application—Civil War and Later." U.S. National Archives and Records Administration, Washington, D.C.

PUBLISHED PRIMARY SOURCES

Bush, A. E., and P. L. Dorman. *History of the Mosaic Templars of America: Its Founders and Officials*. Fayetteville: University of Arkansas Press, 2008.

Ritual No. 1, Ladies' Chamber, Mosaic Templars of America. Little Rock: Arkansas State Archives, 1904.

Washington, Booker T. *Up from Slavery*. New York: Dover Publications, 1995.

JOURNAL ARTICLES

Shaw, Albert. "Negro Progress on the Tuskegee Plan." *Review of Reviews, American Edition* 9, no. 4 (April 1894):436–43.

Washington, Booker T. "The Rural Negro Community." *Annals of the American Academy of Political and Social Science* 40 (March 1912): 81–89. http://www.jstor.com/stable/1012798.

NEWSPAPERS AND PERIODICALS

Freeman (Indianapolis)
Messenger (Tuskegee, Alabama)
Mobile Weekly Press (Alabama)

Montgomery Advertiser (Alabama)
Montgomery Times (Alabama)

WEBSITES

Alabama, U.S., Wills and Probate Records, 1753–1999. Ancestry.com.

Reid, Frank. "The Story of a Farmer." The Literature Network. Accessed December 4, 2021. http://www.online-literature.com/booker-washington/tuskegee-and-its-people/10/.

Secondary Sources

Alabama Historical Commission. "Alabama Historic Cemetery Register." As of December 9, 2021. https://ahc.alabama.gov/cemeteryprogramPDFs/2021_12_14_Alabama_Historic_Cemetery_Register.pdf.

———. "Alabama Register of Landmarks and Heritage." As of December 13, 2021. https://ahc.alabama.gov/AlabamaRegisterPDFs/2021-12_Alabama_Register_of_Landmarks_Heritage_Property_Listing.pdf.

Barnard, Charles, and John Jones. *Farm Real Estate Values in the United States by Counties, 1850–1982*. Statistical Bulletin 751. Washington, D.C.: U.S. Department of Agriculture, Economic Research Service, 1987. https://www.card.iastate.edu/farmland/history/barnard-and-jones-1987-farm-real-estate-values-in-the-united-states-by-counties-1850-1982.pdf.

Blassingame, John W. *The Slave Community: Plantation Life in the Antebellum South*. New York: Oxford University Press, 1979.

Cox, Karen. *Dreaming of Dixie: How the South was Created in American Popular Culture*. Chapel Hill: University of North Carolina Press, 2011.

Edwards, Laura F. "The Politics of Marriage and Households in North Carolina during Reconstruction." In *Jumpin Jim Crow: Southern Politics from Civil War to Civil Rights*, edited by Jane Dailey, Glenda Elizabeth Gilmore, and Bryant Simon, 7-27. Princeton, NJ: Princeton University Press, 2000.

Ellison, Ralph. *Shadow and Act*. New York: Vintage Books, 1964.

Gagnon, Eva Chandler. *Home Place*. Hurtsboro, Ala.: Eva Chandler Gagnon, 1964.

Genovese, Eugene D. *Roll Jordan Roll: The World the Slaves Made*. New York: Vintage Books, 1976.

Hope, Holly. *For the Memorable Fight: Mosaic Templars of America Headquarters Building*. Little Rock: Arkansas Historic Preservation Program, 2004. https://www.arkansasheritage

.com/arkansas-preservation/programs/publications/docs/default-source/ahpp-documents/local-historic-contexts/mosaic_templars_new.

Jones, Tina Cahalan. "Mosaic Templars of America—Reddick Temple #1232, Franklin, Tenn." *From Slaves to Soldiers and Beyond—Williamson County, Tennessee's African American History* (blog), February 26, 2018. http://usctwillcotn.blogspot.com/2018/02/mosaic-templars-of-american-reddick.html.

Landrum, Ardis. "Educating Macon County's Children." In *Alabama African American Heritage*, vol. 1, edited by Black Belt African American Genealogical and Historical Society, 43–44. Selma, Ala.: Black Belt African American Genealogical and Historical Society, 2015.

Mayberry, B. D. *The Role of Tuskegee University in the Origin, Growth and Development of the Negro Cooperative Extension System 1881–1900*. Tuskegee, Ala.: Tuskegee University, 1989.

McIlwain, Charlton D. *Death in Black and White: Death, Ritual and Family Ecology*. Cresskill, N.J.: Hampton Press, 2003.

National Park Service. National Register of Historic Places (database). https://www.nps.gov/subjects/nationalregister/database-research.htm.

Stanley, Tiffany. "The Disappearance of a Distinctively Black Way to Mourn." Atlantic, Jan. 26, 2016. https://www.theatlantic.com/business/archive/2016/01/Black-funeral-homes-mourning/426807/.

Trouillot, Michel-Rolph. *Silencing the Past: Power and the Production of History*. Boston: Beacon Press, 1995.

White, Deborah Gray. *Ar'n't I a Woman? Female Slaves in the Plantation South*. New York: Norton, 1999.

Williams, Shari L. *Silent for a While, but Not Idle: African American Self-Determination Ignites Educational Opportunity in South Macon County, Alabama 1906–1967*. Columbus, Ga.: self-published, 2017.

EPILOGUE

TEACHING THE AMERICAN SOUTH BY LEARNING THE DEAD

This activity calls for students to locate a historic African American cemetery that contains Mosaic Templars of America (MTA) headstones. The goals are that (1) students will learn as much as possible about the deceased members of the MTA and about the community and people who are historically connected to the cemetery and (2) students will develop a political, economic, and social demographic profile for the deceased MTA members buried in the cemetery that will describe the community and people that existed when the MTA members were alive.

Suggested resources include local histories (possibly housed in the public library and in church and college/university archives), findagrave.com, familysearch.org, and Google. Familysearch.org offers free access to U.S. federal census records, vital records, and a multitude of state and local historic records.

Students should pay close attention to census population schedules, agricultural schedules (if researching a rural cemetery), and information in records that provide clues about the economic status of each person studied. There may be an online obituary or historical narrative for one or more of the deceased. Students can visit the selected cemetery in person to identify these graves and take photos of headstones. On an in-person visit, students should take note of the positioning of MTA headstones. For example, are MTA headstones grouped together or are they spread out randomly? What clues, if any, about the person are offered based on the positioning of the headstone? For example, in a grouping of headstones, is there a surname that is common?

If students are unable to visit a cemetery in person, they should find out the names of historic Black churches in the area and look them up on findagrave.com to determine if they have adjacent cemeteries. If a church has an adjacent cemetery, the student should scroll through the photos of the graves to identify MTA headstones. This method will work best for comparison purposes when students locate a cemetery that contains at least ten MTA headstones.

Students should aim to answer the following questions:

- What is the name and age of the cemetery? Is the cemetery affiliated with a church?
- Which burials are marked with an MTA headstone? What are the names of the persons buried? What is the earliest burial? What is the latest burial?
- What is the date of birth and date of death of the person buried?
- What is the name, number, and location of the person's MTA chamber?
- Are there more women or more men with MTA headstones? What are the kinship connections between deceased persons?
- What is the name of the church that is affiliated with the cemetery? When was the church established? Did any of the persons buried participate in the church? If so, how?
- How would you describe the person's economic status based on education level, occupation, and home ownership?
- How did the deceased persons in your cemetery learn about the MTA?
- What struggles challenged African Americans who resided in the community?
- Based on your findings, what are your conclusions about the ways that race, class, and gender affected the deceased persons you are studying in terms of everyday life and their decisions to join the MTA? Be sure to discuss the role of racial conflict in your interpretation.

CHAPTER 5

Jim Crowing the Dead
*A Fight for African American Burial Rights and
Dismantling Racial Burial Covenants*

KAMI FLETCHER

"We can't sell you a plot.... This is a whites-only cemetery. There are no coloreds here," Karla Semien was told, when her husband, Darrell, died at the age of fifty-five. Stunned and unsettled when the employee at Oaklin Springs Baptist Cemetery in Oberlin, Louisiana, refused to sell her a burial plot near her husband's home, his final wish, she and her family knew that they had to go public with the racism they experienced. In a Facebook post describing the encounter, Karla said that the cemetery employee "even had paperwork on a clipboard showing me that only white human beings can be buried here." With nearly three hundred comments and one thousand shares, within hours of her post, media outlets had begun carrying the story, and it made national headlines. The idea of a racially segregated cemetery in Louisiana, the deep South, is likely not surprising. But that this act of blatant racism took place in January 2021 is surprising. The cemetery board president, H. Creig Vizena, fired the worker who refused to sell the burial plot (his eighty-something-year-old aunt) and quickly took steps to change cemetery bylaws to prohibit discrimination by race. He also charged every American cemetery, not just in the South, to examine their bylaws for segregationist language and to promptly remove all racial restrictions, saying, "It's mind-boggling that this still exists."[1] Vizena did not say it's mind-boggling that such racial discrimination *ever* existed—only that it *still* exists. This choice in wording, purposeful or not, coupled with his mentioning the old age of the employee, takes us back to the time of Jim Crow segregation—a nearly eighty-year period in American history that began in 1896, when the U.S. Supreme Court upheld Black-white segregation in all public spaces, including cemeteries. This chapter examines the shift caused by the separate-but-equal Supreme Court ruling that legalized segregated burial, identified here as Jim Crowing the dead, by following newspaper headlines from throughout the entire United States, including in such northern states as Iowa, Illinois, New Jersey, and Ohio, from early segregated cemeteries—those at the turn of the twentieth century—to segregated burials that continued well after the 1964 Civil Rights Act. In the process of tracing this history in headlines, the chapter foregrounds the legal efforts of African Americans to fight against Jim Crowing the dead.

Jim Crowing the dead involved installing and enforcing racial borders around the place Americans most associate with freedom—the cemetery. The cemetery is commonly thought of as the great equalizer, because decedents cannot take riches or any social privileges with them into the afterlife, thus dissolving all divisions and hierarchal rankings, including race. Yet a disconnect existed between the nationally shared idea of equality in death and Jim Crow segregation of the twentieth century. After the 1896 "separate but equal" Supreme Court ruling in *Plessy v. Ferguson*, southern states passed legislation barring African Americans from burial in public cemeteries and used southern customs and norms to relegate these deceased women, men, and children to less desirable segregated sections.[2]

Jim Crowing the dead infused white southern culture into burial grounds and created whites-only racial covenants and "negro" sections. Jim Crow cemeteries, as newspapers called them, segregated whites and African Americans so that, in the words of a Louisiana Episcopalian bishop, "corpses went separate but equal ways to more suitable abodes and bones rose again, but apart."[3] Much more than enforcing literal separation at burial and, according to the bishop, segregation during the afterlife, Jim Crow cemeteries upheld and memorialized white supremacy by serving as the ultimate mainstay of southern tradition. Jim Crow cemeteries, then, functioned as sites of memory for the white community that ignored African American involvement in southern history and leadership in civic engagement, all while inciting white resistance to Black memorialization. For example, in 1906, in an attempt to strip James D. Lynch, the first African American secretary of state of Mississippi, of his title and historic accomplishments, the state's governor, James Vardaman, tried to pass a bill to disinter Lynch from the all-white Greenwood Cemetery.[4] It did not pass, in part because Lynch's family paid for and owned the burial plot, but throughout the twentieth century the issue of burial plot ownership became a point of legal contention as African Americans fought to obtain burial rights. Ultimately, whites constructed Jim Crow cemeteries to subjugate African Americans as they had in life, ex-

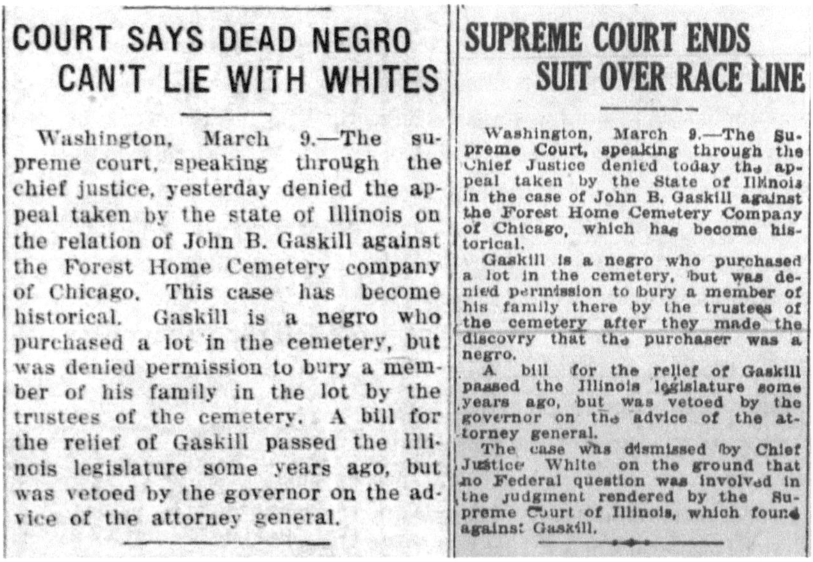

COURT SAYS DEAD NEGRO CAN'T LIE WITH WHITES

Washington, March 9.—The supreme court, speaking through the chief justice, yesterday denied the appeal taken by the state of Illinois on the relation of John B. Gaskill against the Forest Home Cemetery company of Chicago. This case has become historical. Gaskill is a negro who purchased a lot in the cemetery, but was denied permission to bury a member of his family in the lot by the trustees of the cemetery. A bill for the relief of Gaskill passed the Illinois legislature some years ago, but was vetoed by the governor on the advice of the attorney general.

SUPREME COURT ENDS SUIT OVER RACE LINE

Washington, March 9.—The Supreme Court, speaking through the Chief Justice denied today the appeal taken by the State of Illinois in the case of John B. Gaskill against the Forest Home Cemetery Company of Chicago, which has become historical.

Gaskill is a negro who purchased a lot in the cemetery, but was denied permission to bury a member of his family there by the trustees of the cemetery after they made the discovery that the purchaser was a negro.

A bill for the relief of Gaskill passed the Illinois legislature some years ago, but was vetoed by the governor on the advice of the attorney general.

The case was dismissed by Chief Justice White on the ground that no Federal question was involved in the judgment rendered by the Supreme Court of Illinois, which found against Gaskill.

FIGURE 5.1. On March 8, 1915, the United States Supreme Court sided with the Forest Home Cemetery Company's decision not to sell a burial plot to African American John B. Gaskill for his deceased wife, Pinkie. Because Forest Home was a private, rather than a public, entity, the court ruled that its policy of being "maintained for the interment of the remains of persons of the white race only" did not violate Gaskill's constitutional rights. *Left, Dispatch* (Moline, Illinois), March 9, 1915; *right, Evening News* (Wilkes-Barre, Pa.), March 9, 1915.

tending their white supremacy into the grave. Asserting burial rights that helped establish protections from Jim Crow cemeteries, African Americans responded with legal action and challenged postmortem white hostilities.

Using the Fourteenth Amendment's guarantee of citizenship rights, African Americans challenged the rigidity of Jim Crow by demanding the right to purchase burial lots. In 1913, Georgia-born John Barney Gaskill sued Forest Home Cemetery for denying him "right of burial," which he stated "was an infringement of the rights of the relator [John B. Gaskill] under the constitutions of this state and the United States."[5] Gaskill was denied the right to purchase a fifth burial plot in the Cook County, Illinois, cemetery for his deceased wife, Pinkie (Webb) Gaskill, who had died March 16, 1912.[6] Four Gaskill children had already been buried at Forest Home Cemetery, the last one in 1896, the year the Supreme Court ruled racially segregated accommodations legal. Gaskill was completely shocked when he was informed that as of December 31, 1907, Forest Home Cemetery "would be maintained for the interment of the remains of persons of the white race only."[7] Ultimately, on March 8, 1915 (nearly three years after Pinkie's death), the U.S. Supreme Court upheld the Illinois Supreme Court ruling stating that "Forest Home Cemetery did not infringe any right of the relator [John B. Gaskill] under the Constitution of this state, and he has no right respecting such burial under the fourteenth amendment to the Federal Constitution, which only applies to acts of the state."[8] The nation's highest court thus decreed that burial rights and citizenship rights were incongruent and that African Americans could not look to the judicial system to legally enforce rights not first granted to them. Even though the Fourteenth Amendment prohibited discrimination in public accommodations, it made no special provisions for cemeteries, which can be publicly or privately operated. To this point, Forest Home Cemetery was a private corporation, which, the court further stated, gave it the right to sell or deny burial plots to anyone based on its business interests. As attorney Kitty Rogers writes in an article titled "Integrating the City of the Dead," "The passage of public accommodation laws across the country between 1913 and 1955 to protect minorities did not necessarily compel courts to interpret those statutes as covering cemeteries and burial plot purchases by minorities or for minority use."[9]

John Gaskill represented southern African Americans who left the Jim Crow South during the Great Migration seeking freedom and autonomy, only to find themselves fighting fiercely for freedom not only in life but in death. Both Pinkie and John were raised in Georgia during its slaveholding era but both could read and write and had aspirations of moving north to better themselves. By 1900, the couple had been married for twenty-one years, and seven of their ten children were still living. John had left his job in an Atlanta cracker factory and become gainfully employed as a station engineer in Chicago. The Gaskills owned a house on Claremont Avenue in the Forest Glen neighborhood on Chicago's famous South Side. Their twenty-one-year-old daughter, Marjory, was a high school graduate and self-employed music teacher.[10] Their move to Chicago had allowed them to fulfill two dreams that would have been virtually impossible had they remained in the South: owning a home and providing their children with educational opportunities. Yet, while Illinois had passed the racially representative and progressive Civil Rights Act of 1885, when it came to cemeteries and burial the state was closer to Georgia in law and custom. In the words of scholar Helen Sclair, "The problems of Jim Crow had crept northward into Chicago."[11] As Forest Home Cemetery Corporation explained in a letter to John Gaskill, burial rights at the cemetery were privileges extended only to whites—not because of "personal prejudice nor ill will toward colored people, but [because] there had been so much trouble and objection that it was for the best interest of the cemetery to exclude them."[12] More specifically, the letter stated the real reason for barring Black people was the fear of white violence in the form of rioting and destroying cemetery property, as well as the possibility that whites would respond to integration by disinterring their loved ones, which would result in the cemetery's bankruptcy. Because of white interest and white comfort, the Gaskill family was unfairly separated in death, breaking the familial chain visible by headstones.

In addition to pressing for citizenship rights guaranteed under the Fourteenth Amendment, African Americans used different levels of government to demand ownership rights to the burial lots they had purchased. In 1909, when the sexton at Glendale Cemetery in De Moines, Iowa, attempted to bury B. Hicklin, the wife of J. Hicklin, in the cemetery's "colored range," surviving relatives complained to city commissioner Wesley Ash. A self-proclaimed "good friend of the colored people," Ash then contacted J. Gadd, the cemetery's very angry superintendent, and insisted that since the Hicklins had purchased a burial plot, they had the right to bury their loved one anywhere in the city-owned cemetery.[13] African American leaders in Des Moines saw Ash's decision as about more than burial rights; it represented "a distinct victory" over Jim Crow, because "there has long been a well-defined but secretly maintained 'color line' in the management in some Des Moines cemeteries."[14]

For this very reason, various NAACP chapters became involved in burial rights discrimination cases. For example, in 1949 Orville Edder, an attorney representing the NAACP, was called to Klamath Falls, Oregon, to protest what the organization termed "segregation in the cemetery," which violated the "equal rights and protection" guaranteed by the U.S constitution. Deceased veteran Pete Williams, twenty-seven years old at the time of his death, was barred from burial in the brand-new, city-owned Memorial Park Cemetery because of a racial covenant restricting burial to "human dead of the white race as defined by decisions of the United States Supreme Court and none other."[15] When his family and the NAACP pushed back, city officials granted burial but relegated Williams to one of the seventy-two lots designated for non-Caucasians. The NAACP continued to protest, but ultimately Williams was Jim Crowed to the city-owned, all-Black Linkville Cemetery.

In September 1962, the Ohio Civil Rights Commission received a complaint from Ann Smith that "Rose Hill Burial Park was violating the Public Accommodations Law by refusing to sell her a lot for burial of her grandmother Mrs. Annie Wasler."[16] After six months of proceedings, the commission determined that although it had been operating under a "whites-only" rule for forty years, the city-owned Rose Hill Burial Park was in violation of Ohio's public accommodation law.[17]

After *Plessy v. Ferguson*, African Americans had to wage a legal battle for burial rights across the country, but especially in the Jim Crow South, primarily for three key reasons. First, cemeteries were not included in the public accommodations category recognized by state law. During the first half of the twentieth century, cemeteries—other than potter's fields or municipal burial grounds—were started by individuals or corporations and could claim private interests. Cemeteries were not listed in most southern states' public accommodations statutes—an omission interpreted by U.S. court systems as a *purposeful intent* to *exclude them from such laws*.[18] Therefore, some African Americans concluded that the only way to receive burial rights was to establish and buy lots in autonomous burial grounds owned and operated by Black people themselves. Second, purchasing a burial plot was simultaneously viewed as purchasing real estate, where lot owners were guaranteed "a right to control burial."[19] Lot owners also had a "right to realty," which meant the burial plot was viewed as land owned that could be resold or passed on to heirs without the permission of the cemetery owner.[20] Third, cemeteries could legally include racial covenants granting burial rights and privileges to whites while denying them to African Americans. These racial covenants were conveniently embedded in the cemetery regulations that were allegedly needed to keep burial grounds tranquil and safe. If white lot owners might become angry and even pose the threat of violence at the prospect of integration, as was the case at Forest Home Cemetery when John Gaskill tried to bury his wife, then the racist logic supported enforcing racial covenants to keep the peace.

Jim Crow cemeteries of the South were so common that Hubert Humphrey, while running for president in 1952, asserted, "Every southern white supremacist uses the word 'traditions' when he means Jim-Crow cemeteries."[21] The acknowledgment was that Black-white segregation was so bound up in southern culture that whites saw it as part and parcel of their heritage and to challenge or even think of abolishing Jim Crow cemeteries was to destroy their very way of life—and death. In the post–civil rights era, whites held to racial borders around cemeteries, yet African Americans continued to fight in the courts at every level. As the civil rights movement gained momentum in the 1960s, African Americans successfully challenged more and more racial covenant clauses that enshrined white privilege and racial discrimination under the guise of private property ownership.[22] For example, in Lincoln, Nebraska, section 29—labeled the "negroes" section—in the city-owned Wyuka Cemetery was abolished in 1960.[23] On May 3 of that same year, the city-owned Riverview Cemetery in Richmond, Virginia, racially integrated. African Americans also used newly created civil rights organizations to continue the struggle for burial rights. In July 1967, Bernard Hawkins involved the West Virginia Human Rights Commission after he was denied purchase of a burial plot in Sunset Memorial Cemetery because he was deemed to have "a perceptible strain of Negro blood." The Charleston cemetery finally sold Hawkins a plot after a court ruled in July 1968 that "privately-owned public cemeteries must not discriminate against Negroes in the selling of burial plots."[24]

As late as 1987, in some parts of the South, cities still owned and operated Jim Crow cemeteries—such as the whites-only Deerfield Beach Memorial Cemetery and the all-Black Pineview Cemetery in Florida. The two cemeteries made headlines after the 1985 death of Mayo Howard, a police lieutenant who had served on Deerfield Beach's force for twenty-eight years. Because he had been a police officer, the city was financially responsible for his burial. His widow, Evelyn Howard, chose Deerfield Beach Memorial Cemetery as his final resting place and included the name of the cemetery in the funeral program. However, the 1933 cemetery deed included a racial covenant for the "Caucasian race." When mourners arrived at the cemetery, a city employee turned them away and directed them to all-Black Pine View, where a plot had already been selected. After the funeral, Evelyn Howard spent months asking city officials to disinter her husband's body and move it to Deerfield Beach Memorial Cemetery, but after seeing no action she sued the city. Ultimately, the dispute was settled out of court, and the city paid to move Mayo's remains. Evelyn was issued a handwritten apology and $5,000 in damages. "The city should have known that the segregation was occurring [and ensured that] the practice be halted," said Evelyn's attorney.[25] Victorious in court, the attorney scolded city officials as well as cemetery employees by highlighting their awareness of discriminatory practices and that they let these practices persist, in the case of not just Mayo Howard but presumably countless others. Yet the attorney's statement also demonstrates the progress that African Americans had made in the arena of burial rights. In the post–civil rights era, racial segregation is no longer a legally accepted death norm.

The Case of Pondexteur Williams and the Fight for African American Burial Rights

The best-known case of Jim Crowing the dead in the post–civil rights era was that of Pondexteur Williams, who was serving in the U.S. Army at the rank of specialist fourth class when he was killed in the Vietnam War in August 1970. Williams's mother, Mary Campbell, planned to lay her son to rest

FIGURE 5.2. After Army specialist fourth class Pondexteur Williams was killed in the Vietnam War in 1970, his mother, Mary Campbell, successfully sued for the right to bury him in a previously designated whites-only cemetery. *Florida Today* (Melbourne), August 24, 1970.

in Hillcrest Memorial Gardens in Fort Pierce, Florida. But James Livesay, the cemetery manager, refused to allow the burial due to a racial restriction in the cemetery's deed that read, "No bodies except those of persons of the white or Caucasian race may be interred in said lots." When Campbell sued, the case was covered by nearly every newspaper in the country (see figure 5.2), as well as some international press, and even inspired a movie, *Resting Place* (1986). Williams, who turned twenty years old two weeks prior to his death, captured Americans' attention because the burial rights of the soldier, regardless of race, were seen as synonymous with American citizenship rights, even when whites insisted on segregation. In other words, African American soldiers who die for their country should have the right to be buried anywhere in it. Williams's mother and some members of the press linked burial rights with American citizenship rights, making Williams's case a social justice issue that led some to see the absurdity of Jim Crowing the dead. Some whites even publicly expressed shame and guilt for the actions of Livesay, the cemetery manager, but some still cheered on his southern pride. In the immediate post–civil rights era, the fight and resistance to integrating Hillcrest Memorial Gardens became just as important to Black burial rights as it did to uprooting southern cultural death norms.

Jim Crow Cemeteries allowed whites to control Blacks in death as they had in life, but owning a burial plot, which equaled private property, granted African Americans freedom from this control. Livesay knew that cemetery deed contracts were legally binding, and as the manager of Hillcrest Memorial Gardens, he believed he had a responsibility to uphold the rights of the burial lot owner. In his defense of the white lot owners who had purchased property with the expectation that their property and the cemetery would remain accessible only to whites, Livesay said he would protect *any* lot owner, regardless of race. "When her son is buried in Hillcrest," Livesay explained, referring to Mary Campbell and Pondexteur, "I will protect his rights as fervently as I now protect the rights of others."[26] Livesay did not see himself as defending the invisible racial border that segregated the cemetery. Rather, he refused to impede a property owner's right guaranteed in a legally binding agreement. He was quoted many times in newspapers saying that he would bury Williams as soon as he received a court order. For white men such as Livesay who were involved with death work during the post–civil rights era, the rights of *property* ownership dissolved racial boundaries that had previously segregated cemeteries.

In addition, the rights of the African American soldier to his burial plot were interpreted as congruent with American citizenship rights. When deciding in favor of Mary Campbell, Judge William O. Mehrtens of the U.S.

District Court for the Southern District of Florida made it very clear that he believed African Americans deserved and should assert the right to be buried anywhere in a country for which they had died. On August 27, 1970, after deliberating for one short hour in his private chambers with only the lawyers present, Judge Mehrtens ordered the cemetery "to desist from withholding the right of an American citizen to be buried with the same dignity with which he died in the defense of a country not only dedicated to democracy, for itself, but to all others who desire it."[27] The judge did not view the case as being simply about race; indeed, he did not refer to Williams as "Black." Instead, he spoke of Williams as an American hero, who deserved nothing less than a hero's burial.[28]

Some white burial lot holders at Hillcrest Memorial Gardens agreed with the judge. One white lot holder who had recently buried a son who had also died in the Vietnam War told the *Arizona Star*, "They died in the same place and they have a right to be buried in the same place." Another lot holder claimed to have no prior knowledge of the cemetery's racial covenant but nevertheless believed it was her patriotic duty to allow Williams's burial at Hillcrest; "after all," she said, "the boy died fighting for all of us."[29] Both of these white lot owners, like the judge, saw Williams's military service as erasing color distinctions in his burial. In their eyes, Williams did not just legally deserve equal burial rights; he had earned them with his honorable death.

African Americans positioned their rights to burial as social justice issues within the broader pursuit of racial equality—which is why Mary Campbell was prepared to leave her son's body at Lee-Peek Funeral Home (now Sarah's Memorial Chapel), the Black funeral home in the area, "forever if necessary" as she waited for Hillcrest to integrate. She was channeling her grief and mourning into a powerful source of social justice activism. She also debunked white fears about integrated cemeteries by pointing out that her son was not a threat to anyone, noting, "There's nothing he can do to them dead."[30] Williams had arguably ceased to be Black; death had nullified his racialized existence. Under the headline "He Gave His Life—and Then His Death," an August 24, 1970, article in the *New York Daily News* shows that the fight for social justice, the fight against racism, was still fought from the grave. Williams sacrificed his life fighting in Vietnam for freedom and then sacrificed a peaceful death by being buried in an all-white cemetery, away from family and kin, to break the color barrier. Campbell told the newspaper that if her son could not come back and be buried wherever he wanted, then he had died for nothing. He died serving all Americans, including white Americans, and now he couldn't be buried with them. This injustice was further highlighted at his funeral—which occurred while Hillcrest Memorial Gardens still refused to bury his body—when speakers bluntly noted that a burial would not take place after the service and pointed out that the soldier had returned to his country but not to an eternal home.[31]

Newspapers reported on the stark irony that Williams died for a country that refused him a dignified burial. Connecticut's *Hartford Courant* noted, "He didn't die in Vietnam fighting for Blacks only."[32] A white woman who attended the funeral expressed sadness and disbelief: "It's so sad. . . . My son is in a cemetery now [and] I don't know who's next to him, and I don't give a damn."[33] To many, it seemed astonishing that Jim Crow cemeteries still existed four decades after a number of newspapers called for them to be integrated before the 1933 Chicago World's Fair.[34]

White adults and even children wrote to Livesay expressing their disapproval of the cemetery manager's actions and unyielding support for Williams and his. In one newspaper, Fort Pierce mayor Dennis Summerlin described Livesay's actions as "embarrassing to Fort Pierce and futile," adding that "the courts will overrule it." One Tampa woman wrote that Livesay had embarrassed the whole city, while another told Livesay that she was ashamed "there are still [racist] people like you in the world." A soldier from Fort Meade wrote that he would rather be buried in a sewer than in Hillcrest. A ninth-grade boy from New Jersey called Livesay out on his presumed arrogance and superior white status, writing, "You think you are better than another human being because of the color of your skin?"[35] But even supporters evoked racial norms of superiority and inferiority. Mrs. John Diehl, a seventy-two-year-old white woman born and raised in Fort Pierce, offered Campbell one of the spaces in her family plot, right beside Diehl's grandson, who had died as an infant ten years prior. "Our cemetery is a pretty cemetery," Mrs. Diehl said of Hillcrest Memorial Gardens. "The Black cemetery is nothing."[36] Even in Diehl's act of kindness she seems to either acknowledge or assert white supremacy, or both. She admits that Black cemeteries are not comparable to white ones as a result of Jim Crow practices that led to neglect and upkeep of Black graves and thus cannot provide a fit resting place for an American hero. But that begs the question: Can they provide a fit resting place for Black people who are not soldiers?

Proponents of keeping Hillcrest segregated argued that the policy maintained the so-called racial purity of the cemetery, which then increased the value and worth of the burial ground. Blacks countered this assertion with references to the divine. "God carried Williams home to heaven leaving the whites to their white-only burial ground on Earth," wrote news columnist Jim Arpy in "He's Wanted Here," implying that whites at Hillcrest might be left out of an integrated Heaven because of their racism.[37] A year earlier, grieving mother Jimmie Lee Terry had also responded in religious terms when her son, deceased veteran Bill Terry Jr., was refused burial in Birmingham because, as his mother was told, "Elmwood Cemetery has not been opened to Negroes yet." Jimmie Lee retorted, "When the Lord calls us all to the throne, in His eyesight He's not going to pick and choose by color."[38] Jim Crow customs penetrated the holy sanctum of death, and Black folks rebuked them as they would any other evil spirit.

Fort Pierce's Lee-Peek Funeral Home, which cared for the body of Pondexteur Williams until his ultimate interment, received phone calls as late as three o'clock in the morning from white people using racial epithets and threatening violence if Williams were buried at Hillcrest. Security guards were posted at the cemetery, and the lot's area was searched for bombs and booby traps before the grave was dug. E. J. Moulder, a seventy-nine-year-old white male lot owner at Hillcrest, was outraged at the idea of sharing the burial ground with Williams, even if the two lots were not close to each other. Moulder used racial epithets in referring to Williams and threatened to disinter his deceased brother and sister-in-law from the cemetery. "It's degrading to the cemetery," Moulder said. "It's a third rate cemetery now."[39]

The threat of white violence and white harassment in the time leading up to Williams's interment showed how deep rooted was the practice of Jim Crow cemeteries and segregated burial in the South, even during the post–civil rights era. "I don't know why, but that's the way it's been ever since I can remember," Louis Amis said in describing cemetery segregation in Brevard County, Florida. Of the county's seventeen cemeteries, six were segregated, including LaGrange Cemetery, where Amis was caretaker of the Black section.[40] In the post–civil rights era, after removal of the Jim Crow markers designating the Black and white areas, Amis said there was little difference between the two sections except for the style of grave marker or tombstone. Rudy Stone, an African American funeral director, believed that the invisible law of Jim Crow that reached to burials became part of southern culture for Black people as it did for whites. As a professional death worker who saw not racial segregation but separate Black cultural death norms, Stone believed that African Americans held fast to and even enforced Black-only burial grounds.[41] What Stone missed was that these six burial grounds allowed African Americans only burial in a specific Black-only section, which canceled out any choice they might have thought they had. Furthermore, with the impending threat of violence to Williams's grave and his bereaved family, one could ask why African Americans would ever see a Jim Crow, white-only cemetery as a final resting place.

Jim Crowing the Dead as a Catalyst for Autonomous Black Cemeteries

If the only option for burial was the forced choice of claiming a segregated Black-only area (which was no choice at all), some African Americans asserted burial rights aligned with Black separatism to fight Jim Crow cemeteries. These individuals questioned the very notion of being buried in white-only spaces where African Americans were not wanted. Cemeteries, they reasoned, are about community and kinship, so decedents should be among family, where memories are not shrouded in Jim Crow racism. For example, Rev. John Fisher bought shares in the brand-new African American–owned and operated cemetery of Mount Glenwood in Chicago because he was fed up with the way the white-only Oakwoods Cemetery overcharged African Americans. However, the mere rumor of interracial and/or white involvement was enough for Fisher to cease "active participation" with the Mount Glenwood Cemetery Association—a rumor perhaps stemming from the fact that in 1910 lawyer Michael Kannally was listed as a receiver of cemetery stock.[42] Fisher's actions notwithstanding, Black autonomous burial grounds protected African Americans not only from feeling degraded and devalued but from very real harassment and threats of violence, such as those associated with the Pondexteur Williams grave site.

Autonomous Black burial also provided African Americans with wealth-building opportunities free from white control. The Mount Glenwood Cemetery Association was established in 1906 by W. J. Root, James F. Dagley, and Charles O. Patton and on June 6 of that year purchased 141 acres in the small township of Bloom, three miles south of Chicago, for $150,000. The association was not officially dedicated until September 1908 but started selling burial plots in September 1906, three months after its public opening. By August 1910 Mount Glenwood was advertising itself as a way for African Americans not only to be buried with dignity and respect but also to become landowners and receive a 300 percent return on their investment. Prospective buyers of single or family burial lots were told that in no time their lots would be worth $450 each. Family burial lots sold for as little as thirty dollars—two dollars down, and two dollars per month—making this a low-risk investment with a high yield return. By 1922 African Americans who purchased lots for a fifty-dollar flat rate received two shares (worth thirty dollars) of Mount Glenwood Cemetery stock, in addition to a deed.[43] Because of racial discrimination, African Americans had limited opportunities for land ownership and wealth building, and Mount Glenwood presented itself as a surefire option to acquire not just a quick return but generational

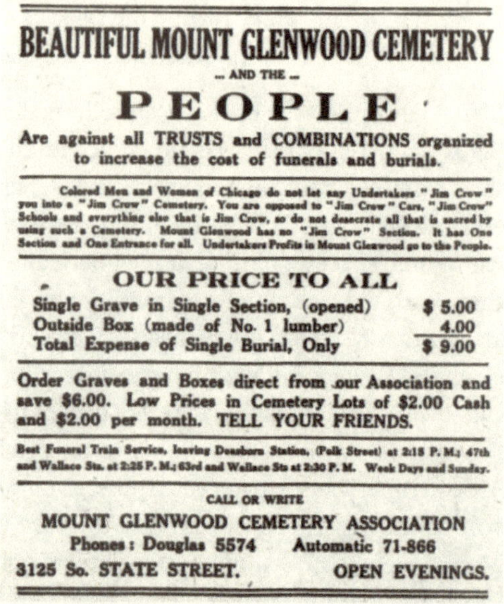

FIGURE 5.3. Along with promoting the sale of burial plots and providing information about their "funeral train services"—days and times when the trolley stops at the cemetery—this newspaper advertisement for Mount Glenwood Cemetery foregrounds its anti-Jim Crow cemetery stance. The beginning of the ad reads, "You are opposed to 'Jim Crow' cars, 'Jim Crow' schools and everything else that is Jim Crow, so do not desecrate all that is sacred by using such a Cemetery. Mount Glenwood has no 'Jim Crow' Section. It has One Section and One Entrance for all. Undertakers Profits in Mount Glenwood go to the People." *Broad Ax* (Chicago), February 1, 1913.

BEAUTIFUL MOUNT GLENWOOD CEMETERY
— AND THE —
PEOPLE
Are against all TRUSTS and COMBINATIONS organized to increase the cost of funerals and burials.

Colored Men and Women of Chicago do not let any Undertakers "Jim Crow" you into a "Jim Crow" Cemetery. You are opposed to "Jim Crow" Cars, "Jim Crow" Schools and everything else that is Jim Crow, so do not desecrate all that is sacred by using such a Cemetery. Mount Glenwood has no "Jim Crow" Section. It has One Section and One Entrance for all. Undertakers Profits in Mount Glenwood go to the People.

OUR PRICE TO ALL
Single Grave in Single Section, (opened) ... $ 5.00
Outside Box (made of No. 1 lumber) ... 4.00
Total Expense of Single Burial, Only ... $ 9.00

Order Graves and Boxes direct from our Association and save $6.00. Low Prices in Cemetery Lots of $2.00 Cash and $2.00 per month. TELL YOUR FRIENDS.

Best Funeral Train Service, leaving Dearborn Station, (Polk Street) at 2:15 P. M.; 47th and Wallace Sts. at 2:25 P. M.; 63rd and Wallace Sts at 2:30 P. M. Week Days and Sunday.

CALL OR WRITE
MOUNT GLENWOOD CEMETERY ASSOCIATION
Phones: Douglas 5574   Automatic 71-866
3125 So. STATE STREET.   OPEN EVENINGS.

wealth, especially with the cemetery's stock increase. By 1919, Mount Glenwood Cemetery Association's total stock was worth $250,000, and capital stock had nearly doubled the original buying price.

Nearly twenty years later, the Burr Oak Cemetery Association followed Mount Glenwood's lead and established an all-Black cemetery in Alsip, Illinois, twenty miles south of Chicago. But after purchasing forty-two acres of land from a Mr. Breen, the association had to fight the white citizens of the town of Worth for its first interment. On February 23, 1927, two Burr Oak Cemetery sextons were arrested as trespassers for digging a grave in preparation for a funeral. The cemetery association was served a writ of injunction by deputy sheriff Carl Carlson.[44] Neither the sextons nor the leaders of the association were shaken, and they stood firm in their decision to properly inter their brethren. Association officials told the *Chicago Tribune* that "another attempt to bury the body will be made either today or tomorrow." This type of resiliency and firm footing in their decision to not only assert burial rights but uphold them for members of their community was respected and commendable. Burr Oak was an autonomously African American cemetery and was not going to be Jim Crowed. Sure enough, the association won the right to bury James Nimmerk at Burr Oak, where he "lies peacefully."[45]

Jim Crow cemeteries intended to memorialize white supremacy provoked Black folks to react fiercely to such an insult in their time of bereavement. In a newspaper ad, the Mount Glenwood Cemetery Association publicly denounced Jim Crow cemeteries (see figure 5.3). The association, which partnered with an activist organization called The People, saw the fight not in local terms but as part of a larger battle against the entire system of Jim Crow, which transcended geographical boundaries. Mount Glenwood is located in Chicago, the destination of many African Americans who moved north during the Great Migration period seeking not only freedom from the rigid racial system of the south but economic freedom and social mobility. Yet even in Chicago and other northern cities, too often Black people still faced discrimination. By empowering lot owners, first financially and then through decision-making power, Mount Glenwood used burial rights as a weapon against Jim Crow. The Mount Glenwood Cemetery Lot Owners Association protected and defended its members while at the same time guaranteeing them the benefits of any and all cemetery improvements. The association made African American lot owners official collaborators with the Mount Glenwood Cemetery Corporation, giving them a voice in the policies and procedures of the cemetery. The organization met frequently, elected officers and committees, and formulated rules for operating.[46]

All-Black cemeteries, contrary to southern white thinking, were places of dignity and honorable memory. Stories of white residents attempting to "save" African Americans from "colored-only" sections of burial grounds by instead having them buried with white decedents reflected white misconceptions. For example, a few days after African American confectioner and barber John Wesley Underhill died on October 26, 1925, he was interred in New Jersey's Union Cemetery but, according to a newspaper story, "not in the Jim crow section reserved for colored folks but in a place of honor among the white folk."[47] The newspaper further reported that the entire town—all 2,500 white residents—attended Underhill's funeral, which was presided over by not one but three white pastors. In Jim Crow cemeteries, white lot owners and cemetery officials decide which African Americans to remember, which to forget, and *how* those African Americans would be remembered or forgotten. In the case of Underhill, he was remembered as the unassuming, wealthy African American who gladly willed his life's savings of $100,000 to his beloved, all-white town of Mays Landing, New Jersey. The true narrative must be more complicated than the one recounted by white residents. To begin with, census records have Underhill listed as a resident of Hamilton, N.J., rather than Mays Landing. What's more, he was born in Wisconsin, and his parents were from Pennsylvania. Underhill had no roots in Mays Landing or even in the state of New Jersey.[48] These missing pieces indicate how whites constructed a memory of an African American that fit their narrative—that of an accommodating and docile African American in a "town largely of Ku Klux persuasion."[49] Admitting that Underhill was the "only colored person in town," Mays Landing residents believed this was his only claim to distinction deserving of memorialization.[50] Jim Crow cemeteries pushed the notion that African Americans deserved memory only when interred with and acknowledged by whites.

All-Black cemeteries were the opposite of white-established and operated Jim Crow cemeteries. They were autonomous burial grounds created to protect against white hostilities while upholding the right to burial of all African Americans. Two years after purchasing land, the Mount Glenwood Cemetery Association officially consecrated the ground with great fanfare. The cemetery was officially dedicated to "colored people of Chicago," and the association arranged a "special train to leave La Salle street station that would stop at both Thirty-First and Sixty-Third Streets."[51] As early as 1910, the Mount Glenwood Cemetery Association advertised the cemetery in newspapers as "beautiful" and "most desirable." The association even handed out free train tickets to get to the cemetery and a coupon discounting the purchase of a burial plot. New African American lot holders were recruited by being told that Mount Glenwood Cemetery "gives every Colored family in Chicago an opportunity to free themselves from the bondage and discrimination of the older Cemeteries."[52] Mount Glenwood Cemetery was the way to freedom, and not buying a lot there was to still be in bondage.

Mount Glenwood Cemetery stood as a symbol of African American pride, demonstrated by its grand Decoration Day observances during the 1910s. Hundreds of visitors—mostly lot owners and their family and friends—visited the cemetery on Memorial Day to celebrate veterans. Well-known pastors gave eloquent and patriotic addresses, while the Della Ridgeway-Brow's Chautauqua Quartet sang several numbers to memorialize members of the Grand Army of the Republic and the United Spanish War veterans. Social fraternities such as the Masons were also represented.

Conclusion

African American grief and mourning were no deterrents to white racism and white violence. During and after Jim Crow segregation, African Americans had to fight to die and mourn in peace. After Pondexteur Williams's mother won the case to bury her son in an honorable veteran's grave, the cemetery sexton still had to check for explosive devices that might have been planted on or near the grave site by white citizens of Fort Pierce. Further, because cemetery manager Livesay received more than two hundred poison-pen letters, many protesting his decision not to uphold the 1954 racial burial covenant even after the federal judge declared burial racial segregation unconstitutional, it did not seem unreasonable to check for bombs or to have a veterans' group guard the lot. "We've had special guards there since this began," Livesay told a newspaper in late August.[53] It may be that one impetus for the guards was to appease white fears that Williams's family would just sneak in and bury the soldier without a court ruling.

Death is thought to be the great equalizer, but with the creation of Jim Crow cemeteries and racial burial divisions, white supremacy and racism remained present in African American death spaces. Jim Crowing the dead took root and became a mainstay of southern death identity, resulting in rigid burial borders. Within the Jim Crow cemetery, not only were whites and Blacks purposely segregated but whites considered African Americans undeserving of burial rights. African Americans were not allowed to own burial lots or purchase the lot of their choosing. Jim Crowing the dead forced African Americans to ponder ridiculous notions about the "color" of a corpse and if racial categories of the living were imprinted on the deceased. In the Jim Crow cemetery, African American decedents were subjugated and whites continued to reign supreme. Southern culture imprinted itself within a set of laws and customs and then embedded itself within the tapestry of this country. Insidious racism lies dormant and reveals itself only where enough Black people gather, live, work, and exist. Jim Crow cemeteries sought to silence the truth of Black life, but through the court system and civil rights organizations, African Americans prevailed in life and death.

Notes

1. "Louisiana Cemetery 'Sorry' after Denying Officer Burial 'Because He is Black,'" BBC, January 29, 2021, https://www.bbc.com/news/world-us-canada-55860238.

2. In 1933, the Denton City Council in Texas passed a city law that limited burial plots to whites. In 1947, the state of North Carolina passed its first Jim Crow law. Pompano Beach, Florida, passed an ordinance in 1955 forbidding burial of persons of "Negro" or African descent in the city-owned cemetery. Orange County, Florida, created the ten-acre "Negro Pauper Cemetery" in 1964.

3. "'These Bones Will Rise Again—Apart,'" *Afro-American* (Baltimore), March 16, 1957.

4. See "Removal of Lynch," *Jackson Daily News* (Mississippi), January 14, 1906; "Vardaman in Role of a Ghoul," *New York Age*, February 8, 1906. In both articles, James D. Lynch is referred to by the wrong name of Charles Lynch and is mistakenly listed as the former lieutenant governor. See also Rowland, *Official and Statistical Register of the State of Mississippi*, 1912, 28, where he is correctly listed as James Lynch, secretary of state.

5. See Rich, *Lawyers Reports Annotated*, 1917B, 947; *Northeastern Reporter with Key-Number Annotations*.

6. "Negro Seeks Writ to Bury His Wife," *Washington Herald*, May 8, 1913.

7. See Rich, *Lawyers Reports Annotated, 1917B*, 947; *Northeastern Reporter with Key-Number Annotations*.

8. Ibid.

9. Rogers, "Integrating the City of the Dead," 1153–66.

10. 1880 United States Census, Atlanta City, Fulton County, Georgia; 1900 United States Census, Chicago City, Cook County, Illinois; 1910 United States Census, Chicago City, Cook County, Illinois.

11. Sclair, "Ethnic Cemeteries," 630; Rosenow, *Death and Dying in the Working Class*, 57–60.

12. See Rich, *Lawyers Reports Annotated 1917B*, 947; *Northeastern Reporter with Key-Number Annotations*.

13. "Sexton Says Color Line is a Fixture," *Des Moines Tribune*, August 6, 1909; "Wesley Ash, for Commissioner," *Iowa Bystander* (Des Moines), February 28, 1908.

14. "Sexton Says Color Line is a Fixture," *Des Moines Tribune*, August 6, 1909.

15. "Jim Crow Ruling Prevents Negro Burial at Cemetery," *Herald and News* (Klamath Falls, Ore.), June 24, 1949.

16. "Cemetery Bars Negro; Probe Seen," *Sandusky Register* (Ohio), February 15, 1963.

17. "Rights Case Ends in Negro's Burial," *Akron Beacon Journal* (Ohio), August 2, 1963.

18. Rogers, "Integrating the City of the Dead."

19. R. S., "Notes: The Cemetery Lot."

20. Ibid.

21. Wilbur Elston, "Red-Tinged Unions Lash at Humphrey," *Minneapolis Sunday Tribune*, March 9, 1952.

22. Rogers, "Integrating the City of the Dead.".

23. Gauger, "'Jim Crow' Ended in Cemetery: Wyuka Trustees Halt Segregation," *Lincoln Journal Star*, May 17, 1960.

24. "Court Rule Lifts Color For Graves," *Beckley Register-Herald* (West Virginia), December 3, 1968.

25. Steven Girardi, "Widow Sues for Reburial Costs," *Sun-Sentinel* (Florida), March 26, 1987. See also "Widow Gets OK to Move Body to White Cemetery," *News-Press* (Fort Myers, Fla.), February 26, 1987; "Deerfield Approves Reburial," *Fort Lauderdale News*, February 25, 1987.

26. "Fight to Bury Black GI in White-Only Cemetery," *Akron Beacon Journal* (Ohio), August 25, 1970.

27. *Piqua Daily Call* (Ohio), August 27, 1970.

28. *Williams et al. v. Livesay et al.*, United States District Court for the Southern District of Florida, Case No. 70-1238.

29. "White-Only Cemetery Suit to Start Today," *Arizona Daily Star* (Tucson), August 27, 1970.

30. "He Gave His Life—and Then His Death," *New York Daily News*, August 24, 1970.

31. Ibid.

32. "Six Feet of Ground in Which to Rest," *Hartford Courant (Connecticut)*, September 1, 1970.

33. Ibid.

34. See *Burlington Free Press* (Vermont), March 29, 1929.

35. "Black GI Buried; Whites Slap Move," *Central New Jersey Home News*, August 31, 1970.

36. *Lancaster-Eagle Gazette* (Ohio), August 22, 1970.

37. Jim Arpy, "He's Wanted Here," *Quad-City Times*, August 31, 1970.

38. "Jim Crow Governs Cemetery," *Sedalia Democrat* (Missouri), November 10, 1969.
39. "Some Whites Angry as Black Vietnam Casualty is Buried," *Missoulian* (Montana), August 30, 1970.
40. Ron Martz, "Segregation Strikes Harder in Death Than in Life," *Florida Today*, June 16, 1974.
41. Ibid.
42. Miles Mark Fisher, "The Master's Slave: Elijah John Fisher," *Chicago Tribune*, November 26, 1910.
43. *Broad Ax* (Chicago), March 4, 1922.
44. "Burial Is Halted by Writ in War over Cemeteries," *Chicago Tribune*, February 24, 1927.
45. "Chicago Cemetery Company Wins," *Afro-American* (Baltimore), March 12, 1927.
46. *Broad Ax* (Chicago), May 24, 1913.
47. "Wills $100,00 to Town, Only Sisters, $5.00: Bronze Coffin and 2,000 Funeral for John Underhill, Mays Landing, N.J.: Whole Village Out for the Last Rites: Hundreds in Tears; Keep Body Out of Jim Crow Cemetery," *Afro-American* (Baltimore), November 7, 1925.
48. 1910 United States Census, Atlantic County, New Jersey, Hamilton Township.
49. "Wills $100,00 to Town."
50. Diner, *In the Almost Promised Land*, 62.
51. *Chicago Tribune*, September 3, 1908.
52. *Broad Ax* (Chicago), June 8, 1912; *Chicago Tribune*, May 26, 1919.
53. *Austin American* (Texas), August 30, 1970.

Bibliography

Diner, Hasia. *In the Almost Promised Land: American Jews and Blacks, 1915–1935*. Baltimore: Johns Hopkins Press, 1995.
The Northeastern Reporter with Key-Number Annotations. Vol. 101, perm. ed., April 1–June 24, 1913. St. Paul, Minn.: West Publishing Company, 1913.
Rich, Burdett, et al., eds. *The Lawyers Reports Annotated, 1917B*. Rochester, N.Y.: Lawyers Co-operative Publishing Company, 1917.
Rogers, Kitty. "Integrating the City of the Dead: The Integration of Cemeteries and the Evolution of Property Law, 1900–1969." *Alabama Law Review* 56, no. 4 (2005): 1153–66.
Rosenow, Michael K. *Death and Dying in the Working Class, 1865–1920*. Urbana: University of Illinois Press, 2015.
Rowland, Dunbar. *The Official and Statistical Register of the State of Mississippi, 1912*. Brandon Printing Company, 1912.
R. S. "Notes: The Cemetery Lot: Rights and Responsibilities." *University of Pennsylvania Law Review* 109, issue 3 (January 1961):378–400.
Sclair, Helen. "Ethnic Cemeteries: Underground Rites." In *Ethnic Chicago: A Multicultural Portrait*, edited by Melvin G. Hollie and Peter d'Alroy Jones, 618–39. Grand Rapids, Mich.: Eerdmans Publishing Company, 1995.

EPILOGUE

TEACHING THE AMERICAN SOUTH BY LEARNING THE DEAD

The cemetery is the place Americans most associate with freedom, namely because death is thought of as the great equalizer. But what happens when racial separatist ideology of the living is applied to the dead, when racial segregation is codified within burial law and creates cemeteries that negate the grief, mourning, and burial rights of bereaved African Americans? As we see in chapter 5, cemeteries can become microcosms of white supremacy that seek to marginalize African American burial rights. These sacred spaces can also become legal battle grounds over rights and freedoms.

As primary sources, newspapers can chronicle the story of African American rights in death, giving personal details that lend themselves to the sympathy and emotion needed to understand grief and mourning.

The following is an exercise designed to use newspapers to help us learn even more about a) racially segregated burial in the post–civil rights era, b) anti-Blackness and American patriotism, and c) Black mothering as activism, using Pondexteur Williams as a case study.

Examine the following newspaper articles and ask and answer the following questions. For even more context and understanding, find and locate the Jim Crow laws surrounding death and burial that were enforced within cities and counties in Florida.

1. Just as there were many whites who vehemently did not believe Williams should be buried in Hillcrest Memorial Gardens, many others held the opposite opinion. One was Mrs. John Diehl, quoted in Figure 5.4, who offered a spot in her family's burial plot to Williams's mother. In response to those who opposed Williams's burial, Diehl said, "I feel that he being Black and can't be buried in Hillcrest, then he didn't have any business going to the war."[1] What conclusions is Diehl drawing, first

about anti-Blackness and patriotism, and second about the dishonoring of Black veterans in life and death? How can these conclusions help us further understand American white supremacy in life and death?

2. Over two hundred white people wrote to cemetery manager James Livesay expressing their strong disapproval and even disgust that Williams's mother had to sue to have her son buried at Hillcrest. At the same time, other whites were adamantly opposed to allowing Williams to be laid to rest at Hillcrest. What can white anger about interracial burial grounds tell us about Florida in the post–civil rights era? Can it tell us something about an established hierarchy that places memorials for white people above those for Black people? Do some whites believe they have a right to control memorialization?

3. From newspaper accounts, it appears that Mrs. Mary Campbell wore all-black clothing, including a lace veil, and carried her Bible to the court cases and many public interactions involving her son. How did she use ritualized mourning wear as activism? How did continually positioning herself as first and foremost a mourning mother shift the narrative, fight racism, and call out the dehumanization of white supremacy?

4. If cemeteries are arguably a place for the living to visit the dead and engage in memory making, how could Williams's family grieve in peace when other lot holders did not want them there and physically engaged in trying to bar their presence?

FIGURE 5.4. This newspaper article highlights the perspective of Mary Campbell, mother of Pondexteur Williams, a twenty-year-old Black soldier killed in Vietnam whose remains were refused burial in an all-white cemetery. *Newark Advocate* (New Jersey), August 2, 1970.

Some Whites Angry as Black Vietnam Casualty Is Buried

FORT PIERCE, Fla. (AP) — A black soldier, who died in Vietnam and lay in a coffin while lawyers battled over his funeral, was buried Saturday in an all-white cemetery as some white grave owners threatened to remove their relatives' bodies.

Hillcrest Memorial Gardens had refused to bury the body of 20-year-old Army Spec. 4 Pondexteur E. Williams since Aug. 20, but a U.S. district judge ordered the burial.

As cemetery manager James A. Livesay supervised final preparations for the burial one elderly man angrily confronted him in his office.

"I don't want my brother and his wife buried here with niggers," shouted E.J. Moulder, 79. He demanded to have grave markers removed from the graves and asked Livesay, "Why didn't you take it to a higher court?"

Later, Moulder said he owns the plot next to that of his brother and sister-in-law for himself and is considering having all the bodies moved out.

"It's degrading to the cemetery," Moulder said. "Why don't they bury him over the hill where he belongs? It's a third-rate cemetery now."

Livesay told a newsman, "This goes on all the time."

"Some people want to remove their loved ones," he said, but added, "I don't anticipate any, though. These first reactions will cool down."

See Photo, Page 2

On his desk was a stack of more than 200 "poison pen letters" from across the country, all received Thursday and Friday. Three secretaries were opening an equally large stack of mail from Saturday.

But Williams was buried, with his mother's bible on his bemedaled chest.

Army riflemen fired 21 rounds into the cloudless sky as Williams' mother, Mary Campbell, soaked her twisted handkerchief and white gloves with tears. She received from Army Maj. Ludwig Benesek the American flag which had draped her son's coffin.

The GI coffin was lowered into a grave in a special section reserved for veterans of the armed forces and their families.

Later, the Army will supply a 12-inch by 24-inch bronze plaque to be set in concrete at the head of Williams' hilltop grave.

Several hundred persons, including many whites, attended the burial, which followed a prayer service on the banks of the Indian River in downtown Fort Pierce.

In permitting the funeral, the cemetery was obeying a court order issued Thursday by U.S. Dist. Judge William O. Mehrtens in Miami.

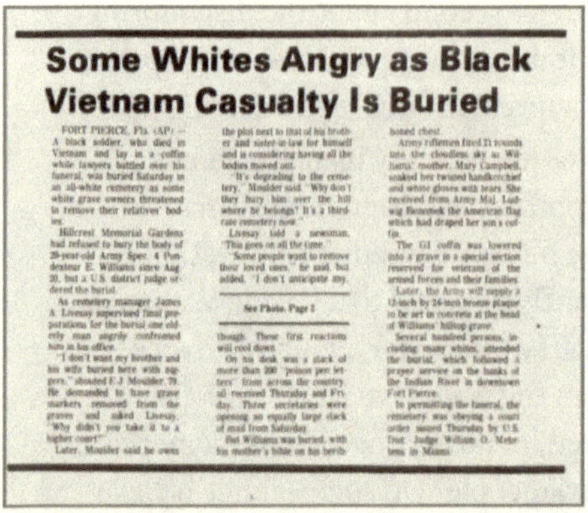

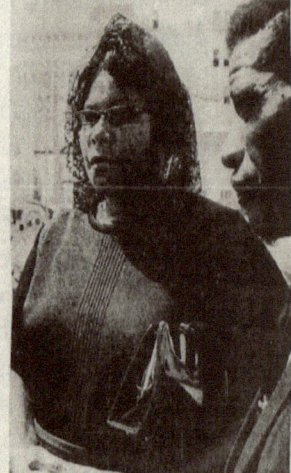

FIGURE 5.5. The story of Pondexteur Williams and his mother's fight to have him buried at Hillcrest Memorial Gardens in Fort Pierce, Florida, was covered by newspapers around the country and abroad. *Missoulian* (Montana), August 20, 1970.

Cemetery ordered to bury black GI

Funeral will be Saturday

By VERNE O. WILLIAMS
Miami News Reporter

A federal judge here today ordered a Fort Pierce cemetery to permit the burial of Spec. 4 Pondexteur E. Williams, the black Vietnam veteran whose body it had turned away because of a whites-only clause in its charter.

Judge William O. Mehrtens told attorneys for Hillcrest Memorial Gardens he expected immediate compliance with his order.

The ruling came after a closed pre-trial conference and without taking any testimony. The suit had been brought by Mrs. Mary Campbell, the soldier's mother. U.S. Attorney Robert Rust of Miami had joined it on instructions from the Justice Department in Washington.

"I'm very grateful," said Mrs. Campbell, who attended the hearing wearing a black dress and a black funeral veil.

Fort Pierce attorney Ralph Flowers, who filed the suit, said the graveside services would be held at 3 p.m. Saturday and that the national commander of the Order of the Purple Heart was expected to be present to honor Spec. 4 Williams.

Williams, 20, of Fort Pierce, was with the First Air Cavalry in Vietnam when he was killed in a Viet Cong mortar barrage on Aug. 8.

A 72-year-old white woman, Mrs. John Diehl, donated a grave next to her infant grandson's for the interment of the soldier but the cemetery then refused burial.

In a letter to Mrs. Campbell on Aug. 21, cemetery director James A. Livesay said that he feared "legal problems" if he allowed the burial, since some 5,000 families in Fort Pierce had been sold plots under a whites-only clause.

However, the suit by Mrs. Campbell pointed out that the cemetery had made a recent newspaper offer to provide a free burial plot to any

Continued on 4A, Col. 4

Miami News Photo by SAL GRISANTI

Soldier's mother waits outside courthouse, Bible in hand

Soldier's mother: 'my prayers answered'

By BILL DOUTHAT
Miami News Reporter

"All these proceedings, papers and hearings — they didn't need any of this to send him over there to die," said Mrs. Roosevelt Campbell.

Mrs. Campbell was bitter today before the Federal District Court ordered Hillcrest Cemetery in Fort Pierce to bury her son's body.

Her son, Pondexteur Eugene Williams, was killed in Vietnam 19 days ago but has not been interred because Hillcrest bars blacks.

After the court ruled in her favor, Mrs. Campbell, dressed in black and clutching a small White Bible, said, "I'm grateful. My prayers have been answered."

She said she hoped her son's body, now in a $120 GI coffin at a Fort Pierce funeral home, would be buried this week.

"I'm just sorry it took so long," said Mrs. Campbell, a large woman who works in a Fort Pierce cafeteria.

Before the hearing began this morning, Mrs. Campbell talked of her two other sons, Andrew, 15, and Alton, 14. "After this, I would not want them to go into the service," she said.

"My son gave his life. There wasn't anything else he could give. Than that."

Mrs. Campbell sat silent through the hearing and afterwards flashed a smile and gave a sigh of relief to the woman sitting next to her, Mrs. Louise Diehl.

They became friends when Mrs. Diehl, a 74-year-old white woman, offered to give a burial plot she owns in Hillcrest to Mrs. Campbell's son.

"I must say I am very happy that freedom and justice prevailed," Mrs. Diehl said.

U.S., Soviet peace team may police the Mideast

Combined Miami News Press Services

SAN CLEMENTE — The United States is prepared to join the Soviet Union in fielding a two-power peacekeeping force — involving American and Russian troops — to maintain a Middle East settlement, high administration officials say.

The disclosure appeared in the 48-page transcript of a background session on foreign policy for editors and publishers from 13 western states who gathered at the presidential compound in San Clemente.

The sources emphasized that such a force — which would resemble in many respects the United Nations emergency force that kept the peace before the six-day war of June, 1967 — would depend upon the consent of the Arabs and the Israelis, and would not, in any case, be assembled until a settlement is achieved in the Arab-Israeli peace talks now under way in New York under the auspices of U.N. negotiator Gunnar Jarring.

Moreover, the sources said, the administration does not envision a joint U.S.-So-

Continued on 6A, Col. 7

Army plane crashes here; 2 injured

By WILLIAM TUCKER
Miami News Reporter

A twin-engine U.S. Army plane lost power on takeoff at Homestead General Airport today and crashed on the edge of the field, critically injuring the two crewmen aboard.

The pilot and co-pilot were rushed by a sheriff's department helicopter to Homestead Air Force Base hospital.

James Hunt, airport manager, said the plane was a

Continued on 4A, Col. 1

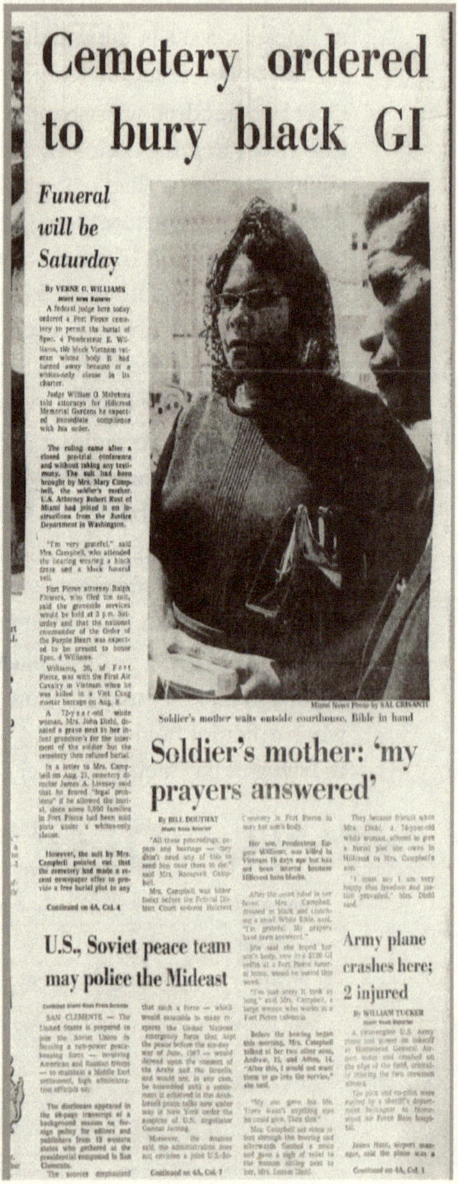

FIGURE 5.6. Ultimately Judge William O. Mehrtens of the U.S. District Court for the Southern District of Florida ruled that Pondexteur Williams be interred in Hillcrest Memorial Gardens. *Asbury Park Press* (Neptune, N.J.), August 28, 1970.

Note

1. "'He Died for Nothing,'" *Newark Advocate*, August 22, 1970.

CHAPTER 6

"We Have No Further Interest in These Patients *until They Die*"

The U.S. Public Health Service's Syphilis Study and African American Cemeteries in Macon County, Alabama

CARROLL VAN WEST

Upon emancipation, African Americans diligently established their own places of community, culture, and faith within the southern public landscape—churches, schools, and cemeteries.[1] Within the institution building of rural African American community in the late nineteenth-century South, the prominence of African American cemeteries cannot be contested—but they are routinely ignored as public landmarks and places of historical merit.[2]

In Macon County, Alabama, however, cemeteries document both past and present meanings of medical experimentation and research in modern American culture and serve as places of commemoration—as sites of conscience—for their southern communities today as they make both profound political and deeply personal statements.

Macon County, Alabama, was the location of one of the most infamous incidents in the medical history of the United States: the study of "Untreated Syphilis in the Negro Male," sponsored by the U.S. Public Health Service (USPHS) from 1932 to 1973. It is often called the Tuskegee Study because the Macon County seat is Tuskegee and a former hospital at Tuskegee Institute (now Tuskegee University) and the Veterans Administration Hospital at Tuskegee were used for some of the medical procedures.[3]

What happened, and did not happen, in Macon County, Alabama, during the syphilis study is of national significance in the history of medicine in the United States.[4] "The Tuskegee Study holds a central place in our understanding of twentieth-century medicine, science, race, and research," as scholars Allan M. Brandt and Larry R. Churchill point out. They emphasize that since "researchers and writers, ethicists and activists have repeatedly turned their attention to the Tuskegee Study in the last quarter-century . . . the study has become more than an important and tragic episode in the ongoing history of human subjects research." In fact, Brandt and Churchill conclude that "the study reels with significance for the most central questions of contemporary medicine and society."[5]

The study reverberates so strongly today because a central concern of the federal physicians leading the study was to acquire family permission to carry out autopsies of the victims upon their death. Medical historian Susan Lederer concluded, chillingly, "The investigators who staffed the study over four decades regarded their African American subjects neither as patients, nor as experimental subjects, but as cadavers, who had been identified while still alive."[6] Her judgment was confirmed by a July 1933 letter where Dr. O. C. Wenger of the USPHS admitted to fellow federal physician Dr. Raymond A. Vonderlehr: "We have no further interest in these patients *until they die*."[7]

Such attitudes long permeated the medical profession in the United States, as explored through recent research from historians Harriet A. Washington, Dorothy Roberts, Rebecca Skloot, and Daina R. Berry and anthropologists Kenneth C. Nystrom and James M. Davidson.[8] "The field of medicine had a kind of schizophrenia in dealing with those of African descent," Davidson concluded. "By the pseudo-scientific measures of the day, they attempted to demonstrate a white superiority and a Black inferiority, even as they were using Black bodies to establish the basic parameters and techniques of their normative knowledge."[9] But the physicians involved in the syphilis study took the exploitation of Black bodies to a new degree of revulsion. As historian James Jones emphasized: "It was as though the PHS had converted Macon County and the surrounding areas into its own private laboratory, a 'sick farm' where [so-called] diseased subjects could be maintained without further treatment and herded together for inspection at the yearly roundups."[10]

The Public Health Service's Vonderlehr was interested in the victims' bodies only for autopsies. The interests of African Americans in Macon County were quite different. They looked at the bodies as those of their husbands, brothers, cousins, and fathers. Within their respective rural communities, they buried the bodies respectfully, quietly, most often with the typical small, unadorned markers found in countless other Black cemeteries across the South. Southern African American cemeteries speak strongly to community, culture, and faith. The ones associated with the syphilis study in Macon County say a bit more. They are evolving from their Jim Crow-era roots as sacred places of community that were hidden from outsider eyes into community-focused and driven places of commemoration—public monuments complete with interpretive markers for the victims of the federal syphilis study. Still, they are reminders of how the dominant culture exploited Black bodies for its own benefit.

Rural African American communities in Macon County have sought to designate their cemeteries as landmarks as they take control of their own narratives of what the syphilis study was about and what such a national public health study plagued by racist norms and dictates means today. There is a tension in these projects. The women who lead the efforts at Creek Stand AME Zion Church Cemetery and Shiloh Missionary Baptist Church Cemetery want to hold the federal government accountable for its betrayal in carrying out medical experimentation on vulnerable citizens. Yet they also convey a strong sense of responsibility to their families and their neighbors. They want to remember the victims on their own terms and insist on privacy and respect to ensure that their association with the syphilis study does not become the only reason their cemeteries are landmarked and remembered. For these communities, cemeteries are both personal and political.

Brief Overview of the U.S. Public Health Service Syphilis Study, 1929-1974

In 1929 the Julius Rosenwald Fund (JRF), in collaboration with the U.S. Public Health Service, approved $50,000 for a pilot syphilis treatment projects in six southern counties, including Macon County, Alabama. In May 1930, Dr. H. L. Harris Jr. of the JRF reviewed the progress of the demonstration project in Macon County and found positive results. He returned in the fall and recommended the implementation of a comprehensive health plan. But after the stock market crash of 1929, there was not enough money to implement this recommendation.[11] A later review by Fisk University sociologist Charles S. Johnson also found that African Americans in Macon County responded positively to the Rosenwald Fund project. He reported that the Rosenwald physicians conducted treatment for typhoid, diphtheria, and smallpox in addition to syphilis. Johnson concluded, "This altogether, with the Red Cross distribution of seeds for gardens and yeast to be used in combating pellagra, constituted one of the most intense concentrations upon a reconstructive health campaign of any rural section in the South."[12]

The USPHS study shared few of the attributes of the initial Rosenwald program. In 1932 Dr. Raymond A. Vonderlehr, the USPHS assistant surgeon general, came to Tuskegee, the seat of Macon County, to identify African

American men who could be in either the scientific sample of subjects or the control group of subjects to be examined in a new project to study untreated syphilis over the long term. Dr. Vonderlehr wanted to focus on African American males between the ages of twenty-five and sixty. (Women were never a focus of the study, even though the health agency understood that untreated, or undertreated, men would continue to pass syphilis to their sexual partners.) Vonderlehr soon encountered resistance from the African American communities, as they were convinced that his call for men over the age of twenty-five meant that the program was really for military draft physicals. The agency countered this concern by increasing the number of men and women tested. Since initially federal officials agreed with the request of Macon County's Board of Health to treat individuals outside of the survey parameters, the 1932 survey took more time and cost much more money than the agency had predicted.[13]

Medical practice in Alabama was segregated by law. To have medical facilities and qualified personnel available for the study the USPHS turned to Tuskegee Institute and the Veterans Administration Hospital located at Tuskegee for assistance. Tuskegee administrators debated the correct course of action. On September 17, 1932, the director of the institute's Andrew Hospital, Dr. Eugene H. Dibble Jr., asked institute president Dr. R. R. Moton to support the USPHS request for assistance. Dibble argued that involvement with the federal program could benefit the professional training of Tuskegee's students and that the results of the research could potentially raise the institute's standing and reputation: "While this would not bring any additional compensation to our hospital, it would certainly not cost us any more and would offer very valuable training for our students as well as for the Internes. As Dr. [Taliaferro] Clark said, our own hospital and Tuskegee Institute would get credit for this piece of research work. He also predicts that the result of this study will be sought after the world over."[14] Dr. Moton also heard from the U.S. surgeon general himself, Dr. Hugh Smith Cumming, who urged the Tuskegee president to cooperate.[15] Dr. Moton agreed to provide facilities and personnel for the subjects' medical sessions, but the USPHS never viewed or treated Tuskegee as an equal, nor did the USPHS allow Tuskegee meaningful input in the study. Control over the study, and decisions on its funding, rested solely with the U.S. Public Health Service.

Local African American professionals were needed to make the study work. Dr. Jesse Peters, of the Veterans Administration Hospital, carried out the x-rays and autopsies of the subjects.[16] The USPHS hired former Tuskegee nurse Eunice Rivers to be the key community contact person. She was well known to the African American communities of Macon County, starting with her involvement in the Tuskegee Movable School project in 1923.[17] She knew the roads to the local communities and where to meet with the research subjects. Rivers took subjects to medical offices at Tuskegee Institute and at the nearby Veterans Administration Hospital. She served as the liaison between the patients and the medical professionals from 1932 until her retirement in April 1970, almost the entire length of the study. Rivers remains a polarizing figure in the Black community, sometimes presented as an individual worthy of sympathy in such popular culture productions as the 1997 television movie *Miss Evers' Boys* while at other times seen as a professional who deserved censure for not protecting victims from the study.[18]

Ultimately the USPHS identified approximately four hundred men to receive no treatment, or limited and ineffective treatment, for syphilis. The first group received a complete examination, including x-rays and spinal taps, carried out by staff and faculty at Tuskegee Institute. Although segregated practices dominated southern health care, white USPHS physicians participated in the field testing of the study's victims. In the initial study, the USPHS had no plans to offer any medical treatment for latent syphilis, which was assumed to be noncontagious, nor did they inform the patients of the nature of the study. When the agency wrote the subjects about the forthcoming spinal tap procedure, the letter's misleading language called the procedure a "special" treatment process.[19]

The three primary federal officials who instituted the Tuskegee study and guided it during its formative years were Dr. Hugh Smith Cumming, the U.S. surgeon general, Dr. Taliaferro Clark, the author of the initial Rosenwald Fund report, and Dr. Raymond Vonderlehr, the USPHS assistant surgeon general. All three medical professionals received degrees at the University of Virginia, which, according to historian Gregory Dorr, "was an epicenter of eugenical thought, closely linked with the national eugenics movement and with the Virginia antimiscegenation movement and tied to the state mental health professionals who promoted eugenic sterilization."[20] The institutional ties between their University of Virginia training and their USPHS careers "imbued" PHS officers in the Division of Venereal Diseases with "a common institutional heritage."[21] This outlook reflected a belief in Black inferiority and a faith that the exploitation of Black bodies was for the greater scientific good. Unfortunately, such faith has a long history in medical practice. Historian Todd L. Savitt explored the roots of the practice in the Old South. Scholars Dorothy E. Roberts and Harriet Washington have investigated the history of experimentation on the bodies of people of color up to the present.²² "For much of our nation's history," Washington distressingly concludes, "Black patients were commonly regarded as fit subjects for nonconsensual, nontherapeutic research.²³

In June 1933, as the new syphilis study was just underway, Vonderlehr succeeded Clark as chief of the Venereal Diseases Division. Sociologist Susan E. Bell points out that "over the next four decades the head of the Division of Venereal Disease (VD) is usually recruited from a man who has worked on the Tuskegee Syphilis Study."²⁴

Thus, the racist intellectual assumptions that undergirded the syphilis study remained unchallenged and continued as the decades passed. Dr. Vonderlehr in particular continued to pursue his eugenics-infused theory that "race-linked pathology" would somehow prove fundamental biological differences between the races.²⁵ His USPHS colleagues agreed that the project—studying untreated late latent syphilis in a large sample of rural African Americans—had too much potential for medical knowledge for it ever to end, no matter the price paid by the African American victims. Treatment was far from their minds, but not all subjects had symptoms, and many received some treatment from ingesting oral doses of aspirin, mercury iodide (or protiodide of mercury), iron, and placebos. The patients were not informed about the nature of the study, its purpose, or its dangers. Since the project had come to be viewed as a long-term study, rather than a short-term review, Vonderlehr instituted a group of just over two hundred men as a control sample.²⁶

The new USPHS procedures underscored how the study was now a case of human experimentation that ended with a subject's death, with autopsies a key part of the project. The officials understood that autopsies would be controversial in any southern rural community. Wenger told Vonderlehr, "If the colored population becomes aware that accepting free hospital care means a post-mortem, every darkey will leave Macon County."²⁷ The federal physicians took steps to secure the involvement of Tuskegee officials in the autopsies and made sure that local Macon County doctors understood the importance of postmortem examinations. The USPHS found that Nurse Rivers was a crucial person to develop trust with the subjects' families and convince them to proceed with autopsies. Families who participated received fifty dollars as a burial stipend, meaning that federal funding for the syphilis project directly touched the victims' final resting places in Macon County. Families, not federal funds, paid for the headstones for the graves.

The program continued until an interagency whistleblower brought it to newspapers in 1972, and scandal erupted. The federal government ended the program in March 1973.²⁸ That spring a federal review panel ruled, "The scientific merits of the Tuskegee Study are vastly overshadowed by the violation of basic ethical principles pertaining to human dignity and human life imposed on the experimental subjects."[29]

In July 1973 local African American attorney Fred Gray filed a lawsuit on behalf of the Macon County victims. The following year, the lawsuit was settled with a $10 million out-of-court settlement, giving $37,500 to each surviving subject, $15,000 to the heirs of any deceased subject, $16,000 to the surviving victims of the study, and $5,000 to the heirs of deceased victims of the study.[30]

By identifying the victims, Gray's lawsuit allows historians today to locate the cemeteries where they were buried. In the 2010s, families associated with the Creek Stand AME Zion Church Cemetery and the Shiloh Missionary Baptist Church Cemetery took steps to commemorate the victims buried within their properties, with exhibits located on or near the site, interpretive markers on the properties, and listings of the cemeteries in the National Register of Historic Places for their significant association with the U.S. Public Health Service Syphilis Study. The churches connected with both cemeteries had an additional tie to the study, as they served as locations for the "roundups" held by USPHS officials, including Nurse Eunice Rivers, in the early 1950s. The "roundups," a term used by USPHS administrators, described the yearly visits that USPHS physicians made to Macon County to examine the study's subjects. Historian James Jones explains that young USPHS physicians, all white, eagerly participated in the roundups because they "gave them a chance to sharpen their diagnostic skills by observing the complications of late syphilis. Thus, in addition to collecting blood samples and stimulating the subjects' interest, the roundups served as a training program for young officers."[31] The agency would send letters to the participants telling them to meet Nurse Rivers and the medical team at various locations, mostly churches and schools, scattered throughout the county.

Creek Stand AME Zion Cemetery

Creek Stand AME Zion Cemetery is an isolated place, located off a dirt road, in the southern half of Macon County. Compared to grand, decorative cemeteries found in the urban South, it is a most unassuming place. The cemetery lies on either side of the concrete-block church building. The grave markers come in a range of sizes, materials, and styles; some are more prominent than others and are arranged in rows with some family grouping. In these general characteristics, Creek Stand AME Zion Cemetery differs little from thousands of other rural African American cemeteries across the South. But church members understand that the cemetery's statement of community, faith, and permanence matters. They want to tell their story and pay appropriate respect to their members who were victims of the USPHS syphilis study.

In 2011 congregation member Shari Williams and pastor Katrina Love invited me to their cemetery because they were aware that I had worked with other southern African American communities to list their properties in the National Register of Historic Places.[32] As they carried out research about their church and cemetery for an exhibit in the church's fellowship hall, they located the multiple property nomination materials that the Middle Tennessee State University (MTSU) Center for Historic Preservation had previously prepared for the National Register about the USPHS syphilis study in Macon County.[33] They wanted to talk, show me what they had done, and discuss next steps. The multiple property nomination had identified the church cemetery as potentially eligible for listing in the National Register. Williams and Love wanted to explore that option and find out what research and community input would be necessary for it to be listed.

Williams and Love's activism for taking control of the cemetery's story and remembering the victims of the syphilis study on their terms, by way of the National Register and interpretive markers and exhibits at their church, mirrored a similar interest from Elizabeth Sims, Barbara Mahone, Shirley Johnson, and Felecia Chandler at the Shiloh Missionary Baptist Church in northern Macon County. Women descendants of the syphilis study victims led their communities in telling the story of the study and the legacy of the victims buried in their cemeteries.

The message of these two women at Creek Stand has been exceedingly clear from the beginning. They first want to acknowledge and identify their congregation's beginnings as a church started by formerly enslaved citizens—people who survived one era of government-sponsored brutality and oppression to build a lasting community they controlled. In 1893–94, local white farmer Dr. James E. Ellison transferred the land to Stephen Pace, George Washington Pace, Sidney Mahone, Russell Dawkins, and Taylor Robinson, who became the first trustees of the church and cemetery.[34] Community members consider Creek Stand to be one of the oldest African American rural communities in south Macon County, where slaves and former slaves, such as Stephen Pace, were buried in unmarked graves even before the cemetery was formally established.[35] Beedie Pace (1852–1902) was also born into slavery, and his grave has the cemetery's oldest known marker.[36]

FIGURE 6.1. Creek Stand AME Zion Church Cemetery, facing northwest (photograph by the author)

The congregation wanted to use the cemetery to tell two stories: (1) of its roots and identity as a proud African American community and (2) of the syphilis study in their own words and terms. In 2006, using a listing of syphilis study victims, members confirmed that their cemetery contained the tombstones for six victims: Albert Daniels Sr., Ephron Julkes, Fonzie Mahone, Elmore Pace, John Shaughter, and Ed Sparks. They also determined that four other victims—Clark Daniel, Ernest Lloyd, Albert Julkes, and Henry Pace—were buried at the cemetery but either their markers were temporary and have been lost or they were buried in unmarked graves.[37]

In my two visits with members of Creek Stand AME Zion Church, we discussed how the graves of the syphilis victims were not set aside or identified with any sort of special marker. Not one of the tombstones included an inscription identifying the victim as associated with the syphilis study. Rather, the victims' burials were spaced throughout the cemetery and most typically placed among the tombstones of other family members. The congregation members explained that the families knew who the victims were and where they were buried. In their discussions with me over the last ten years, none of them have expressed a desire for a special marker or designation because such treatment, the descendants believe, would only perpetuate government control over their bodies. Identifying the victims would privilege one fact of their father's or brother's life—a fact that was imposed on them without their consent—and ignore who they were to their families and friends. Descendants of victims at other cemeteries in Macon County have shared similar thoughts with me. As Macon County syphilis study participant Herman Clark from the Shiloh community once explained to journalist Jean Heller, "We were so poor, and poor people couldn't get a doctor and couldn't get medicine, and that's how they got us to cooperate. They blackmailed us."[38] During our visits victims' families at Creek Stand scoffed at the idea of some sort of designated tombstone. The minor federal death benefit of fifty dollars defrayed a bit of the cost of burial. But the descendent families clearly and correctly emphasized that they had retrieved their loved ones' bodies after autopsy and that the family made all arrangements for the burial and chose the type of gravestone they could afford and thought was appropriate.[39]

In 2010 the congregation and pastor Katrina Love took the first public steps to assert their control over the story of Creek Stand AME Church Cemetery by submitting an application for it to become part of the Alabama Historical Commission's historic cemetery program. In May 2011 the commission, the congregation, and several descendants of syphilis study victims gathered at the church for a ceremony to unveil a metal monument detailing the cemetery's history. The marker was at the location where "roundups" and victim burials took place, but its text emphasized how formerly enslaved people had gained the property and established the church and cemetery in the 1890s. Congregation members reserved the story of the cemetery's association with the syphilis study to exhibits in the church fellowship hall because there they were not limited to the word count of a typical metal marker.

Then the congregation and Love reached out to the MTSU Center for Historic Preservation for assistance in developing an individual nomination of the cemetery to the National Register of Historic Places. Shari Williams of the congregation collaborated with center faculty and staff on the nomination. For the congregation, it was upsetting to learn that the property served in the 1950s as one of the infamous "roundup" locations, where officials of the U.S. Public Health Service, including nurse Eunice Rivers, met community members to monitor the progress of the disease in their bodies—that the very ground of the cemetery had been violated by the federal physicians. The Center for Historic Preservation shared images, taken by an official USPHS photographer and now housed in the National Archives, of a roundup session at the church property in 1952.[40] The Center also shared a USPHS memo from 1955 that listed Creek Stand AME Zion Church as a lo-

FIGURE 6.2. Creek Stand AME Zion Church Cemetery, facing southeast
(photograph by the author)

cation for meetings with Nurse Rivers and the physicians. The memo stated, "The Government doctor will be here next week. Be sure to meet him at the time and place listed below that is nearest your home."[41] It is difficult to determine from existing records when roundup sessions began at Creek Stand and when they ended. Church members emphasized that Rivers visited local families and continued monitoring victims until they died or until the study ended in the early 1970s.[42]

The National Register process of exchanging information and documents, and then preparing draft statements of historical significance that the congregation reviewed and approved, took several years of collaboration. In February 2016 the Keeper of the National Register formally designated the cemetery as a historic property. Congregation members use the metal state historical marker to introduce their story as one of the area's oldest African American communities. Visitors are then welcome to see the history exhibit inside the church and to pay respect to those buried in the cemetery. The members tell their story of community, faith, and identity, on their terms, saying the names of the victims in their exhibit text, recognizing that the study is an important part of their story but that it is not the only story worth telling. They also include sections of narrative from the National Register multiple property nomination and use several of the USPHS photographs taken during a "roundup" at the church in the 1950s. The quiet dignity of this unassuming place, after decades of government-sponsored racism and cultural inequality, makes a powerful, lasting statement.

Shiloh Missionary Baptist Church Cemetery

Like Creek Stand AME Church Cemetery, Shiloh Missionary Baptist Church Cemetery is strongly associated with the USPHS Syphilis Study—more victims of the study are buried here than in any other cemetery in the county.[43] But to congregation and community members the cemetery is most important as a 150-year-old statement of African American empowerment through faith and community, nestled as it is in the hills south of the town of Notasulga, about a third of a mile south of the Shiloh Missionary Baptist Church, which owns the property. Its location reflects a Reconstruction-era African American settlement trait of locating rural neighborhoods and institutions away from established white communities but in close enough proximity that residents could walk or travel by horseback to employment in the towns.[44]

The cemetery is similar to many other rural African American cemeteries in the South in its lack of large, architecturally ornate tombstones or landscaped roads and plantings. The estimated number of all burials, determined by a count of headstones and of rectangular-shaped depressed areas, is approximately three hundred. As in many other rural southern African American cemeteries, the tombstones and grave markers vary in materials and design. The artistry of various markers ranges from formal to hand engraved. Religious symbols include the cross, book outlines representing the Bible, and hands clasped in prayer.

The cemetery has scattered markers with standardized designs from two major sources, fraternal lodges and the Veterans Administration. African American fraternal organizations, points out historian Jacqueline Moore, "provided opportunities not found in the larger society for Blacks to practice leadership skills, as well as places where they could meet socially in a friendly environment."[45] Liberty Chamber 2076 of Notasulga, Alabama, was the most active such group at the Shiloh cemetery, installing standardized markers primarily for women members but also sponsoring the tombstone for Rev. Sam Moss (d. 1918), who was the minister at Shiloh Missionary Baptist Church for fifteen years. The Liberty Chamber was the local chapter of the Mosaic Templars of America, an African American fraternal organization established in 1883 in Little Rock, Arkansas, that embraced both men and women. The organization at its height in the 1920s had over 100,000 mem-

FIGURE 6.3. Shiloh Missionary Baptist Church Cemetery, facing north (photograph by the author)

bers and chapters throughout the South.[46] Veterans Administration markers honor servicemen and women from World War II through the Vietnam War. The congregation takes great pride in the number of veterans buried at the cemetery.

The victims of the USPHS syphilis study are not officially designated in any manner, and their graves are found throughout the cemetery, typically arranged in family sections. Charlie Pollard, who is one of the study's most recognized victims, due to his interview in *Ebony* magazine in 1972 and subsequent testimony before Congress, is buried at Shiloh. His tombstone, erected in 2000, bears the inscription "father." Nearby is the grave marker of his descendant Elizabeth Sims (d. 2010), who spent her last years of life working with multiple local, state, and national partners to fulfill her vision of having three adjacent sites associated with the syphilis study—the cemetery, Shiloh Rosenwald School, and Shiloh Missionary Baptist Church—listed as national landmarks. She told the local newspaper in 2008, "So many people, young and old, know absolutely nothing about the trials that went on here. I'm hoping to get recognition for those men."[47]

For decades, members of the Shiloh Missionary Baptist Church understood the impact of the study on their community. In 1972 church member

Charlie Pollard first approached civil rights attorney Fred Gray to represent him, and eventually hundreds of others, in a federal lawsuit. Pollard was one of Jean Heller's interviewees for an influential *New York Times* exposé of the program in July 1972 and then in November of that year was featured in an extensive story about the program in *Ebony* magazine.[48] At a Senate hearing in 1973 about the abusive program, Pollard testified that no USPHS official ever gave him an opportunity for informed consent.[49] "All I knew was that they just kept saying I had the bad blood—they never mention syphilis to me, not even once," he told James T. Wooten of the *New York Times* in 1972.[50]

In 1996 a group of community members and academics produced a report about the study and its legacy, urging the federal government to offer a formal apology. In the spring of 1997, officials at the White House agreed. Attorney Fred Gray gathered four surviving victims—Pollard, Herman Shaw, Fred Simmons, and Carter Howard—for a press conference at Shiloh Missionary Baptist Church. Gray cuttingly told the reporters, "These men were taken advantage of by being used as human guinea pigs." Herman Shaw thought that a monument should be built "so our children, grandchildren, and great grandchildren could see what we went through."[51] Pollard and his neighbors attended a ceremony at the White House on May 16, 1997, when President Bill Clinton offered an official apology on behalf of the United States government. Later that summer, Jean Heller, one of the original journalists covering the story, wrote about the lasting legacy of the syphilis study nearly twenty-five years after it ended: a "deep-seated distrust" that African Americans everywhere held against the medical establishment.[52]

The legacy that concerned Herman Shaw most, however, was a wish for a place where his descendants "could see what we went through." In 1999, the Tuskegee History Center opened in downtown Tuskegee and featured a major exhibit about the study. In 2009, the recently established Bioethics Center at Tuskegee University finished a major exhibit about the syphilis study.[53] These institutional responses, no matter how respectfully executed, meant little to Elizabeth Sims and members of Shiloh Missionary Baptist Church. They wished for people to understand by going to the actual place where these African American men gathered, and where federal physicians repeatedly violated their rights and bodies. Sims particularly took Clinton's words—"Let us resolve to hold forever in our hearts and minds the memory of a time not long ago in Macon County, Alabama, so that we can always see how adrift we can become when the rights of any citizens are neglected, ignored and betrayed"—as a call for action.[54]

FIGURE 6.4. Shiloh Missionary Baptist Church Cemetery, including Charlie Pollard grave, facing west (photograph by the author)

It is this call for action that gives Shiloh Missionary Baptist Church Cemetery much of its meaning. As Elizabeth Sims explained to me in 2007:

> Most people look at this as a historic project. I look at it as being personal simply because it is the life I lived. I and 5 of my sisters and brothers attended this Shiloh Rosenwald School, I have been a member of this church since the age of 9, and both grandfathers and my great grandfather were in the Tuskegee Syphilis Study. My maternal grandfather was blinded by this study and my grandmother died at a very young age and her last child was born with mental problems. My grandfather was already blind by the time I was born in 1949. So his blindness occurred between 1932–1949.[55]

Sims was a determined leader. Although the project undoubtedly took longer than she wished, within ten years the community foundation achieved its overriding goal, which Sims called her "Plan A," of having all three related community institutions—the church, cemetery, and school—listed for their national significance in the National Register of Historic Places. The restoration of the school came first, thanks to a grant from Lowe's Companies Inc. and successful partnerships with Tuskegee University and Auburn University.[56]

FIGURE 6.5. Shiloh Missionary Baptist Church Cemetery, interpretive marker, facing south (photograph by the author)

Community members then raised money from donations and private foundations for the cemetery. They designed and installed their own interpretive marker, emblazoned with the logo of the Shiloh Community Restoration Foundation, along the state highway that fronts the cemetery. They wanted their own memorial with their own words, because the victims buried there belonged to their community and to their families, and they too wanted them buried as everyone always had been, in a dignified manner that spoke to their strength and character, qualities that the federal experiment could never take away from them.[57] Barbara Mahone, a descendant of a syphilis study victim and later chair of the Shiloh Community Restoration Foundation, asserted that Shiloh had "a story that reminds us how far we have come as citizens in the last 100 years and reflects the best we can be. Its story also reminds us of what happens when we turn away from our core values and forget the basic dignity of all citizens. This story is about the best and the worst of humankind and a determined perseverance through it all."[58]

It matters to the Shiloh community, as it did to the congregation of Creek Stand AME Zion Church, that visitors come to their community and stand where the syphilis study victims stood as they waited for the federal physicians, where they worshipped as community members, where their funerals were held, and where they were buried. The actual place allows today's descendants to tell the story, directly and without being filtered.[59] A core concept in public history is shared authority. In the case of Shiloh Cemetery, the descendants hold almost all of the authority: it was their community that was victimized and thus it is their story to control. To avoid victimizing families once again in the name of history, the descendants needed to decide how much individual information to share. They already have shared so much in preserving and taking care of the very place where the syphilis study occurred, then opening it to those of us who can never really understand its meaning. At the end of the chapter is a list of study victims at both cemeteries that the congregations are willing to share.

In 2016 the MTSU Center for Historic Preservation collaborated, pro bono, with the community foundation on the exhibits to be installed in the Shiloh Rosenwald School, which operates now as a community center. The descendants chose the three themes—the school, the community, and the syphilis study. They controlled the language of each exhibit panel. The primary interpretive panel about the study reads:

> Shiloh School and the Public Health Service Syphilis Study
>
> On cold days in the 1950s and 1960s, patients such as Charlie Pollard, would wait here, peering out the large windows for staff from the U.S. Public Health Service to arrive by automobile. From here, nurses and physicians took Pollard and the others to Tuskegee for what were called examinations.
>
> These men were innocent victims of one of the nation's most infamous medical scandals, the U.S. Public Health Service's study of untreated syphilis among African American men in Macon County, which lasted from 1932 to 1972. The doctors called places like Shiloh "roundup" locations, where men would gather for what they thought would be medical treatment from U.S. government physicians. Instead, their health was merely monitored, with no treatment provided. In 1997 at a White House ceremony President Bill Clinton offered an apology from the nation to seven surviving victims, among whom was Charlie Pollard, who is buried in nearby Shiloh Cemetery.[60]

Medical historians who were asked by the community foundation to review the interpretive panel questioned the use of the word "victim," rather than "patient" or "subject," but the community members insisted on using that term because, as Felecia Chandler said, "they were never informed, they never had a choice."[61]

In 2009 historian Susan M. Reverby considered what places such as the Shiloh cemetery mean in the twenty-first century: "For the families, the Study is etched in their memories and identities. I learned this once again as I came to the Shiloh church. It was in its school and yard that Nurse Rivers recruited dozens of the men, and it is in the church's graveyard up the road that they are buried. It is where Lucious Pollard, a man in the Study who died of syphilis, has his picture and words 'gone but not forgotten' carved on his headstone." Reverby concludes, "'Tuskegee' is one of the foundational stories of American racism in the twentieth century, and it anchors our beliefs about race, medicine, and science."[62] This rural cemetery tells a most powerful story, yet it remains centered in the community, protected by the community, and told most powerfully through the community's own exhibits and historic markers.

Creek Stand AME Zion Church Cemetery and Shiloh Missionary Baptist Church Cemetery are sacred places of community, faith, and memory for two rural African American neighborhoods in Macon County, Alabama. By their efforts to preserve and tell their side of the Tuskegee Study story, however, a group of dedicated and determined African American women—Shari Williams, Rev. Katrina Love, Elizabeth Sims, Shirley Johnson, Barbara Mahone, and Felecia Chandler—have quietly established two of the most powerful public monuments about American history in not only the Alabama Black Belt but in the nation as a whole. Cemeteries need not be covered by architecturally pleasing sculptures and crypts to be monumental—they can be monumental in the stories they preserve and commemorate and, in the case of these two unassuming places in Macon County, by the counternarratives of American history that they represent.

Appendix

**IDENTIFIED SYPHILIS STUDY VICTIMS BURIED AT
CREEK STAND AME CHURCH CEMETERY**

Albert Daniels Sr.	Ernest Lloyd	Henry Pace
Clark Daniel	Fonzie Mahone	John Shaughter
Albert Julkes	Elmore Pace	Ed Sparks
Ephron Julkes		

**IDENTIFIED SYPHILIS STUDY VICTIMS BURIED AT
SHILOH MISSIONARY BAPTIST CHURCH CEMETERY**

Frank Cooper	Charlie Pinkard	Will Pollard
Joseph Holliday	Charlie Pollard	Jethro Potts
Dave Mahone	Elbert Pollard	Albert Robinson
Richard Mims	Lucious Pollard	Herman Shaw
Julius Mott	Osburn Pollard	Anderson Sinclair
Charles Pinkard		

Notes

1. Foner, *Reconstruction*, 88–102. In a 2008 essay I explored how churches, schools, and cemeteries were often located in very close proximity to each other in rural southern African American communities. West, "Sacred Spaces of Faith, Community, and Resistance."
2. Rainville, *Hidden History*; Schexnayder and Mainhein, *Fragile Grounds*.
3. For pivotal historical studies see Jones, *Bad Blood*; Reverby, *Tuskegee's Truths*; Washington, *Medical Apartheid*.
4. Corbie-Smith et al., "Attitudes and Beliefs of African Americans toward Participation in Medical Research"; Green, Mckiernan-González, and Summers, *Precarious Prescriptions*; Alford, *Tuskegee's Forgotten Women*.
5. Brandt and Churchill, "Preface," xv.
6. Lederer, "Tuskegee Syphilis Study in the Context of American Medical Research," 266.
7. O. C. Wenger to R. A. Vonderlehr, July 21, 1933, Center for Disease Control Papers, Tuskegee Syphilis Study Administrative Records, 1930–1980, box 5, folder correspondence, National Archives–Southeast Region.
8. Berry, *Price for Their Pound of Flesh*; Roberts, *Killing the Black Body*; Washington, *Medical Apartheid*; Skloot, *Immortal Life of Henrietta Lacks*; Nystrom, "Bioarchaeology of Structural Violence and Dissection"; Davidson, "'Resurrection Men' in Dallas."
9. Davidson, "'Resurrection Men' in Dallas," 194.
10. Jones, *Bad Blood*, 187.
11. Reverby, *Tuskegee's Truths*, 18, 34.
12. Charles S. Johnson, *Shadow of the Plantation*, cited in Reverby, *Tuskegee's Truths*, 59.
13. Brandt, "Racism and Research," 21–22.
14. Eugene H. Dibble Jr. to Dr. R. R. Moton, September 17, 1932, R. R. Moton Papers, General Correspondence, box 180, folder 1516, Public Health Service, Tuskegee University Archives, Tuskegee, Ala.
15. Cumming's letter is cited in Jones, *Bad Blood*, 102.
16. Rivers, "Health Work with a Movable School"; also see analysis of Rivers's career in Susan Smith, *Sick and Tired of Being Sick and Tired*, 106–9; Ethan Bernal, "Rivers' Role: A Deeper Look into Nurse Eunice Rivers Laurie," *Tuskegee News*, March 14, 2013.
17. Mayberry, "Tuskegee Movable School."
18. Smith, "Neither Victim nor Villain" 95–113; Reverby, "Rethinking the Tuskegee Syphilis Study"; Michael Marriott, "First, Do No Harm: A Nurse and the Deceived Subjects of the Tuskegee Study," *New York Times*, February 16, 1997; "How Nurse Eunice Rivers Became Involved in the Tuskegee Syphilis Study: A Tale of Prejudice, Betrayal, and Neglect," *Atlanta Daily World*, February 6, 2018.
19. Brandt, "Racism and Research," 23.
20. Dorr, "Assuring America's Place in the Sun," 276.
21. Lombardo and Dorr, "Eugenics, Medical Education, and the Public Health Service," 303.
22. Savitt, "Use of Blacks for Medical Experimentation and Demonstration"; Roberts, *Killing the Black Body*; Washington, *Medical Apartheid*.
23. Washington, *Medical Apartheid*, 13.
24. Bell, "Events in the Tuskegee Syphilis Study," 35.
25. Lombardo and Dorr, "Eugenics, Medical Education, and the Public Health Service," 313.
26. Reverby, *Examining Tuskegee*, 41–50.
27. O. C. Wenger to R. A. Vonderlehr, July 21, 1933, Center for Disease Control Papers,

Tuskegee Syphilis Study Administrative Records, 1930–1980, box 5, folder correspondence, National Archives–Southeast Region.

28. "HEW to End Ala. Study of Syphilis," *New York Times*, October 28, 1972.

29. Jones, *Bad Blood*, 210–11; Reverby, *Tuskegee's Truths*, 171 (quote).

30. Gray, *Tuskegee Syphilis Study*, 80–99. In an appendix to the book, Gray lists the names of the subjects associated with the study.

31. Jones, *Bad Blood*, 186.

32. For example, see "Rural African American Churches in Tennessee, 1850–1970" multiple property nomination form for the National Register of Historic Places, Tennessee Historical Commission, 1999, National Park Service, https://npgallery.nps.gov/NRHP/AssetDetail/55b6bcf1-2b93-4289-ad38-d19bc6304540; "The Civil Rights Movement in Selma, Alabama, 1865–1972," multiple property form for the National Register of Historic Places, Alabama Historical Commission, 2013, National Park Service, https:npgallery.nps.gov/NRHP/AssetDetail/ bbb16bcf-ee90-45a4-ba0d-8cbe29ca91a0.

33. "The U.S. Public Health Service Syphilis Study, Macon County, Alabama, 1932–1975," multiple property nomination form for the National Register of Historic Places, Alabama Historical Commission, 2010, National Park Service, https://catalog.archives.gov/id/77835306.

34. Macon County Deed Book 4 (1894), 169–71, Macon County Register of Deeds, Tuskegee, Alabama.

35. See the website for The Ridge project, which is being carried out by Auburn University and the local communities of Macon County, www.digtheridge.com.

36. Matthew Busch, "Descendant of Macon County Slaves to Help Commemorate History," *Birmingham News*, May 27, 2011.

37. Shari L. Williams to Elizabeth Moore, fieldwork coordinator, Middle Tennessee State University Center for Historic Preservation, September 18, 2011, USPHS Syphilis Study Files, MTSU Center for Historic Preservation; also see Shari L. Williams, "Creek Stand African Methodist Episcopal Zion Church Cemetery," Alabama Historic Cemetery Register application, Alabama Historical Commission, Montgomery, 2010.

38. Jean Heller, "The Legacy of Tuskegee," *Tampa Bay Times*, July 20, 1997.

39. Notes from field visits to Creek Stand AME Zion Church, September 2011 and April 2013, Creek Stand AME Zion Church National Register File, Middle Tennessee State University Center for Historic Preservation.

40. Photographs of Participants in the Tuskegee Syphilis Study, Record Group 442, Records of the Centers for Disease Control and Prevention, 1921–2002, National Archives–Southeast Region.

41. Public Health Service to Dear Sir, October 18, 1955, CDC Papers, Tuskegee Syphilis Study Administrative Records, 1930–80, box 16, folder Alabama-Misc., National Archives–Southeast Region. Also cited in Reverby, *Tuskegee's Truths*, 102.

42. Notes from community discussion with Shari Williams, Willie Pace, Katrina Love, Hattie Lloyd Youson, Jerry Washington, and Alfonso Tolbert at Creek Stand AME Church, September 2011, Creek Stand AME Zion Church National Register Nomination File, Middle Tennessee State University Center for Historic Preservation.

43. "Shiloh Cemetery," Shiloh Community Restoration Foundation, https://shiloh commfound.com/shiloh-community-restoration-foundaton/syphilis-study/cemetery/.

44. Aiken, *Cotton Plantation South since the Civil War*, chap. 5.

45. Moore, *Booker T. Washington, W.E.B. DuBois, and the Struggle for Racial Equality*, 6.

46. Blake Wintory and Ashan R. Hampton, "Mosaic Templars of America," *Encyclopedia*

of Arkansas, last updated August 19, 2021, https://encyclopediaofarkansas.net/entries/mosaic-templars-of-america-1186/.

47. Jeff Thompson, "Shiloh Starts Down Road to Washington," *Tuskegee News*, January 10, 2008.

48. Jean Heller, "Syphilis Victims in U.S. Study Went Untreated for 40 Years," *New York Times*, July 26, 1972; Slater, "Condemned to Die for Science.".

49. "Blacks Tell of U.S. Deceit in Syphilis Study," *Miami Herald*, March 9, 1973.

50. James T. Wooten, "Survivor of '32 Syphilis Study Recalls a Diagnosis," *New York Times*, July 27, 1972.

51. Sonya Ross, "Syphilis Patients to Get Apology," *Cincinnati Enquirer*, April 9, 1997.

52. Jean Heller, "The Legacy of Tuskegee," *Tampa Bay Times*, July 20, 1997.

53. Lynch, *Origins of Bioethics*, 43–78.

54. "Remarks of the President in Apology for Study Done in Tuskegee, May 16, 1997," Office of the Press Secretary, the White House, William J. Clinton Papers, Clinton Presidential Library, National Archives.

55. Elizabeth Sims, email message to the author, September 24, 2007, Shiloh Missionary Baptist Church Cemetery National Register Nomination Files, Middle Tennessee State University Center for Historic Preservation.

56. Jeff Thompson, "Shiloh's New Team Puts Project on Its Shoulders," *Tuskegee News*, August 20, 2009.

57. Notes taken from field visits to the cemetery with Elizabeth Sims and Edie Powell, January 2008 and July 2009, and with Felecia Chandler and Barbara Mahone, August 2014, Shiloh Missionary Baptist Church Cemetery National Register Nomination Files, Middle Tennessee State University Center for Historic Preservation.

58. Barbara Mahone to the author, December 12, 2014; notes taken from field visits to the cemetery.

59. "My Soul Looks Back in Wonder, Tuskegee, Alabama," *Philadelphia Sun*, January 3, 2014.

60. Shiloh Community Exhibit, Shiloh Rosenwald School, Notasulga, Ala., installed 2016; "Shiloh Rosenwald School to Debut New History Exhibit," *Tuskegee News*, August 4, 2016; Rosanna Smith, "Shiloh Rosenwald School Opens as New Permanent History Exhibit," WSFA 12 News, August 13, 2016.

61. Comments by Felecia Chandler, Notes from Planning Session, Shiloh Exhibit Project, 2016, Files, Middle Tennessee State University Center for Historic Preservation.

62. Reverby, *Examining Tuskegee*, 238–39.

Bibliography

Aiken, Charles S. *The Cotton Plantation South since the Civil War*. Baltimore: Johns Hopkins University Press, 1998.

Alford, Deleso A. *Tuskegee's Forgotten Women: The Untold Side of the U.S. Public Health Service Syphilis Study*. New York: ABC-CLIO, 2018.

Bell, Susan E. "Events in the Tuskegee Syphilis Study." In *Tuskegee's Truths: Rethinking the Tuskegee Syphilis Study*, edited by Susan M. Reverby, 34–40. Chapel Hill: University of North Carolina Press, 2000.

Berry, Daina R. *The Price for Their Pound of Flesh: The Value of the Enslaved from Womb to Grave in the Building of the Nation*. Boston: Beacon Press, 2017.

Brandt, Allan M. "Racism and Research: The Case of the Tuskegee Syphilis Experiment." *Hastings Center Report* 8, no. 6 (1978): 21–29.

Brandt, Allan M., and Larry R. Churchill. "Preface." In *Tuskegee's Truths: Rethinking the Tuskegee Syphilis Study*, edited by Susan M. Reverby, xv–xvi. Chapel Hill: University of North Carolina Press, 2000.

Clinton, William J., Papers. Clinton Presidential Library, National Archives. Little Rock, Arkansas.

Corbie-Smith, Giselle, Stephen B. Thomas, Mark V. Williams, and Sandra Moody-Ayers. "Attitudes and Beliefs of African Americans toward Participation in Medical Research." *Journal of General Internal Medicine* 14, no. 9 (1999): 537–46.

Davidson, James M. "'Resurrection Men' in Dallas: The Illegal Use of Black Bodies as Medical Cadavers." *Journal of Historical Archaeology* 11, no. 3 (2007): 193–220.

Dorr, Gregory M. "Assuring America's Place in the Sun: Ivey Foreman Lewis and the Teaching of Eugenics at the University of Virginia, 1915–1933." *Journal of Southern History* 66, no. 2 (May 2000): 257–96.

Foner, Eric. *Reconstruction: America's Unfinished Revolution, 1863–1877*. New York: Harper and Row, 1988.

Gray, Fred D. *The Tuskegee Syphilis Study: The Real Story and Beyond*. Montgomery, Ala.: NewSouth Books, 1998.

Green, Laurie B., John Mckiernan-González, and Martin Summers, eds. *Precarious Prescriptions: Contested Histories of Race and Health in the United States*. Minneapolis: University of Minnesota Press, 2014.

Jones, James J. *Bad Blood: The Tuskegee Syphilis Experiment*. New York: Basic Books, 1993.

Lederer, Susan. "Tuskegee Syphilis Study in the Context of American Medical Research." In *Tuskegee's Truths: Rethinking the Tuskegee Syphilis Study*, edited by Susan M. Reverby, 266–75. Chapel Hill: University of North Carolina Press, 2000.

Lombardo, Paul A., and Gregory M. Dorr. "Eugenics, Medical Education, and the Public Health Service: Another Perspective on the Tuskegee Syphilis Experiment." *Bulletin of the History of Medicine* 80, no. 2 (2006): 291–316.

Lynch, John A. *The Origins of Bioethics: Remembering When Medicine Went Wrong*. East Lansing: Michigan State University Press, 2019.

Mayberry, B. D. "The Tuskegee Movable School: A Unique Contribution to National and International Agriculture and Rural Development." *Agricultural History* 65, no. 2 (1991): 85–104.

Moore, Jacqueline M. *Booker T. Washington, W.E.B. DuBois, and the Struggle for Racial Equality*. Wilmington, Del.: Scholarly Resources, 2003.

Moton, R.R., Papers. Tuskegee University Archives. Tuskegee, Ala.

Nystrom, Kenneth C. "The Bioarchaeology of Structural Violence and Dissection in the 19th-Century United States." *American Anthropologist* 116, no. 4 (December 2014): 765–79.

Records of the Centers for Disease Control and Prevention, 1921–2002. National Archives–Southeast Region.

Rainville, Lynn. *Hidden History: African American Cemeteries in Central Virginia*. Charlottesville: University of Virginia Press, 2014.

Reverby, Susan M. *Examining Tuskegee: The Infamous Syphilis Study and Its Legacy*. Chapel Hill: University of North Carolina Press, 2009.

Reverby, Susan M. "Rethinking the Tuskegee Syphilis Study: Nurse Rivers, Silence, and the Meaning of Treatment." In *Tuskegee's Truths: Rethinking the Tuskegee Syphilis Study*, edited by Susan M. Reverby, 365–85. Chapel Hill: University of North Carolina Press, 2000.

Reverby, Susan M., ed. *Tuskegee's Truths: Rethinking the Tuskegee Syphilis Study*. Chapel Hill: University of North Carolina Press, 2000.

Rivers, Eunice. "Health Work with a Movable School." *Public Health Nurse* 18 (November 1926): 575–77.

Roberts, Dorothy. *Killing the Black Body: Race, Reproduction, and the Meaning of Liberty*. New York: Pantheon, 1997.

Savitt, Todd L. "The Use of Blacks for Medical Experimentation and Demonstration in the Old South." *Journal of Southern History* 48, no. 3 (1982): 331–48.

Schexnayder, Jessica H., and Mary H. Mainhein. *Fragile Grounds: Louisiana's Endangered Cemeteries*. Jackson: University Press of Mississippi, 2017.

Skloot, Rebecca. *The Immortal Life of Henrietta Lacks*. New York: Crown Books, 2010.

Slater, Jack. "Condemned to Die for Science." *Ebony*, November 1972, 177–90.

Smith, Susan L. "Neither Victim nor Villain: Nurse Eunice Rivers, the Tuskegee Syphilis Experiment, and Public Health Work." *Journal of Women's History* 8, no. 1 (Spring 1996): 95–113.

Smith, Susan L. *Sick and Tired of Being Sick and Tired: Black Women's Health Activism in America, 1890–1950*. Philadelphia: University of Pennsylvania Press, 1995.

Tuskegee Syphilis Study Administrative Records, 1930–1980. National Archives–Southeast Region.

USPHS Syphilis Study Files. Middle Tennessee State University Center for Historic Preservation, Murfreesboro.

Washington, Harriet A. *Medical Apartheid: The Dark History of Medical Experimentation on Black Americans*. New York: Harlem Moon, 2006.

West, Carroll Van. "Sacred Spaces of Faith, Community, and Resistance." In *"We Shall Independent Be": African American Place Making and the Struggle to Claim Space in the United States*, edited by Angel D. Nieves and Leslie M. Alexander, 439–62. Boulder: University Press of Colorado, 2008.

EPILOGUE
TEACHING THE AMERICAN SOUTH BY LEARNING THE DEAD

Part One:
The Historic Cemetery at Creek Stand AME Zion Church

Now that we know the background of the U.S. Public Health Service Syphilis Study, let's next consider one of the cemeteries where the victims of the study are buried.

FIGURE 6.2. Creek Stand AME Zion Church Cemetery, facing southeast (photograph by the author) (see also p. 181)

FIGURE 6.6. Creek Stand AME Zion Church Cemetery, facing northeast (photograph by the author)

FIGURE 6.1. Creek Stand AME Zion Church Cemetery, facing northwest (photograph by the author) (see also p. 179)

FIGURE 6.7. Amy Pace grave marker, Creek Stand AME Zion Church Cemetery (photograph by the author)

FIGURE 6.8. Ned Pace grave marker, Creek Stand AME Zion Church Cemetery (photograph by the author)

FIGURE 6.9. Lelar Hubbard grave marker, Creek Stand AME Zion Church Cemetery (photograph by the author)

How would you describe the cemetery?

Are the grave markers similar?

What questions about the people buried at the cemetery would you want to pursue?

What are online resources you can use to find out more about those buried here?

Does the cemetery strike you as a place that reflects the class and wealth of the victims?

Why would this place still matter to the community?

What does the cemetery's setting and its markers imply about the syphilis study and its victims?

Part Two:
The Historical Marker at Shiloh Missionary Baptist Church Cemetery

What story is conveyed by the historical marker at Shiloh Missionary Baptist Church Cemetery?

How is this marker different from others you have seen at historic places or along highways?

Do the size and design of the marker reflect a community need to state clearly and loudly why the cemetery matters?

The marker faces a state highway. How does that location reflect the community's resistance to government erasure of the cemetery's story—in the present, and for the future?

FIGURE 6.5. Shiloh Missionary Baptist Church Cemetery, interpretive marker, facing south (photograph by the author)
(see also p. 186)

Part Three:
Documenting the Landscape

Why do cemeteries matter to the study of the U.S. Public Health Syphilis Study?

Are the cemeteries properties of commemoration or properties of victimization?

Should the stories and locations of these cemeteries be shared with others? Why?

CHAPTER 7

Profane Memorials

Burying the Martyrs of the Civil Rights Movement

ADRIENNE CHUDZINSKI

The Southern Poverty Law Center (SPLC) recognizes forty "civil rights martyrs" in the Civil Rights Memorial located at its central office in Montgomery, Alabama. According to the SPLC website, "The martyrs include activists who were targeted for death because of their civil rights work; random victims of vigilantes determined to halt the movement; and individuals who, in the sacrifice of their own lives, brought new awareness to the struggle."[1] Seven of the forty individuals remembered in the SPLC's memorial died as adolescents—including fourteen-year-old Emmett Till and the four girls (ages eleven through fourteen) who were killed in the Sixteenth Street Baptist Church bombing. Unlike activist martyrs, these child victims were not targeted for their involvement in civil rights organizations. Instead, they died at the hands of white southerners who attempted to intimidate and terrorize Blacks.

To many Americans, the lynching of Emmett Till, a Chicagoan who was murdered in 1955 in Mississippi for offending a white woman, served as a watershed event of the civil rights movement. Till's death propelled civil rights into mainstream American consciousness by attracting widespread national attention for the cause while simultaneously evolving into a rallying cry for movement organizers. Similarly, the Sixteenth Street Baptist Church bombing shocked and horrified many in the nation as it reminded global audiences of the United States' tragic legacy of racial inequality.[2] In the wake of the bombing, Martin Luther King Jr. traveled to Birmingham to deliver a eulogy in honor of the four children who perished in the blast. Although the victims were not participants in the civil rights movement,

FIGURE 7.1. Maya Lin, Civil Rights Memorial, 1989, monumental sculpture, Southern Poverty Law Center, Montgomery, Alabama (photograph by the author)

FIGURE 7.2. Virgil Ware is remembered along with the victims of the Sixteenth Street Baptist Church bombing at the Civil Rights Memorial (photograph by the author).

King implied that they were an integral force in the larger struggle, stating, "They are the martyred heroines of a holy crusade for freedom and human dignity."[3]

Though public remembrance celebrates these children as martyrs, their final resting places are not afforded the same degree of reverence. Following his funeral, Till was buried at Burr Oak Cemetery just outside Chicago in Alsip, Illinois. In 2005, Till's remains were exhumed as part of an ongoing FBI investigation, and he was reburied in a new casket. While Till's body remains at its original grave site, his casket has undergone several transformations. What initially served as a sacred vessel containing the young martyr later suffered desecration in an abandoned shed. Today, the casket in which Till was first buried has finally earned a position of national prominence and esteem at the National Museum of African American History and Culture. Similarly, though Americans have revered the victims of Birmingham's church bombing—Addie Mae Collins, Denise McNair, Carole Robertson, and Cynthia Wesley—as martyred heroines for the past sixty years, their physical remains rest beneath a sea of headstones in a dilapidated cemetery. Worse still, the body of one of the victims is presumably missing, while another is misidentified on her grave maker.

The local and national struggles to restore a degree of reverence and respect to the burial site of each of these victims have endured for the past half century. This is surprising given the amount of public attention paid to both of these crimes over the last sixty years. The narratives that emerged in the immediate wake of these events took on a moral, uplifting quality as civil rights leaders such as King reminded the nation that "unearned suffering is redemptive."[4] In this sense, the sacrifices of civil rights activists, and of these martyred children, were understood as moral offerings in the name of freedom, equality, and national progress. This concept of redemptive suffering provided a righteous rationale for the otherwise meaningless acts of racial violence and brutality that plagued the Black freedom struggle. But this emotional salve does not come without a cost. The personal identities of these victims were sacrificed even as many remembered them as sacred symbols of the civil rights movement. To address the incongruences in public and private forms of remembrance, it is also necessary to focus on the cultural afterlife of these prominent public deaths and to explore the tension that separates revered historical narratives from the reality found within cemeteries and public sites of remembrance.

Sacrificial Lamb of the Movement: Emmett Till

During the summer of 1955, fourteen-year-old Emmett Till of Chicago traveled to Mississippi for a summer-long visit with his cousins and uncle, Moses Wright.[5] Wright was a sharecropper, and his children worked alongside their father in the summer months. Till joined his cousins and their friends after they worked in the fields all day and sought refreshment at Bryant's Grocery and Meat Market, owned by Roy Bryant and his wife, Carolyn. On August 24, the boys entered the market a few at time and purchased candy and other small food items. Unaware of, or perhaps skeptical about, the severe level of racial intolerance in the South, Till allegedly made inappropriate, flirtatious comments to Carolyn Bryant while in the store. Over fifty years later, in a 2007 interview with historian Timothy B. Tyson, Carolyn Bryant recanted her original testimony and admitted what many had suspected for decades. When asked if Till grabbed her and made unseemly comments, she said, "That part's not true."[6] After Tyson asked Bryant to clarify, she claimed that she could not remember any specific details, only that she felt intense pressure from her husband's family to lie under oath about Till's behavior in the store.[7] Nevertheless, Till's cousin Simeon Wright, who was with the group that afternoon, agreed that upon exiting the grocery, young Emmett defied strict southern racial standards by letting out a "wolf whistle" directed at Carolyn Bryant.[8]

Terrified of the possible ramifications of Till's actions, the boys decided to keep a low profile and not inform Moses Wright about the episode. Three days later, after returning to town, Roy Bryant heard about the incident and set out to find young Till. Arriving at the home where Till was staying at 2:30 a.m., Bryant threatened the residents of the house before abducting the boy. Aided by his stepbrother, J. W. Milam, Bryant reportedly tortured and beat the boy for hours before shooting him in the head. Till's body was found in a river three days later, weighed down by a seventy-five-pound cotton gin that had been tied around his neck. "The boy was so badly beaten that" his great-uncle Moses Wright "could identify Emmett only by his father's ring."[9]

Considering his alleged "crime," Till's fate was not unusual in the South. Yet, the combined factors of his young age and geographic origins as a northerner made his case particularly startling to Americans living outside of Mississippi.[10] As the 1950s marked the beginning of an era in which civil rights, specifically race relations in the South, emerged as a national political issue, Till's story received widespread attention. "The youth of the victim helped bring the horror home with more impact to many white as well as Negro parents and other persons humane enough to believe a youngster enjoys a certain amount of immunity even for misdeeds," journalist Alfred Duckett wrote in the *Chicago Defender*. "The news significance lay in the age of the victim contrasted to the brutality of the crime."[11]

Amid the contentious debate surrounding the events leading up to Till's murder, his mother, Mamie Till-Mobley, attempted to assert control over Emmett's memory by carefully framing and shaping both the visitation and the funeral services.[12] Through the use of these initial memorialization efforts, Mamie was able to create a narrative in which Emmett took on the role of a young martyr in the struggle for racial equality.

According to Mamie, "We learned from Uncle Crosby that they were trying to bury Bo [Emmett] in Mississippi and I told him to stop the burial at any cost and to bring my baby—what was left of him out of Mississippi."[13] Southern law enforcement grudgingly returned Till's body to Illinois, yet an agreement between the sheriff in Mississippi and the funeral director in Chicago nearly kept the family from actually seeing Emmett's remains. Apparently, Chicago funeral director A. A. Rayner promised law enforcement in Mississippi that he would keep Till's casket closed or, more accurately, "nailed shut."[14] Though it is unclear precisely why Rayner agreed to the sheriff's terms, it is possible he acquiesced to ensure that Till's body would be sent northward to Chicago and not buried in Mississippi. Once the sealed casket arrived in Illinois, Rayner's initial unwillingness to open it may have been spurred in part by a desire to shield and protect the slain child's mother from the gruesome realities of Till's torture and subsequent murder. Nevertheless, Mamie demanded the funeral director allow her to view the mangled corpse of her only son and thus forgo any agreement he may have made to keep the casket sealed. According to Till-Mobley, "I asked him, 'Mr. Rayner, do you have a hammer? I haven't signed anything, and I haven't made any promises, and if you can't open . . . that box, I can.'"[15]

After privately viewing her son's body, Mamie chose to hold public visitation services. She firmly believed it was essential that she show Emmett's body in an open casket so that "everybody can see what they did to my boy."[16] In choosing to show her son's corpse publicly, Mamie effectively began the process of meaning making and memorialization surrounding Emmett and the nature of his death. Rather than characterizing Emmett as a helpless victim of Southern insensibility, Mamie portrayed her son as a martyr, a sacrifice in the larger struggle for civil rights. As the narrator of a documentary about Till noted, "Mamie's decision would make her son's death a touchstone for a generation: At a church on the South Side of Chicago, Emmett Till's mutilated body would be on display for all to see."[17]

Tens of thousands of individuals visited Roberts Temple Church of God in Chicago on September 3, 1955, to view Till's mutilated corpse.[18] The *Chicago Defender* reported, "Officials of the funeral home where the angry, the awed and the curious filed in to view the remains of the boy . . . declared they had never seen anything like it."[19] The predominantly African American crowd believed that everyone who wished should view the body; parents brought their young children as a way to teach them about the severe implications of racial injustice.[20] News of Till's crowded funeral services spread across the nation as media outlets such as the *Associated Press* and the *New York Times* provided coverage of the event.[21]

Carefully constructing her personal narrative surrounding Till's death, Mamie used specific, deliberate language that effectively determined the way in which civil rights activists and sympathizers would remember and honor her son.[22] In an interview with the *Chicago Defender*, Mamie described the rationale behind her decision to publicly discuss the details of her son's murder: "I think that the large class of decent people in this county are guilty of the sins of omission when they fail to speak out for the right and take a stand against injustice. These are the people I am appealing to."[23] By allowing the publication of photographs of Emmett's desecrated and disfigured body in Jet Magazine, Mamie expanded her memorialization efforts and ensured that all Americans, not just those living in Chicago, could see the extreme effects of Southern racial intolerance.[24]

The ways in which Mamie presented and displayed the corpse of her son and spoke about the larger meaning surrounding his death meant that members of the African American community, and also civil rights activists, would come to remember and revere Till as "the sacrificial lamb" of the civil rights movement.[25] In fact, the timing of Till's murder in 1955 played a large part in his transformation into a martyr, as it coincided with the emergence of the civil rights movement on a national stage. Specifically, the visual imagery of Till's mutilated corpse proved to be a key component in civil rights leaders' efforts to earn and maintain national attention for crimes of racial violence.

Till's lynching motivated individuals who were virtually unknown outside of local civil rights organizations—such as Rosa Parks and Martin Luther King Jr.—to stand up and speak out against the evils and injustices of Jim Crow.[26] When asked why she remained in her seat in a move that effectively began the Montgomery bus boycott, Parks replied, "I thought about Emmett Till, and I could not go back."[27] By invoking the memory of the boy's decimated corpse, Parks reminded Americans of the brutal side of Jim Crow and garnered public support for the civil rights movement. Similarly, other civil rights leaders such as Medgar Evers, Fred Shuttlesworth, and King utilized Till's memory to garner support for the cause. Shuttlesworth explained, "The fact that Emmett Till, a young Black man, could be found floating down the river in Mississippi, as, indeed, many had been done over the years, this set in concrete the determination of people to move forward."[28]

Following his funeral in 1955, Till was buried at Burr Oak Cemetery in Alsip, Illinois, about twenty miles southwest of Chicago. Burr Oak was established in 1927 in response to the Great Migration of African Americans out of the South and into major western and northern metropolises such as Chicago. In the late 1920s, the town of Alsip was predominantly white, and local residents were not happy about the prospect of having an African American cemetery so close to their homes. In fact, "armed police" attempted to block the first burial at Burr Oak but eventually conceded the land after a deputy sheriff arrived to oversee the dedication and burial.[29] By the time Till was buried nearly thirty years later, the cemetery was firmly established in the community.

Marking Till's grave site is a flat headstone that lies flush against the cemetery lawn. Along with his name and the dates of his birth and death, the marker bears the simple inscription "In Loving Memory" and features a permanent vase for floral offerings and a small photograph of the youth encased in an oval-shaped locket frame. In 2005, Till's body was exhumed by the FBI as new evidence led to a reinvestigation of the historic case. At this time, Till's corpse was removed from his original casket and placed in a new casket for reburial. Surviving members of Till's family entrusted the original casket to Carolyn Towns, director of Burr Oak Cemetery. In exchange, Towns vowed to raise money to create a museum in Till's honor that would display the casket and raise public awareness of Till's murder. Many, including Till's surviving family, supported the proposed museum, as the city of Chicago lacked any significant form of tribute to the "martyred" child.[30]

Yet, in the midst of the project, Towns was embroiled in a macabre scandal that made national headlines. As Black Entertainment Television (BET) reported, Towns "was convicted and sentenced to 12 years in prison for her role in stealing more than $100,000 in a scheme involving digging up bodies and reselling plots."[31] Till's body was not included in the list of those unlawfully exhumed, yet investigators discovered that Towns and her associates had seemingly discarded his casket in a shed that was abandoned but for a family of possums that had taken up residence.[32]

Till's family soon realized that Towns's conviction meant another missed opportunity to memorialize the slain youth in his hometown of Chicago. Simeon Wright, Till's cousin from Mississippi, criticized the city of Chicago for allowing fifty-six years to pass without creating a memorial or a museum for Emmett: "It is a sad commentary that this is his hometown. Even in the place that he was killed, they're building a memorial to him."[33] While there are undoubtedly many groups and organizations that would support the initiative to create a memorial for Till, it is unclear why Chicago has failed to prioritize this project. Perhaps the delay stems from a lack of funding and clear leadership. Yet the problem is also related to the difficulty of connecting Till's murder to the larger community of Chicago. For many, Till's murder was a southern issue and thus should be remembered that way: removed from Chicago, deep in the southern landscape of Mississippi.

Following the discovery of the Burr Oak Cemetery scandal, Till's surviving family members chose to donate his original casket to the Smithsonian Institution's National Museum of African American History and Culture (NMAAHC).[34] According to NMAAHC director Lonnie Bunch, "Part of the responsibility of a national museum is to help people to remember, and through this donation we will ensure that future generations will remember how the death of a child, a mother's courage, helped to transform America."[35] The casket is now on display in an exhibition titled "Defending Freedom, Defining Freedom: The Era of Segregation 1876–1968," and Till's story has shifted from its relatively inaccessible position in regional peripheries to the center of the larger national narrative surrounding the African American experience.

Though Till's physical remains are still interred at Burr Oak cemetery, the story of his life and legacy is most visible at the NMAAHC. Till's cousin, Simeon Wright, who shared a bed with the teen the night he was abducted in Mississippi, said that in looking at the casket, "I see something that held the object of a mother's unconditional love. And then I see a love that was interrupted and shattered by racial hatred without a cause."[36] Wright's emphasis on Till's personal relationship with his mother helps to remind the public that before his horrific murder, the fourteen-year-old had an individual identity that was largely unrelated to the Black freedom struggle. By insisting that her son's corpse be visible and by rejecting social pressure to remain silent, Mamie Till-Mobley refused to allow her son to become another nameless victim of racial violence. At the same time, she played an instrumental role in defining the imagery of the murder and creating an accompanying narrative that not only transformed her son into a martyr but made his death a touchstone moment in the national civil rights movement.

In this sense, contemporary public remembrance of Till reflects his death and burial in 1955. Mamie took a very private moment, the murder of her only child, and made it public. She publicly mourned Emmett and invited the rest of the nation to do so as well by viewing his body and attending his funeral. While Bur Oak Cemetery remains open to the public, its geographic location in a small suburb of Chicago ensures that Till's grave site has remained a relatively private space for surviving family to remember the boy they lovingly called Bobo. Yet, just as they did with the images of his desecrated body, Till's family has chosen to share his casket with the rest of the nation in an effort to educate and inspire positive change. This parallel is explicit at the NMAAHC. Curator Paul Gardullo and director Lonnie Bunch explained, "Our decision to display Emmett's casket as his mother displayed it at Roberts Temple Church of God in Christ on Chicago's South Side in September of 1955—open, for all the world to see—is a choice that daily pays tribute to her courage and, hopefully, acts as a source of inspiration for our many visitors to find a small piece of that courageous act in their own lives toward creating a more just, equal and fair society."[37] For the "sacrificial lamb" of the civil rights movement, it is the final resting place of the casket, rather than of the bodily remains, that conveys the legacy of Till's involuntary martyrdom.

Perhaps this is for the best. In recent years, the details of the sordid reburial scheme at Burr Oak have only become more unsavory. Along with Towns, three other cemetery employees were found guilty on charges of digging up nearly three hundred graves, desecrating corpses, and reburying the decedents in an unmarked mass grave.[38] The cemetery was in disarray as local law enforcement and federal investigators worked to uncover the extent of the damage caused by those who perpetrated these grisly crimes. After a visit to the cemetery in 2011, one observer remarked, "Crime tape from the investigation into the reburial scheme still covered the grounds. Dirt streaked Till's marker, and it was hard to imagine any improvement in the whole grim scene."[39] During her next visit, just five years later, much had improved. Shortly after news of the scandal broke, a court-appointed trustee was given the responsibility of managing the cemetery. In 2014, Burr Oak Cemetery unveiled a memorial monument created to honor all those buried at the historic African American cemetery, especially those affected by the recent scandal.[40]

Till and his mother, who is also buried at Burr Oak, are implicitly included as honorees at this site. Yet it makes sense, given the circumstances surrounding his death and burial, that public remembrance of Till is less conspicuous in this space. After all, it was the graphic images associated with Till's death and Mamie's bold decision to display his corpse that catapulted this case into its position of historic and national prominence. The same articles—in both historically African American newspapers and in those read by a wider national audience—that gave front-page coverage to Till's funeral and included photographs of an inconsolable Mamie at the grave site made only passing reference to the cemetery in which the teen was buried.[41] And as the civil rights movement gained momentum in the late 1950s and early 1960s, it was evident that this public remembrance of Till set the tone concerning the representation and memorialization of the civil rights deaths that would follow—beginning with another instance of murder involving innocent children.

The Sixteenth Street Baptist Church Bombing and Birmingham's "Four Little Girls"

After attending their Sunday school class on September 15, 1963, five girls ventured into the ladies' room at Birmingham's Sixteenth Street Baptist Church to smooth their dresses and freshen up before assisting with the youth day service. At 10:22 a.m., a bomb erupted at the church, killing four of the five girls in the restroom and injuring many others. In the wake of the bombing, Martin Luther King Jr. traveled to Birmingham to eulogize the victims and to create a narrative that would garner sympathy and support for the murdered children and, by extension, the larger civil rights struggle they came to represent. King comforted the mourners in Birmingham by explaining, "They are the martyred heroines of a holy crusade for freedom and human dignity." He promised, "The innocent blood of these little girls may well serve as a redemptive force that will bring new light to this dark city."[42]

The reverberations of the Sixteenth Street Baptist Church bombing were felt on an unprecedented level. The murders of these four adolescents attracted national attention that has continued through the present day—in 2013, the girls received the nation's highest civilian honor, the Congressional Gold Medal. Yet, despite public awareness of the crime, many in the nation are woefully unfamiliar with the legacies of personal suffering and individual loss that accompanied and outlasted the bombing in Birmingham. Nowhere is this disparity more clear than at Birmingham's Greenwood Cemetery.

Located on land adjacent to the Birmingham airport, Greenwood Cemetery (or Woodlawn Cemetery, as it was previously named) served as the final resting place of three of the four victims of the bombing: Addie Mae Collins, Cynthia Morris Wesley, and Carole Robertson. Unfortunately for the families of these victims, and the thousands of other decedents buried at Greenwood, the cemetery fell into a state of disarray after its owners and caretakers went bankrupt and abandoned their post in the late twentieth century. Rather than being a serene resting place for the movement's revered martyrs, the cemetery soon became a mess of opened graves with broken headstones. In some cases, uprooted trees caused caskets to surface and expose their contents. After one particularly strong storm, human remains littered the cemetery lawn.[43]

In 1997, filmmaker Spike Lee released *4 Little Girls*, a feature-length documentary about the Sixteenth Street Baptist Church bombing and the long struggle for justice in Birmingham. Earning praise and acclaim from popular audiences and film critics alike, Lee's documentary reminded the nation of the bombing and cemented its place in the civil rights narrative for a new generation of Americans. In a single remark, CBS news correspondent Walter Cronkite described the impact of the Birmingham bombing on the national consciousness: "This was the awakening."[44] Just as the bombing alerted the nation to, as Cronkite put it, "the depth of the problem and the depths of the hate" in Birmingham, Lee's documentary revealed the enduring legacy of racial violence: the pain, grief, and trauma that continued to plague those who survived the city's most violent and turbulent decades.[45] While the bombing has always been a fixture in the national narrative of the civil rights movement, public awareness about the victims of this crime and their families increased as a result of Lee's film.

In response, *People* magazine published an article that featured Junie and Sarah Collins, sisters of the deceased Addie Mae. In the years after the bombing, Junie told the magazine, she never smiled or discussed her sorrow with others. For Sarah, sleeping through the night without a panic attack was a feat.[46] After describing the surviving sisters' decades-long struggle to find a measure of peace and serenity in the wake of the blast, the article revealed that one aspect of the ordeal continued to disturb the Collins family: "the forlorn state of Addie's grave site."[47]

At the time of Addie Mae's burial, the Collins family did not have enough money for a proper headstone (or any type of permanent marker, for that matter).[48] For decades, a small wooden plaque served as the only indicator of the location of Addie Mae's grave site. After learning about the inadequate marker in 1990, Ken Mullinax, press secretary to local congressman Earl F. Hilliard, purchased a headstone for Addie Mae. In addition to listing her birth and death dates, the marble headstone described Addie Mae as a "civil rights martyr" and declared, "She died so freedom might live."[49] But even after the headstone was installed, the cemetery itself remained in a poor state. *People* reported, "The grass is overgrown, and a dirt road leading there is rutted, but Junie and Sarah can't afford to move their sister."[50] The condition of their sister's grave site, Junie explained, "is like an open sore to us."[51]

For the Collins sisters, the magazine article proved to be an unexpected blessing as the renewed national interest in the 1963 bombing resulted in an outpouring of public support. *People*, along with several other "media organizations," created a fund to assist the sisters in their goal of reburying Addie Mae, and by the end of 1997, the Collins family had raised enough money to move Addie Mae's grave to a better-maintained location.[52] In January 1998, Sarah hired Jim Stokes of the Superior Concrete Company to open Addie Mae's grave and retrieve her casket for reburial. Supervising the intended exhumation, Sarah grew anxious when the casket that supposedly held her sister's remains revealed an elderly individual wearing dentures and not the body of a child.[53] As workers widened their hole and dug deeper into the earth to check for another casket, Sarah was horrified to discover an otherwise vacant burial plot in what was supposed to be her sister's final resting place. Although Sarah had been unable to attend her sister's funeral and burial in 1963—she spent several months in the hospital recovering from her own injuries from the blast—she recalled visiting Addie Mae's grave site on various occasions in the years after the bombing. She told the *Los Angeles Times*, "I've been going there, talking to her for years. Then to find out that she really wasn't there... It was really hurtful."[54]

Since 1998 the Collins family, with the assistance of reporters, researchers, and local community members, have searched for an answer to the question of Addie Mae's missing remains. Many agree that the most likely explanation is that Addie Mae's headstone was simply misplaced by Congressman Hilliard and the Collins family, who gauged the location of Addie Mae's grave by using the small wooden marker that mourners placed in the ground during the 1963 burial. As it turned out, the wooden marker was a poor indicator of the burial plot's location, and no one in the Collins family or the local community was able to recall the exact location of Addie Mae's grave. The Collins siblings who were able to attend their sister's 1963 funeral were so distraught at the time that they can recall little other than King's presence, the large crowds, and their own feelings of profound grief. And although Cynthia Wesley was buried in close proximity to Collins, no one in attendance at either interment can agree upon the location of Addie Mae's burial site. In total, three of the four victims were buried in this space within a span of two days, but unlike Collins, Cynthia Wesley and Carole Robertson were interred in family plots, making the location of their caskets a certainty. Since they discovered this mystery nearly two decades ago, the Collins family has maintained the belief that Addie Mae's remains are likely buried in a nearby plot.

For much of the 1990s and early 2000s, the issue of Addie Mae's misplaced casket remained a local matter, but the year 2013—the fiftieth anniversary of the bombing—brought a new wave of national attention to Birmingham and, along with it, public outcry over the uncertain location of the decedent's body. Supporting the effort to locate Addie Mae's remains, one online commenter exclaimed, "This is just not right! We mourn and grieve over these children every year—as we should—but don't take the time and effort to find the final resting place of one of them? Why?"[55] After years of searching in vain for Addie Mae's grave, the Collins family confronted a harsh reality: though civic and national leaders revered Addie Mae in her symbolic form as a martyr, her physical body remains lost indefinitely.

Finally, in 2016, the Collins family received promising information after ground-penetrating radar scans suggested that Addie Mae is buried behind, rather than in front of, her headstone. One of those who replaced the original wooden marker with the marble headstone explained, "We felt confident that was the general area where her body was. But we were not being scientific in knowing for a fact that her body was in that exact location at that angle."[56] During the attempted disinterment in 1998, the family and contractors never considered looking behind the grave but now admit that location is plausible as it is in closer proximity to the burial site of Cynthia Morris Wesley, another of the bombing victims. Though the question of Addie Mae's grave site has not been definitively answered, for Sarah and her family, the ground scan evidence of a small casket behind the tombstone is enough. "I'm so happy we found where Addie's grave is located," she told a reporter. "I am just real happy."[57]

In the case of the Sixteenth Street Baptist Church bombing, the public's neglect of Addie Mae Collins's personal identity in favor of her symbolic role in the movement is not unique. In fact, the friends and families of each of the four young women killed that September morning have struggled in various ways over the past half century to sustain a memory of their loved ones that is at odds with the more mythical remembrance of the movement and its valorization of the murdered girls. This tension can be seen in one family's decades-long effort to recognize their murdered sister according to her biological ancestry and corresponding legal name.

Though she was named Cynthia Diane Morris at birth, by the early 1960s much of Birmingham's Black community recognized Cynthia as a Wesley.[58] She began using this surname shortly after moving in with Claude Wesley, the principal of Lewis Elementary School, and his wife, Gertrude, who worked alongside her husband as a teacher. Unable to have children of their own, the Wesleys were interested in adopting a child who demonstrated educational potential and who might benefit from the financial support they could provide. As a single mother of eight children, Estelle Morris was receptive to the Wesleys' offer to care for and educate her youngest daughter, Cynthia.[59] Though Estelle agreed to let Cynthia move in with the Wesleys, she was adamant that their arrangement remain informal.[60] Agreeing to this request, the Wesleys never pursued legal guardianship of Cynthia or filed formal adoption papers in Jefferson County. Nevertheless, Gertrude and Claude introduced Cynthia as their adopted child to their friends and used their own last name on her elementary and high school enrollment records.

As a result of her established, though not legal, identity within Birmingham's affluent Black community, local newspapers identified Cynthia as a Wesley instead of as a Morris—a misnomer that the national press published and reprinted endlessly for several decades. Yet the media are not solely responsible for the perpetuation of this error. At the time of her death in 1963, the Morris family could not afford the costs associated with a funeral, so Cynthia's final arrangements were handled by Gertrude and Claude.[61] As a result, Cynthia's postmortem medical records misidentified

FIGURE 7.3. Memorial plaque, Sixteenth Street Baptist Church, Birmingham, Alabama (photograph by the author)

her legal name, and her death certificate reflected her informal adoption by the Wesleys rather than her biological parentage. A few days after the bombing, when county coroner J. O. Butler requested demographic data for Cynthia's death certificate, he looked to Claude and Gertrude Wesley for this information. Butler listed Claude Wesley as the official "informant" on the document, and Claude provided his own name for the section marked "father," listed Gertrude as mother, and identified his adopted daughter as "Cynthia D. Wesley."[62] Butler signed the death certificate on September 18, 1963—the day of Cynthia's funeral—and the local registrar received the record the following day.[63] By this time, the local and national media had been referring to Cynthia by her adopted last name of Wesley for four days. The legal documents merely offered official confirmation of Cynthia's new surname in the formal record.

Even with these changes in the legal record, the modifications in Cynthia's name did not end with the filing of her death certificate. Though Claude listed only a middle initial of "D" on Cynthia's postmortem records, the funeral program for the joint obsequies identified the teen as "Cynthia Dianne Wesley"—adding an extra "n" to the victim's middle name.[64] Despite this error, the funeral program recognized Cynthia as "the adopted daughter of Mr. and Mrs. Claude A. Wesley" and thus made an implicit acknowledgment of the informal agreement between Estelle Morris and the Wesleys.[65] In addition, the program provided a few details about Cynthia's high school and extracurricular activities, both of which reflected her membership in Birmingham's affluent Black community. Finally, the last line of the program's biography hinted at the unusual nature of Cynthia's living arrangement. The program announced Cynthia's "immediate survivors are her mother, father, seven sisters and brother, an aunt, and Mr. and Mrs. Claude A. Wesley."[66] Though the program did not list Claude and Gertrude as Cynthia's mother and father, it did identify the Wesleys as her "adoptive parents" in an earlier sentence. Moreover, the acknowledgment of the Morris family in this paragraph is largely indirect; while it noted that the Wesleys adopted Cynthia and that she had seven biological siblings, it failed to acknowledge the Morris surname. Although Claude and Gertrude Wesley did not list the Morris family name or provide any of Cynthia's biological family members' names on the funeral program, neither did they claim to be the exclusive parents of this child. In this way, they extended a minor degree of recognition to the Morris family while maintaining their status as Cynthia's adoptive parents.

In choosing the best way to remember Cynthia, Claude and Gertrude also had to consider the expectations of the local congregation and community that likely knew the teen only as their child. In this sense, the program and the funeral services reflected the tenuous and flexible nature of Cynthia's identity as a member of both the Morris and Wesley families. Despite its shortcomings, the program from the joint funeral is one of the only sources from the twentieth century (and perhaps the only remaining source from the 1960s) to acknowledge that Cynthia was an integral part of two different families in Birmingham. The funeral program, more so than any other form of remembrance for Cynthia, signals an attempt to demonstrate the teen's attachment to two distinct communities in Birmingham. It would also be the last time in many decades in which the Morris family's biological connection to the young victim would be formally or publicly recognized.

After the funeral services, Cynthia's body was interred in a Wesley family plot at Birmingham's Woodlawn Cemetery. Seemingly unnoticed amid the groundswell of grief, anger, and hopelessness that consumed much of Birmingham's Black community after the church bombing, Cynthia's name changed one final time before her burial. Though all official and unofficial documents prior to her interment list Cynthia's middle name as "Diane" or "Dianne," the headstone above her grave identifies the teen as "Cynthia Dionne," changing all but her first name from the record on her birth certificate.[67] King repeatedly extolled Cynthia and the other victims as "martyred heroines" and countless others have marked her death as a turning point in the civil rights movement, yet the various families and communities of which Cynthia was a member cannot agree on her name. Given her symbolic prominence as a martyred heroine of the movement, it is disturbing that few are aware of the inaccuracies and inconsistencies that mar public remembrance of Cynthia as an individual.

For decades Cynthia's biological family was distraught over public remembrances that failed to properly identify her as a member of the Morris family. Eunice, Cynthia's biological sister, explained that the omission of the Morris surname in public references to Cynthia felt like "opening an old wound that has never healed." She said, "It is the hurt that I still feel because of so much rejection when I tell my story."[68] Nevertheless, the debate over Cynthia's legal name ceased at the request of Estelle Morris, who feared that a public dispute would turn into a distasteful confrontation in the local and national press. Fate Morris, Cynthia's biological brother, remembered asking his mother if the problem of Cynthia's surname bothered her. Estelle admitted that the erasure of the Morris last name was upsetting, but she refused to pursue the issue. When Fate offered to try to correct the error, his mother replied, "No. I don't want to drag her name through the mud."[69] But after Estelle died in 1988, the surviving Morris children, Eunice and Fate, decided to renew their efforts to inform the public about Cynthia's biological family.

Up to this point, the Morrises' attempts to correct this inaccuracy were limited to conversations with other family members and private requests made to Gertrude Wesley, asking that she publicize the details of the informal adoption within the local community. But after nearly thirty years of what the Morrises described as polite resistance (Eunice asserts that in their private conversations, Gertrude agreed to publicly address the problem, but when given the opportunity she remained silent), Eunice and Fate grew impatient with the Wesleys' quiescence. In the early 1990s, Eunice contacted the media in Birmingham and found a few local outlets that were willing to report the Morris family's story.[70] Because they helped her initiate what she called the "recognition process," Eunice said there is "a special place" in her heart for these local reporters and television stations.[71] The Morrises wanted the public to acknowledge or validate their familial claims to Cynthia so that, as Eunice explained, "my family will stop being treated as strangers."[72] Through this process of public recognition, it seems that the family also hoped they might claim a piece of Cynthia's martyrdom, a place in the dominant narrative of the bombing. Public veneration of these girls as martyrs has obscured not only the families of these children but also the sense of loss those families endured. Yet, in the specific case of Cynthia, it also prevented public acknowledgment of the Morris family's biological connection to the victim—a connection, they contend, that would "correct history and bring [their] sister home."[73] This final statement indicated a desire not only to correct history but to remove Cynthia's remains from the Wesley plot and reinter them at a different site.

Eunice and Fate were encouraged by the small bit of recognition that the Morris family earned from this local coverage, though it did little to alter public remembrances of their deceased sister. Few in Birmingham, or in the nation for that matter, knew the Morris surname in conjunction with the church bombing or its resultant casualties. Yet the country continued to recall the fatal blast itself. Marking its anniversary every five or ten years, national media outlets published short articles informing the public about the civil rights progress that had been made in the years after the event.

In an attempt to gain support for her family's efforts to recognize Cynthia as a Morris, Eunice prepared a short manuscript titled "The Forgotten Ones: Cynthia Morris Wesley," which she hoped to have published as a book. Eunice used a plural descriptor in the main title, though Cynthia's is the only name to appear in the manuscript's secondary heading. From Eunice's commentary throughout, it is clear that the title is meant to describe not only Cynthia but the entire Morris family. As the Morris surname has been omitted in references to Cynthia, Eunice suggested, her entire family has been forgotten or subject to the process of historical erasure. .

Although Eunice was unable to find a publisher for her family memoir, she and Fate finally achieved a measure of success in their goal of correcting Cynthia's misnomer. On October 9, 2002, nearly forty years after the bombing, Cynthia's death certificate was amended based on Eunice's testimony.[74] In addition to correcting her name to read "Cynthia Diane Morris," instead of "Cynthia D. Wesley," officials revised the parents' names from "Claude A. Wesley" and "Gertrude Turner" to "Charlie Morris" and "Estelle Merchant."[75] Throughout her battle to prove that Cynthia remained a Morris for her entire life, Eunice was adamant that she did not want money or fame but desired only for Cynthia to be remembered as *both* a Morris and a Wesley.[76]

The Morrises achieved another small victory when in 2013 a few sources began to refer to Cynthia's last name as "Morris Wesley."[77] For the first time, in speeches, articles, and interviews that coincided with the fiftieth anniversary of the bombing, some started referring to, and thereby *remembering*, Cynthia as both a Morris and Wesley—a more complete version of her living identity. Despite these incremental changes, the process of revising or updating old mentions and ensuring that new references include the correct version of the victim's name has proved to be slow and arduous. The majority of public references to the victims of the bombing continue to identify Cynthia only as a Wesley. In memorials at Sixteenth Street Baptist Church, on markers installed by the National Park Service, and in the national legislation honoring the slain girls, Cynthia exists as the daughter of Gertrude and Claude Wesley. Moreover, there remains the question of Cynthia's final resting place. To Fate Morris, any progress in terms of public remembrance of Cynthia is incomplete without a change in the location of her grave. In

2013 he made his desire to relocate Cynthia's remains explicit when he told the *Birmingham News* that he would like to have "his sister's body moved and relocated near his late parents."[78] This request would require the disinterment of Cynthia's remains from their current location at Woodlawn Cemetery and their removal to Inglenook Cemetery, just over three miles away.[79] Fate's wish has remained unfilled, likely due to the difficulty of obtaining permission from the surviving members of the Wesley family and the expense associated with relocation and reinternment.

Though the location of Cynthia's final resting place remains contested by her brother, public remembrance of the four victims has continued to expand. In 2011, nearly fifty years after the bombing and fourteen years after the release of Lee's documentary, Birmingham decided it was time to honor the victims of the bombing with a public memorial in the city and announced a competition for artists to design it. By a stroke of luck, sculptor and native Alabamian Elizabeth MacQueen happened to see an advertisement for the design contest and, with only four days to meet the submission deadline, she scrambled to develop a proposal for the planned Four Spirits Memorial.

MacQueen knew the design contest might finally give her the opportunity, and the reason, to return to her hometown. In 1963 she was fourteen years old and living just outside of Birmingham in the community of Mountain Brook. As a white teen, MacQueen was isolated from the violence of the city, and her parents and teachers did not address the subject. After the church bombing, MacQueen recalls, "I didn't hear a word about it that day, not from my parents, not from anyone. When we got to school on Monday, there was kind of a whoosh. Just whisperings."[80] But the bombing would alter MacQueen's life in a way she had never imagined when fifty years later her proposal won the design competition and she was selected as the sculptor to create Birmingham's first public memorial for the victims of September 15, 1963.

Though it took nearly half a century for the city to welcome a memorial to these victims, MacQueen's design ultimately benefited from the passage of time, because the sculptor was able to learn more about each of the victims' individual identities from friends and family who, in decades past, had been unwilling to share the extent of their grief. After researching the case and talking with local residents, civic leaders, and the victims' families, MacQueen rejected the mythic characterization of the girls as martyrs. She explained, "The girls would not have volunteered to die that day. So, I oppose the use of the word sacrifice, as if falsifies history. It is erroneous."[81] MacQueen also disliked forms of remembrance that described the victims as little girls. With the exception of eleven-year-old Denise McNair, MacQueen asserted, "they were mature, in their menses, blooming breast buds, becoming young women." She continued, "Do we think because they might have been mature it would not hold as much tragedy or injustice as if they had been little innocent girls?"[82] Instead of adhering to the traditional, mythic representations of the crime, MacQueen designed a memorial that depicted the victims alive and in motion, each engaging in a distinct activity that MacQueen imagined might reflect their individual identities and personalities.

On September 14, 2013, one day shy of the fiftieth anniversary of the bombing, MacQueen unveiled the memorial at Kelly Ingram Park. The park, which shares an intersection with Sixteenth Street Baptist Church and the Birmingham Civil Rights Institute, is located in the city's historic "civil rights district" and features memorials honoring Martin Luther King Jr. and those who participated in Project C, also known as Project Confrontation, or the Birmingham Campaign, a series of sit-ins, boycotts, and marches during the spring of 1963. The newest memorial in the park, Four Spirits, depicts the four girls gathered around a bench. Cynthia sits on the edge of the bench reading a book, while Carole looks back at the others, midstride, and beckons as she heads in the direction of the church across the street. Addie Mae rests in a kneeling position as she ties the sash on Denise's dress. The youngest victim, meanwhile, reaches skyward toward the six doves that fly overheard. The doves represent the lives of the six children killed on September 15, 1963. In this way the memorial remembers the often-overlooked murders of Virgil Ware and Johnny Robinson, two boys who were murdered in related incidents the same day.

MacQueen's memorial reflects the historical debate surrounding the public remembrance of racial violence in Birmingham and its place in the national mythology of the civil rights movement. Though the Four Spirits Memorial depicts the victims as teenagers instead of as little girls, MacQueen retains other features of the mythic memory of the bombing in her representation. In King's redemptive interpretation of the bombing, the victims' innocence plays a central role in their qualification for collective martyrdom. While the Four Spirits sculpture disregards the concept of martyrdom, it still alludes to the girls' innocent nature as it shows the young ladies reading quietly or helping one another instead of engaging in protest. Finally, by ignoring the defining role of violence in the girls' deaths, MacQueen rejects the notion that the crime might have served a "redemptive" purpose in the larger story of the struggle for freedom and equality. Though MacQueen's decision to omit any references to the bombing works to highlight the individual *lives* of the girls, it simultaneously erases the role of the perpetrators

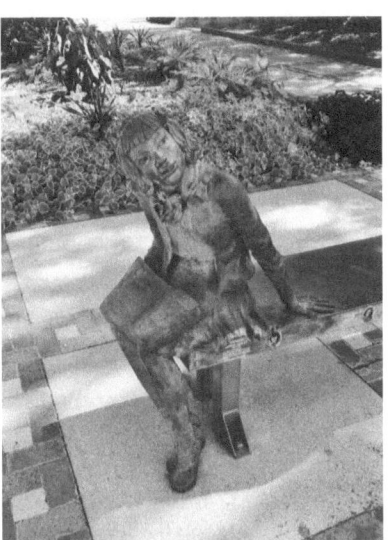

FIGURE 7.4. The Four Spirits Memorial depicts Addie Mae Collins tying the ribbon on Denise McNair's dress (photograph by the author).

FIGURE 7.5. In this detail from the Four Spirits Memorial, Cynthia Morris Wesley looks up from reading a book (photograph by the author).

FIGURE 7.6. The Four Spirits Memorial identifies Cynthia Morris Wesley by her biological and adoptive surnames (photograph by the author). The marker reads, "Cynthia D. Morris Wesley / murdered / Girl Scout, loved reading / sang in the choir, ushered in the church, / played piano and clarinet, loved dogs, / aspired to be a teacher like her parents // born: April 30, 1949.

and, by extension, the responsibility of all those in Birmingham and beyond who supported their racist ideology, if not their methods.

MacQueen ultimately achieved her goal of creating a memorial in honor of four real people—Addie Mae Collins, Denise McNair, Carole Robertson, and Cynthia Morris Wesley—instead of the angelic, indistinct martyrs that are revered in the mythology of the movement. When asked about the memorial at the 2013 dedication, Chris McNair—who, other than his wife, Maxine, was the only parent still living—announced, "I'm pleased with it."[83]

Conclusion:
Private and Public Remembrances

The private and public spaces in which these victims are memorialized expose the challenges of confronting America's enduring legacies of racial violence. Perhaps civil rights icons are best remembered in spaces that acknowledge the contributions they made to the Black freedom struggle. For instance, it is fitting to honor King on the National Mall in Washington, D.C., a space in which he captivated and inspired national audiences with his calls for equality, justice, and a more perfect form of democracy. But are these highly visible sites the most appropriate places in which to recall and reflect on the deaths of innocent children such as Emmett Till, Addie Mae Collins, Denise McNair, Carole Robertson, and Cynthia Morris Wesley? As Paul Gardullo and Lonnie Bunch remind us, in Till's case it is not only "the brutal murder of an innocent Black boy but also . . . the tremendous bravery of his mother in response to that violence" that is on display at the NMAAHC.[84] In this sense, it is apt to remember these victims in public spaces that provide additional context and position their murders within a larger narrative of racism and intolerance in the United States.

Nevertheless, problems of representation and remembrance remain. The existence of alternate forms of public remembrance should not mitigate the reverence that is due at their grave sites or excuse the deplorable condition of the cemeteries in which a few are buried. Further, though each of these child-victims has been labeled a martyr of the movement, none knowingly or willingly gave their lives in service of the Black freedom struggle. Their deaths were not personal choices but rather the atrocious consequences of deeply entrenched racial loathing. A brutal lynching and a murderous bombing cost Emmett Till, Addie Mae Collins, Denise McNair, Carole Robertson, and Cynthia Morris Wesley more than their lives; their personal identities were sacrificed as well.

The recent proliferation of memoirs, public lectures, popular films, and commemorative ceremonies related to the civil rights movement indicates that there is space for these long-silenced voices and concealed personal identities to emerge in new and existing forms of public remembrance. Cemeteries and grave sites—as one of the most personal forms of public remembrance—certainly provide a space through which the individual identities could be reclaimed. In the specific cases of Burr Oak and Greenwood Cemeteries, despite the historic instances of negligence, abandonment, and even criminal activity, there is reason to be cautiously optimistic about the prospect of renewed remembrance of the civil rights victims buried on their grounds. As previously mentioned, new management at Burr Oak has worked to restore and revitalize the cemetery while instilling a new sense of reverence—through the creation of a memorial monument—for those buried at the site. Conditions are improving at Greenwood Cemetery in Birmingham, as well; in 2016 it earned a place on the Alabama Historic Cemetery Register, and since the city has taken over the cemetery after it was abandoned by its previous owners, thousands of dollars from the city's treasury have been spent on cleanup, maintenance, and preservation efforts.[85] Yet, given the location of the cemeteries, on the peripheries of Chicago and Birmingham, far from the bustling downtown in one city and the historic civil rights district in the other, it is likely that any effort to emphasize or enhance the grave sites of these civil rights martyrs will fail to attract widespread attention.

After all, the public desire to turn the senseless murder of innocents into something meaningful—the blood sacrifice of martyrs—reflects the dominant narrative of the civil rights movement in the United States. This mythology of the movement is one of inspiration; it reassures Americans that the once festering sores of racism have been healed by the inexorable moral progress of the nation. But it is also a narrative of containment, as it frees Americans from engaging with the horrific realities and legacies of racial violence.

In this sense, the mythic rendering of the past may do more harm than good in terms of public remembrance. Though the mythology of the movement offers Americans hope and optimism in the face of persistent violence and conflict, it is ultimately damaging to the communities and individuals it silences and neglects. By disregarding individual trauma and loss, this myth offers a narrative centered on the virtue of redemptive suffering. In the process, it denies space for conversations about public deaths and meaningless violence—discussions that may in turn promote tolerance, empathy, and understanding among diverse national audiences. Ignoring the enduring legacies of racial violence does not ease the frustration, pain, and trauma that characterized the Black freedom struggle but rather stunts opportunities for national unity based on a shared understanding of the past. The repercussions of the myth's disregard for individual suffering and loss are visible in contemporary questions about public deaths and the value of Black lives in this nation. To confront this imbalance in the dominant narrative of the movement and to prevent further disparities, we must constantly consider the damage we do to a symbol when we disregard or neglect that which it represents. Though collectively these children may be sacred symbols of the civil rights movement, the current state of their physical remains suggests that their individual identities matter little to a nation plagued by chronic racial violence.

Notes

1. "Civil Rights Martyrs."
2. For instance, editorial articles in national publications asked, "What kind of creature is it that would snuff out the lives of children innocently at church on a Sunday morning?" The *New York Post* declared, "There could be no more ghastly illumination of the utter depravity of the racists than the murder of four little children while attending Sunday school." See *Washington Post* editorial reprinted in "Round Up of Editorial Views on Birmingham," 4.
3. King, "Eulogy for the Young Victims of the Sixteenth Street Baptist Church Bombing."
4. King, "I Have A Dream."
5. For more on Till's trip to Mississippi see Metress, *Lynching of Emmett Till*; Nelson, "Murder of Emmett Till"; Hudson-Weems, *Emmett Till*.
6. Tyson, *Blood of Emmett Till*, 21.
7. Tyson, *Blood of Emmett Till*, 21, 103–7.
8. Until the publication of Timothy Tyson's *The Blood of Emmett Till*, there remained uncertainty concerning the actual conversation between Carolyn Bryant and Emmett Till. The complexities surrounding this debate are discussed in detail in Tyson's book, in which Bryant admits to lying under oath and exaggerating the extent of any wrongdoing by Till. See Tyson, *Blood of Emmett Till*. For corroboration about the whistle, see Simeon Wright, *Simeon's Story*, 51.
9. Nelson, "Murder of Emmett Till."
10. This point is evidenced through national news coverage of Till case. "In his death, Emmett Till not only brought Negro reporters into the heart of the white man's kingdom—the courtroom—but he brought white reporters into the Deep South in unprecedented numbers to cover a racial story." Roberts and Klibanoff, *Race Beat*, 86.
11. Duckett, "Teenagers Give Meaning to Money," 5.
12. "Instead of fainting, I realized that here's a job that I got to do now and I don't have time to faint; I don't have time to cry," Mamie Till-Mobley said of the moment when she first saw Emmett's mutilated corpse. "I've got to make a decision and my decision was that there is no way I can tell the world what I see. The world is going to have to look at this."

They're going to have to help me tell the story." "Emmett Till's Mother Remembers Her Son," 6.

13. Payne, "Mamie Bradley's Untold Story: Installment VII," 8.

14. Mamie Till Mobley asserted that the funeral director at A. A. Rayner and Sons funeral home, where Emmett's body was prepared, agreed to honor the request of Mississippi law enforcement to keep the casket sealed to preclude the physical display of the corpse. Nelson, "Murder of Emmett Till."

15. Nelson, "Murder of Emmett Till."

16. Barrow, "Here's a Picture of Emmett Till," 4. An article marking the fortieth anniversary of Till's murder recounts Mamie Till-Mobley's initial conversation with the funeral directors in Chicago: "The undertaker politely asked, 'Do you want me to fix him up?' Mrs. Till did not hesitate: 'No, you can't fix that. Let the world see what I saw.'" See "Killed for Whistling at a White Woman," 24–32.

17. American Experience, "Murder of Emmett Till."

18. Reports of exactly how many mourners came to view Till's corpse vary greatly. In a 2003 article reviewing the history of Till's case, *Jet* claimed that "more than 200,000 people lined up for blocks outside the A.A. Rayner Funeral Home in Chicago to view the teenager's disfigured body over the four days it lay in state," while the *New York Times* estimated "10,000 persons" in attendance. West, "Mamie Till-Mobley," 17; "Slain Youth's Body Seen by Thousands," s9.

19. Robert, "Thousands at Rites for Till," 1.

20. Henry Caise, a mortician at the funeral home where Till's body was shown, said of those who attended Till's visitation, "Well, they brought the children with them because Emmett was fourteen years old and they wanted the younger kids to see what happened to Emmett. They were mad, they were angry." Nelson, "Murder of Emmett Till."

21. While there was some television coverage of the Milam/Bryant trial, it appears that print media such as newspapers and magazines were most successful in reaching a broad national audience.

22. According to Moses Wright's brother-in-law, Crosby Smith, the murder of Till had a powerful impact on the African American community: "'What we saw in the death of Emmett Till was a signal from God that things would never be the same again in Mississippi." Shostak, "Crosby Smith," 324.

23. Payne, "Mamie Bradley's Untold Story: Installment VIII," 8.

24. *Jet* originally published the pictures of Till in his casket in its September 15, 1955, issue. "Nation Horrified by Murder," 6–9. Speaking at Mamie Till-Mobley's funeral in 2003, the Reverend Jesse Jackson reminded mourners of the significant contributions she made in connection with her son's murder: "In many ways, the killers saw [Till's death] as a hole, but Mamie saw an earthquake, and she used the aftershocks of the earthquake to wake up and shake up a nation." West, "Mamie Till-Mobley."

25. Historian Clenora Hudson-Weems argues that the impetus of the modern civil rights movement was Till's death and not the Montgomery bus boycott, which began about three months later. Hudson-Weems asserts, "The impetus that Till's murder gave to African-American activists clearly places him, with others, at the head of the Civil Rights Movement, not in the background." Hudson-Weems, *Emmett Till*, 6.

26. In a letter read at Mamie Till-Mobley's 2003 funeral, Rosa Parks wrote, "The heinous crime which murdered your boy, your baby at 14 years of age shall never be forgotten. The news of the crime caused many people to participate in the cry for justice and equal rights including myself." West, "Mamie Till-Mobley."

27. "Recalling the Life of Rosa Parks"; Rothman, "Rosa Parks 'Transformed a Nation' on This Day."

28. *Eyes on the Prize*, "Interview with Reverend Fred Shuttlesworth."

29. "Burr Oak History."

30. Keith Beauchamp, director of the documentary *The Untold Story of Emmett Louis Till*, said of Mamie Till-Mobley, "She really wanted a mausoleum and a museum. She really wanted something to recognize the legacy of her son in history." FitzPatrick, "Proposed Emmett Till Museum Lost in Burr Oak Scandal."

31. Danielle Wright, "Hope for Emmett Till Memorial Lost."

32. Ibid.

33. FitzPatrick, "Proposed Emmett Till Museum Lost in Burr Oak Scandal."

34. For national coverage of the Burr Oak Cemetery scandal see Bowean, "Burr Oak Cemetery Scandal"; FitzPatrick, "Proposed Emmett Till Museum Lost"; Danielle Wright, "Hope for Emmett Till Memorial Lost."

35. Christina Wright, "Emmett Till's Casket Headed to Smithsonian."

36. Callard, "Emmett Till's Casket Goes to the Smithsonian."

37. Gardullo and Bunch, "Why Emmett Till's Case Matters to American History and Our Future."

38. Rogers, "New Burr Oak Cemetery Monument Dedicated."

39. Alessio, "Why Has Chicago Failed to Honor the Grave of Emmet [sic] Till?"

40. Knowles, "Officials Tout Burr Oak Cemetery's Monument."

41. "10,000 View Body of Youth Lynched for Whistling at White Woman"; "Emmett Till Funeral Saddens City, Nation."

42. King, "Eulogy for the Young Victims of the Sixteenth Street Baptist Church Bombing."

43. Bryant, "Birmingham Spends $250,000 for Cemetery Care."

44. Lee, *4 Little Girls*.

45. Ibid.

46. Smith, "The Day the Children Died."

47. Ibid.

48. "Collins Family Attorney and Birmingham City Council Member Discuss Addie Mae Collins Case."

49. "Addie Mae Collins"; Temple, "1963 Bombing Victim's Family Eager to Locate Site of Grave."

50. Smith, "The Day the Children Died."

51. Ibid.

52. "Collins Family Attorney and Birmingham City Council Member Discuss Addie Mae Collins Case."

53. Underwood, "Sister of 16th Street Church Bombing Victim Pleads for Help."

54. Moehringer, "A Child Lost to Racial Hate Lost Again in Birmingham."

55. Comment of "BK1022," in response to Underwood, "Sister of 16th Street Church Bombing Victim Pleads for Help."

56. Pia, "Addie Mae Collins May be Buried on the Other Side of her Tombstone."

57. Pia, "Missing Remains of 1963 Church Bombing Victim Believed to be Found."

58. "Cynthia Diane Morris Birth Certificate."

59. Ravitz, "Siblings of the Bombing."

60. Davis, "Forgotten Ones," 4.

61. Ibid., 7.

62. "Cynthia Wesley Death Certificate."
63. Ibid.
64. "Joint Obsequies."
65. Ibid.
66. Ibid.
67. "Cynthia Dionne Wesley."
68. Davis, "Forgotten Ones," 8-9.
69. Ravitz, "Siblings of the Bombing."
70. Davis claimed that two local television stations and a Birmingham newspaper picked up the story: "We were tired of being left out, so we contacted Channel 13 News. They were fascinated by out [sic] story and did a story on us." She added, "We then contacted The Birmingham News, and they contacted Channel 6 News for us. Thanks are to at [sic] Birmingham News and Channel 6 for starting the beginning of my recognition process." Though Davis does not give a specific date for these stories, she mentions that they were aired around the "time the movie *4 Little Girls* came out," which would mean the late 1990s. Davis, "Forgotten Ones," 10.
71. Ibid.
72. Ibid., 12.
73. Morris, "Cynthia Morris—NOT Cynthia Wesley."
74. "Alabama Amendment to Record of Death."
75. Ibid.
76. Davis, "Forgotten Ones," 12.
77. See, for example, McWhorter, "Stark Reminders of the Birmingham Church Bombing."
78. Bryant, "Sixteenth Street Families Reject Congress Medal," 1A.
79. "Estelle Morris."
80. MacQueen, "We Lived in a Bubble."
81. Ibid.
82. Ibid.
83. Gordon, "Four Spirits Unveiled Across from Sixteenth Street Baptist Church."
84. Gardullo and Bunch, "Why Emmett Till's Case Matters."
85. Alabama Historic Cemetery Register, chrome-extension://efaidnbmnnnibpcajpcglcke findmkaj/https://ahc.alabama.gov/cemeteryprogramPDFs/Alabama_Historic_Cemetery _Register.pdf; Bryant, "Birmingham Spends $250,000 for Cemetery Care."

Bibliography

"Addie Mae Collins." Find a Grave. http://www.findagrave.com/cgi-bin/fg.cgi?GRid =6433252&page=gr.

"Alabama Amendment to Record of Death." Cynthia Wesley File, Civil Rights Memorial Records, Southern Poverty Law Center, Montgomery, Alabama.

Alessio, Carolyn. "Why Has Chicago Failed to Honor the Grave of Emmet [sic] Till?" *America: The Jesuit Review*, December 5, 2016. https://www.americamagazine.org/politics -society/2016/12/05/why-has-chicago-failed-honor-grave-emmet-till.

Barrow, John. "Here's a Picture of Emmett Till Painted by Those Who Knew Him." *Chicago Defender*, October 1, 1955.

Bowean, Lolly. "Burr Oak Cemetery Scandal: Some Remains May Never Be Identified, In-

vestigators Say." *Chicago Tribune*, August 8, 2009. http://articles.chicagotribune.com
/2009-08-08/news/0908070241_1_family-graves-scandal-remains.
Bryant, Joseph D. "Birmingham Spends $250,000 for Cemetery Care." AL.com, July 4,
2011. http://blog.al.com/spotnews/2011/07/birmingham_spends_250000_for_c
.html.
———. "Sixteenth Street Families Reject Congress Medal." *Birmingham News*, April 12,
2013.
"Burr Oak History." Burr Oak Cemetery. http://theburroakcemetery.com/burr-oak
-history/.
Callard, Abby. "Emmett Till's Casket Goes to the Smithsonian." *Smithsonian Magazine*, November 2009. https://www.smithsonianmag.com/arts-culture/emmett-tills-casket-goes
-to-the-smithsonian-144696940/.
"Civil Rights Martyrs." Southern Poverty Law Center. http://www.splcenter.org/civil
-rights-memorial/civil-rights-martyrs.
"Collins Family Attorney and Birmingham City Council Member Discuss Addie Mae Collins Case." CNN, October 25, 2000. http://www.cnn.com/TRANSCRIPTS/0010/25/mn.19
.html.
"Cynthia Diane Morris Birth Certificate." Cynthia Wesley File, Civil Rights Memorial Records, Southern Poverty Law Center, Montgomery, Alabama.
"Cynthia Dionne Wesley." Find a Grave. http://www.findagrave.com/cgi-bin/fg.cgi?page
=pv&GRid=6433296&PIpi=1714291.
"Cynthia Wesley Death Certificate." Cynthia Wesley File, Civil Rights Memorial Records, Southern Poverty Law Center, Montgomery, Alabama.
Davis, Eunice. "The Forgotten Ones: Cynthia Morris Wesley." Unpublished manuscript.
Cynthia Wesley File, Civil Rights Memorial Records, Southern Poverty Law Center, Montgomery, Ala.
Duckett, Alfred. "Teenagers Give Meaning to Money: It's the Worst." *Chicago Defender*, October 1, 1955.
Elliot, Robert. "Thousands at Rites for Till." *Chicago Defender*, September 10, 1955.
"Emmett Till Funeral Saddens City, Nation." *Chicago Defender*, September 17, 1955.
"Emmett Till's Mother Remembers Her Son on His 50th Birthday." *Jet*, August 12, 1991.
"Estelle Morris." Find a Grave. https://www.findagrave.com/memorial/136861450
/estelle-morris.
Eyes on the Prize. "Interview with Reverend Fred Shuttlesworth." November 7, 1985. Film and Media Archive, Washington University in St. Louis, American Archive of Public Broadcasting (GBH and the Library of Congress). http://americanarchive.org/catalog
/cpb-aacip-151-086348h395.
FitzPatrick, Lauren. "Proposed Emmett Till Museum Lost in Burr Oak Scandal." *Chicago Sun-Times*, July 11, 2011.
Gardullo, Paul, and Lonnie G. Bunch, III. "Why Emmett Till's Case Matters to American History and Our Future." CNN, July 14, 2018. https://www.cnn.com/2018/07/14/opinions
/emmett-till-case-casket-gardullo-bunch-opinion/index.html.
Gordon, Tom. "Four Spirits Unveiled Across from Sixteenth Street Baptist Church." Weld for Birmingham (news website), September 14, 2013.
Hudson-Weems, Clenora. *Emmett Till: The Sacrificial Lamb of the Civil Rights Movement*.
Troy, Mich.: Bedford Publishers, 1994.
"Joint Obsequies for Carol Denise McNair, Addie Mae Collins, and Cynthia Dianne Wesley." September 18, 1963. Albert Burton Boutwell Papers, 1949–1967, collection number

264, Archives Department, Birmingham Public Library. https://cdm16044.contentdm.oclc.org/digital/collection/p4017coll8/id/13949.

"Killed for Whistling at a White Woman." *Emerge*, August 1995.

King, Martin Luther, Jr. "Eulogy for the Young Victims of the Sixteenth Street Baptist Church Bombing." Delivered at the Sixteenth Street Baptist Church, Birmingham, Alabama, September 18, 1963. https://mlkscholars.mit.edu/updates/2015/invoking-dr-king.

———. "I Have a Dream." Speech presented at the March on Washington for Jobs and Freedom, Washington, D.C., August 28, 1963. https://www.npr.org/2010/01/18/122701268/i-have-a-dream-speech-in-its-entirety.

Knowles, Francine. "Officials Tout Burr Oak Cemetery's Monument, Renovation," *Chicago Sun-Times*. August 30, 2014. https://chicago.suntimes.com/city-hall/2014/8/30/18589234/officials-tout-burr-oak-cemetery-s-monument-renovation.

Lee, Spike, dir. *4 Little Girls*. Forty Acres and a Mule Filmworks and HBO, 1997.

MacQueen, Elizabeth. "We Lived in a Bubble." Kids In Birmingham 1963. http://kidsinbirmingham1963.org/category/elizabeth-macqueen/.

McWhorter, Diane. "The Stark Reminders of the Birmingham Church Bombing." *Smithsonian Magazine*, November 1, 2013. http://www.smithsonianmag.com/history/the-stark-reminders-of-the-birmingham-church-bombing-4304931/.

Metress, Christopher, ed. *The Lynching of Emmett Till: A Documentary Narrative*. Charlottesville: University of Virginia Press, 2002.

Moehringer, J. R. "A Child Lost to Racial Hate Lost Again in Birmingham." *Los Angeles Times*, January 19, 1998. http://articles.latimes.com/1998/jan/19/news/mn-9918.

Morris, Fate. "Cynthia Morris—NOT Cynthia Wesley—Issue Proclamation." Online petition. Change.org, 2014. https://www.change.org/p/cynthia-morris-not-cynthia-wesley-issue-proclamation.

"Nation Horrified by Murder." *Jet*, September 15, 1955.

Nelson, Stanley, dir. "The Murder of Emmett Till." *American Experience*. Aired January 20, 2003, on PBS. https://www.pbs.org/wgbh/americanexperience/films/till/.

Payne, Ethel. "Mamie Bradley's Untold Story: Installment VII." *Chicago Defender*, March 7, 1956.

———. "Mamie Bradley's Untold Story: Installment VIII." *Chicago Defender*, March 8, 1956.

Pia, Brian. "Addie Mae Collins May Be Buried on the Other Side of Her Tombstone." ABC 33/40 News, October 27, 2016. https://abc3340.com/news/abc-3340-investigates/abc-3340-news-investigates-search-for-addie-mae-collins.

———. "Missing Remains of 1963 Church Bombing Victim Believed to Be Found." KLEW News, May 3, 2017. https://klewtv.com/news/nation-world/addie-mae-collins-mystery-solved.

Ravitz, Jessica. "Siblings of the Bombing: Remembering Birmingham Church Blast 50 Years On." CNN, September 17, 2013. https://www.cnn.com/2013/09/14/us/birmingham-church-bombing-anniversary-victims-siblings/index.html.

"Recalling the Life of Rosa Parks." *News and Notes*, National Public Radio, October 25, 2005. https://www.npr.org/templates/story/story.php?storyId=4973330.

Roberts, Gene, and Hank Klibanoff. *The Race Beat: The Press, the Civil Rights Struggle, and the Awakening of a Nation*. New York: Knopf, 2006.

Rogers, Phil. "New Burr Oak Cemetery Monument Dedicated." NBC Chicago, August 29, 2014. https://www.nbcchicago.com/news/local/New-Burr-Oak-Cemetery-Monument-Dedicated—273248811.html.

Rothman, Lily. "Rosa Parks 'Transformed a Nation' on This Day." *Time*, December 1, 2014. http://time.com/3603948/jesse-jackson-rosa-parks/.

"Round Up of Editorial Views on Birmingham: New Outrage in Birmingham." *Chicago Defender*, September 21, 1963.

Shostak, David A. "Crosby Smith: Forgotten Witness to a Mississippi Nightmare." *Negro History Bulletin* 38, no. 1 (December 1974/January 1975): 320–25.

"Slain Youth's Body Seen by Thousands." *New York Times*, September 5, 1955.

Smith, Kyle. "The Day the Children Died." *People*, August 11, 1997. https://people.com/archive/the-day-the-children-died-vol-48-no-6/.

Temple, Chanda. "1963 Bombing Victim's Family Eager to Locate Site of Grave." *Birmingham News*, January 14, 1998.

"10,000 View Body of Youth Lynched for Whistling at White Woman." *Philadelphia Tribune*, September 10, 1955.

Tyson, Timothy B. *The Blood of Emmett Till*. New York: Simon and Schuster, 2017.

Underwood, Madison. "Sister of 16th Street Church Bombing Victim Pleads for Help Finding Her Sister's Lost Grave." AL.com, September 15, 2014. http://www.al.com/news/birmingham/index.ssf/2014/09/sister_of_16th_street_church_b.html.

West, Malcolm R. "Mamie Till-Mobley, Civil Rights Heroine, Eulogized in Chicago." *Jet*, January 27, 2003.

Wright, Christina M. "Emmett Till's Casket Headed to Smithsonian." CBS News, August 28, 2009. https://www.cbsnews.com/news/emmett-tills-casket-headed-to-smithsonian/.

Wright, Danielle. "Hope for Emmett Till Memorial Lost." BET.com, July 11, 2011. http://www.bet.com/news/national/2011/07/11/hope-for-emmett-till-memorial-losto.html.

Wright, Simeon. *Simeon's Story: An Eyewitness Account of the Kidnapping of Emmett Till*. Chicago: Lawrence Hill Books, 2010.

EPILOGUE

TEACHING THE AMERICAN SOUTH BY LEARNING THE DEAD

To a society plagued by political divisiveness, racial tension, and seemingly endless eruptions of violence, the history of the civil rights movement offers meaningful, and often uplifting, examples of strength, sacrifice, and perseverance in the pursuit of liberty and equality. These narratives are meant to inspire, to teach Americans how to confront contemporary obstacles, just as civil rights activists challenged oppressive racial inequality and injustice. They are reminders that "we shall overcome." Yet, as is discussed in the chapter "Profane Memorials," much of this history—or, rather, mythology—amplifies heroic leaders and redemptive sacrifices as it tempers instances of trauma, brutality, and defeat. Revisiting the question posed at the conclusion of that chapter, about how and where civil rights activists and casualties should be remembered, proves to be a useful exercise for scholars and students alike.

The following activity asks students to consider public remembrance of the civil rights movement by identifying and analyzing grave sites of both celebrated civil rights activists and ordinary people who died as a result of movement-related violence. This lesson encourages students to practice their historical research skills by identifying and analyzing specific details related to each decedents' life, legacy, and grave site. The following list focuses on the modern civil rights era and is thus composed of individuals who lived and died during the twentieth and twenty-first centuries. Yet, educators could (and should) expand the limits of this list to fit the needs of their classrooms and to assess a broader chronology of the Black freedom struggle in the United States.

Instructions for Educators

Assign each student several names from the following list. Try to select at least one well-known person and one individual with whom students may be unfamiliar. Ask students to complete the worksheet and answer the following questions for each of their assigned names.

After students have completed the following activity, divide them into small groups to discuss the legacies and public memories of the individuals they researched. Have students consider the following questions:

1. Was it easier/more difficult to research any particular individual? Why might this be?
2. Did you uncover anything unexpected or surprising?
3. What types of variation do you notice in terms of burial site, memorials, and public remembrance for each person?
4. Are there any common themes or trends that emerge in terms of how the lives and legacies of these individuals are marked at their grave sites and/or memorials?

Next, ask each group to select two or three of the individuals they discussed to present to the class. (This may be done in a subsequent class period.) Following the presentations, initiate a class-wide conversation about public remembrance of both the modern civil rights movement and the activists/martyrs they assessed. Does it seem as if any of these people are "forgotten"? What about their remembrance suggests this? Are there any movies, books, television series, or songs that feature the individuals they researched? Is remembrance of these individuals uniform or even? What may account for discrepancies in public memory of the movement and its martyrs?

Name:
Birth Date:
Death Date:
Cause of Death:
Burial Place:
Additional Memorials/Monuments:
How was this individual related to the civil rights movement?
How is this person remembered at a grave site?
Is there a headstone/marker?
Does the marker bear an inscription? What does it say?

Are there other memorials in honor of this individual? Where are these memorials?

Beyond the life of the individual listed, what specific actions/events do these memorials acknowledge?

Was this individual cremated? How might that change public remembrance?

TABLE 7.1. Civil Rights Grave Sites

	Name	Grave Location
1.	A. Philip Randolph	Cremated
2.	Addie Mae Collins	Greenwood Cemetery, Birmingham, Ala.
3.	Andrew Goodman	Mount Judah Cemetery, Ridgewood, N.Y.
4.	Bayard Rustin	Cremated
5.	Benjamin O. Davis Jr.	Arlington National Cemetery, Arlington, Va.
6.	Booker T. Washington	Tuskegee University Campus Cemetery, Tuskegee, Ala.
7.	Carole Robertson	Greenwood Cemetery, Birmingham, Ala.
8.	Carter G. Woodson	Lincoln Memorial Cemetery, Suitland, Md.
9.	Charles Alfred Anderson	Greenwood Cemetery, Tuskegee, Ala.
10.	Cynthia Morris Wesley	Greenwood Cemetery, Birmingham, Ala.
11.	Daisy Bates	Haven of Rest Cemetery, Little Rock, Ark.
12.	Denise McNair	Elmwood Cemetery, Birmingham, Ala.
13.	Dorothy Height	Fort Lincoln Cemetery, Brentwood, Md.
14.	Ella Baker	Flushing Cemetery, Flushing, N.Y.
15.	Emmett Till	Burr Oak Cemetery, Alsip, Ill.
16.	Fannie Lou Hamer	Fannie Lou Hamer Memorial Garden, Ruleville, Miss.
17.	Fred Hampton	Bethel Cemetery, Haynesville, La.
18.	Fred Shuttlesworth	Oak Hill Cemetery, Birmingham, Ala.
19.	George Lee	Green Grove Cemetery, Humphreys County, Miss.
20.	Hosea Williams	Lincoln Cemetery, Atlanta, Ga.
21.	Huey Newton	Cremated
22.	James Alexander Hood	Pleasant Gap Cemetery, Canton, Ga.
23.	James Chaney	Okatibee Cemetery, Meridian, Miss.
24.	James Reeb	Cremated
25.	Jimmie Lee Jackson	Heard Cemetery, Marion, Ala.
26.	Johnny Robinson	New Grace Hill Cemetery, Birmingham, Ala.
27.	Julian Bond	South View Cemetery, Atlanta, Ga.

TABLE 7.1. Civil Rights Grave Sites (*continued*)

	Name	Grave Location
28.	Malcolm X	Ferncliff Cemetery, Hartsdale, N.Y.
29.	Marcus Garvey	National Heroes Park, Kingston, Jamaica
30.	Martin Luther King Jr.	Martin Luther King Jr. Center, Atlanta, Ga.
31.	Medgar Evers	Arlington National Cemetery, Arlington, Va.
32.	Michael Schwerner	Cremated
33.	Paul Robeson	Ferncliff Cemetery and Mausoleum, Hartsdale, N.Y.
34.	Ralph Abernathy	Lakewood Park Cemetery, Affton, Mo.
35.	Rosa Parks	Woodlawn Cemetery, Detroit, Mich.
36.	Roy Wilkins	Pinelawn Memorial Park, East Farmingdale, N.Y.
37.	Septima Clark	Old Bethel United Methodist Church Cemetery, Charleston, S.C.
38.	Stokely Carmichael (Kwame Ture)	Canakry, Guinea
39.	Thurgood Marshall	Arlington National Cemetery, Arlington, Va.
40.	Viola Liuzzo	Holy Sepulchre Cemetery, Southfield, Mich.
41.	Virgil Ware	St. Luke Baptist Church, Pratt City, Ala.
42.	Vivian Malone Jones	Westview Cemetery, Atlanta, Ga.
43.	W. E. B. Du Bois	W. E. B. Du Bois Memorial Centre for Pan African Culture, Accra, Ghana
44.	Whitney Young	Ferncliff Cemetery, Hartsdale, N.Y.

Suggested Resources for Educators and Students

Ancestry.com

Clio, https://www.theclio.com/web/

Cobb, Charles E., Jr. *On the Road to Freedom: A Guided Tour of the Civil Rights Trail*. Chapel Hill: Algonquin Books of Chapel Hill, 2008.

Dwyer, Owen J., and Derek H. Alderman. *Civil Rights Memorials and the Geography of Memory*. Chicago: Center for American Places at Columbia College Chicago, 2008.

Find a Grave, https://www.findagrave.com/.

Gallard, Frye. *Alabama's Civil Rights Trail: An Illustrated Guide to the Cradle of Freedom*. Tuscaloosa: University of Alabama Press, 2010.

Romano, Renee C., and Leigh Raiford, eds. *The Civil Rights Movement in American Memory*. Athens: University of Georgia Press, 2006.

CHAPTER 8

Cemeteries and Community

Foregrounding Black Women's Labor and Leadership in Sacred Site Remembrance Practices

KANIQUA L. ROBINSON AND
ANTOINETTE T. JACKSON

Black Women and Death Care Labor:
A Black Feminist Epistemology

An article about the University of South Florida's African American Burial Ground and Remembering Project (AABGP) includes this statement from Antoinette T. Jackson, an applied cultural anthropologist and the project's principal investigator (PI): "Working with communities and finding out about their heritage, I often find myself in cemeteries."[1] Jackson underscores that as a Black woman born in New Orleans and raised by parents who were born and raised in Louisiana, she draws knowledge from her direct connection to Black churches and the burial practices of Black families in New Orleans and Independence, Louisiana.

Black burial traditions, particularly in Louisiana, are all encompassing and often part of everyday living. At Macedonia Free Will Baptist Church, for example—her family's church in Independence—Jackson learned that death was part of life and that it was the responsibility of the living to bury, mourn, celebrate, and tell the stories of those who had died through singing, Sunday testimonials, memorial and remembering days, obituary notices, funeral programs, reciting memorable quotes and phrases of the deceased, and, when possible, visiting graves in the Macedonia Church cemetery located immediately behind the church. At Macedonia, Jackson recalls, people often talked about death and prepared for it by leading others in prayer, by intentionally giving thanks and praise each Sunday as if it would be their last

FIGURE 8.1. Macedonia Baptist Church Covenant Pamphlet, which outlines the mission and guiding or aspirational principles of the church

prayer, by offering testimonials about overcoming trials and tribulations, and by sharing stories and insights about life with those who would be expected to carry on after they were gone. Sometimes people even joked about wanting lots of mourning and crying at their funeral or asked that certain songs be sung, particular music be played, or specific types of food be provided at the funeral repast. Jackson also remembers visiting Macedonia as a youth in the summertime and spending hours in the cemetery with her siblings, listening to her uncles tell stories about the people and family members buried there. History came alive through hearing those stories.

It is instilled in people raised in the southern Black church tradition, especially in small, rural places like Independence, Louisiana, that honoring the dead is the responsibility of the living. Jackson has also been grounded in this tradition through witnessing strong women leaders in church and civic activities via the Order of Eastern Star, a female benevolent society. As she was growing up and visiting Independence, Jackson watched her paternal grandmother, Mrs. Oral Lee Jackson, her aunts, and other women in the community who were Eastern Star members take on projects to help people in need, from hospital visits to delivering food and medicine. She recounts hearing the pride in her grandmother's voice when she would recite her formal title as a member of Rose of Sharon Chapter number 22 OES.

Most memorable, however, were the funeral rituals when a member of the Order of Eastern Star died. For Jackson, seeing women in charge and in uniform performing funeral rites imprinted powerful images and messages that have helped shape how she thinks about death, female leadership, and the honor and responsibility associated with bringing dignity to the dead. On her maternal and paternal side, Jackson is descended from a family of ministers, Masons, and caregivers of the living and the dead, and she has been influenced by both male and female leadership models. For Jackson, the work today of connecting family cemetery histories and rural or small church funeral practices to a larger understanding of Black history and heritage requires calling on insights learned through intimate connections to New Orleans and Independence, grounded in southern Black church funeral and burial practices.

Examining these burial sites today within their social, political, and economic context gives us a greater understanding of the community's past. The AABGP seeks to identify, interpret, and record unmarked, and previously erased, African American burial grounds and sacred sites in Florida, specifically Zion Cemetery in Tampa and Oaklawn, Evergreen, and Moffett Cemeteries in St. Petersburg. This project also aims to engage members of the living community to understand the ways in which they interpret these sites and how they choose to remember them.

Jackson was intentional about assembling a research team and applying for funding from the University of South Florida Research Task Force on Understanding and Addressing Blackness and Anti-Black Racism in Local, National and International Communities. Established in response to the 2020 deaths of George Floyd, Breonna Taylor, and Ahmaud Arbery due to police brutality, systemic racism, and institutional violence, the task force oversaw a $500,000 fund to be used for projects that contribute to understanding racial oppression. After being selected to receive one of the task force grants, Jackson and the AABGP team used the opportunity to speak directly to the institutional racism and white supremacy that perpetuate the historical erasure of the Black experience. In actively identifying and documenting African American burial grounds in Florida, AABGP is doing resistance work, building on the Black intellectual tradition to "validate Black humanity."[2] The Black intellectual tradition, as defined by Derrick Alridge, Cornelius Bynum, and James Stewart, is "a system of thought specifically designed to challenge Jim Crow, lynching, disfranchisement, discrimination, and other forms of racial oppression that were now facts of law, not just facts of Black life."[3] The AABGP team brings forth this tradition in examining the deathways and related institutions of the Black community, which not only honored the deceased but were defiant acts against the structural dehumanization of Black people.

In critically understanding the communities connected to the cemeteries, the AABGP team interrogates the multiple social positions/roles of people in the building of social infrastructures in the communities they serve. Southern cemeteries are sacred places within African American communities, with complex histories of race and gendered oppression of those buried and of those tasked with memorialization and remembrance practices. Centering Black women in discussions of southern cemeteries and remembrance practices can challenge and expand lessons we learn and communicate about power, knowledge creation, leadership, and place making in American history. We employ a Black feminist anthropological approach as a theoretical frame in retelling and reconstructing these community stories and focusing on Black women in connection to these southern cemeteries. Such an approach is an appropriate theoretical frame for this study, as it incorporates the Black intellectual tradition and feminism in its foundation. Black feminist anthropology is grounded in the works of Ida B. Wells, W. E. B. Du Bois, Anna Julia Cooper, St. Clair Drake, Katherine Dunham, and many other scholars from multiple disciplines who have criticized racism and its social, political, and economic consequences.[4] The gendered focus on Black feminist anthropology draws from the feminist movement, which itself has historically focused on white women.

In addition, Black feminist anthropology situates Black women's identity as a point of departure for gathering and analyzing research. As Irma McClaurin notes, "The politics of Black feminist anthropology can be found in our self-conscious positioning of ourselves as Black women (first) who do anthropology (second)."[5] Patricia Hill Collins argues that marginalized groups are positioned in a manner that challenges the core of power structures and are thus able to ask different questions than nonmarginalized groups.[6] This approach posits that scholars must apply an intersectional lens to their work to fully illuminate Black women's lives and power within the context of multiple and layered forms of structural oppression. The African American Burial Ground and Remembering Project follows in this tradition of bringing visibility to lived experiences of Black people in America as it seeks to reclaim African American burial grounds and sacred sites as an integral part of America's story. Yet these histories have often been literally paved over in acts of structural racism. The roles of Black women as researchers and leaders in the work of honoring the dead and in the preservation of cemeteries and sacred sites in communities where they reside have primarily been rendered invisible. Grounded in her own racialized and gendered position, Jackson deliberately chose women as co-PIs on the AABGP to aid in dissecting the multilayered and intersecting oppression of the cemeteries and communities. Jackson sought to embrace the varied experiences and racial, ethnic, and gendered positionalities these women embody, not only for the insight they bring to the research goals and objectives of the project but also for the tensions they excite in terms of project management/leadership and thinking outside the box in terms of doing research in community.

In this chapter, we discuss research we conducted associated with Oaklawn, Evergreen, and Moffett Cemeteries, referred to as the Oaklawn Cemetery Complex (OCC), and institutions connected to death and deathways in St. Petersburg, Florida. These cemeteries, now paved over by parking lots and highways, were connected historically to the African American communities of Methodist Town and the Gas Plant District. Black women have been integral in death care labor and the memorialization of these sites. We argue that to fully capture the numerous laboring roles and responsibilities of Black women, researchers must disaggregate their study findings and practices to make Black women's roles visible and to illuminate the significance of their work within the communities they serve. In this chapter we bring to the center the multifaceted roles of Black women as essential to creating and sharing ways of knowing, enhancing, and complicating southern cemetery histories. In doing so, we have been intentional about our approach to discussing our research to make visible the often underacknowledged experiences and labor of Black women.

History of Oaklawn Cemetery Complex, from Creation to Destruction

Many drivers traveling across Interstate 175, one of two short spurs running from I-275 into downtown St. Petersburg, Florida, have no idea, as they slow down along the ramp, that they are cruising over the former site of three burial grounds—Moffett, Evergreen, and Oaklawn Cemeteries. For them, this mile-long stretch of highway serves as a primary exit for Tropicana Field, the Bayfront/All Children's Hospital complex, the Salvador Dalí Museum, and the University of South Florida's St. Petersburg campus.

Discussed collectively here as the Oaklawn Cemetery Complex, these three sites were built during the late nineteenth and early twentieth centuries, then condemned and abandoned during the 1920s. All three cemeteries were founded during the period in U.S. history when racial segregation was legal. For African Americans and their families, this meant that cemeteries were typically segregated or partitioned along racial lines, with certain cemeteries or areas within cemeteries designated for whites only. "White only" spaces, from cemeteries to parks to schools, excluded Black people

FIGURE 8.2. Oaklawn, Evergreen, and Moffett (St. Petersburg) cemeteries are shown in this overlay image with Tropicana Field and the interstate (courtesy of the University of South Florida African American Burial Ground and Remembering Project).

from access or use.[7] Segregation limited burial options for Black people, often dictating location, legal/legislative protections, and resources available for perpetual care and upkeep. Moffett, Evergreen, and Oaklawn Cemeteries tell the history of segregation, even in death, in St. Petersburg. Today these three burial grounds are unmarked, erased from the physical landscape, or paved over in the name of urban development.

The roughly two-acre Moffett (also known as "Moffett's" and "St. Petersburg Cemetery"), the oldest of the three, was founded by David Moffett, who purchased the land in 1888. Initially the cemetery was for Black and

white Civil War veterans, but in 1902 it was opened to all Black residents, with Sallie Ross being the first civilian burial. Evergreen, similarly, about two acres in size and used by African Americans, was founded by 1905. That year also saw the founding of the larger, twelve-acre Oaklawn Cemetery, which contained both Black and white graves that were segregated into sections by race. The Independent Order of Odd Fellows (IOOF) and the Carpenters' and Joiners' Union of America (CJU) bought a parcel of land north of Moffett Cemetery, which became Oaklawn Cemetery. Today, the site of Oaklawn Cemetery is under VIP Parking Lot 1 of Tropicana Field, and Moffett and Evergreen Cemeteries are now under Interstate 175 and the I-275 overpass on Fifth Avenue (see Appendix A).[8]

How did we get to this level of Black cemetery erasure? In 1908 Evergreen, which was located west of Moffett and south of Oaklawn, was bought by Senator Samuel D. Harris, an undertaker who also purchased Bussey's Funeral Home.[9] Harris eventually owned all three cemeteries but sold them to J. H. Endicott and Sarah K. Cowen in 1921. After several additional changes in ownership, the cemeteries were condemned and closed by city ordinance in February 1926 "for the protection of public health." A subsequent ordinance called for the removal of the burials to be Under Ordinance 440-A, to either Royal Palm Cemetery (for whites only) or Lincoln Cemetery.[10]

Lincoln Cemetery, for African Americans, in nearby Gulfport opened in 1926—the same year the other three burial grounds were condemned and ordered closed. Some graves were relocated shortly thereafter, while others were moved two decades later, when the Royal Court housing project—later known as Laurel Park—was built. In each case, former cemeteries made vulnerable by time, limited resources, and redevelopment complicated the process of locating graves and identifying bodies. Some were moved with ceremony. In 1953, the *St. Petersburg Times* reported the relocation of graves for Civil War veterans Joseph Brownlow, John W. Sharter, and John Lasker. Others were moved without fanfare, if they were moved at all.[11]

The process of burial removal from these cemeteries was disjointed at best. Following the implementation of Ordinance 440-A, only fifty burials were removed from Evergreen and Moffett, while there is no documentation of removals from Oaklawn Cemetery. In 1949, developers Donald Rosselli, Ed Harris, and Gust Blair acquired ownership of the Oaklawn Cemetery land and built the Royal Court Apartments for Black residents, with burials underneath the construction.[12] Moffett and Evergreen Cemeteries, which were combined under the name Moffett Cemetery in 1953, continued to change ownership until 1958, when Grady Swope took over the land with the intention of erecting apartment buildings for Black residents. Before construction began, McRae Funeral Home led the effort to relocate the burials from Moffett Cemetery to Lincoln Cemetery, which was to be done by September 1958.[13]

The official story was that all human remains were exhumed and reinterred—until, that is, the apartments were demolished in 1971, revealing that several burials remained under the structure. More bodies turned up in 1976 as construction began on the interstate. By 1990, when construction started for Tropicana Field (then called the Florida Suncoast Dome), the city expressed confidence that the site was fully cleared. However, recent research by the Florida Public Archaeology Network FPAN has found that a complete survey was never done. In early 2021, Cardno, a firm specializing in site evaluation prior to construction, worked with FPAN to conduct a ground-penetrating radar survey on Lot 1 of Tropicana Field and discovered at least three burials and other partial graves and locations where there could have been grave removals.[14] This research was cut short due to COVID-19 restrictions. However, the preliminary findings add validity to concerns of community residents and local citizens about the erasure of historic Black cemeteries in the Tampa Bay area. At present, the city of St. Petersburg is considering proposals to redevelop the area surrounding Tropicana Field, while there are discussions about shortening or removing I-175. Both possibilities raise new concerns about disturbing historic grave sites and questions about what comes next in terms of memorialization.

The Network of Death Surrounding Oaklawn Cemetery Complex

As we sought to preserve the histories of the Oaklawn Cemetery Complex, we recognized that we must begin with researching the people and communities who were erased with the paving of the burial grounds. AABGP works to amplify the complex lived experiences of Black people and include their narratives in conversations on the future of these sites.[15] These cemeteries are *lieux de mémoire*, sites of memory, as they speak to the heritage of the community. *Lieux de mémoire*, as defined by Pierre Nora, are objects, places, or concepts "where memory crystalizes and secretes itself."[16] In other words, these sites, which are material, functional, and symbolic in nature, are historically significant representations of a community's collective memory. *Lieux de mémoire* are established to limit forgetfulness and evoke a historical consciousness in the community. Though the cemeteries have been erased, AABGP has investigated other sites of memory that speak to the past and present Black community in St. Petersburg and that provide cultural and social context for the burial grounds. As Nora argues, for *lieux de mémoire* to exist there must be a "will to remember."[17] The Black community has worked to preserve the collective memories of its past through maintaining sites that speak to its heritage. In investigating the Oaklawn Cemetery Complex, we investigated the sites of memory that intersected death and deathways of the Black community in St. Petersburg. We researched what Lynn Rainville describes as multiple points in the network of death—those social institutions involved in the deaths and deathways of the community.[18] For this study, we recognized the network of death as including the church, funeral homes, benevolent societies, and hospitals. We used our positionality to critically examine the history of this network of death to avoid an androcentric view of the past. As Black women from the U.S. South, we know that women occupy nontraditional and often informal leadership roles that are vital to the Black community, from church secretary to kinship roles such as aunt or mother. Our work illuminates the ways in which Black women have maintained these institutions and have been integral to their preservation.

One way of knowing Black history is by researching and learning about Black churches and the centrality of these sites within Black communities. Antoinette Jackson writes about the importance of Black churches in her book *Heritage, Tourism, and Race: The Other Side of Leisure*, stating that "adopting a critical spatial perspective means interrogating the Black church and other unconventional sites as ways of knowing and engaging Black leisure history."[19] The Black church has been critical in the social, spiritual, economic, and political uplift of the African American community. It has also been a significant carrier of Black cultural tradition. Cheryl Townsend Gilkes explains that upholding cultural traditions can be an act of political resistance, especially as pressure is applied from outside the Black community to abandon tradition.[20] Black women have helped to facilitate and maintain these traditions, which ensured the survival of the church. Exploring the numerous roles of women, such as serving as Sunday school teachers and missionaries and hosting teas, offers us insight into the resiliency of the churches and community.

The Oaklawn Cemetery Complex was located in close proximity to the Gas Plant District, a historically African American community. The community—so named because there was an actual gas plant in the neighborhood—was located west of Ninth Street South and south of First Avenue South in St. Petersburg. In her article "I AM: The Story of the Gas Plant Neighborhood," Gwendolyn Reese explains that "the neighborhood was home to many people, me included, who still have pleasant memories of growing up there. The communal fish fries on Friday, crab boils on Saturday and barbecues were a major part of the social life of the neighborhood."[21] Near the Gas Plant District was another historically African American community called Methodist Town, named after the historic Bethel African Methodist Episcopal (AME) Church, which was established in 1894. Located west of Ninth Street North and north of First Avenue North, Methodist Town was a close-knit community with its own extensive social network. According to Irene Williams Griffin, a longtime resident, "Black people served their own people. They had grocery stores, dry cleaners, restaurants. They had their own lounges and they had their barber shop, wood yard, furniture transfer.... They just had a lot of things going for them."[22] As Methodist Town grew, Bethel AME became a business, social, and spiritual center for the community.

For our project at the Oaklawn site, we began with a focus on examining the Black churches in the area. There are more than forty-five Black churches that have been active in St. Petersburg, both historically and currently. They represent such denominations as Baptist, Church of God in Christ, Methodist, African Methodist Episcopal, Church of God, Seventh-Day Adventist, and Jehovah's Witnesses. When available, we reviewed archival information on the churches and documented church history, leadership, and location. Formal histories of the churches generally centered on the leadership and vision of the pastors, who were largely male.[23] Several Black churches in St. Petersburg employed a gendered structure or division of labor, with women having supportive yet powerful roles in the church and community.

Black women, when not in traditional leadership positions, have created roles for themselves that have been integral to the resilience of the church. As Cheryl Townsend Gilkes argues, "When blocked from the most visible leadership positions, women find ways to make their voices heard and their power felt in alternate spaces of their own creation, spaces that give them limited access to the sacred platforms."[24] To understand how Black women have shaped the Black church experience in Gas Plant and Methodist Town, we examined newspaper archives, specifically the Black section of the *St. Petersburg Times* (now known as the *Tampa Bay Times*). We also examined obituaries of people buried in the Oaklawn Cemetery Complex. These obituaries, some of which are in the *Tampa Bay Times* archives, document the multiple affiliations of deceased individuals, such as their organizational memberships, church affiliations, and other responsibilities to their home and community. These death notices are a treasure trove of information that tells how these individuals created a community.

Historic Bethel African Methodist Episcopal Church, the first African American church in St. Petersburg, provides a great opportunity for understanding how Black women have created their own institutional space. Since its founding, only men have been selected to be pastors of Bethel. A pastor not only represents the church in the community but is the spiritual and logistical leader of the congregation. The women of Bethel, on the other hand, were, and still are, more active in less public roles. According to Daphne C. Wiggins, "Whether in their roles as soloists, ushers, nurses, church mothers, Sunday school teachers, missionaries, pastor's aides, deaconesses, stewardesses, or prayer warriors, women are at the core of the Black Church, which could not exist without them."[25] They managed its daily activities, finances, fundraising, and other logistical duties necessary for the church to function. The church secretary, who assisted the pastor in his administrative duties, was responsible for bookkeeping, filing, and other tasks involved in the daily management of the church.

Among the most notable activities held by women of Bethel AME were the "calendar teas," which raised money for the church, its events, and other needs. Ada L. Kelly, a parishioner who chaired one of the teas, recalls that "most of the times the Women's Day Tea was given to buy different things for the church, to have the seats covered, to buy rugs."[26] Church teas were hosted by women in their homes and, particularly as they became more popular, at the church.[27] This tea tradition has been a significant aspect of the church's history, not only in providing financial support but also in celebrating major events. At various times the Women's Day Committee, the Usher Board, and the Gospel Chorus hosted annual teas. Teas were held to celebrate the church's anniversary and Valentine's Day and to honor special guests. Even as the church has changed over time, women continue to hold the traditional calendar teas to benefit the church.[28] Other African American churches in St. Petersburg enjoyed calendar teas as well. In the "Local and National Negro News" section of the *St. Petersburg Times*, the calendar teas were highly advertised as major social events, complete with a listing of all the women involved in their organizing and execution.[29]

Black women also have played an active role in the preservation of Bethel AME Church's history. P. H. Wright, a Black woman congregant, wrote a piece for the church's *Women of Purpose* newsletter entitled "HERstory of Historic Bethel AME," which documents the multiple contributions of women to the church.[30] Annie Reddick, who was mentioned in Wright's work, developed and managed the church's archives. Women have contributed to preserving the church's past in less formal ways too. In a 1999 article published in the *Tampa Bay Times* highlighting Bethel AME's 105th anniversary, Waveney Ann Moore describes the involvement of women in the church's legacy and describes how women have been integral to the church's membership by using their own kinship networks. For example, former St. Petersburg police chief Goliath Davis attended Bethel AME with his grandmother, Hattie Lilly, while church member Tereatha Mae Brown brought her seven sons and three daughters with her to Bethel AME.[31] As W. E. B. Du Bois pointed out, "Black women (and women whose grandmothers were Black) . . . are the main pillars of those social settlements which we call churches; and they have with small doubt raised three-fourths of our church property."[32]

Another arena where Black women's labor was invaluable was the funeral home industry. Funeral homes provide important context to our work on the Oaklawn Cemetery Complex, as they provide insight into the social, political, and economic nature of death. Black funeral homes have been critical to the deathways of African Americans since the end of the Civil War, when the funeral industry became more formalized.[33] In the face of racial segregation and death, Black funeral homes provided proper and respectful burials for African Americans and thus contributed to the long tradition of homegoings. Among the Black funeral homes and undertakers that have operated in St. Petersburg are Creal-Williams Funeral Home, Arch of Royal Funeral Home, Clarke Mortuary, Sanchez-Arch Royal Funeral Home, Sanchez Rehoboth Mortuary and Cremations Services, and McRae Funeral Home, which was responsible for the removal of bodies from Moffett to Lincoln Cemetery in the 1950s.

Although Black funeral homes in St. Petersburg were dominated by men, women played active roles in the ownership of three of them. Williams Funeral Home was founded by Fred and Nathanial Williams in about 1926, but when the brothers died, Nathaniel's wife, Florence Williams, managed the business with Robert Creal, who was appointed its director in 1950. It was later renamed Creal-Williams Funeral Home. Although Florence Williams did not have complete ownership, she helped to maintain the business after the death of her husband. By contrast, the original owner of Sanchez-Arch Royal Funeral Home was a Jesse Marie Calhoun, a Black woman. She was married to R. C. Calhoun, the architect of First Baptist Institutional Church in the Gas Plant District. Bought in the late 1950s, the funeral home was originally called Arch Royal, but the name changed to Sanchez-Arch Royal Funeral Home when Calhoun's nephew, Irving Sanchez II, took over the business in the 1960s. Sanchez's son, Irving Sanchez III, continued the legacy of his aunt and father when he, along with his wife, Judy Sanchez, founded Sanchez Rehoboth Mortuary and Cremation Services in St. Petersburg.[34]

Just as the labor of women was critical to the functioning of the Black church, the women auxiliaries, or sister organizations, of benevolent societies were instrumental in homegoing services. African American fraternal organizations and benevolent societies were created to provide social support and encourage economic cooperation in Black communities and were active from Reconstruction into the twentieth century. The fraternal orders help establish record keeping involving births, marriages, deaths, and adoptions—a vitally important service, since African Americans were often not adequately documented. These organizations also offered assistance with funerals to ensure that homegoing services and cemetery plots were respectful.[35]

The African American Burial Ground and Remembering Project team identified several benevolent societies that were active in St. Petersburg, including the Knights of Pythias and the Independent Order of the Oddfellows. Since the original Knights of Pythias, founded in 1864 by white men, refused to accept Black members, African Americans created their own fraternal order of the same name. In St. Petersburg, the group was referred to as the St. Petersburg Colored Chapter of the KOP. The women's auxiliary is called the Order of Calenthe, and only women who are married to a Knights of Pythias member can join. In the "Card of Thanks" section of the *St. Petersburg Times*, where the family and friends of the deceased acknowledged the people who showed kindness and offered help during the time of bereavement, the Order of Calanthe was often credited for its role in homegoing services.[36]

Several entries in the "Card of Thanks" section also expressed gratitude to doctors and staff at Mercy Hospital, another key institution in the network of death.[37] Mercy was the only St. Petersburg hospital that admitted African American citizens in the period between 1923 and 1966. Prior to its establishment in 1923, there were two hospitals in the city—St. Petersburg Sanitorium and St. Petersburg Emergency Hospital, later called Samaritan Hospital—and both treated only white patrons. Charles M. Roser, a prominent developer, moved Samaritan Hospital to the Gas Plant District and designated it for Black patients.[38] According to the *Tampa Bay Times*, it was at Mercy Hospital that "Black women gave birth to generations of children. That was also where Black workers received treatment if injured while building the Don CeSar resort, the Gandy Bridge, and the Renaissance Vinoy Resort or when felled by the sunstroke when laying the city's brick streets."[39] Mercy was staffed by only white doctors from Mound Park Hospital, now Bayfront Health St. Petersburg, until Dr. James Maxie Ponder, an African American physician, was hired in 1926. The hospital eventually hired additional African American doctors, including Dr. Breaux Martin, Dr. Fred W. Alsup, Dr. Orion T. Ayer Sr., Dr. Ralph M. Wimbish Sr., Dr. Harry F. Taliaferro, and Dr. Eugene C. Rose.[40]

Also staffing Mercy Hospital was a group of registered nurses and volunteers who were predominantly Black women. Nurses had a wealth of responsibilities, including dealing with infectious diseases, accident victims, and obstetrics.[41] The Registered Nurses Club, founded in 1946 by Marie Yopp, was the first African American registered nurses' organization in St. Petersburg.[42] Other women involved in the club's founding include Catherine James, Emma Yvonne Taylor, Hannah Singleton, Effra Mae Clark, Deloris Gordon, Mattie C. Bennet, and Sadie Henry. The Gray Ladies of Mercy

Hospital provided volunteer support to the nurses and physicians by answering phones, greeting visitors, running errands, and feeding patients.[43] They also helped with various events such as Christmas celebrations.[44]

Mercy Hospital closed its doors in 1966, five years after Mound Park Hospital began to admit African American patients.[45] Yet even today, the labor of Black women continues as they lead the efforts to preserve the site. The Mercy Hospital Alumni Association consists of former employees, mainly nurses, who worked at the institution.[46] At one point, it included about one hundred members, but its numbers have declined significantly in recent years due to the age of the members and the fact that a few have moved out of the area.[47] Ann Gethers, the association's first president, organized the first reunion of personnel in 1993 and has continued to plan activities with members.[48] Her stories, and those of other hospital personnel, have helped preserve the memory of Mercy Hospital as a vital part of St. Petersburg's Black history.

Conclusion: Beyond the Oaklawn Cemetery Complex

In 2013, three Black women—Alicia Garza, Patrisse Cullors, and Opal Tometi—started the #BlackLivesMatter movement to bring attention to the systematic threat on Black lives. The movement has grown into a global network that aims to recognize and fight against the inequalities that render Black lives inferior and invisible. However, as the movement developed, the deaths of Black women and girls were pushed to the periphery of this global network. Kimberlé Crenshaw, who coined the term "intersectionality," saw this gap in coverage of the Black experience and, with the African American Policy Forum, formed the hashtag #SayHerName in December 2014 to highlight Black women and girls who have been victims of police violence and other forms of anti-Black violence.[49] The need for the #SayHerName campaign also highlights the invisibility of Black women's experience, in understanding their roles in the larger Black community around sacred site place making and remembrance.

The African American Burial Ground and Remembering Project contributes to these efforts to move the experiences of Black women to the center of the conversation on death care labor. In our research, we learned of the multiple roles Black women held, from professional to personal. Black women have been the cornerstone of the African American community, yet their labor is rendered invisible in the male-centered recounting of the Black past. Further, racism involved in the disjointed removal of burials in

St. Petersburg's Oaklawn Cemetery Complex and the paving of Tropicana Field contributed to the silencing of their narratives. Taking a Black feminist approach to this multifaceted study, we are actively honoring the work of Black women in the community while also interrogating the silencing processes that have pushed their stories to the periphery.

Black women are essential to sustaining community infrastructure through their laboring roles, particularly in preservation efforts associated with southern cemetery sites in the United States. They are particularly essential in leadership, research, and advocacy roles, as their lived experiences often give them a foundation from which to ground knowledge and direct research that centers communities most affected by the erasure of Black sacred sites and most in need of specific solutions that speak to the specific needs and traditions in communities that have often gone underrepresented and underresourced. In the case of Antoinette Jackson's leadership, this connection to Black cemeteries as sites of knowledge, history, and expectation that the living learn from and honor the dead is evident, particularly in the many links and collaborations she is bringing together at local and national levels. The differentiated accounting of church spaces, the funeral industry, and cemeteries, and the related types of labor associated with church affiliation and service, poignantly unveils complex articulations of power and access to resources often ignored when addressing African Americans' burial practices. To access African American engagements with the living and services associated with bringing dignity to the deceased, it is important to focus on strategies happening from within communities such as St. Petersburg. In June 2021, Jackson formed a team and launched the Black Cemetery Network (BCN) as a platform for advocacy and education at the national level and the promotion of #BlackGravesMatter for social justice outreach to draw attention to the erasure of Black cemeteries from the landscape. Centering southern cemeteries—sites such as those in Florida—as well as churches and associated sites of service that attend to the needs of the living and the dead in small and large communities, will enrich the study of death care and provide lessons we can learn and share.

Notes

The authors wish to thank the many researchers, scholars, artists, and community outreach activists and advocates on the African American Burial Ground and Remembering Project, including Dr. Julie Buckner Armstrong, Dr. Kathryn Weedman Arthur, Dr. Cheryl Rodriguez, Alanah Cooper, Dr. Anna R. Dixon, Lesleyanne Drake, Jessica Gantzert, Charles (Fred) Hearns, Kaleigh Hoyt, Khalia Jenkins, Walter Jennings, Verna Peddi, John Pendygraft, Andrew M. "Drew" Smith, and David Shedden.

1. "Research Project to Recover, Engage Public."
2. Alridge, Bynum, and Stewart, introduction to *The Black Intellectual Tradition*, 9.
3. Ibid.
4. McClaurin, introduction to *Black Feminist Anthropology*, 5.
5. Ibid., 16.
6. Collins, *Black Feminist Thought*.
7. Jackson, *Heritage, Tourism, and Race*.
8. Shedden, "St. Petersburg African American Burial Ground and Gas Plant Neighborhood Timeline."
9. Grismer, *Story of St. Petersburg*, 106.
10. St. Petersburg Ordinance 425-A (February 1926); "Title and Synopsis of Proposed Ordinance No. 440-A Title," *St. Petersburg Times*, March 17, 1926.
11. "Clearing of Old Cemetery Recalls Historical Facts," *St. Petersburg Times*, May 23, 1933; Paul Mitchell, "Veterans Groups Fight Moffett Cemetery Grave Desecration," *St. Petersburg Times*, November 9, 1949; "Rubbish Again Marks Veterans' Graves," *St. Petersburg Times*, August 16, 1951; Don Branning, "Bones of Two Negro Confederate Soldiers Moved to New Cemetery," *St. Petersburg Times*, July 1, 1958.
12. O'Sullivan, Hinder, and McKendry, "Oaklawn Cemetery Ground Penetrating Radar Survey."
13. "More Bodies Found at Site of Apartment," *St. Petersburg Times*, August 22, 1958; Pat Fenner, "Finding Relatives' Graves Is Proving a Difficult Task," *St. Petersburg Times*, November 1, 1987.
14. Patrick Tyler, "Human Bones Found at Scene of Mattress Fire," *St. Petersburg Times*, February 11, 1976; Paul Guzzo, "Are There Graves under Tropicana Field Parking Lots? Archaeologists Want to Find Out," *Tampa Bay Times*, July 2, 2020; Dan Matics, "Tropicana Field Parking Lot May Be Site of Forgotten African American Cemetery," WTVT-TV Fox 13 News, March 29, 2021.
15. The AABGP digital archive is available via the University of South Florida Digital Commons (https://digitalcommons.usf.edu/african_american_burial_grounds_ohp/). This includes an oral history database of people associated with the cemeteries and a project StoryMap.
16. Nora, "Between Memory and History," 7.
17. Nora, "Between Memory and History," 19.
18. Rainville, *Hidden History*.
19. Jackson, *Heritage, Tourism, and Race*, 71.
20. Gilkes, "'Together and in Harness,'" 629.
21. Reese, "I AM: The Story of the Gas Plant Neighborhood."
22. Quoted in Curtin, "Neighbors Reunite to Remember."
23. Wiggins, *Righteous Content*, 2.
24. Gilkes, *If It Wasn't for the Women*, 7.
25. Wiggins, *Righteous Content*, 2.
26. Quoted in Moore, "Spiritual Revival."
27. Wright, "HERstory of Historic Bethel AME."
28. Moore, "Spiritual Revival."
29. Peterman, "Librarian Is Quiet, Unassuming."
30. Wright, "HERstory of Historic Bethel AME."
31. Moore, "Spiritual Revival."
32. Du Bois, *Darkwater*.
33. Smith, *To Serve the Living*.

34. "Irving Sanchez III Oral History Interview," African American Burial Grounds Oral History Project, 2021, https://digitalcommons.usf.edu/african_american_burial_grounds_ohp/4/.

35. Smith, *To Serve the Living*, 40.

36. See, for example, *St. Petersburg Times*, March 8, 1953; *St. Petersburg Times*, May 17, 1953.

37. See "Card of Thanks" entries in the *St. Petersburg Times*, September 18, 1949; January 31, 1954; July 15, 1956; August 17, 1958; and October 13, 1964.

38. Reese, "Mercy Hospital and its Pioneering Physicians."

39. Eastman, "Mercy's History Hangs over City Purchase," 4.

40. Reese, "I AM: Mercy Hospital and Its Pioneering Physicians, Part 2."

41. Shonel, "Keeping the History of Mercy Hospital Alive."

42. Yopp was also the first Black registered nurse at the African American health clinic that was located in a converted house adjacent to Mercy Hospital. Miller, "For Decades, She Nursed a Community in Need."

43. The Gray Ladies, formally known as the Red Cross Hospital and Recreation Corps, were an all-female volunteer unit that began at the Walter Reed Army Hospital in 1918. Reese, "Mercy Hospital and Its Pioneering Physicians, Part 2."

44. Duckworth, "Mercy Hospital Reunion Would Reunite a Family."

45. Eastman, "Mercy's History Hangs over City's Purchase."

46. There is conflicting information about when the organization was founded. According to a 2016 newspaper article (Shonel, "Keeping the History of Mercy Hospital Alive"), the alumni association was established in 1993. However, obituaries in the *St. Petersburg Times* as early as the late 1980s mention the association. See "Faney," Funeral Notices, *St. Petersburg Times*, May 8, 1980.

47. Shonel, "Keeping the History of Mercy Hospital Alive."

48. Duckworth, "Mercy Hospital Reunion Would Reunite a Family."

49. Crenshaw, "Demarginalizing the Intersection of Race and Sex"; Crenshaw et al., *Say Her Name*.

Bibliography

Alridge, Derrick P., Cornelius L. Bynum, and James B. Stewart. Introduction to *The Black Intellectual Tradition: African American Thought in the Twentieth Century*, edited by Derrick P. Alridge, Cornelius L. Bynum, and James B. Stewart, 9–19. Champaign: University of Illinois Press, 2021.

Black Cemetery Network. https://Blackcemeterynetwork.org/.

Collins, Patricia Hill. *Black Feminist Thought: Knowledge, Consciousness, and the Politics of Empowerment*. New York: Routledge Classics, 2009.

Crenshaw, Kimberlé. "Demarginalizing the Intersection of Race and Sex: A Black Feminist Critique of Antidiscrimination Doctrine, Feminist Theory and Antiracist Politics." *University of Chicago Legal Forum* 1989, no. 1 (1989): 139–67.

Crenshaw, Kimberlé W., Andrea J. Ritchie, Rachel Anspach, Rachel Gilmer, and Luke Harris. *Say Her Name: Resisting Police Brutality against Black Women*. New York: African American Policy Forum and Center for Intersectionality and Social Policy Studies, 2015. https://scholarship.law.columbia.edu/cgi/viewcontent.cgi?article=4235&context=faculty_scholarship.

Curtin, Patty. "Neighbors Reunite to Remember//Methodist Town Still Exists." *Tampa Bay Times*, July 6, 2006.

Davis, Dána-Ain, and Christa Craven. *Feminist Ethnography: Thinking through Methodologies, Challenges, and Possibilities*. Lanham, Md.: Rowman and Littlefield, 2016.

Du Bois, W. E. B. *Darkwater: Voices from within the Veil*. New York: Harcourt, Brace, and Company, 1920. Project Gutenberg e-book, 2005. https://www.gutenberg.org/files/15210/15210-h/15210-h.htm.

Duckworth, Erika N. "Mercy Hospital Reunion Would Reunite a 'Family.'" *St. Petersburg Times*, August 8, 1993.

Eastman, Susan. "Mercy's History Hangs over City's Purchase." *Tampa Bay Times*, January 14, 1998; updated September 12, 2005.

Floyd-Thomas, Juan Marcial. *Liberating Black Church History: Making it Plain*. Nashville: Abingdon Press, 2014.

Gilkes, Cheryl Townsend. *If It Wasn't for the Women*. Maryknoll, N.Y.: Orbis Books, 2001.

———. "'Together and in Harness': Women's Tradition in the Sanctified Church." In *African American Religious Thought*, edited by Cornel West and Eddie S. Glaude Jr., 629–50. Louisville: Westminster John Knox Press, 2003.

Glaude, Eddie S., Jr. "Of the Black Church and the Making of a Black Public." In *African American Religious Thought*, edited by Cornel West and Eddie S. Glaude Jr., 338–65. Louisville: Westminster John Knox Press, 2003.

Grismer, Karl H. *The Story of St. Petersburg*. St. Petersburg, Fla.: P. K. Smith, 1948.

Harris, Ida. "Black Funerals Are a Radical Testament to Blackness." *Yes!*, August 21, 2019. https://www.yesmagazine.org/issue/death/opinion/2019/08/21/funeral-Black-african-american-radical-Blackness.

Holloway, Karla FC. *Passed On: African American Mourning Stories*. Durham, N.C.: Duke University Press, 2003.

Jackson, Antoinette. *Heritage, Tourism, and Race: The Other Side of Leisure*. New York: Routledge, 2020.

———. "Intangible Cultural Heritage and Living Communities." *Anthropology News* 55, no. 3 (2014): e21–e61.

———. "Shattering Slave Life Portrayals—Uncovering Subjugated Knowledge in U.S. Plantation Sites in South Carolina and Florida." *American Anthropologist* 13, no. 3 (2011): 448–62.

———. *Speaking for the Enslaved: Heritage Interpretation at Antebellum Plantation Sites*. New York: Routledge, 2012.

Kottak, Conrad P. *Anthropology: Appreciating Human Diversity*. New York: McGraw Hill, 2021.

Lynd, Robert S., and Helen M. Lynd. *Middletown: A Study in Contemporary African Culture*. New York: Harcourt, Brace, and Company, 1929.

McClaurin, Irma. Introduction to *Black Feminist Anthropology: Theory, Politics, Praxis, and Poetics*, edited by Irma McClaurin, 1–23. New Brunswick, N.J.: Rutgers University Press, 2001.

McGrew, J. H. *A Study of Negro Life in Tampa*. Typescript report, 1927. State Library of Florida, Florida Memory. https://www.floridamemory.com/items/show/326639?id=1.

McKittrick, Katherine. *Demonic Grounds: Black Women and Cartographies of Struggle*. Minneapolis: University of Minnesota Press, 2006.

Miller, Betty Jean. "For Decades, She Nursed a Community in Need." *Tampa Bay Times*, March 14, 1994; updated October 6, 2005.

Moore, Waveney Ann. "Spiritual Revival: Bethel AME Church, Once the Center of St. Petersburg's Black Community, Searches for a New Mission—and Younger Worshipers—As It Celebrates Its 105th Birthday." *Tampa Bay Times*, Nov. 21, 1999.

Nora, Pierre. "Between Memory and History: Les Lieux de Memoire." In "Memory and Counter-Memory." Special issue, *Representations* 26 (Spring 1989): 7–24.

O'Sullivan, Rebecca, Kimberly D. Hinder, and Erin McKendry. "Oaklawn Cemetery Ground Penetrating Radar Survey at Tropicana Field Parking Lots 1 and 2." Draft report. Cardno, Riverview, Fla., July 19, 2021.

Peterman, Peggy M. "Librarian Is Quiet, Unassuming." St. Petersburg Times, April 11, 1965.

Rainville, Lynn. *Hidden History: African American Cemeteries in Central Virginia*. Charlottesville: University of Virginia Press, 2014.

Reese, Gwendolyn. "I AM: Mercy Hospital and Its Pioneering Physicians, Part 2." *Weekly Challenger*, December 13, 2018.

———. "I AM: The Story of the Gas Plant Neighborhood." *Weekly Challenger*, May 13, 2021.

———. "Mercy Hospital and Its Pioneering Physicians." *Weekly Challenger*, November 2, 2018.

"Research Project to Recover, Engage Public on Lost History of African American Burial Grounds in Tampa Bay." University of South Florida St. Petersburg Campus News, Dec. 21, 2020. https://www.stpetersburg.usf.edu/news/2020/research-project-to-recover-engage-public-on-lost-history-of-african-american-burial-grounds-in-tampa-bay.aspx.

Shedden, David. "St. Petersburg African American Burial Ground and Gas Plant Neighborhood Timeline and Bibliography 1888–2022." African American Burial Ground and Remembering Project, University of South Florida Libraries, November 1, 2022. chrome-extension://efaidnbmnnnibpcajpcglclefindmkaj/http://aae.lib.usf.edu/wp-content/uploads/2022/04/St.-Petersburg-African-American-Burial-Ground-Gas-Plant-Neighborhood-Timeline-Bibliography_Nov.-1-2022.pdf.

Shonel, Raven Joy. "Keeping the History of Mercy Hospital Alive." *Weekly Challenger*, July 28, 2016.

Smith, Suzanne E. *To Serve the Living: Funeral Directors and the African American Way of Death*. Cambridge, Mass.: Harvard University Press, 2010.

Wiggins, Daphne C. *Righteous Content: Black Women's Perspectives of Church and Faith*. New York: New York University Press, 2004.

Wright, P. H. "HERstory of Historic Bethel AME." *Historic Bethel AME Church Women of Purpose*. Website of the Historic Bethel AME Church. chrome-extension://efaidnbmnnnibpcajpcglclefindmkaj/https://h7jaf7.a2cdn1.secureserver.net/wp-content/uploads/2020/08/Women-of-purpose.pdf.

EPILOGUE

TEACHING THE AMERICAN SOUTH BY LEARNING THE DEAD

The Black Cemetery Network (BCN) was developed to bring public awareness to the erasure of Black cemeteries in the United States. These cemeteries tell stories of the Black people and their communities that have been silenced by forces of institutional racism and not included in the U.S. public memory. This network, started by a Black woman scholar-activist, aims to bring attention to these hidden narratives. On the Black Cemetery Network website (https://Blackcemeterynetwork.org) is an interactive map of African American cemeteries. This archive includes the history, resources, and contact information about each cemetery.

For this exercise, make sure you use the sources available to you on the Black Cemetery Network website. Choose an African American cemetery from the BCN archival map. Once you have identified a site, locate one church that either owned or was associated with the cemetery. Another option is to research/identify a funeral home that has directly worked with the cemetery or a benevolent society, or any health care facility that existed during the time in which the cemetery was active and served the African American community.

After you have found a cemetery and a church, funeral home, benevolent society, or hospital/health care facility, research the roles and positions Black women held and complete the following questions:

1. What roles, positions, and responsibilities did Black women hold in this network of community burial practices and sacred site remembrance?
2. Explain your research process, including any obstacles you encountered while searching for the roles of Black women. What can this tell us about how women's roles within these institutions are valued?

3. How do your research and findings compare and contrast with the discussions and findings regarding the roles and responsibilities of African American women in relation to cemeteries and sacred site maintenance and remembrance practices presented in this chapter? How do you explain these similarities and/or differences?

CHAPTER 9

Permanent Reconstruction in Richmond's Black Cemeteries

ADAM ROSENBLATT,
ERIN HOLLAWAY PALMER, AND
BRIAN PALMER

If you travel toward East End and Evergreen Cemeteries from downtown Richmond, Virginia, your roughly ten-minute car trip will first take you past another cemetery, Oakwood. Oakwood is larger than the two historic African American burial grounds and separated from them by a creek and a roadway. The three cemeteries are so close they could almost be mistaken for a single unit. But there are some glaring differences. Oakwood's well-manicured lawns are cut regularly. It has a security gate and paved roads. Its headstones are largely clean, legible, and upright.

Large swaths of the grounds at East End and Evergreen, on the other hand, are heavily overgrown. Vegetation covers hundreds of headstones, some of them broken, fallen, or with faded inscriptions. Small, metal grave markers, originally intended as temporary substitutes for headstones, are often mangled. Even if they're still legible, many have been scattered, meaning that knowledge of someone's burial site is lost. Oakwood Cemetery has trash bins for visitors. At East End and Evergreen, despite efforts to reclaim and secure the cemeteries, people still pull up to dump their old tires, mattresses, couches, bags of debris, and the occasional dead dog.

Other differences between these spaces of the dead are social and symbolic rather than physical. Oakwood's prominent Confederate section runs along East Richmond Road, in a neighborhood that is predominantly African American. This section of Oakwood, a public, once segregated cemetery, is immaculate and hypervisible—a different world from East End and Evergreen. The conditions of the burial grounds speak volumes about how the dead of different races have been treated in American history and memory.

FIGURE 9.1. Oakwood Cemetery's Confederate section (May 23, 2015).

FIGURE 9.2. When volunteers began working at East End in the summer of 2013, the cemetery was impassable. Nearly two years later, much of it was still thickly overgrown (May 6, 2015).

Even Google Maps reinforces the inequities of these two sites. When we zoom out far enough to see nearly the entirety of Richmond, we find both Hollywood and Oakwood Cemeteries clearly labeled. From there, we zoom in three more times to find Evergreen Cemetery labeled as a place worthy of recognition. For East End, still one more click. Anyone wishing to assert that this discrepancy results simply from the difference in acreage (Oakwood is significantly larger than Evergreen or East End) would have to explain why small recreational areas such as Powhatan Playground and Libby Hill Park are labeled when the cemeteries are not. While a complex and confidential set of factors goes into determining what places are named, and when, on tools such as Google Maps, the disparity illustrates how new technologies often maintain rather than disrupt our unseen bordering and memory practices. Only some places are recognized as places.

This chapter is about the structural forces that make East End and Evergreen, as well as other historic African American burial grounds, seem "abandoned." The cemeteries mirror racial inequalities that are deeply embedded in Virginia, the South, and the United States as a whole; yet they also carry those inequalities forward in new ways that compound and complicate them. Structurally neglected cemeteries show us whose dead are taken care of, and who has not had the deeply human privilege of caring for their dead. They tell us whose histories are recognized and reaffirmed, and whose are treated as an afterthought. Last but not least, the structural neglect of these cemeteries makes them both evidence of and agents in the unraveling of community. As Joseph Bottum puts it, "The living give us crowds. The dead give us communities."[1]

This chapter is as much about community and repair as it is about injustice. We write as collaborators who have come together through our work in neglected African American burial grounds. For years, Brian and Erin worked to restore East End, also documenting its history and its transformation on a website, in articles, photography, essays, and an oral history project featuring descendants of the people buried in the cemetery. In 2017, to formalize the reclamation effort, they founded the nonprofit Friends of East End Cemetery with other longtime volunteers. Adam is working on a book, *Cemetery Citizens*, about grassroots efforts to reclaim burial grounds of the marginalized dead. These include African American burial grounds, psychiatric hospital cemeteries, and other sites. His many visits to East End to work alongside Brian and Erin and conduct interviews with other volunteers led him to join the Friends of Geer Cemetery, a nonprofit working to restore a historic African American burial ground in Durham, North Carolina. In 2021, he cofounded the Durham Black Burial Grounds Collaboratory,

FIGURE 9.3. Volunteers excavated and removed more than 1,500 illegally dumped tires from East End (April 18, 2015).

a university-cemetery partnership modeled on Richmond's East End Cemetery Collaboratory, of which Brian and Erin are founding members. Adam teaches community-engaged courses at Duke University that bring students into cemetery reclamation efforts. Brian and Erin have visited Geer to volunteer and document the site multiple times, and these exchanges in both directions are fueling the nascent grassroots network of people working in African American cemeteries.

In this chapter, we describe the efforts to reclaim, celebrate, and build community in these beautiful places. Using Robert Meister's notion of "permanent reconstruction," we argue that East End, Evergreen, and other African American burial grounds are far from being merely "heritage" spaces that need to be maintained—though they are certainly that.[2] They also offer a future-oriented portrait of the kind of daily practices—the *work*—that is necessary to move forward in a country whose history, political landscape, and physical spaces have all been shaped by white supremacy.

First, we root East End and Evergreen in their historical context, highlighting stories of Black prosperity, civil society, and resistance, as well as the story of the cemeteries' eventual decline. We go on to critique the discourse of "abandonment" that is often used in describing spaces such as East End and Evergreen. We suggest that structural violence and a dynamic we call "care disruption" offer a more accurate understanding. If structural forces such as Jim Crow and community displacement determine the fate of the cemeteries, then reclaiming them goes far beyond mere historic preservation. We analyze the reclamation efforts that had been making these degraded and disrupted spaces public again. As this work was gradually transforming the cemeteries into energized places of public activity, it also attracted interest and intervention from new parties. We analyze the role of a local nonprofit, the Enrichmond Foundation, which acquired Evergreen in 2017 and East End in 2019, and then—well after we had originally drafted this chapter—suddenly dissolved and abdicated its responsibilities for the cemeteries.

East End, Evergreen, and the "Afterlife of Jim Crow"

In Virginia, racial segregation shaped every institution and was the guiding logic of physical space. Even before the 1896 *Plessy v. Ferguson* decision legalized segregation, Jim Crow had been tightening its grip on the South. Virginia had already passed two laws restricting voting rights for African American men.[3] Then, in 1902, a new state constitution, the product of a convention that was all white and all male, instituted a poll tax and permitted registrars to administer literacy tests. Taken together, these measures disenfranchised ninety percent of Black male voters and roughly fifty percent of white male voters.[4] Carter Glass, a member of the constitutional convention and later a U.S. congressman and senator, declared, "Discrimination! Why that is precisely what we propose; that, exactly, is what this Convention was elected for—to discriminate . . . with a view to the elimination of every negro voter who can be gotten rid of."[5]

In 1900, Virginia's legislature passed a law requiring separate or partitioned railroad cars for Blacks and whites but did not immediately enforce it.[6] That happened four years later, when the Virginia Passenger and Power Company imposed racial separation on a Richmond streetcar line. Black citizens launched a boycott that helped bankrupt the company.[7] Their protest, however, did nothing to stop the rolling tide of Jim Crow. The legislature made segregation of streetcars mandatory in 1906.[8] In 1924, the Racial Integrity Act was signed into law, barring interracial marriage and defining as "white" a person "who has no trace whatsoever of any blood other than Caucasian."[9] This pseudoscientific legal definition of whiteness enabled the state to apportion civil rights and privileges to whites while denying them to people of color. The Massenburg Law, which established racial segregation in all public accommodations, followed two years later.[10]

FIGURE 9.4. Maggie L. Walker's family plot at Evergreen Cemetery (May 2, 2015)

Places such as Evergreen and East End (founded in 1891 and 1897, respectively) are themselves products of Jim Crow, which demanded the separation of the Black dead from the white. In death as in life, separate would never be equal. As conditions in the cemeteries deteriorated in the 1960s, both became burial grounds of last resort for people who couldn't afford interment elsewhere. But when they were thriving, they served African Americans at all socioeconomic levels, including the wealthy. "The situation of the Cemetery is high, dry and rolling and accessible to the Richmond Traction Street Railway and Seven Pines Railway lines," reads a recurring 1902 advertisement placed in the *Richmond Planet*, the city's Black newspaper, by the East End Memorial Burial Association of Richmond.[11] Funerals of prominent Black Richmonders were front-page news. A subheadline in the June 26, 1900, paper described "Imposing Funeral Services" for Thomas Mitchell, brother of the *Planet*'s editor and the newspaper's manager.[12] While the burial at Evergreen Cemetery wasn't mentioned, the *Planet* ran a story a little over a year later about the dedication of a large memorial to Mitchell, also on the front page: "When the cemetery was reached a strange sight met the eye. All around the square, in the centre of which stood the great monument, were, what seemed to be black walls, formed by the thousands of spectators who filled the grounds. To the north and west there were two solid lines of humanity. People had crowded to the grounds hours ahead of the parade to secure event standing room."[13]

The *New Journal and Guide* of Norfolk, Virginia, a widely read Black newspaper, reported extensively on the funeral of the first woman in the United States to charter a bank, Maggie L. Walker. A breathless headline promises (and delivers) "Exclusive Pictures of Impressive Final Rites for Mrs. Maggie L. Walker, Prominent Business and Fraternal Leader." The December 29, 1934, story has rare details of the burial service itself. One photo shows the officiant, the Rev. W. T. Johnson of First African Baptist Church, "committing the remains to the grave as dusk settled over the hill-top family plot."[14]

As late as the 1950s, Black Richmonders of some means were being laid to rest at the cemeteries. The Rev. Daniel J. Bradford was buried at East End in March 1951. The November 16, 1957, edition of the *Afro American*, the *Planet*'s successor, reported that real estate broker Benjamin Harrison Beverly was interred in his family's plot at East End.[15] He's listed in the Richmond city directories in 1954 and 1955 as a salesman for Spottswood W. Robinson Jr., a realtor (and father of the noted civil rights attorney Spottswood W. Robinson III), who was buried at Evergreen in 1955 and later reinterred at city-owned Riverview Cemetery, which did not open to African Americans until 1968.[16]

Evergreen occupies fifty-nine acres; East End, adjacent to it, sits on sixteen. How many people are buried at the cemeteries remains a mystery, since records are patchy. Estimates range from as low as ten thousand to more than sixty thousand at Evergreen and upwards of fifteen thousand at East End. These cemeteries are dense with the dead. By way of comparison, city-owned Oakwood Cemetery sprawls across 199 acres and contains roughly 100,000 interments; Hollywood, a tourist attraction in the center of town that features prominent Confederate graves and monuments, totals 135 acres and has about eighty thousand burials.

With no perpetual care funds, which were not legally mandated by the state of Virginia until after World War I, East End and Evergreen relied on financial support from the Black community's extensive network of social, professional, religious, and philanthropic organizations. Records of these contributions are literally etched in the headstones and markers laid at both cemeteries. Institutions such as First African Baptist, Richmond's oldest Black church, and the National Ideal Benefit Society commissioned headstones for members, as did employees' groups such as the Porters of Byrd St. Station and Nurses Local Association 1. The Independent Order of St. Luke, which began as a burial society (and sold burial insurance), other charitable groups, churches, mutual aid societies, and fraternal organizations often helped people pay expenses incurred when a relative died.

Segregation, Black disenfranchisement, and white political hegemony are the more obvious of the structural forces that shape East End and Evergreen. But displacement is as much a part of their history, and as powerful a shaper of their fates. By the early twentieth century, Richmond's Jackson Ward had become one of the nation's most prosperous African American neighborhoods, nicknamed the Harlem of the South. In 1954, the city's white power brokers and state legislators in the all-white General Assembly created the Richmond-Petersburg Turnpike Authority and approved construction of the highway through Jackson Ward, overruling Richmond voters who had twice voted down similar proposals. The construction razed a vast swath of Black businesses, homes, and institutions, tearing the community apart. In 1970, more than eight hundred homes and businesses were leveled in mostly Black Fulton, uprooting thousands of people. Isolated and unattractive housing projects were constructed in the place of what had been vibrant neighborhoods with walkable streets. Such acts of destruction, under the guise of "urban renewal" (or, as James Baldwin famously put it, "negro removal"), were visited upon communities of color across the country—in New Orleans, Montgomery, Detroit, New York.

Furthermore, as Zach Mortice explains, "the Great Migration of blacks to northern cities dispersed the descendant communities and weakened ties to their ancestral burial places."[17] From 1920 to 1930, U.S. census figures show a decline in Richmond's Black population, even as others were drawn to the city for jobs in the tobacco factories and other industries, causing an increase in the African American population the following decade. By the time East End and Evergreen began their decline, the Great Migration had been underway for nearly fifty years. The network of descendants now stretches far beyond Richmond, sometimes with very few links back to the city or its cemeteries.

The neglect of Evergreen and East End means more than just violence against the dead and their descendants. It is part of a sustained, systematic project of forgetting. Between 1790 and 1860, more than 700,000 enslaved people were sold or otherwise relocated from the Upper South (Maryland, Virginia, and the Carolinas) to the Lower South.[18] By the 1840s, Richmond had become the northern hub of the interstate slave trade.[19] Yet there is no visible evidence of that massive crime—and major source of the city's wealth—which was centered in Shockoe Bottom. The area is now filled with bars and restaurants. The African Burial Ground, at Fifteenth and East Broad Streets in Richmond, was a graveyard for enslaved and free people of African descent. It was also the site of the gallows where the leaders of a slave rebellion in 1800 were hanged.[20] Until 2011, these graves were hidden underneath the pavement of a Virginia Commonwealth University parking lot. Thanks to community activism, it is now part of the Richmond Slave Trail and marked by plaques. But the site continues to feel marginal, wedged between Interstate 95 and the train tracks.

Until very recently, Confederate monuments were inescapable in Richmond, the former capital of the Confederacy. The massive Black Lives Matter protests that began in May 2020, following the murders of George Floyd, Breonna Taylor, Ahmaud Arbery, and other African Americans, achieved what once seemed unimaginable: the removal of those monuments. The statues, however, are only one piece of a much more complex landscape of memory and public space in Richmond and beyond. The pristine Confederate graves in public cemeteries such as Oakwood, and the even more idyllic private Hollywood, have benefited from a century and a half of public funding, both direct and indirect. For example, the United Daughters of the Confederacy (the group perhaps most responsible for propagating "Lost Cause" and "loyal slave" mythology) and other Confederate memorial associations have received annual allotments from the state legislature to maintain thousands of Confederate graves since 1902.[21] East End and Evergreen received no such aid until 2017, when Virginia passed the largely symbolic Historical African American Cemeteries and Graves Act.

Paradoxically, desegregation also had an adverse impact on the cemeteries, speeding up their decline. As formerly white cemeteries began to accept African Americans for burial, locals were faced with the choice between historic but poorly tended, isolated graveyards and safe, well-maintained, easily accessible locations. By the end of the 1970s, burials at East End had all but ceased. At Evergreen they continued in one irregularly maintained section until 2016, even as the rest of the cemetery was engulfed by forest.

Mortice explains how this common history, which cuts across African American cemeteries in the United States, produces dilemmas in the present:

Before a cemetery can be restored, all the assorted stakeholders—preservationists, archaeologists, anthropologists, historians, community members, descendants of the deceased—must determine that it is worthy of restoration in the first place. Should a cemetery be saved because of its age? Because it served a spectrum of the black community, from barbers to businessmen? Because its plots are filled with notable historical figures . . . ? These questions are further complicated by the fact that the descendant communities are often impoverished. African-American cemeteries are attached to communities that have been redlined and segregated out of billions of dollars of wealth that could have been passed down

FIGURE 9.5. Medical students from Virginia Commonwealth University unearth one half of a broken headstone on a sodden spring afternoon at East End (April 12, 2019).

through the generations, and the usual perpetual care funds that are replenished regularly in burial businesses that cater to whites simply aren't available."[22]

The overgrown, dilapidated state of East End and Evergreen obscures the rich history of Richmond's African American community. It also reinforces the insidious logic of white supremacy and Black inferiority. This is the afterlife of Jim Crow. If segregation, disenfranchisement, and displacement have degraded the condition of the cemeteries, that very degradation perpetuates racist notions of individual and societal worth—who matters, who doesn't.

And yet, at the same time that white supremacists were stripping African Americans of their hard-won rights, Black people were building schools, businesses, and churches, knitting together a community with fraternal organizations and mutual aid societies. Several of the most prominent leaders and entrepreneurs organized opposition to streetcar segregation, launching and funding the 1904 boycott. Among them were Maggie L. Walker, John Mitchell Jr. (both buried at Evergreen), and Richard F. Tancil (buried at East End).

All three of these leading lights were born during slavery; they were members of what historian Robert F. Engs called "freedom's first generation."[23]

Tancil (ca. 1852–1928), went on to earn an undergraduate degree and later, in 1883, his medical degree from Howard University. He established a practice in Richmond, just a few blocks from where Brian and Erin live in the historic Church Hill neighborhood, and served as the director of the (segregated) Richmond Hospital.[24] Mitchell (1863–1929) was the fearless editor of the *Richmond Planet*, called the most radical Black newspaper in the South at the time.[25] Walker (1864–1934), in addition to chartering a bank, rescued and ran a major, national Black philanthropic organization, the Independent Order of St. Luke. She published the *St. Luke Herald*, a newspaper, as well.[26] Tancil and Mitchell also founded banks.

With the exception of Walker, whose life and legacy are celebrated locally, these eminent African Americans, and many others like them, remain largely unknown even in Richmond. And if the elite are not widely recognized as central figures in the city's history, those who did not rise to prominence during their lifetimes are more invisible in death. Describing Durham's Geer Cemetery, historian William Sturkey makes the connection between neglected cemeteries and the ongoing erasure of African Americans in local histories. To him, the focus on Confederate monuments risks becoming yet another process in which white lives are placed at the center of our national narratives: "As we spend hundreds and thousands of hours and dollars worrying about abstract Confederate monuments and the legacies of wealthy white elites, nary a nickel goes toward maintaining the graves of actual people who built our society. As important as those white families were, it was other people who did the digging, laid the bricks, raised the crops, and cared for their children. It was black people. And today, we allow a forest to silently swallow the bones and headstones of those who have truly been erased from history."[27]

Beyond "Abandonment"

Local media often refer to East End and Evergreen as "neglected" or "abandoned."[28] This vocabulary implies that the local Black community simply has not cared enough about its dead or the spaces they inhabit.[29] One can detect an echo here of popular arguments that blame African American men for not taking responsibility as fathers, or that hold "Black culture" responsible for various social problems. What all of these arguments and narratives do is mask the role of systemic injustice—how factors such as mass incarceration, educational inequities, and housing and employment discrimination constrain people's choices, their life courses, and even their ability to care for the dead.[30]

What looks like "lack of care" is driven not by individual or communal choices to let cemeteries decline but rather by structures preventing people from sustaining the forms of care that keep burial grounds accessible and maintained. The notion of structural violence, which the Metta Center for Nonviolence defines as "the hidden violence in our midst, built into the structure of society itself and therefore more difficult to pinpoint and eradicate," is one powerful lens for describing how race continues to shape the "life chances" of people in the United States today.[31] Yet it strikes us as important to call attention to *care*—the ability to receive care, and to perform it—as subject to similar hidden forces.

In the long history of "Western" thought, care has often been subordinated to questions of violence, rights, and justice.[32] But care is bound up with a community's well-being in much the same way as violence. Caring for the dead, far from being oriented only toward the past, is a way of constructing community and memory. Historian Thomas Laqueur writes, "As far back as people have discussed the subject, care of the dead has been regarded as foundational—of religion, of the polity, of the clan, of the tribe, of the capacity to mourn, of an understanding of the finitude of life, of civilization itself."[33] Attacks on this foundational institution, care of the dead, have been manifold and ever present in the African American experience—from the bodies of dead or ill enslaved people that were thrown overboard during the Middle Passage, through the untold number of places where people were buried with no permanent marker, far from their loved ones. For this reason, funerals have often been important sites of Black resistance. The 1800 uprising of enslaved people in Richmond, which led to the hanging of the rebellion's leader, Gabriel, and twenty-five other resistance fighters, began at a child's funeral.[34] This tradition continued in the large, politicized funerals for Medgar Evers and Emmett Till in the mid-twentieth century.[35] More recently, as poet Claudia Rankine wrote in the *New York Times Magazine*, "The Black Lives Matter movement can be read as an attempt to keep mourning an open dynamic in our culture because Black lives exist in a state of precariousness. Mourning then bears both the vulnerability inherent in Black lives and the instability regarding a future for those lives. Unlike earlier Black-power movements that tried to fight or segregate for self-preservation, Black Lives Matter aligns with the dead, continues the mourning and refuses the forgetting in front of all of us."[36]

The slow, structural neglect of East End and Evergreen is not as spectacular as the public lynchings and other forms of necroviolence—violence against the dead—that have been central to the treatment of Black bodies in America.[37] But it, too, works to cast the Black dead out of the fabric of white-dominant society—out of "grievability"—and out of a world where care binds the living to the dead.[38] What we see at East End and Evergreen, then, is not "abandonment." In fact, anyone who spends a few daylight hours there will see people arriving, sometimes alone and sometimes in groups, to mow a small section, or leave flowers on a grave; at least one family has even held a multigenerational reunion in front of the family plots, singing songs in celebration. The cemeteries have never been fully "abandoned" by mourners and caregivers, even as their communities have been displaced and impoverished by policies that targeted Black neighborhoods and obstructed the creation of Black wealth—or outright stole what capital African Americans were able to generate.[39] Descendants did not stop visiting, even as tangles of vines, trash, and vandalism diminished the pride that went into the cemeteries' founding and the many burials there.

Rather than abandonment, East End and Evergreen have experienced decades of what we call "care disruption." Care disruption refers to the social, political, economic, and cultural structures that prevent people and places from being cared for and/or giving care and obscure the ethical importance of care itself to the survival and thriving of living communities.

Care disruption almost always appears alongside structural violence. Just as care labor and the caring professions are less visible and less valued than other forms of "productivity," the care disruption that communities experience often goes unnamed. Care and care disruption are, notoriously, hard to measure—one reason they are not taken seriously.[40] Yet care disruption is both a result and a further driver of all other forms of structural violence; it fully pervades the life of a community. Despite the intertwined traditions of mourning and resistance to which Rankine and others allude, there is still much more to say about the disruption of African American care for the dead in places such as East End and Evergreen—and about the work that is being done to address it.

Reclamation

Since the 1980s, there have been periodic efforts to clear and maintain East End and Evergreen. National Park Service ranger James (Jim) Bell ran a long-standing volunteer program in the late 1990s through the early 2000s. In 2008, John Shuck, a retired bank analyst and "cemetery buff," began visiting the cemeteries to take photographs. He soon felt compelled not only to document them, but also to do something about their neglected state. So Shuck joined an ongoing volunteer cleanup effort at Evergreen. In 2013, after a dispute between the organizers of the Evergreen cleanup initiative and the cemetery's owners, UK Corporation, Shuck and others moved their project next door. Until 2020, the initiative at East End had been sustained by volunteer labor and small donations from private citizens, local businesses, and organizations.

Brian and Erin started working at the cemetery in December 2014. They had moved from Brooklyn, New York, to Hampton, Virginia, in 2013 to devote themselves to a documentary begun the previous year. Originally, the film, *Make the Ground Talk*, centered on another African American cemetery, where Brian's great-grandparents, both born into slavery, are buried. That graveyard is difficult to access—hidden within the confines of Camp Peary, a top-secret military base and CIA training facility near Williamsburg. They wound up exploring other historic Black cemeteries on the Virginia Peninsula and were struck and saddened by the tumbledown state of so many of them. When friends in Richmond told them about Evergreen (East End is often overshadowed by its larger, better-known neighbor), they were intrigued—little suspecting that their first visit, in spring 2014, would mark the beginning of a yearslong engagement with the place. They were overwhelmed by the sheer size of the cemeteries and the extent of the overgrowth, but the power of the history they saw lying dormant at these sites compelled them to join the cleanup effort at East End.

Small groups and individuals have begun working in other Black cemeteries and burial grounds around the country. While there are too many sites to name here, they include Hunts Point Slave Burial Ground in the Bronx, Pierce Chapel Cemetery in Harris County, Georgia, Olivewood Cemetery in Houston, Lincoln Memorial Park in Miami, and Geer Cemetery in Durham, North Carolina. The efforts to reclaim these spaces have important differences in their organizational structures and styles, their visions of what a preserved or reclaimed cemetery looks like, and how they tell their stories. Yet all of these reclamation efforts exist because of how white supremacy has shaped physical space and disrupted the care of the dead.[41] All persist because some people believe these places matter.

Before being halted by COVID-19 in March 2020, work days at East End accomplished an extraordinary transformation. A place originally defined by a logic of segregation emerged as a pluralistic space where people of different races, religions, ethnicities, ages, and walks of life worked together. As they involved local churches, university students, Scout troops, and so on, the Friends of East End created links between the cemetery and various institutions that had excluded the people buried at East End when they were alive.

FIGURE 9.6. English ivy, an invasive species, still blankets large swaths of East End. Here, University of Richmond volunteers work to remove thick tangles of it, revealing a headstone in the process (February 20, 2016).

The diversity of the volunteers tells only one part of the story, however. The cemetery's fate is still being shaped by racial and other power dynamics. Among the volunteers, some were cemetery enthusiasts, history buffs, and environmentalists. Some of them tended to present a "color-blind" account of their work in the space. They emphasized the right of all people to a dignified burial, or the land's status as a green space and "historical asset" for the city.[42] They generally avoided talking about race or about the causes—beyond the standard references to "neglect"—of the cemeteries' decline. A video called *Discover!*, produced by Enrichmond, the nonprofit that acquired ownership of both cemeteries before it dissolved, has only this to say about the long history that produced Evergreen's current conditions: "Over several decades, it's fallen into disrepair."[43] This passive language makes the cemetery's condition seem like a natural event, rather than the result of discriminatory practices and policies.

For other volunteers, work in the cemetery—clearing graves while also telling the stories of all the dead buried there—was a way to grapple with race or was even a form of resistance to white supremacy. On the website they designed for East End, when interacting with the public at the cemetery, and in other journalistic and documentary projects, Brian and Erin insist that East End and Evergreen are not simply isolated places of forgotten history. They are in constant dialogue with Confederate graves, monuments, and other memory sites throughout the South. In a section of the website called "Connecting a Community," Brian and Erin map connections between the lives of people buried at East End and other sites in Richmond that are crucial to Black history and Black life. These include the Navy Hill School, the first public school in Richmond to employ Black teachers (at least two of them, Rosa Dixon Bowser and Harvey Grant Lewis, are buried at East End), and the funeral homes that served Richmond's African American population.[44] At the beginning of this chapter, we described how searches on Google Maps isolate landmarks and assign priority to some places over others, often leaving a place like East End unnamed and unmapped. The East End Cemetery website does the opposite: it reestablishes East End as part of a fabric of interconnected places, literally tracing the paths of generations of African Americans in Richmond. Brian and Erin also connect their work at the cemetery and their storytelling to the broader Movement for Black Lives.

Care, Disrupted

Enrichmond's acquisition of East End and Evergreen would not have been possible without significant financial and administrative support from state agencies, principally the Virginia Outdoors Foundation (VOF). In effect, VOF backed a favored nongovernmental entity and used state money to subsidize the purchase of two sacred African American sites by a white-led organization with no experience owning, restoring, or managing fragile historic cemeteries. If VOF conducted any due diligence to determine whether Enrichmond had the capacity to take on East End and Evergreen, it presented no evidence thereof. Enrichmond was not required to produce a preservation plan or environmental impact study before taking over the cemeteries. The very ownership structure—Evergreen and East End were purchased by a limited liability company created by Enrichmond's executive director, not the nonprofit itself—insulated Enrichmond from accountability and meaningful oversight, giving it license to learn cemetery restoration on the fly.

Even with abundant support from the state—and additional aid from local governments and federal agencies such as AmeriCorps—Enrichmond proved unable to care for the cemeteries. In fact, the nonprofit, which also served as a fiscal agent for several dozen Richmond-area volunteer groups, abruptly announced its dissolution in June 2022, leaving tens of thousands of dollars unaccounted for.[45] Board members resigned and refused to answer questions from groups whose money Enrichmond held.[46] The longtime executive director, who had quietly left the foundation several months earlier, has been silent.[47] Meanwhile, as of November 2022, the cemeteries are in legal limbo.[48]

Enrichmond's implosion followed years of conflict with community members, notably the Friends of East End, over its treatment of the cemeteries, lack of transparency, and resistance to public engagement. Prior to its acquisition of East End and Evergreen, Enrichmond had played no discernible role in their reclamation. This inexperience—coupled with hubris and insularity—manifested itself throughout Enrichmond's tenure. In one telling instance, in July 2020, Enrichmond allowed a local TV news crew to film exposed human remains at East End; the video and images circulated online until community outcry compelled their removal.[49] A few days earlier, without notice, Enrichmond had pulled up hundreds of American flags placed by volunteers at veterans' graves, bagged them up along with floral arrangements left by family members, and thrown them in a dumpster at Evergreen. The periodic removal of flags and flowers is standard practice at regularly maintained cemeteries but had not been so at East End and Evergreen. These items were tangible signs of care and commitment in long-abused spaces, and their summary disposal triggered fierce community backlash.

Not long before, Enrichmond had effectively evicted the Friends of East End from the cemetery. In May 2020, it demanded that all volunteers sign a new agreement before resuming work at East End and Evergreen, which had been interrupted by the pandemic. Not only did the agreement restrict access to East End, it also laid claim to intellectual property, including research and photographs, and asserted the right to use and distribute volunteers' likenesses. The Friends of East End refused to sign, as did their academic partners at the University of Richmond and Virginia Commonwealth University. The Friends also sought pro bono legal representation and entered monthslong negotiations, which came to an impasse when Enrichmond stopped responding to the Friends' lawyers. As a result, the Friends of East End were forced to suspend their on-site work in November 2020, ending a thriving, seven-year-long reclamation effort. Enrichmond never managed to fill the vacuum left at East End, substituting aggressive, intermittent mowing and weed whacking for consistent, painstaking care.

When Enrichmond dissolved, it abandoned the cemeteries, leaving little behind but its heavily promoted blueprint for the transformation of Evergreen. In March 2020 it unveiled a $19 million master plan for Evergreen, which focuses heavily on construction: a visitors' center ($1.85 million), "Memorial Meadow" ($1.26 million), a sewer system ($195,000), a fiber-optic cable system ($30,000), and a trail network "suitable for mountain

FIGURE 9.7. One of East End's fragile courtesy markers has been damaged by landscapers. Enrichmond hired the crew in fall 2020 to clear it of overgrowth, after months of neglect (October 7, 2020).

biking" with trailhead and overlooks (no cost estimate). The plan allocates no funds to finding, documenting, and mapping the thousands of graves, marked and unmarked, that remain obscured by overgrowth.[50]

From our perspective, then, it is crucial that people concerned about the fate of these cemeteries, and the history and community they embody, understand how "neglect" and care disruption work. Often neglect is carried out through a lack of attention, maintenance, and funds. But not always. By alienating East End's long-standing caretakers, hoarding resources, and causing physical damage to grave markers via reckless landscaping in areas that volunteers had tended previously by hand, Enrichmond showed that it is possible to deploy the rhetoric of caretaking and stewardship while simultaneously disrupting real care for a sacred site.

Ever Unfinished

The English ivy, privet, wild grapevine, and greenbrier that grow over graves and cover cemeteries are key players in their daily life and have a more ambivalent role to play than it initially seems. As the weeds that cover up history, erasing lives and creating obstacles for people wishing to locate and care for their dead, they must be eliminated. In other words, the main "work that plants do" in these cemeteries is the work of erasure and forgetting; when we go back to the contrast between the clear and well-maintained white cemeteries and these African American sites, tall grasses and vines come to seem like a nonhuman extension of Jim Crow—they are an inexorable force, enveloping, destroying, and returning to nature a site that community members had intentionally carved from nature to place and honor their dead.[51]

But for the Friends of East End and other volunteers, the weeds have also been a call to action and raison d'être (the group's logo, a stylized rendering of curling vines, elegantly speaks to this).[52] Without weeds to clear from plots and grave markers, there would still be plenty of work to do; but it would largely consist of more specialized and less accessible tasks—such as the cleaning of headstones or genealogical research about names found on the markers. Weeding and clearing brush are tasks that one can jump right into, on almost any day, tasks that can easily be shared with Scout troops, visiting families, students, and other groups. "We're sort of building a new community around this place," Erin said about the Friends of East End's work during Adam's first visit to the cemetery, in October 2017. While taking care to consult with archaeologists and follow best practices in cleaning and resetting headstones, the Friends treat the cemetery as a living place to inhabit—not as a dead piece of history to be "preserved." Perhaps this marks an important distinction between historic preservation and *reclamation*.[53]

On a cemetery work day in March 2019, Brian, Erin, and Adam gathered at East End with ten others, some of whom were volunteering for the first time. Early in the day, working quietly by herself, Erin discovered a grave marker in a partially cleared section. It was one of the small metal markers intended for temporary use, which are easily kicked up or displaced by people, animals, and lawn mowers. This one had been dislodged from its original position and was caked with dirt. Erin showed volunteer Hanan DuVerney how to scrub the marker without damaging it. Until spring 2020, East End was a place of reclamation but also a place of teaching, where people with expertise (often self-taught) passed it along to others.

Hanan's brushing revealed the name Pernett Anthony and a date of death: May 1964. After the work day, back at home, Erin would use city and state records to identify the deceased as Pernett Anthony Jr., born November 19, 1923, in Hanover County, Virginia. He was the son of Pernett Anthony and Mary Johnson, and the husband of Magnolia Thompson. He died May 29, 1964, at the age of forty years, in Richmond. We know very little else about what happened "between the dashes" of his birth and death dates. And because the records for burials at the cemetery are scattered, this man's ex-

FIGURE 9.8. A volunteer washes Pernett Anthony Jr.'s newly uncovered grave marker (March 30, 2019).

act burial location will likely never be known. Having cleaned the marker and made the name visible, the Friends of East End placed it upright in the ground in the spot where it had been found. The work is never perfect; the work is never done. But it goes on.

In fact, cemetery reclamation is a task that keeps growing. Every section that is cleared generates new obligations for the maintenance of that area over time. Otherwise, especially in the lush ecosystems of the South, the work that was done can disappear under the vines again, in the space of just a few months.

Nearly every volunteer Adam has interviewed gives voice to this theme, often with ambivalence. Brian admits feeling overwhelmed by the work, especially when he first started. In conversation with Adam, he recalled "feeling like 'we'll never finish.' . . . Then I realized that wasn't the point." Instead, he said, "It's the looking, it's the clearing that matters."[54] In a separate interview, longtime Friends of East End volunteer Melissa Pocock told Adam, "It will never end, that work."[55]

Reclamation at East End, Geer, and other Black cemeteries comes to seem more like a work of art, or a practice, than a project to complete. This emphasis on process is crucial, especially for understanding the ways in which reclaiming Black cemeteries can be one limited form of "reparations" for America's violent racial inequality, an idea that both white and Black vol-

FIGURE 9.9. Every summer, pokeweed takes over a section of East End that was once among the most heavily overgrown. As volunteers expand the cleared area, the pokeweed spreads, creating still more work during the hottest months of the year (July 27, 2019).

unteers with the Friends of East End have voiced.[56] Political theorist Robert Meister has written, "The paradigmatic constitutional argument of the Second Reconstruction, based on *Brown [v. Board of Education]*, is that national recovery from a history of racial oppression requires both a continuing awareness of the dangers of relapse and a constant vigilance against the repetition of past patterns and practices. This argument implies that we can never recover from our past unless we believe ourselves to be in permanent recovery—that we are never in greater danger of reviving racism than when we believe ourselves to have overcome it."[57]

In its own small but significant way, the daily or weekly work in Black cemeteries echoes these implications of *Brown*; like postslavery and post–Civil War reconstruction in the country as a whole, cemetery reconstruction can advance in meaningful ways but never *conclude*. Every day of labor lays the groundwork for further labors ahead.

Philosopher Jill Stauffer builds on the notion of "permanent recovery" in Meister's work. But she locates the source of many of these forms of repair—and the solidarity needed to sustain them—outside of the formal institutions of courts and legislatures. In this way, her work speaks even more directly to the grassroots, volunteer efforts at East End. She writes, "Reconciliation can never be finished, and as it continues it will likely be punctuated by disturbing ruptures, unexpected truths, and new problems necessitating new attention to the work of reconciling. Minimal solidarity, sometimes more than that, may be achieved after violence.... Institutions may help or hinder in that solidarity's formation—and the rule of law can be a big help here—but solidarity is also anarchic: it may come from elsewhere."[58]

Reclamation efforts at East End and Evergreen show us one model of that anarchic solidarity, which one could witness every Saturday as people gathered with gardening gloves, clippers, and rakes. Disturbing ruptures and new problems are part of the work. Sometimes they arise from outside (vandalism, dumping), sometimes from within (different visions of the reclamation process among volunteers). Sometimes they foreground the question of who is "inside" and who is "outside"—as occurred when Enrichmond made legal claims of ownership alongside a moral claim of representing "the community," boxing longtime volunteers and community members out of funding opportunities and the decision-making process (ultimately clearing away thousands of dollars of the public's money far more effectively than any acre of the cemetery).

What neither Meister nor Stauffer offers in their visions of permanent reconstruction or reconciliation is a discussion of how often violence disrupts quotidian, overlooked acts of care—including the care for graves and the dead. We have thus highlighted the role that embodied care plays in cemetery reclamation, and how that care becomes political. In a society where the dead, and thus history, are to have any significance, there is no model of permanent reconstruction that does not also require perpetual care.

Notes

1. Bottum, "Death and Politics."
2. Meister, *After Evil*.
3. Tarter, "Disfranchisement."
4. Ibid.
5. J. Douglas Smith, *Managing White Supremacy*, 26.
6. Wynes, "The Evolution of Jim Crow Laws in Twentieth Century Virginia," 417.
7. Kelley, *Right to Ride*, 145–46.
8. Murray, *States' Laws on Race and Color*, 484.
9. Wolfe, "Racial Integrity Laws."
10. Wynes, "Evolution of Jim Crow Laws," 420.
11. "Notice!!!"
12. "Col. Mitchell Gone."
13. "Monument Unveiled."
14. "Exclusive Pictures of Impressive Final Rites for Mrs. Maggie L. Walker."
15. "Rev. Beverly Mourns for His Brother."
16. Ryan Smith, "Riverview Cemetery."

17. Mortice, "Perpetual Neglect."
18. Murphy, "Securing Human Property."
19. "Introduction," *To Be Sold*.
20. DeFord, «Gabriel's Rebellion.»
21. Levin, "Pernicious Myth of the 'Loyal Slave.'"
22. Mortice, "Perpetual Neglect."
23. Engs, *Freedom's First Generation*. Maggie Walker's mother, Elizabeth Draper Mitchell, was free by the time Walker was born in 1864. Both John Mitchell Jr. and Richard F. Tancil were enslaved at birth.
24. Mitchell, "Dr. Richard Fillmore Tancil."
25. McCrery and Somay, "John Mitchell Jr."
26. Branch, "Maggie Lena Walker."
27. Sturkey, "Geer Cemetery."
28. See, for example, Lazarus, "Evergreen Cemetery Sold to Enrichmond Foundation."
29. As Brian wrote in an op-ed for the *New York Times*, "People often ask me how these cemeteries got so bad. Why can't they be like the Confederate Section of Oakwood or Hollywood Cemetery, the immaculate burial ground of thousands of Confederate soldiers? The subtext is: Why can't black people take care of their own stuff?" Palmer, "For the Forgotten African-American Dead."
30. See, for example, Dyson, *Is Bill Cosby Right?*; Mychal Smith, "Dangerous Myth of the 'Missing Black Father.'"
31. "Structural Violence." On structural violence as a way to understand "unequal life chances," see Galtung, "Violence, Peace, and Peace Research."
32. See, for example, Gilligan, *In a Different Voice*; Held, *Ethics of Care*; Noddings, *Caring*; Tronto, *Moral Boundaries*.
33. Laqueur, *Work of the Dead*, 9.
34. Egerton, "Gabriel's Conspiracy and the Election of 1800," 202.
35. Stanley, "Disappearance of a Distinctively Black Way to Mourn."
36. Rankine, "'Condition of Black Life Is One of Mourning.'"
37. De León, *Land of Open Graves*, 62–85.
38. On "grievable" and "ungrievable" lives, see Butler, *Frames of War*.
39. See, for example, Coates, "Case for Reparations"; Presser, "Their Family Bought Land One Generation after Slavery."
40. See O'Connor, "'You Choose to Care.'"
41. See Wessler, "Black Deaths Matter."
42. See "Evergreen Cemetery Public Input Summary."
43. *Discover!*
44. Hollaway Palmer and Palmer, "Context."
45. Oliver, "Enrichmond Foundation's Collapse Throws Nonprofits in Limbo."
46. Thompson, "Over $100k Tied Up in Dissolved Richmond Nonprofit."
47. Williams, "Enrichmond Foundation Is Dissolving."
48. Khalil, "Volunteer Groups Affected by Enrichmond Dissolution Plan Next Steps."
49. Suarez, "Human Remains Found at East End Cemetery."
50. "Historic Evergreen Cemetery Master Plan."
51. Thank you to Angela Naimou for the phrase "the work that plants do."
52. See Friends of East End website, https://friendsofeastend.com.
53. For a view of preservation as an effort to create places of vibrant democratic life, see Page, *Why Preservation Matters*.
54. Brian Palmer, conversation with Adam Rosenblatt, October 15, 2017.

55. Melissa Pocock, interview by Adam Rosenblatt, March 30, 2019.
56. Maurice Fountain, Interview by Adam Rosenblatt, October 14, 2017; Erin Hollaway Palmer, conversation with Adam Rosenblatt, October 15, 2017.
57. Meister, *After Evil*, 101.
58. Stauffer, "Speaking Truth to Reconciliation."

Bibliography

Bottum, Joseph. "Death and Politics." *First Things*, June 2007. http://www.firstthings.com/article.php3?id_article=5917.
Branch, Muriel. "Maggie Lena Walker (1864–1934)." In *Encyclopedia Virginia*, February 15, 2023. https://encyclopediavirginia.org/entries/walker-maggie-lena-1864-1934/.
Butler, Judith. *Frames of War: When Is Life Grievable?* London: Verso Books, 2016.
Coates, Ta-Nehisi. "The Case for Reparations." *Atlantic*, June 2014. https://www.theatlantic.com/magazine/archive/2014/06/the-case-for-reparations/361631/.
"Col. Mitchell Gone." *Richmond Planet*, June 26, 1900.
DeFord, Susan. "Gabriel's Rebellion." *Washington Post*, February 6, 2000. https://www.washingtonpost.com/archive/lifestyle/2000/02/06/gabriels-rebellion/33c9061a-e33d-4f18-bf02-fe3cd294f5df/.
De León, Jason. *The Land of Open Graves: Living and Dying on the Migrant Trail*. Oakland: University of California Press, 2015.
Discover! Enrichmond. Accessed June 6, 2019. https://enrichmond.org/evergreen-cemetery/discover/.
Dyson, Michael Eric. *Is Bill Cosby Right? Or Has the Black Middle Class Lost Its Mind?* New York: Civitas Books, 2008.
Egerton, Douglas R. "Gabriel's Conspiracy and the Election of 1800." *Journal of Southern History* 56, no. 2 (May 1990): 191–214.Engs, Robert F. *Freedom's First Generation: Black Hampton, Virginia, 1861–1890*. Philadelphia: University of Pennsylvania Press, 1979.
"Evergreen Cemetery Public Input Summary." Enrichmond, December 7, 2017. https://enrichmond.org/wp-content/uploads/2017/12/Evergreen-Cemetery-Public-Engagement-Summary-web_120717.pdf.
"Exclusive Pictures of Impressive Final Rites for Mrs. Maggie L. Walker, Prominent Business and Fraternal Leader." *New Journal and Guide*, December 29, 1934.
Galtung, Johan. "Violence, Peace, and Peace Research." *Journal of Peace Research* 6, no. 3 (1969): 167–91.
Gilligan, Carol. *In a Different Voice: Psychological Theory and Women's Development*. Cambridge, Mass.: Harvard University Press, 1982.
Held, Virginia. *The Ethics of Care: Personal, Political, and Global*. New York: Oxford University Press, 2006.
"Historic Evergreen Cemetery Master Plan." Enrichmond Foundation and Pond and Company, November 2019.
Hollaway Palmer, Erin, and Brian Palmer. "Context." East End Cemetery. https://eastendcemeteryrva.com/context/.
"Introduction." *To Be Sold: Virginia and the American Slave Trade*. Online exhibition. Library of Virginia. https://www.virginiamemory.com/online-exhibitions/exhibits/show/to-be-sold/introduction.
Kelley, Blair L. M. *Right to Ride: Streetcar Boycotts and African American Citizenship in the Era of Plessy v. Ferguson*. Chapel Hill: University of North Carolina Press, 2010.

Khalil, Jahd. "Volunteer Groups Affected by Enrichmond Dissolution Plan Next Steps." VPM, October 28, 2022. https://vpm.org/news/articles/36872/volunteer-groups-affected-by-enrichmond-dissolution-plan-next-steps.

Laqueur, Thomas W. *The Work of the Dead: A Cultural History of Mortal Remains*. Princeton, N.J.: Princeton University Press, 2018.

Lazarus, Jeremy M. "Evergreen Cemetery Sold to Enrichmond Foundation." *Richmond Free Press*, June 2, 2017. http://richmondfreepress.com/news/2017/jun/02/evergreen-cemetery-sold-enrichmond-foundation/.

Levin, Kevin M. "The Pernicious Myth of the 'Loyal Slave' Lives On in Confederate Memorials." *Smithsonian Magazine*, August 17, 2017. https://www.smithsonianmag.com/history/pernicious-myth-loyal-slave-lives-confederate-memorials-180964546/.

McCrery, Anne, Errol Somay, and *Dictionary of Virginia Biography*. "John Mitchell Jr. (1863–1929)." In *Encyclopedia Virginia*, February 15, 2023. https://encyclopediavirginia.org/entries/mitchell-john-jr-1863-1929/.

Meister, Robert. *After Evil: A Politics of Human Rights*. New York: Columbia University Press, 2012.

Mitchell, Susan. "Dr. Richard Fillmore Tancil." East End Cemetery. https://eastendcemeteryrva.com/person/dr-richard-fillmore-tancil/.

"Monument Unveiled." *Richmond Planet*, August 31, 1901.

Mortice, Zach. "Perpetual Neglect: The Preservation Crisis of African-American Cemeteries." *Places*, May 30, 2017. https://doi.org/10.22269/170530.

Murphy, Sharon Ann. "Securing Human Property: Slavery, Life Insurance, and Industrialization in the Upper South." *Journal of the Early Republic* 25, no. 4 (Winter 2005): 615–52.

Murray, Pauli, ed. *States' Laws on Race and Color: And Appendices Containing International Documents, Federal Laws and Regulations, Local Ordinances and Charts*. N.p.: Woman's Division of Christian Service, Board of Missions and Church Extension, Methodist Church, 1951. http://hdl.handle.net/2027/mdp.39015046394402.

Noddings, Nel. *Caring: A Feminine Approach to Ethics and Moral Education*. Berkeley: University of California Press, 1984.

"Notice!!!," *Richmond Planet*, February 1, 1902.

O'Connor, Kate Eliza. "'You Choose to Care': Teachers, Emotions and Professional Identity." *Teaching and Teacher Education* 24, no. 1 (January 1, 2008): 117–26. https://doi.org/10.1016/j.tate.2006.11.008.

Oliver, Ned. "Enrichmond Foundation's Collapse Throws Nonprofits in Limbo." Axios Richmond, July 21, 2022. https://www.axios.com/local/richmond/2022/07/21/enrichmond-foundation-collapse-throws-nonprofits-in-limbo.

Page, Max. *Why Preservation Matters*. New Haven, Conn.: Yale University Press, 2016.

Palmer, Brian. "For the Forgotten African-American Dead." *New York Times*, January 7, 2017. https://www.nytimes.com/2017/01/07/opinion/sunday/for-the-forgotten-african-american-dead.html.

Presser, Lizzie. "Their Family Bought Land One Generation after Slavery. The Reels Brothers Spent Eight Years in Jail for Refusing to Leave It." ProPublica, July 15, 2019. https://features.propublica.org/black-land-loss/heirs-property-rights-why-black-families-lose-land-south/.

Rankine, Claudia. "'The Condition of Black Life Is One of Mourning.'" *New York Times Magazine*, June 22, 2015. https://www.nytimes.com/2015/06/22/magazine/the-condition-of-black-life-is-one-of-mourning.html.

"Rev. Beverly Mourns for His Brother." *Richmond Afro-American*, November 16, 1957.

Smith, J. Douglas. *Managing White Supremacy: Race, Politics, and Citizenship in Jim Crow Virginia.* Chapel Hill: University of North Carolina Press, 2003.

Smith, Mychal Denzel. "The Dangerous Myth of the 'Missing Black Father.'" *Washington Post*, January 10, 2017. https://www.washingtonpost.com/posteverything/wp/2017/01/10/the-dangerous-myth-of-the-missing-black-father/?utm_term=.e547fda06535.

Smith, Ryan K. "Riverview Cemetery." *Richmond Cemeteries* (blog), March 24, 2017. https://www.richmondcemeteries.org/riverview/.

Stanley, Tiffany. "The Disappearance of a Distinctively Black Way to Mourn." *Atlantic*, January 26, 2016. https://www.theatlantic.com/business/archive/2016/01/black-funeral-homes-mourning/426807/.

Stauffer, Jill. "Speaking Truth to Reconciliation: Political Transition, Recovery, and the Work of Time." *Humanity* 4, no. 1 (Spring 2013): 27–48.

"Structural Violence." Metta Center for Nonviolence, April 13, 2010. https://www.mettacenter.org/glossary.

Sturkey, William. "The Geer Cemetery: A Lesson in Black History." *Durham Herald Sun*, February 5, 2019. https://www.heraldsun.com/opinion/article225427335.html.

Suarez, Chris. "Human Remains Found at East End Cemetery This Summer May Have Been Used in Medical Experiments." *Richmond Times-Dispatch*, October 27, 2020. https://richmond.com/news/local/human-remains-found-at-east-end-cemetery-this-summer-may-have-been-used-in-medical/article_89f27342-fbe4-516e-91f2-5cb3e4fc27f8.html.

Tarter, Brent. "Disfranchisement." In *Encyclopedia Virginia*, July 19, 2016. https://www.encyclopediavirginia.org/Disfranchisement#start_entry.

Thompson, Cameron, "Over $100k Tied Up in Dissolved Richmond Nonprofit, City Hopes to Help." WTVR, July 18, 2022. https://www.wtvr.com/news/local-news/over-100k-tied-up-in-enrichmond-foundation-july-18-2022.

Tronto, Joan C. *Moral Boundaries: A Political Argument for an Ethic of Care.* New York: Routledge, 1993.

Wessler, Seth Freed. "Black Deaths Matter." *Nation*, October 15, 2015. https://www.thenation.com/article/archive/black-deaths-matter.

Williams, Michael Paul. "Enrichmond Foundation Is dissolving. Its Death Calls for More Transparency Than It Demonstrated in Life." *Richmond Times-Dispatch*, July 8, 2022. https://richmond.com/news/local/govt-and-politics/williams-enrichmond-foundation-is-dissolving-its-death-calls-for-more-transparency-than-it-demonstrated-in/article_47d997a9-3f2f-5557-997c-8e9dab0ed98a.html.

Wolfe, Brendan. "Racial Integrity Laws (1924–1930)." In *Encyclopedia Virginia*, February 6, 2023. https://encyclopediavirginia.org/entries/racial-integrity-laws-1924-1930/.

Wynes, Charles E. "The Evolution of Jim Crow Laws in Twentieth Century Virginia." *Phylon* 28, no. 4 (1967): 416–25. https://doi.org/10.2307/274293.

EPILOGUE

TEACHING THE AMERICAN SOUTH BY LEARNING THE DEAD

We believe that when students visit historic African American cemeteries such as East End and Evergreen, they need the following three things: context, direct experience, and opportunities to reflect. This three-part design incorporates what we know about effective experiential learning and pedagogy. But it also serves as a guide by which cemetery visitors can respectfully be present in a sacred but marginalized burial ground and actively participate in honoring its dead. We do not cast volunteers, especially short-term ones, as saviors of the cemetery or rescuers of forgotten graves. Rather, we ask them to engage with its rich history, form relationships with the place and its people, and ask critical questions.

The first two parts, context and direct experience, generally happen in sequence. At East End, after a brief introduction to the cemetery and its history, visitors would be put to work. There were many tasks for them to help with, which could be adjusted based on age, ability, size of the group, and other factors. During the autumn and winter, conditions were good for clearing new sections and finding graves that were hidden. In spring and summer, often the most urgent task was removing new growth to maintain sections that had already been cleared. Regardless, Brian and Erin tried to give volunteers at least some exposure to all of the activities going on in the cemetery, especially the intimate contact with individual plots that makes volunteering not only a form of beautification or "yard work," but also an act of care.

As volunteers were working, Brian and Erin provided much of the broader context that we explained earlier in this chapter, describing the cemetery's founding, its connections to Richmond's diverse and complex African American social fabric, the reasons for the cemetery's decline, and the ongoing disparities between white and Black cemeteries. If time permitted, they'd lead visitors on a tour, stopping at graves that bring these histories to life. Some of them are the graves of prominent people, such as physician and banker Richard F. Tancil. Dr. Tancil's grave marker bears the tender, short inscription "Well Done," chosen by his wife, who signed it simply "Widow."[1] Visitors were often stunned to hear that the grave marker they saw is actually a replica that the Friends of East End commissioned after Dr. Tancil's original marker was stolen in 2015.

Other graves Brian and Erin showed to East End visitors do not have the same dramatic history, nor do they belong to history's "notables." Rather, they illustrate the variety of markers people were able to afford, the businesses and civic organizations they belonged to (which often helped make these purchases possible), and the way ordinary people remembered their loved ones. As visitors walked around the cemetery, they saw the work that had been done to reclaim it and the challenge of clearing new sections while also maintaining old ones.

The following are some prompts for reflection, the final pillar of the learning experience, that Brian, Erin, and Adam have developed together. Some of them are appropriate for impromptu oral discussion, but most require some individual time to reflect and write down answers before sharing and group discussion.

1. If you have any deceased relatives or loved ones, do you know where they are buried? If they did not choose to be buried, or if that is not your cultural or family tradition, what other markers, rituals, or forms of commemoration have they had? Write a list of the laws, financial arrangements, environmental protections, and forms of access that you think have helped enable and protect those burials or other commemorations. It is OK if you are guessing at this point. (Teachers may design a longer assignment where students conduct research on their family's burial/commemoration practices and obtain richer, more accurate information than this initial list. It is also interesting to compare how much individual students know about their family's burial or commemoration practices, whether this has been discussed in their households growing up, and why they think that is or is not the case.) Also list any factors that may have interfered with your relatives' or loved ones' resting places or rituals of care and memory—or that threaten to do so in the future.

2. During your experience today at the cemetery, were there any graves that you reacted to particularly strongly? Why? If you volunteered, was there a particular task that had a special impact on you? Why? How do

you think you will/would share this experience with others who have never visited a place like it?

3. The following are excerpts from two obituaries for William Custalo, an entrepreneur who died in 1907 and is buried at East End. Here is an excerpt from the *Times-Dispatch*, which was then the newspaper of the Richmond's white establishment:

> "UNCLE BILLY" DEAD.
> **Wealthiest Colored Man in Richmond Passes Away.**[2]
>
> William Custalo, well-known as "Uncle Billy," and probably the wealthiest colored man in business in this city, died at his home on North Ninth Street yesterday at 1 o'clock, after a brief illness. For more than thirty years Sustalo [sic] conducted a saloon at the corner of Seventh and Broad Streets, and not a more orderly place of its kind could be found in the city.... Custalo was held in high esteem by his own people, and was much thought of by the white population here as well. Though a saloon-keeper he was a prominent church worker. He was a member of the Odd-Fellows, Masons and Knights of Pythias. He was also a director of The Mechanic's [sic] Savings Bank.

This excerpt comes from the *Richmond Planet*, the city's African American newspaper at the time:

> **William Custalo is Dead.**
>
> William Custalo went home Monday night, September 2d from his place of business as well as usual. He ate his supper and later retired. His wife has no further recollection of anything happening until about 2, when she heard something fall in the hallway. She went to the door and down the hall steps, when she observed something white lying on the floor....
>
> A doctor was hastily summoned and it was ascertained that Mr. Custalo had suffered from a stroke of paralysis and that there was little or no hope of his recovery. He never rallied. One time, after repeated efforts, he answered his wife's appeals by a pressure of the hand several times repeated. He died Saturday, September 7th, 1907 and the news was immediately communicated over the entire city, both white and colored people joining in the expressions of regret at his sudden taking off....
>
> The funeral took place last Tuesday from the Second Baptist Church. Rev. W. T. Johnson, D.D., delivered a most impressive dis-

course from the subject, "Thy Will be Done." Mr. Custalo had been a faithful member of this church for many years. . . .

The floral designs were numerous and costly. The casket was cloth-covered with heavy silver bar extension handles. The casket plate contained the Knights of Pythias emblem and the Masonic emblem. He was an Odd Fellow also. He was also a member of the board of directors of the Mechanics' Savings Bank, being on the Finance Committee of that institution. . . .

Interment was in East End Cemetery. William Custalo was a landmark so to speak and his death will tend to cast a gloom over this entire community. He was upright, conscientious, and faithful. His troubles are over and on the other side of the River he will "rest 'neath the shade of the trees."

Compare and contrast these two obituaries. What does each communicate about Mr. Custalo? How do they prioritize, include, and exclude certain kinds of information? What do they say about the communities to which Mr. Custalo belonged in life, and about the mourning of his death?

4. Volunteers are needed for many things in our community, some of which seem more urgent than caring for a cemetery. Having visited the cemetery, what would you say is the value in this kind of work? How does it relate to other projects of community building or social justice?

Notes

1. Mary Tancil actually died before her husband; our best guess is that she had commissioned the headstone long before.
2. "'Uncle Billy' Dead," *Times-Dispatch*, September 8, 1907.

CONTRIBUTORS

Adrienne Chudzinski: Adrienne Chudzinski is a history instructor at Stanford Online High School in Palo Alto, California. She received her PhD from Indiana University, and her research explores the rich political and cultural afterlife of racial violence in Birmingham, Alabama, as it relates to the mythology of the civil rights movement and public memories of the Black freedom struggle in the United States. Chudzinski taught previously at Miami University, has worked in several history museums, including the National Museum of American History and the Rutherford B. Hayes Presidential Library and Museum, and served as an editorial assistant at the *American Historical Review*.

Kami Fletcher: Kami Fletcher is an associate professor of history at Albright College. She received her PhD in history from Morgan State University in 2013. Her research centers African American burial grounds and late nineteenth- / early twentieth-century Black male and female undertakers. She is the author of "Real Business: Maryland's First Black Cemetery Journey's into the Enterprise of Death, 1807–1920" (*Thanatological Studies*, April 2015) and coeditor of *Till Death Do Us Part: American Ethnic Cemeteries as Borders Uncrossed*, which examines the internal and/or external drives among ethnic, religious, and racial groups to separate their dead (University Press of Mississippi, March 2020). Fletcher's work has been featured on the websites *Black Perspectives*, *The Order of Good Death*, and *Death & the Maiden* and the podcast *The Rise of Charm City*. She serves on the international board of the journal *Mortality: Promoting the Interdisciplinary Study of Death and Dying* and is an associate member of the Death and Culture Network based at the University of York. For more, visit www.kamifletcher.com and contact her on Twitter using @kamifletcher36.

Joy M. Giguere: Joy M. Giguere is an associate professor of history at Penn State York, where she teaches courses on American history, the history of technology, the history of Western medicine, African American history, the Civil War era, and the history of death and mourning. Her research has been published in a variety of history journals, and she is the author of *Characteristically American: Memorial Architecture, National Identity, and the Egyptian Revival* (Knoxville: University of Tennessee

Press, 2014). Her forthcoming book is *Pleasure Grounds of Death: The Rural Cemetery in Nineteenth Century American Society and Culture* (University of Michigan Press).

Erin Hollaway Palmer: Erin Hollaway Palmer is an editor and graphic designer. Since 2004, she has worked for a variety of national magazines, including *National Geographic Adventure*, *Parade*, and, most recently, *Inc*. She is a founding member of the Friends of East End Cemetery, the all-volunteer nonprofit devoted to the reclamation and documentation of that historic African American burial ground in Richmond, Virginia.

Antoinette T. Jackson: Dr. Antoinette Jackson is professor and chair of the department of anthropology at the University of South Florida (USF) in Tampa, founder of the Black Cemetery Network, and director of the USF Heritage Research Lab. Her most recent book, *Heritage, Tourism, and Race: The Other Side of Leisure*, was published by Routledge in April 2020.

Scarlet Jernigan: Scarlet Jernigan received her PhD in history at Texas Christian University. Her dissertation, "To Live on Mulberry and Sleep Forever on the Banks of the Ocmulgee: Mapping Antebellum Macon, Georgia, and Its Necropolis," explores the central Georgia city's migration patterns as well as its socioeconomic hierarchy and networks manifested in both life and death. Her research interests include the "good death," religious and gendered epitaphal language, necrogeography, and sectional cultural differences. She has published two articles, "'Why Should a Christian Desire to Sleep Here?' The Unitarian Rural Cemetery Movement and Its Adoption in Macon, Georgia" in *Georgia Historical Quarterly* (Winter 2015) and "Northside 'Hypocrites' versus Southside 'Racists': Three Atlanta Southern Baptist Churches Respond to Changes in the Racial Status Quo" in *Baptist History and Heritage Journal* (Fall 2013).

Brian Palmer: Brian Palmer is a Richmond, Virginia–based journalist whose work has appeared in *the New York Times*, *the Nation*, and *Smithsonian Magazine*, and on The Root, BuzzFeed, PBS, and the radio show *Reveal*. He received the Peabody Award, the National Association of Black Journalists Salute to Excellence Award, and the Online Journalism Award for "Monumental Lies," a 2018 *Reveal* story about public funding for Confederate sites. Palmer is currently the Joan Konner Visiting Professor of Journalism at Columbia Journalism School. He earned his bachelor's in East Asian studies from Brown University and his master's in photography from the School of Visual Arts.

Lynn Rainville: Lynn Rainville is an author, speaker, and public historian who studies ordinary Virginians doing extraordinary things in the past. Since earning a PhD in Near Eastern archaeology, she has spent two decades studying historic cemeteries, gravestones, enslaved communities and their descendants, town poor farms, and Virginia's role in World War I. Her grant-funded research has produced numerous articles and books, including *Hidden History: African American Cemeteries in Central Virginia* (University of Virginia Press, 2014); *Sweet Briar College* (Arcadia, 2015); *Virginia and the Great War* (McFarland, 2017); and *Invisible Founders: How Two Centuries* *of African American Families Transformed a Plantation into a College* (Berghahn Books, 2019). In 2019 she was appointed the inaugural director of institutional history at Washington and Lee University, where she is also a professor of anthropology. For more information, see www.lynnrainville.org.

Kaniqua L. Robinson: Dr. Kaniqua L. Robinson is an assistant professor of anthropology at Furman University. Her research focuses on the politics of memory and race. Dr. Robinson is the research consultant and memorialization specialist for the Black Cemetery Network.

Adam Rosenblatt: Adam Rosenblatt is associate professor of the practice in international comparative studies and cultural anthropology at Duke University. He is the author of *Digging for the Disappeared: Forensic Science after Atrocity* (Stanford University Press, 2015) and has written extensively about mass graves, forensic science, and movements to care for the marginalized dead. His second book, *Cemetery Citizens: Reclaiming Buried Pasts to Revise the Present*, will be out in early 2024. Adam lives in Durham, North Carolina, where he is the cofounder of the Durham Black Burial Grounds Collaboratory and a board member of the Friends of Geer Cemetery.

Ashley Towle: Ashley Towle is assistant professor of history at the University of Southern Maine. She earned her PhD in history from the University of Maryland in 2017 and a BA from Gettysburg College in 2009. She is the author of *African Americans, Death and the New Birth of Freedom: Dying Free during the Civil War and Reconstruction* (2023).

Carroll Van West: Carroll Van West received a doctorate in history from the College of William and Mary. He currently serves as Tennessee state historian as well as the director of the Tennessee Civil War National Heritage Area. West serves on the board of advisers for the National Trust for Historic Preservation and continues to work extensively with the National Register of Historic Places program. He has worked with museum and preservation projects in many states and has been recently working on historic preservation issues in Alabama, Mississippi, and Montana. Dr. West's research interests lie in nineteenth- and twentieth-century southern and western history as well as architecture and material culture. He has written numerous articles and book reviews in southern and western history. He regularly speaks to history, museum, preservation, and civic groups and conferences in Tennessee and across the nation.

Shari L. Williams: Dr. Shari L. Williams is the first African American woman to earn a PhD in history from Auburn University. She is an independent social and cultural historian who studies the modern American South with a focus on the past, present, and future of rural historic landscapes and cultural traditions in Alabama's Black Belt through the lens of race, gender, and class. Her publications include articles for the Encyclopedia of Alabama and the self-published book *Silent for a While, but Not Idle: African American Self-Determination Ignites Educational Opportunity in South Macon County, Alabama 1906–1967*. Dr. Williams is the executive director of the Ridge Macon County Archaeology Project located in Warrior Stand, Macon County, Alabama. The Ridge Project provides educational resources and programs centered on racial/cultural groups that, from the 1800s, populated communities along the historic Federal Road through the region, and it works to document and preserve the area's historic cemeteries.

INDEX

Page numbers followed by *f* and *t* refer to figures and tables, respectively.

AABGP. *See* African American Burial Ground and Remembering Project
abolitionists, 28, 30
African American Burial Ground and Remembering Project (AABGP), 231, 233–35, 239, 244, 245–46
African American Policy Forum, 245
afterlife: African traditions, 94; cultural, 9, 200; romanticization of, 5–6; seen as integrated, 159–60; segregation during, 150
Alabama Historic Cemetery Register, 114, 219
Albemarle Charlottesville Historical Society, 101, 102
Ali, Muhammad, 51; grave of, 52*f*
Alridge, Derrick, 233
Alsip, Ill., 203
American identity, 5
antebellum period, 6
anti-Blackness, 116, 122
Antioch (Macon County, Ala.), 121
Antioch Baptist Church (Macon County, Ala.), 123
Antioch Missionary Baptist Church Cemetery (Macon County, Ala.), 122, 135*f*
Arbery, Ahmaud, 233
architecture, 53, 81, 93
Ash, Wesley, 153
attuned spaces, 125

Bates, Lehman D., II, 101
BCN (Black Cemetery Network), 246, 251

Becker, Ernest, 3
BeCville Project, 101
Bederman, Gail, 40–41n35
Bell, John F., 91
Bell, Susan E., 176
belonging, communities of, 2, 5
benevolent societies, 8, 84, 88, 93, 232, 243–44
Benson, Arzela, 119*t*
Berry, Daina R., 172
Bethel African Methodist Episcopal Church (St. Petersburg, Fla.), 241–42
Bioethics Center (Tuskegee University), 184
Birmingham Campaign (Project Confrontation, Project C), 216
Black Cemetery Network (BCN), 246, 251
"Black Experience with Death, The" (M. Jackson), 3
Black feminist anthropology, 10, 234
#BlackGravesMatter, 246
Black intellectual tradition, 233–34
#BlackLivesMatter movement, 245
Black separatism, 161
Blassingame, John, 125
Blood of Emmett Till, The (Tyson), 220n8
"Blue and the Gray, The" (Finch), 68
body, after death: Black mourning and, 124–25; corpse care, 4; embalming and sanitization, 3; meaning making and, 202–3, 205
Bond, Joseph, 29–31, 34, 41nn37–39
Bonner, James C., 42n65
Boone, Daniel, 54
Borom, Abe, 133, 139*t*
Borom, Charlie, 135, 139*t*

Boromville (Macon County, Ala.), 121, 137
Boromville AME Zion Church Cemetery (Macon County, Ala.), 122, 136*f*
Brandt, Allan M., 171–72
Breckinridge, William C. P., 70
Bristow, Benjamin H., 69–70
Brown, Ellen, 119*t*
Brown, Francis, 119*t*
Brown, Malinda, 119*t*
Brown, W. L., 100
Brundage, W. Fitzhugh, 34
Bryant, Carolyn, 200–201, 220n8
Bryant, James, 101
Bryant, Roy, 200–201
Buckner, Annie, 92
Buckner, Anthony, 92
Buckner, George W., 92–93
Buckner, John T., 92
Buckner, Louisa E., 93
Buckner, Mary Churchman, 93
Buckner, Robert, 97
Buckner, Susie, 92
Bullock, Burkley, 100
Bunch, Lonnie, 204–5, 218
burial grounds. *See* cemeteries
burial plots: ownership of, 25, 86, 150; as private property, 157; purchase of, 8, 151, 153; as real estate ownership, 154, 157; size of, 90
burial rights, 12; Black cemeteries as guaranteeing, 154; Black resistance and struggle for, 8, 151–52, 157; Black separatism and, 161; changing white opinions of, 158, 159, 160; discrimination cases, 153; post–civil rights era, 155, 157, 160; refusal of, seen as embarrassing, 159; of soldiers, 157–60
burial societies, 4, 85, 94
Burnside, Ambrose, 60–61
Burr Oak Cemetery (Alsip, Ill.), 199, 203–4, 206, 219
Burr Oak Cemetery Association (Alsip, Ill.), 162
Burton, Ida, 101, 111
Burton, Kristen D., 42n56
Bush, Charles E., 115, 116–17
Bynum, Cornelius, 233

calendar teas, 242
Calhoun, Jesse Marie, 243
Campbell, Mary, 155–60, 164; news coverage of case, 156*f*, 157, 158, 169, 169*f*
Campbell, Thomas M., 117
Carpenters' and Joiners' Union of America (CJU), 237
Carter, Eliza, 97
Carter, Narcissie, 119*t*; headstone, 114*f*
Cary, Jesse, 86, 87, 99
Cary, Nancy Baker Gatewood, 86, 87, 88, 95
Cave Hill Cemetery (Louisville, Ky.), 56*f*; Ali burial, 51; antebellum burials of people of color, 58; Black burials in, as exceptions, 72; Civil War and, 59, 60–62; Confederate burial section, 64*f*, 71; Confederate identity and, 7; Decoration Day ceremonies initiated at, 65; dedication of, 55–57; diversity in, 51; epilogue on, 80–83; as exclusively white, 51, 54, 58, 71–72; landscaping of, 53, 54–55, 57–58, 71; as learning center, 72; Monument to the Unknown Union Dead, 68*f*, 75n46; postbellum period, 62–71; racial discrimination ended in, 72; in twentieth century, 71; in twenty-first century, 72
cemeteries: as analytical tool, 2; as associated with freedom, 150, 168; communities in absence of, 10; community building and, 7; as cultural institutions, 5; examination of, 11; excluded from public accommodations category, 154; family visits to, 232; as "great equalizer," 150; individual remembrance and, 219; integration of, during civil rights movement, 154–55; kinship and, 161; located on city outskirts, 3; as neighborhoods of dead, 96; politicization of, 60–62; as private interests, 151, 152, 154; reality in, versus historical narratives, 9; remembrance as monumental in, 188; residential segregation preserved in, 84; seen as necessities only, 5–6; as sites of memory, 5, 239; as sites of power, 5; as to be avoided, 6; upkeep of, 10; urban, 90
cemeteries, Black, 1–2, 182, 203, 233; advertising of, 161–62, 162*f*, 163, 164; autonomous, 161, 164; as both personal and political, 173; burial rights and, 154; community and, 4, 161, 233–35; community and, epilogue on, 251; as constructing meaning from antebellum South, 7; created by formerly enslaved people,

4; destroyed by "urban renewal," 9–10, 236–39; dignity and honor of, 163, 164; disrepaired state of, 9, 10, 12, 159, 200, 207, 208, 218, 254f; erasure of, 233, 238–39, 245–46; family histories and, 233; founding of, 58–59; freedom and, 4, 164; as Jim Crow segregation resistance, 154, 161–65; kinship and, 161; paved over, 9–10, 235, 236–37f, 237–38, 246; peripheral locations of, 17, 48, 219; preservation of, 100; remembrance and, 4, 233; restoration of, 100; as sites of resistance, 4, 233; southern, as sacred places, 234; Tuskegee Study victims and, 172–73; white disdain for, 159; white misconceptions of, 163

cemeteries, Jim Crow, 154, 159, 165; epilogue on, 168–70; examples of, 149, 150, 151, 154, 155–60; existing into 1980s, 155; as upholding white southern norms, 150, 160, 165; as white control of Blacks in death, 157

cemeteries, segregated, 8, 120; arguments by proponents of, 159; Black burials in, 93, 95; court rulings upholding, 149–50, 151f; desegregation of, 95; founding of Black cemeteries and, 85, 98; in twenty-first century, 149

cemeteries, slave: as representing ownership of parts of plantations, 4; as sites of resistance, 4

cemeteries, white: court cases challenging restrictions, 8; existing into 1980s, 155; restrictions on Black visitors, 58–59, 71–72, 73n2

cemetery associations, 1

Chambliss, Polly, 134, 139t

Chandler, Felecia, 178, 188

Charlottesville, Va., 8, 84; Black-founded organizations, 89; racial and economic disparity addressed in, 101–2; Unite the Right violence, 101

Charlottesville Unity Days, 102

churches, Black: Black cultural traditions and, 240; founding of, 86, 87–88, 93–94, 123; as institutions, 8, 93–94; southern, funeral and burial traditions, 232, 233

Churchill, Larry R., 171–72

churchyards, 6, 93; clergy buried in, 93; MAT headstones in, 119–20t

citizenship, 1–2, 86, 151, 153, 157–60

Civil Rights Act of 1866, 1

Civil Rights Act of 1875, 2

Civil Rights Act of 1885, 152

Civil Rights Act of 1964, 51, 150

civil rights martyrs, 198, 204; meaning making and, 219–20; murdered children as unintentional, 215–18; portrayal of murdered children as, 200, 202, 205, 207, 208, 212; public reverence versus private remembrance, 9, 199–200, 209–10, 212, 213, 220

Civil Rights Memorial, Montgomery, Alabama, 199f

civil rights movement, 115, 154, 198; cemetery lot and burial deed ownership and, 8; children's murders as watersheds, 9, 198, 201, 205, 207, 212, 220n2, 221n25; epilogue on, 227–30; mythology of, 122, 215–16, 218, 219–20; narrative of, 227; remembrance of, 219

CJU (Carpenters' and Joiners' Union of America), 237

Clark, Herman, 180

Clark, Taliaferro, 174, 175

Clark, William B., 33

class: beneath Jim Crow segregation ceiling, 115, 131; middle, 8, 37, 115, 131; MAT membership and, 115; mutual aid societies and, 8; slaveholding, 19, 23, 27, 29, 31, 32–34; working, 8, 27, 82, 115, 131

Clay, Henry, 54

Clinton, Bill, 184, 187

Cole, George E. "Buck," 99

Coles, Addie Golden, 99

Cole[s], Jane, 86, 98

Cole[s], Jesse, 86

Collins, Addie Mae, 9, 200, 207; Four Spirits Memorial, 216, 217f; grave site, 208–10; missing remains of, 208–10; symbolic role versus personal identity, 209–10

Collins, Junie, 208

Collins, Patricia Hill, 234

Collins, Sarah, 208–9, 210

communities: Black, cemeteries and, 161, 239–40; Black, construction of, 7; cemeteries absent in, 10; commitment to, 8; of exclusion and belonging, 2, 5

community building, 7

community connections, 96

Confederate Burial Memorial Association, 64

Confederate Decoration Day, 11, 63–71, 75n51

Confederate grave sites, 7, 59–62, 64f, 71, 72, 254f; beautification of, 64, 69; reburials, 63
Confederate identity, 7, 60–61
Confederate monuments, 11, 12, 70–71, 71f; rural cemeteries as precursors to, 7
Confederate Soldiers' Monument (Louisville, Ky.), 70–71, 71f
Cooper, Anna Julia, 234
Cooper, Frank, 188t
Cooper Chapel AME Zion Church, Warrior Stand, 120, 123
corpse care, 4
Coulter, E. Merton, 62
Court of Calanthe, 89
Creal-Williams Funeral Home (St. Petersburg, Fla.), 243
Creek Stand (Macon County, Ala.), 121, 137; white residents of, 122
Creek Stand AME Zion Church (Macon County, Ala.), 179, 181; Tuskegee Study victims and, 186
Creek Stand AME Zion Church Cemetery (Macon County, Ala.), 9, 114, 122, 134f, 142n4, 179f, 181f; Tuskegee Study victims and, 173, 177–82, 188, 194–97, 194f
Creek Stand School (Macon County, Ala.), 128–29
Crenshaw, Kimberlé, 245
Cronkite, Walter, 207
Cullors, Patrisse, 245
Cumming, Hugh Smith, 174, 175

Dabney, Jeanetta, 99
Daniel, Clark, 179, 188t
Daniels, Albert, Sr., 179, 188t
Daughters of Samaria, 85
Daughters of the Good Samaritan, 33
Daughters of Zion, 84–87; as defunct, 89, 95; esteem for, 93; leaders of, 88; membership changes, 89; timing of, 86; variant of national organizations, 88
Daughters of Zion Cemetery (Charlottesville, Va.), 8, 92, 98f, 109f, 111f; audio tour, 112f; biographical inscriptions in, 93–94; decline of, 89–90, 95, 100; deed for, 86; epilogue on, 107–12; founding of, 85, 98; interment dates, 100; map of, 96f, 100; online resources, 97, 102, 104n37, 108; preservation of, 100–102; rate of interments, 96; restoration of, 100–102; site of, 90; University of Virginia and, 99

Davidson, James M., 172
Davis, Eunice (Morris), 213–14, 223n70; "The Forgotten Ones," 214
Dawkins Church (Sweet Pilgrim Baptist Church), 121, 123
Dawkins Crossroads (Macon County, Ala.), 137
death: as accepted, by enslaved Black people, 3; as central to lives of African Americans, 3; changing ideas about, in nineteenth century, 7; contemplation of meaning of, 6; domestication of, 40n27; as form of freedom, 3; as "great equalizer," 1, 8, 165, 168; inequality preserved in, 150, 168; as part of life, 3, 231–32; romanticization of, 5–6; societal aversion to, 3
death benefits, 117, 126, 130
death care labor, 245
deathscapes, 8, 100
deathways, 2, 3, 233; Black social institutions and, 10; commemoration, 31; community and, 239–40; geography, 16, 22–27, 31–33; slaveholder responsibilities, 32
Declaration of Independence, 1
Decoration Day, 101, 164
Deerfield Beach Memorial Cemetery (Deerfield Beach, Fla.), 155
Delaney, Ted, 100, 105n77
desecration, 9, 59–60, 199, 203, 205, 206
disinterment, 150, 153, 155, 160, 204, 206, 210, 215. *See also* exhumation
Dorr, Gregory, 175
Douglass, Frederick, 40–41n35
DOZ. *See* Daughters of Zion
Drake, St. Clair, 234
Du Bois, W. E. B., 85, 234; on Black women, 242
Dunham, Katherine, 234

East End Cemetery (Richmond, Va.), 10, 253, 254f
Eastern Cemetery (Louisville, Ky.), 54, 58–59
Eastern Stars, 85
Ebenezer Baptist Church (Charlottesville, Va.), 87, 89, 94, 100
economic stratification, 131, 138
Edder, Orville, 153
Ellison, Clara, 119t, 130, 133–34, 137, 139t; headstone, 134f, 138
Ellison, Isom, 133, 139t
Ellison, Lewis, 133
Ellison, Ralph, 123

emotionalism, 125
enslaved people: burial in Black cemeteries, 7, 32; Civil War impression of, 59, 92; death as representing freedom to, 4; demographics of, 37, 38n4; gendered oppression of, 124; infant deaths among, 124; mourning and, 124–26; white disdain and fascination for, 123–24
epitaphs, 6, 28–29; family and, 28, 41n40, 91; of men, 28; of women, 31
eugenics, 175, 176
Evergreen Cemetery (Richmond, Va.), 10, 253
Evergreen Cemetery (St. Petersburg, Fla.), 233, 235; erasure of, 236–37*f*
Evers, Medgar, 203
exclusion, 72; communities of, 2, 5
exhumation, 199, 204, 208, 238, 243. *See also* disinterment

family: ancestral, 4; Black, depictions of, 33; history, cemeteries as repository of, 33; separate burial locations of, 93; white, depictions of, 28, 31. *See also* kinship
family lots, 6, 39n18, 90; of Black families, 92–93; of families separated by slavery, 33; of planters, 25, 27
farmers, 8, 115, 123, 134; assets and properties, 131–33, 132*f*
Fifteenth Amendment, 1
Finch, Francis Miles, 68
First Baptist Church (Charlottesville, Va.), 87, 94
First Baptist Institutional Church (St. Petersburg, Fla.), 243
Fisher, John, 161
Fleming, J. P., 99
Florida Public Archaeology Network (FPAN), 239
Floyd, George, 233
Forest Home Cemetery Company (Cook County, Ill.), 151, 151*f*, 154
"Forgotten Ones, The" (Davis), 214
4 Little Girls (film), 207–8, 223n70
Four Spirits Memorial (Kelly Ingram Park, Birmingham, Ala.), 215–18, 217*f*
Fourteenth Amendment, 1, 151–52, 153
FPAN (Florida Public Archaeology Network), 239
Frankfort Cemetery (Frankfort, Ky.), 54
fraternal organizations, 85, 116, 164, 182, 244
Freemasons, 85, 87, 164

French, Scot, 105n77
French, Stanley, 5–6
funeral homes, 3, 91; as Black social institutions, 10, 243
funeral processions, 5, 125. *See also* homegoings
funeral rites rituals, 4, 232–33
funerals, 3, 231–32; burial refusal and, 159; development of, 4; for enslaved persons, 42n56; "proper," 4, 126
funerary culture, 4

Gagnon, Eva Chandler, 122–26, 138, 139; *Home Place*, 122
GAR (Grand Army of the Republic), 67, 69
Gardullo, Paul, 205, 218
Garza, Alicia, 245
Gaskill, John B., 151–53, 151*f*, 154
Gaskill, Pinkie (Webb), 151–53, 151*f*
Gas Plant District (St. Petersburg, Fla.), 235, 240, 243, 244
Gatewood, Armstead, 87
gender: epitaphs and, 6, 27–28; femininity and, 30–31; gendered oppression, 124, 234; manhood, in epitaphs, 27–28; monuments and, 30–31; mutual aid societies and, 85; norms of, in southern funeral culture, 4; property rights and, 86. *See also* manhood; women; women, Black; women, white
generational gaps, 89, 95–97
Genovese, Eugene, 123
Germany, Adaline/Adeline, 119*t*, 121, 140*t*
Germany, Henry, 140*t*
Gethers, Ann, 245
Gilkes, Cheryl Townsend, 240, 241
Glendale Cemetery (Des Moines, Iowa), 153
Goff, Lisa, 102
Goins, Martha Patsy, 86, 88
Goins, Robert, 86, 88
Goldin, Claudia, 38n6, 38n9
Goodall, Lindsey Baxter, 88
"good dead" traditions, 94
Good Samaritans, 85, 88, 89
Gorer, Geoffrey, 3
GPR. *See* ground-penetrating radar
Grand Army of the Republic (GAR), 67, 69
grave markers, 8, 10, 109*f*; of civil rights martyrs, 9, 200, 204; design of, 90, 204; as distinguishing Black and white graves, 160; kinship and, 93; materials of, 90, 91; misidentifications on, 9, 200, 212–15;

grave markers (*continued*)
    occupations and, 93; as primary sources for research, 107–12; standardization of, 91; symbols and, 91; of unknown individuals, 68*f*, 75n46, 101. *See also* monuments
graveyards. *See* cemeteries
Gray, Fred, 177, 184
Gray Ladies of Mercy Hospital (St. Petersburg, Fla.), 244–45
Grear, Ada, 120*t*
Great Depression, 115, 118
Great Migration, 152, 163, 203
Greenberg, Kenneth S., 30
Green Mount Cemetery (Baltimore, Md.), 54
Greenwood Cemetery (Birmingham, Ala.), 207, 212, 215, 219
Green-Wood Cemetery (Brooklyn, N.Y.), 54
Greenwood Cemetery (Louisville, Ky.), 58–59
ground-penetrating radar (GPR), 41–42n46, 90, 101, 209–10, 239

Hailstock, George, 95
Hand, Winny (Swanson), 134
Hann, Carrie, 120*t*, 121, 133, 134, 137, 140*t*; headstone, 135*f*
Harris, Alax/Alex, 140*t*
Harris, Susan, 119*t*, 121, 140*t*
Harte, Brett, 34
Hawkins, Bernard, 155
Hebrew Cemetery (Charlottesville, Va.), 84, 89
Heller, Jean, 180, 184
Henderson, Mary L., 119*t*
Henderson, Tatum Feebee, 120*t*
Hendon, Leila, 119*t*
Heritage, Tourism, and Race (A. Jackson), 240
Herndon, Jesse, 93
Hicklin, B., 153
Hicklin, J., 153
Hillcrest Memorial Gardens (Fort Pierce, Fla.), 157–60
Hilliard, Earl F., 208, 209
historical methods, 50
historical silences, 34
history: Black, ignorance of, 12; family and community, 232; mapping of, 90; medical, racism in, 171, 172, 175–76, 187
"history hunt" exercise, 111*f*
Holliday, Joseph, 188*t*
Holloway, Karla FC, 4

Hollywood Cemetery (Richmond, Va.), 255
homegoings, 4–5, 10, 125–26, 243
Home Place (Gagnon), 122
hospitals, 3, 63; as Black social institutions, 10, 244–45
Household of Ruth, 89
Howard, Carter, 184
Howard, Evelyn, 155
Howard, Mayo, 155
Hubbard, Lelar, grave marker of, 195*f*
Hudson, H. J. T., 33
human experimentation, 9, 171, 172–73, 175–76
Humphrey, Edward P., 56–57
Humphrey, Hubert, 154

"If We Must Die" (McKay), 3
Improved Order Shepherds and Daughters of Bethlehem, 89
Independence, La., 231
Independent Order of Odd Fellows (IOOF), 85, 88, 237, 244
Independent Order of Saint Luke, 85
Independent Society, 33
Inglenook Cemetery (Birmingham, Ala.), 215
inscriptions, 88; biographical, 93–94; segregation documented by, 98; slavery memorialized by, in Black cemeteries, 98; standardized, 91; types of, 90–91
"Integrating the City of the Dead" (Rogers), 152
intersectionality, 234, 245
IOOF. *See* Independent Order of Odd Fellows

Jackson, Antoinette T., 231, 246; *Heritage, Tourism, and Race*, 240
Jackson, Benson, 133, 140*t*
Jackson, Maurice, 3
Jackson, Oral Lee, 232
Jackson, Parthenia, 120*t*, 133–34, 140*t*; headstone, 134*f*
Jefferson Graded School (Charlottesville, Va.), 94
Jefferson High School (Charlottesville, Va.), 95
Jefferson Masonic Lodge, 87, 93
Jernigan, Scarlet, 6–7
J. F. Bell Funeral Home (Charlottesville, Va.), 91
Jim Crow segregation, 3–4; Black cemeteries as resistance to, 162*f*, 163; Black funeral development and, 4; Black intellectual

tradition as challenging, 233; brutality of, 203; burial patterns and, 8; legislation of, 123; northward extension of, 152–53; origins of, 149–50; reunification and, 116
Johnson, Andrew, 63
Johnson, Lucy, 97
Johnson, Michael P., 124
Johnson, Philip, 97
Johnson, Shirley, 178, 188
Johnson/Johnston, Delila, 97
Johnson/Johnston, Phillip, 97
Johnston, William Butler, 22, 27, 30
Jones, James, 172, 177
Julius Rosenwald Fund (JRF), 173
Julkes, Albert, 179, 188*t*
Julkes, Ephron, 179, 188*t*

Keatts, Chester W., 115
Kelser, Robert, 91
Kentucky, 53, 62–71; Confederate identity and, 7, 66–71
Kentucky Women's Confederate Monument Association, 70
Key, Carrie, 119*t*, 140*t*
Key, Cornelia, 119*t*
Key, Wyatt, 140*t*
King, Martin Luther, Jr., 203; site of remembrance, 218; Sixteenth Street Baptist Church victims and, 198–99, 207, 212, 216
King, Robert, 101, 111
kinship, 134–38; beliefs about, 8; Black cemeteries and, 161; fraternal organization membership and, 121–22; interments and, 96, 100; networks, 7
Kitchen, Aaron, 135, 140*t*
Kitchen, Martha, 119*t*, 130, 133, 135, 139*t*, 140*t*; headstone, 136*f*
Kitchen, William, Sr., 140*t*
Knights of Pythias, 85, 88, 244
Kruger-Kahloula, Angelika, 17, 32
Kübler-Ross, Elisabeth, 3

ladies' memorial associations (LMAs), 11, 64–65, 70
landscape design, 8, 23, 100; exercise, 81
landscapes, 53, 54–55, 57–58, 59–60, 69, 72, 90; didactic, 16; of memory, 30
Laurel Grove Cemetery (Savannah, Ga.), 32
Laurel Hill Cemetery (Philadelphia, Pa.), 54
Lederer, Susan, 172

Lee, Edmund Francis, 55
Lee, Spike, 207–8
Lee-Peek Funeral Home (Fort Pierce, Fla.), 158, 160
Lewis, Belle, 119*t*, 137
Lewis, C. E., 99
Lewis, G. W., 100
Lewis, Margaret, 99
Lewis, Mary Nelson, 100
Lewis, M. T., 86, 87, 93
Lewis, P. C., 99
Liberty Chamber (MAT chamber), 182–83
Lincoln Cemetery (Gulfport, Fla.), 238, 243
Linkville Cemetery (Klamath Falls, Oreg.), 153
Livesay, James, 157, 159, 164–65
Liz (enslaved woman), 126
Lloyd, Ernest, 179, 188*t*
LMAs. *See* ladies' memorial associations
Lone Star Chamber number 1, 122
Lost Cause myth, 6, 63, 65; narrative emergence, 123; white women and, 11
Louisville, Ky.: Confederate identity and, 60; in nineteenth century, 53; social complexity of, 72; in twenty-first century, 51; Union and, 61–62
Louisville Cemetery (Louisville, Ky.), 58–59
Love, Katrina, 178, 180, 188
Lynch, James D., 150

Macedonia Free Will Baptist Church (Independence, La.), 231–32
Macedonia Free Will Baptist Church Covenant, 232*f*
Macon, Ga.: antebellum demography, 16–22; antebellum period, 16–33; deathways geography, 22–27; demographics, 6–7, 18*f*, 20*f*, 21*f*, 33, 38n9; Oak Ridge excluded from map of, 32; postbellum period, 33–35; socioeconomic groupings, 17, 18*f*, 19, 20*f*, 21*f*, 25, 26*f*, 35–37, 36*t*, 42n62, 42–43n65; urban geography, 16–22, 18*f*, 20*f*, 21*f*, 38–39n12
Macon County, Ala., 121*f*, 171, 172–74
MacQueen, Elizabeth, 215–18
Mahone, Barbara, 178, 188
Mahone, Dave, 188*t*
Mahone, Fonzie, 179, 188*t*
manhood, 27, 29, 30, 40–41n35. *See also* gender
marginality, 16, 33
Marshall, Pearlie, 119*t*
Mary (enslaved woman), 126

Masonic lodges, 93
MAT. *See* Mosaic Templars of America
material culture, 9
MAT headstones, 8, 114, 114*f*, 127*f*, 134*f*, 135*f*, 136*f*, 138; criteria for, 127–28; description of, 127–28; epilogue on, 147–48; meanings of, 139; Precinct Four Zephroes and, 119–20*t*, 120–21; request forms, 127, 128*f*
Mayo, Maria Harris, 88
Mayo, Thadeus, 88
Mays Landing, N.J., 163–64
McBryde, Jayne, 119*t*
McClaurin, Irma, 234
McIlwain, Charlton D., 124–25
McKay, Claude, 3
McNair, Chris, 218
McNair, Denise, 9, 200, 207; Four Spirits Memorial, 216, 217*f*
McNair, Maxine, 218
McRae Funeral Home (St. Petersburg, Fla.), 243
Mehrtens, William O., 157–58
memoirs: Black, 122, 138, 214; white, 122–26, 138
Memorial Day, 69, 70, 101, 164
Memorial Park Cemetery (Klamath Falls, Oreg.), 153
Memorial to the Unknown (Daughters of Zion Cemetery, Charlottesville, Va.), 101
Mercy Hospital (St. Petersburg, Fla.), 244
Mercy Hospital Alumni Association, 245
Methodist Town (St. Petersburg, Fla.), 235
Middle Tennessee State University (MTSU) Center for Historic Preservation, 178, 180, 187
Milam, J. W., 201
Mims, Richard, 188*t*
Miss Evers' Boys (TV movie), 175
Missouri, 13n8
Mitford, Jessica, 3
Moffett Cemetery (St. Petersburg, Fla.), 233, 235, 236, 243; erasure of, 236–37*f*
monuments, 7, 9, 206; of slaveholders, 30, 34, 41n37; Tuskegee Study and, 173, 184, 188; Union versus Confederate, 70–71
Mooney, Gwen, 72
Moore, Adeline, 137
Moore, Eliza, 140*t*
Moore, Emmaline, 137
Moore, Everena/Everline, 120*t*
Moore, Frances, 120*t*, 137, 140*t*
Moore, Malinda, 119*t*
Moore, Moses, 137, 140*t*
Moore, Nettie, 119*t*, 121, 137, 140*t*
Moore, Turner, 121, 137, 140*t*
Moore, Waveney Ann, 242
Moores Choice Chamber (MAT Precinct Four chamber), 118, 121, 122
Morris, Charlie, 214
Morris, Estelle (Merchant), 210–11, 213, 214
Morris, Fate, 213–15
Mosaic Templars of America (MAT), 8, 114, 182–83; chambers, lodges, and temples, 117–18, 122; epilogue on, 147–48; financial policies, 117, 130; founding of, 115; goals of, 118; Great Depression insolvency, 118; kinship and, 121–22; organization of, 117–18; prominence of women leaders, 117; *Ritual No. 1, Ladies' Chamber*, 129–30, 129*f*; rituals, 116; socioeconomic class and, 115
Most Worshipful Zipporah (MWZ), 129, 130
Moton, R. R., 174
Mott, Julius, 188*t*
Mound Park Hospital (St. Petersburg, Fla.), 244, 245
Mount Auburn Cemetery (Cambridge, Mass.), 5, 7, 23, 54, 74n28
Mount Glenwood Cemetery (Chicago, Ill.), 161–63, 162*f*, 164
Mount Glenwood Cemetery Association (Chicago, Ill.), 161–63, 164
Mount Zion Baptist Church (Charlottesville, Va.), 87, 93, 94
MTSU Center. *See* Middle Tennessee State University (MTSU) Center for Historic Preservation
mutual aid societies, 4, 8, 11, 33, 85–87
Mvskoke (Muscogee) Creek Nation, 113, 142n1
MWZ (Most Worshipful Zipporah), 129, 130

NAACP (National Association for the Advancement of Colored People), 153
narratives: historical, 34; historical, versus reality, 9, 200, 227; white northern, 164; white southern, 29, 30
narratives, slavery, 27–28; deathways responsibilities and, 32; "faithful slave," 65; as paternalistic, 33, 35, 98–99; promoted by slaveholders, 32
National Association for the Advancement of Colored People (NAACP), 153
National Grand Temple (MAT headquarters) (Little Rock, Ark.), 117

National Museum of African American History and Culture (NMAAHC, Washington, D.C.), 199, 204–6
National Negro Business League (NNBL), 117
National Register of Historic Places, 114, 142n4, 177, 178, 180–82, 185
necrogeography exercises, 82–83
Nelson, William "Bull," 59–60
Nimmerk, James, 162
NMAAHC (National Museum of African American History and Culture, Washington, D.C.), 199, 204–6
NNBL (National Negro Business League), 117
Nora, Pierre, 5
Nystrom, Kenneth C., 172

Oakes, James, 29, 31
Oak Hill Cemetery (Charlottesville, Va.), 84
Oaklawn Cemetery Complex (OCC, St. Petersburg, Fla.), 233, 246; community and, 239–45; erasure of, 236–37f; history of, 236–39; paving over of, 9–10
Oaklin Springs Baptist Cemetery (Oberlin, La.), 149
Oak Ridge Cemetery (Macon, Ga.), 7, 16, 17, 35; class in, 22–23; deathways geography, 31–33; designated as Black cemetery, 32; elitism in, 22–23; enslaved and free Black burials in, 32; postbellum period, 33; racial burial segregation in, 31–33; racial disparities in, 22–23; white view of, 32
Oakwood Cemetery (Charlottesville, Va.), 85, 89, 90, 95, 100
Oakwood Cemetery (Richmond, Va.), 253, 254f, 255
obituaries, 95, 241; racism in, 92, 97, 98, 99
OCC. See Oaklawn Cemetery Complex
Ocmulgee River, 16–17, 23, 25, 27
O'Donovan, Susan E., 34
Ohio Civil Rights Commission, 153
Old Macon Cemetery (Macon, Ga.), 23
Order of Calenthe, 244
Order of Eastern Star, 232–33
Order of Elks, 85, 88
Order of the Good Samaritan, 33
Oser, Jennifer Lynn, 85, 89

Pace, Albert, 128
Pace, Amy, grave marker of, 195f
Pace, Elmore, 179, 188t
Pace, Henry, 140t, 179, 188t

Pace, Ned, grave marker of, 195f
Pace, Sallie, 119t, 128, 137, 140t
parking lots paved over Black cemeteries, 9–10, 235, 236–37f, 237–38, 246
Parks, Rosa, 203, 221
Parrish, Shirley, 101
Passed On (Holloway), 4
Patton, Samuel, 60
Peters, Jesse, 174–75
Petrella, Christopher, 12
Pineview Cemetery (Deerfield Beach, Fla.), 155
Pinkard, Charles, 188t
Pinkard, Charlie, 188t
Plessy v. Ferguson, 150, 154
politicization, 5, 59
Pollard, Charlie, 183–84, 187, 188t; grave of, 185f
Pollard, Elbert, 188t
Pollard, Lucious, 188, 188t
Pollard, Osburn, 188t
Pollard, Will, 188t
Ponder, James Maxie, 244
Porter, Woodford, Sr., 51
postbellum period, 16, 33–35, 62–71, 99
potter's fields, 39n18, 154
Potts, Jethro, 188t
Powers, Georgia, 51
Precinct Four (MAT): Black schools in, 123; cemetery map, 121f; churches founded in, 123; land values, 132f; material assets, 132f
Precinct Four Zephroes, 116, 117; actions, symbols, and rituals of, 128–30; burial locations, 119–20t; chamber size, 122; chambers of, 118; kinship, 122, 139–40t; literacy, resources, and class distinctions, 130–33; material assets, 131–38; with MAT headstones, 119–20t, 120–21, 126; profiles of, 133–38, 136f; research sources, 122; residences of, 121
Preer, Tolbert, 140t
Prentice, George D., 68–69, 73n4
Preservation Piedmont, 102
Preservers of the Daughters of Zion Cemetery, 90, 97, 100–102; educational projects, 107–12
private remembrance, 9, 200, 218–20
Project Confrontation (Project C; Birmingham Campaign), 216
pseudoscience, 172
public accommodations, 152, 153–54; access to, 1

public remembrance, 9, 34, 200, 205, 206, 215, 218–20; community and, 233; epilogue on, 227–30; historical debate about, 216

racial covenants, 150, 154, 155; ruled unconstitutional, 165; whites claiming unawareness of, 158
racism: Black cemetery erasure and, 245–46, 251; Black intellectual tradition and, 234; civil rights murders and, 216, 218; institutional, 116, 233; narrative of, 218; spaces of death as challenging, 7; structural, 116, 234; systemic, 233
Rainey, Joseph H., 1–2
Rayner, A. A., 201–2, 221n14
Reconstruction, 2, 7–8, 34
Reddick, Annie, 242
redemptive suffering, 200, 207, 216
Reese, Octavia, 120*t*, 137
Registered Nurses Club (St. Petersburg, Fla.), 244
Reid, Dow, 136–37
Reid, Eliza, 120*t*, 121, 137, 138, 140*t*, 144n60
Reid, Frank, 121, 136–37, 138
Reid, Harbard/Harbord, 134, 137, 140*t*, 144n60
Reidy, Joseph, 38n9
religious revivals, 86
Resting Place (TV movie), 157
Reverby, Susan M., 187–88
rhetorical spaces, 5
Richmond, Va., 10
Ritual No. 1, Ladies' Chamber, Mosaic Templars of America (MAT publication), 129–30, 129*f*
Rivers, Eunice, 174–75, 176, 177, 181, 187–88
Roberts, Dorothy, 172, 175–76
Robertson, Carole, 9, 200, 207; Four Spirits Memorial, 216; grave site, 209
Roberts Temple Church of God (Chicago, Ill.), 202, 205
Robinson, Albert, 188*t*
Robinson, Johnny, 216
Rogers, Kitty, 152
Rose Hill Burial Park, Ohio, 153
Rose Hill Cemetery (Macon, Ga.), 6–7, 16, 17, 22, 35; burial patterns, 24*f*, 26*f*; class in, 22–27; deathways geography, 24*f*, 26*f*; elitism in, 22–27; epilogue on, 48–50; epitaphs in, 28, 31, 49; landscaping of, 23, 39n17; modern map of, 48–49; monuments in, 27–31, 34, 41; postbellum decay of, 34, 42n53; racial disparities in, 22–27; slavery narratives in, 27–31
Rose of Sharon Chapter number 22 OES, 232
rural cemeteries, 6, 11, 17, 71; aesthetic of, 54; historical narratives in, 34; list of major, 80; segregated spaces in, 58–59; visitor behavior in, 74n28
rural cemetery movement, 5–7; classism and elitism and, 23, 27; as cultural phenomenon, 54; landscaping and, 16, 23, 31–32, 54–55

Sanchez, Judy, 243
Sanchez-Arch Royal Funeral Home (St. Petersburg, Fla.), 243
Sanchez Rehoboth Mortuary and Cremation Services (St. Petersburg, Fla.), 243
Sanders, Harland, 51; grave of, 52*f*
Sass, Shelley, 100
Savitt, Todd L., 175
#SayHerName, 245
schools, Black, 94, 143–44n45; founding of, 123, 142n15; as institutions, 8
Sclair, Helen, 152
secret societies, 85
segregation. *See* cemeteries, segregated; Jim Crow segregation
self-determination, 113, 122
Semien, Darrell, 149
Semien, Karla, 149
sentimentalism, 33–34
Shaughter, John, 179, 188*t*
Shaw, Herman, 184, 188*t*
Shealey's Pride Chamber (MAT Precinct Four chamber), 118
Shiloh Community Restoration Foundation, 186
Shiloh Missionary Baptist Church (Notasulga, Ala.), 182–87
Shiloh Missionary Baptist Church Cemetery (Notasulga, Ala.), 9, 114, 142n4, 178, 183*f*, 185*f*, 187; state historical marker, 181, 196, 196*f*; Tuskegee Study interpretive markers, 186, 186*f*; Tuskegee Study victims and, 173, 177, 182–87, 188
Shiloh Rosenwald School (Macon County, Ala.), 183, 187–88
Shobe, Benjamin, 51
shrouds, 4
Shuttlesworth, Fred, 203

Simmons, Fred, 184
Simmons, William J., 72
Sims, Elizabeth, 178, 183, 184–85, 188
Sinclair, Anderson, 188*t*
sites of memory, 5, 98, 239; Jim Crow segregation cemeteries as, 150
Sixteenth Street Baptist Church (Birmingham, Ala.), 9, 198, 206–8; memorials at, 211*f*, 214
Sixteenth Street Baptist Church bombing: fiftieth anniversary of, 214–15; omitted from Four Spirits Memorial, 216, 218; public memorials, 215–18, 217*f*, 219; unaddressed by white community, 215; victims as not "little girls," 215–16; victims memorialized, 199*f*, 199–200
Skloot, Rebecca, 172
Skocpol, Theda, 85, 89
Slaughter, Martha, 88
Sloane, David, 39n18
Smith, Ann, 153
Smith, Crosby, 221n22
Smith, Dede, 102
Smith, Jane, 102
Smith Prospect Chamber (MAT Precinct Four chamber), 118
Smithsonian Institution (Washington, D.C.), 204–6
social justice, 157, 158
social networks, 96
socioeconomic stratification, 133, 136
soldiers, 164; Black, 157 (*see also* United States Colored Troops); burial rights as earned by, 158
Southern Poverty Law Center (SPLC), 198
Sparks, Ed, 179, 188*t*
SPLC (Southern Poverty Law Center), 198
Spring Grove Cemetery (Cincinnati, Ohio), 54
Stewart, James, 233
Strangers Row (Rose Hill Cemetery, Macon, Ga.), 23, 25
St. Rose, Edwina, 100, 101, 102
structural uncaring, 10
Sullivan, Theresa, 99
Sumner, Charles, 1–2
Sunset Memorial Cemetery (Charleston, W.Va.), 155
Swanson, Weny/Winny, 140*t*
Sweet Pilgrim Baptist Church (Macon County, Ala.), 121, 123

Sweet Pilgrim Cemetery (Macon County, Ala.), 121, 122, 135*f*
Sweet Pilgrim Zephroes, 136–37

"Talented Tenth," 85
Tatum Home Chamber (MAT Precinct Four chamber), 118, 121, 122
Taylor, Breonna, 233
Taylor, Frazine, 138
Terry, Egbert, 95
Terry, Margaret, 95
Thirteenth Amendment, 62
Thlucco, Tustanagee, 113
Thompson, Steve, 100–101
Till, Emmett, 9, 11, 198, 220n8; burial and reburials of, 199, 203–6; caskets of, 9, 199, 202, 204–6; funeral of, 202–3, 206, 221n18, 221n20; historical legacy of, 222n30; invocation of, 203; murder of, 200–201; news coverage of, 201, 202–3, 220, 221n18
Till-Mobley, Mamie, 11, 201–3, 206, 220–21n12, 221n14, 221n16; civil rights influence of, 205, 221n26; Till's remembrance and, 222n30
Tolbert, Effie, 119*t*, 140*t*
Toler, Betsy, 88
Tometi, Opal, 245
Tonsler, Benjamin, 94, 98
Tonsler, M. T., grave of, 98*f*
Toscano, David J., 102
Towns, Carolyn, 204, 206
"Tribute to the Ancestors, A" (Parrish), 101
Tropicana Field (St. Petersburg, Fla.), 236–37*f*, 238, 246
Trouillot, Michel-Rolph, 138
Truatt, Alexander, 87
True Reformers, 85, 89
Tuskegee History Center (Tuskegee, Ala.), 184
Tuskegee Institute (Tuskegee, Ala.), 116–17, 171
Tuskegee Plan, 116–17
Tuskegee State Normal School (Macon County, Ala.), 113
Tuskegee Study: acknowledgment of, by accountable institutions, 184; Black professionals and, 174–75; exposure and ending of, 176–77; as foundational story of American racism, 171, 188; government accountability for, 173, 184; introduction to, 171–72; overview of, 173–77

Tuskegee Study victims, 9; autopsies of, 172, 176; burial locations of, 176, 177, 179–82, 188, 188*t*, 194*f*; choice of word "victim," 187; epilogue on, 194–97; family and community care for, 172–73, 178, 180, 186–88; graves as not officially designated, 179–80, 183; identification of, 177; lawsuit on behalf of, 177, 184; legacy of, 184, 186; remembrance of, 173, 178–81, 185–87; white interest in death of, 172

Tyson, Timothy, 200; *The Blood of Emmett Till*, 220n8

Underhill, John Wesley, 163
undertakers, 91
Union grave sites, 60, 61–64, 68*f*, 72; lack of respect for, 66–69; monuments and, 70, 75n46
United States Colored Troops (USCT), 53; grave sites of, 67, 76n69
University of South Florida Research Task Force on Understanding and Addressing Blackness and Anti-Black Racism in Local, National and International Communities, 233
University of Virginia (Charlottesville), 99, 101, 175; *Gone but Not Forgotten* exhibit, 102
upkeep, cemetery, 2, 10, 42n53; as political act, 12; women and, 11, 61
USCT. *See* United States Colored Troops
USPHS. *See* U.S. Public Health Service
U.S. Public Health Service (USPHS), 171–72, 173–78, 180–82, 184
U.S. Supreme Court, 149–50, 151*f*

Veterans Administration Hospital (Tuskegee, Ala.), 171, 174–75
Victoria Tabernacle, 85, 89
Vietnam War, 155, 158
violence, white, 207, 233; civil rights murders, 198, 200, 203, 205, 207, 216, 218, 220; epilogue on, 227–30; threat of, cemetery integration and, 153, 154, 160, 161, 164
Vizena, H. Creig, 149
Vonderlehr, Raymond A., 172, 173–76

Walters Choice Chamber (MAT Precinct Four chamber), 118, 121, 122
Ware, Virgil, 199*f*, 216
Warren, Jamie, 4

Warrior Stand (Macon County, Ala.), 113–14, 120, 121, 137
Warrior Stand Cemetery (Macon County, Ala.), 122, 134*f*
Washington, Booker T., 113–14, 116–17; on Black landownership, 137, 138; call for self-determination, 122; MAT joined by, 117
Washington, Harriet A., 172, 175–76
Wasler, Annie, 153
Watson, Caroline, 97
Wells, Ida B., 234
Wenger, O. C., 172
Wesley, Claude, 210–12, 214
Wesley, Cynthia Morris, 9, 200, 207; death certificate misidentifications, 210–11, 214; Four Spirits Memorial, 216, 217*f*; funeral program, 211–12; grave site, 209, 214–15; Morris family disconnected from memory of, 212–15; name of, 210–15; news coverage and, 210–11, 213–14; symbolic role versus personal identity, 212
Wesley, Gertrude (Turner), 210–12, 213, 214
Wesley Chapel (Charlottesville, Va.), 94
West Virginia Human Rights Commission, 155
White, Debra Gray, 124
white supremacy, 233; Black cemeteries as resistance to, 4, 10; cemeteries as resistance to, 233; Confederate monuments and, 12; extended into grave, 151; funeral processions as resistance to, 5; male power and, 30; memorialized by burial patterns, 8; memorialized in Jim Crow segregation cemeteries, 150, 162–63, 165; "tradition" and, 154; white nationalists and supremacists, 101, 116
Whitsett-Hammond, Bernadette, 100, 101
Whittaker, Robert Leo, 94
Williams, Florence, 243
Williams, Henry, 33
Williams, Pete, 153
Williams, Pondexteur, 155–60, 156*f*, 161, 164; news coverage of, 157, 158, 169, 169*f*, 170*f*
Williams, Shari, 178, 180, 188
Williams Funeral Home (St. Petersburg, Fla.), 243
women: domains of, in antebellum America, 30–31; mourning and, 30–31, 41n39; property rights and, 86
women, Black: centering of, 245; creation and maintenance of cemeteries, 11; death care

and, 235, 245; deathways and, 10, 232–35; deathways and, epilogue on, 251; enslaved, corpse care and, 4; enslaved, gendered oppression of, 124; funerary interests of, 8; hospitals and, 10, 244–45; leadership and, 246; leadership of, 232–33, 234–35, 240, 241–43; motherhood and, 11; mutual aid societies and, 8, 86–87; social institutions and, 10; stereotypes of, 128, 139; Tuskegee Study remembrance and, 188; violence against, 245. *See also* gender

women, white: cemetery upkeep and, 11, 61, 66, 67, 69; Civil War funerals and, 61; Confederate commemoration and, 7; corpse care of enslaved people and, 4; death work and, 7; feminist movement focused on, 234; memorial associations and, 64–65, 70; "white womanhood" concept, 65. *See also* gender

Woodlawn Cemetery (Birmingham, Ala.). *See* Greenwood Cemetery (Birmingham, Ala.)

Wright, Dow, Jr., 134, 140*t*
Wright, Dow, Sr., 134, 140*t*
Wright, Elizabethada, 5
Wright, Emmaline, 120*t*, 121, 140*t*
Wright, Fletcher, 140*t*
Wright, Moses, 200–201
Wright, P. H., 242
Wright, Pollie, 119*t*, 133, 134, 139*t*, 140*t*; headstone, 135*f*
Wright, Simeon, 201, 204, 205

Yopp, Marie, 244

Zephroes, 8, 115, 116; Sweet Pilgrim, 136–37. *See also* Precinct Four Zephroes
Zephroe Temple number 1, 122
Zion Cemetery (Tampa, Fla.), 233
Zion Hall (Charlottesville, Va.), 88–89
Zion Union Church (Charlottesville, Va.), 94
Zipporah (biblical figure), 128